Contents

The
Crag Guide
to
England and Wales

David Jones

The Crowood Press

First published in 1989 by
The Crowood Press
Ramsbury, Marlborough
Wiltshire SN8 2HE

British Library Cataloguing in Publication Data

Jones, David
   Crag guide to England and Wales.
   1. Great Britain. Mountains. Visitors' guides
   I. Title
   914.1'04858

   ISBN 1 85223 238 2

Picture Credits

Front cover: Phil Davidson on the Cromlech Boulders, Llanberis Pass, Wales
(photo by David Jones).
Back cover: Joe Healey on Citadel, Gogarth, North Wales
(photo by David Jones).

All maps by David Jones

Typeset by Keyboard Services, Luton, Beds
Printed in Great Britain by Biddles Ltd, of Guildford and King's Lynn

Acknowledgements

In writing this guide I have received support from everyone, and my thanks go out to anyone who has helped this project come to fruition. I thank particularly Malcolm McPherson who helped me with the word processor, without which I would never have finished this book before the year 2000. I thank also every guidebook author there has ever been, for it is their hard work which has enabled me to climb on most of the crags in Britain over the past 20 years. The following people also deserve a mention: Felicity Butler, Phil Davidson, Mark Edwards, Rowland Edwards, Andy Fanshawe, Mick Fowler, Joe Healey, Bradley Jackson, Gordon Jenkins, Fred Simpson, Gordon Stainforth, Dave and Moira Viggars, Paul Williams, Stew Wilson, Bill Wright, Harrow School and Miranda Ruffell.

Thanks go to everyone who helped in getting all the photographs together, and especially to Steve Ashton, Mike Browell, Compass West School of International Rock Climbing, Paul Cornforth, Adrian Gostick, Tony Greenbank, Joe Healey, Guy Mclelland, Bob Moulton, Bernard Newman, Jerry Peel, Francis Ramsey, Ian Roper, Fred Simpson, and Ken Wilson.

Finally, where would we all be without the Ordnance Survey maps, undoubtedly the finest in the world? My thanks to them!

Preface

For most people, writing a guidebook to a local area that they know intimately is a gigantic task; to attempt a guide covering all the crags in England and Wales is an almost suicidal one, believe me. I make no excuses for missing out any crags or for falling short of the most up-to-date information on every crag. The reason I have attempted this guide alone is that I believe guidebooks are far better produced by one person than a committee, not least because the user can relate quite quickly to the author's style and gain a far better understanding of the comments made. Certainly, in all my research over several years, guides by single authors have been far superior to those of committees. If anything over the years has prompted me to think of strangling guidebook writers it is their assumption that the reader has an OS map and knows the way to the crag. In this book my first intention is to get you to the crag without an OS map, just a simple road atlas to the UK.

All road distances are in imperial measurements, like all the road signs in the UK, and heights are in feet. There is quite a simple reason for this — of a weekend I want to leave the metrication of design and engineering behind and enjoy the change to a more traditional lifestyle. May yards, feet and inches continue as long as you get your change from a round of beers in pounds, shillings and pence at The Douglas Arms in Bethesda.

To have included every piece of rock in England and Wales would have meant at least a two-volume book. There is always the possibility that I have missed out your favourite bouldering area. I therefore ask that you write to me with the details so it can be included in a future edition. I would also be very grateful to hear of any errors made in descriptions, however minor. Please send new details or comments to: David Jones, Ivy Cottage, West Bank, Winster, Derbyshire, DE4 2DQ

Introduction

The achievement of a first ascent has long been regarded by climbing literature as the ultimate success. The spirit to conquer the unclimbed has lived with us in print since the mid-nineteenth century, when alpine exploration was in its golden age. At a time when the choice of Burgundy or Bordeaux was as important as climbing a particular mountain, lengthy preparation included local guides, load carriers and even geological instruments. Mountaineering literature has always described the whole affair in a very grandiose way. Indeed many of the first ascensionists' essays of adventure and peril were achievements in themselves, and as beautiful as many of our finest prose essays.

At the turn of the century, when rock climbing was gathering momentum in the mountains of England and Wales, the achievement of a first ascent became very fashionable. The Victorian pioneers, quite without conscience, dismissed thoughts that an odd shepherd or young lad might have already achieved such a climbing feat and proclaimed themselves as gallant pioneers. To safeguard their afternoon's outing as a great historic occasion, the particulars of the ascent and the people involved were recorded, and in 1909 the first ever guidebook to an area in England and Wales, Lliwedd, was published.

It was around the early 1920s that a new approach to rock climbing really became popular. At that time protection was non-existent and this approach was very sensible for those who were not of great skill or ability; the thought of climbing unguided by person or by book was more for those of a suicidal nature. This changed very slowly over the years with the improvement of equipment, but in 1978 it could still be claimed that you had not actually done a route if you had used a friend for protection.

It was not until the beginning of the 1980s that real gains were made. The introduction of the friend and the death of the Whillans harness showed the way forward. The early years of the decade saw the introduction of chalk, excellent double-rope techniques, perfected belay plates, comfortable harnesses, rocks, RPs and, most useful of all, bolts. Indeed, the sting had been taken out of climbing, and its popularity has grown enormously ever since.

What of the 1990s and the future? Virtually every piece of rock in England and Wales has now been climbed in some fashion, and documented into precise guidebooks that lead the climber very confidently up the routes. The future must be to discard the route descriptions, leave the guide at home, go to the crag and climb routes completely on sight. Those who prefer a route description should not feel offended, for I do not seek guidebook eradication in any way. But to climb without route knowledge on a fully developed cliff, use the modern protection which allows you to climb and retreat in safety. This is definitely the way to enjoy real adventure in rock climbing. Certainly the days have gone when you turn up at a crag without a route description and have to set forth in danger.

GUIDE USE

This guide serves three main purposes. Firstly, it gives an overall impression of the climbing on offer in England and Wales to people who live here and also to visiting climbers from abroad. Secondly, it enables those who cannot afford the 50-volume set of guidebooks, costing around £350, a way of having a guide to every crag in the country. And thirdly, it presents a modern style to climbing – arriving at a crag and climbing the lines on it that appeal to you, in search of adventure rather than route ticking. I forgot, fourthly, the ideal gift for the crag ticker.

England and Wales have been split up into the areas listed in the Contents. Each chapter covers a wide area and within it there are sections that fall naturally into weather patterns, rock type or ease of access. The whole country is covered by maps which are also listed in the Contents and shown on the overall map on both inside covers. Use this to locate an area map, then find any crag by its number index. Each section has separate numbering and appears at the top of each page.

Some of the crags are major and others minor. The larger crags are in circles to help those new to an area. Several crags in the guide have restrictions and these have been made quite clear. It has often taken a lot of work to gain access for the climber to these crags, but most organisations such as wildlife and nature conservancy groups have been very co-operative and it would be a great shame on climbing as a whole if these restrictions were ever to be breached. The national body for climbing in Britain is the British Mountaineering Council, which has various meetings to arrange access agreements to the crags. As yet there are no publications of the restrictions and the only way to find out the latest access agreement is to phone the Council on 061 273 5835. All sea cliffs affected by the tide have been given a tide rating. This is the amount you have to add or subtract from high tide at London Bridge on your given day. All large-format newspapers publish high tide at London Bridge daily, so you can easily work out high tide at any crag in the country for the weekend, for example. In summer, note that tides are Greenwich Mean Time.

Each crag has a description of the climbing found on it, but there is no regular format since each crag varies so much. Generally, the better crags have larger descriptions. Every crag has details of how to locate it. The idea is that all you have is a basic road map to England and Wales. The big floppy car atlas is perfect. I used the very reasonably priced *Ordnance Survey Superscale Atlas of Great Britain* to write the guide. If you use this you will have the advantage that I like of working on one page and not across folds, so you will have great ease in using it successfully. It also shows campsites and all the up-to-date motorways and road numbers. Those without a car have my sympathy, nevertheless the details should be quite clear to the person you have hitched a lift with. All distances are meant to be accurate. The mileometer on most cars proves very effective here and can be used with ease. All distances are if anything slightly under, so always travel the distance stated.

At the end of each crag is a guide reference (see Appendix 1 at the back of the guide) which shows the actual guide area publication with all the routes in. Virtually every piece of rock in England and Wales that has been climbed upon is documented somewhere. Most of the routes are listed and described in various climbing guidebooks which are in theory readily available from most climbing shops. In practice you often walk away empty-handed since even the best shops cannot afford to stock the 50 or so volumes that cover England and Wales. Also, guides often go out of print or a new edition is still in the pipeline and you are left stuck. If you cannot get hold of a guide to a particular area, this guide will at least enable you to find the crags and get out climbing. The publication dates of the guides are listed with the references, but areas do change slightly from time to time when guidebooks are updated. Also, with the availability of this guide, topos and crag updates will be worth publishing in club journals and climbing magazines.

NOTES FOR FOREIGN CLIMBERS

Rock climbing techniques in Britain differ slightly from those in Europe. The general absence of bolts and pegs will no doubt horrify many climbers, especially the French. However, after spending all your holiday money on bizarre-looking protection devices, the delights of the British crags can be sampled. Most of the pitches are up to 140ft and wander around a lot, so double 9mm ropes are useful. The best length is 40m; 50m is all right but the last 10m is almost never used. Protection varies from brass RPs to friend 4s (see page 11).

The climbing season in Britain varies considerably. The warm summer starts around 1 June and lasts until mid-September. April to October is classified as British Summer Time and is climbable if the rain ever stops. The winter, November to late March, is only for the very enthusiastic as snow often falls during this period. Mild spells have been known in Cornwall at Christmas, but so have wet gales.

One can climb relatively cheaply in Britain; camping fees are quite low and there are no motorway tolls (just traffic jams). Very cheap beer and good quality food are often available in pubs which, except on Sundays, open till late in the evening. Banks open Mon.–Fri., 9.30 a.m. to 3.30 p.m., and exchange all major currencies. General shopping times are 9 a.m. to 5 p.m., sometimes with an extra hour either way, but in the country this is unlikely. Petrol stations are self-service, 7 a.m. to 10 p.m. North Wales is terrible, though, so never drop below half a tank. Motorway services are now very good, with a 24-hour service but are quite expensive for eating.

It is essential to avoid bank holidays in Britain as shops close and the roads are completely impossible. They fall on 1 Jan., Easter Fri. and Mon., May Day (first Monday in May), Whitsun (last Monday in May) and Aug. Bank Holiday (last Monday in August). It is traditional for it to rain on these days also.

Car hire and rail travel in Britain is expensive, but standards are very good; coach travel is cheap and very effective. Cars should always be left locked and bags watched at very busy crags near the cities, which attract non-climbers. Most climbing areas have good equipment shops where you can buy the essentials. The best guide to living as a climber is *The Alternative Guide to Climbing* by Gill Fawcett. It is well worth getting. Good luck.

GRADES

UK	France	Germany	USA	Australia
Diff	2	I	5.2	10
V Diff	3	II	5.4	12
Severe	4	III	5.5	14
Hard Severe	5a	IV	5.6	15
Very Severe	5b	V	5.8	17
HVS	5c	VI	5.9	18
E1, 5b	6a	VII-	5.10b	19
E2, 5c	6a	VII	5.10c	21
E3, 5c	6b	VII-	5.10d	22
E3, 6a	6b	VIII-	5.11b	23
E4, 6a	6c	VIII	5.11c	24
E4, 6b	7a	VIII	5.11d	25
E5, 6a	7a	VIII-	5.12a	26
E5, 6b	7b	IX-	5.12b	27
E6, 6b	7c	IX-	5.12c	29
E6, 6c	8a	X	5.13	32
E7, 8, 9	8b, 8c	XI-	5.14	40

METRIC EQUIVALENTS

Miles	Km	Miles	Km	Feet	Metres
0.1	0.16	10	16	10	3
0.2	0.32	11	17.7	15	4.6
0.3	0.5	13	21	20	6
0.4	0.64	14	22.5	30	9
0.5	0.8	15	24	40	12
0.6	0.96	20	32	50	15
0.7	1.13	25	40	80	24
0.8	1.3	30	48	100	30
0.9	1.45	40	64	150	45
1.0	1.6	50	80	1,000	300

SAFETY NOTES

Anybody visiting the British crags from the Continent will be stunned by the lack of expansion bolts for protection. They are found only on the hardest routes on limestone. Why only the hardest and only on limestone? The first reason is pure selfishness in that the best climbers of the time feel it is essential for safeguarding their difficult routes. Ninety-five per cent of British climbers approve of bolts, indeed it is a rare sight ever to see someone pass a bolt and not clip it. The problem lies in the other five per cent, who take such a strong dislike to the placing of bolts that they go along with a hammer and chop the heads off. It's only a matter of time before someone does it to them and sees if they like it. So the placing of bolts relates to the attitude of a handful of choppers. The second reason for the lack of bolts on some routes is the type of rock. A bolt on gritstone would last about five seconds – don't bother – Welsh rock about one day, limestone two months to two years depending on the difficulty of the route, and slate, well, for ever.

The rest of us, outside this pathetic bolting–chopping syndrome, put up with ordinary protection. Nearly all routes can be well protected using natural runners placed when climbing.

Most of the reasonably hard routes around E5 can be climbed on sight, but even so I would always advise abseil inspection first, especially to those from abroad who might end up at the crux having run out of the right-sized nuts. The other routes are all quite straightforward to protect. One should, however, be realistic about the grades climbed at, since harder climbs often need far less protection than the low-grade climbs. Overleaf are two suggested gear racks for different standards of climbing.

Diff to E1 Rack

3 screw-gate karabiners
15 karabiners
Belay plate
Rocks 1–6 on wire
Rocks 6, 7, 8, 9 on rope
Hex 7, 8 on rope
2 moacs
Friends no. 3
4 tape extensions
2 long tapes

E1 to E6 Rack

1 screw-gate karabiner
24 lightweight karabiners
Belay plate
2 sets of RPs
2 sets rocks 1–5
2 sets rocks 6, 7, 8 on rope
Baby moac
Friends, selection
6 tape extensions
1 long tape

Additional Notes

(1)   Double 9mm ropes are standard in Britain since protection rarely falls in a straight line and rope drag becomes impossible.

(2)   If a crag specification is loose, rock helmets can be thoroughly recommended, especially in the lower grades.

(3)   All belays should be dynamic, i.e. to the person and not the rock. This takes shock out of the system, the major contributory factor to any piece of equipment failing.

(4)   Friends should become second nature and beginners should know how to get them out. Also only use in an emergency in parallel, smooth-sided limestone cracks.

(5)   A fall on a rope can flick out the runners beneath it, so try and place runners on alternate ropes if possible.

(6)   Don't ever feel too embarrassed to use a top rope on short gritstone routes with no protection, especially when climbing in damp conditions.

(7)   In the mountains in summer, respect the weather and make an effort to have a map, compass, jumper and cagoule.

(8)   Always use two anchors for belays, screw-gate or double opposing krabs.

(9)   Always tie on with a figure of eight knot – the bowline if tied incorrectly fails, the figure of eight generally does not.

(10)   A second should always be willing to be lifted off the ground in

a fall to reduce shock loading. In the event of a leader possibly grounding out, the second should run downhill fast!

Sea Cliffs

Climbing is obviously more dangerous on sea cliffs than on inland crags. However, the lure is there so one should simply go well-prepared. The first and most important fact to remember is that climbing gear sinks! Never mind the cost, if you fall in the drink while traversing with a huge heavy rack strapped to you, you will be lucky to avoid drowning. A shoulder bandolier must be used on sea cliffs where there is any possibility of falling in. Don't get too ambitious on your first route in a new area. If the sea is rough, forget dynamic belay tactics and get well-secured to the bottom of the cliff. Find out the tide times and write them down. Birds often nest and can suddenly fly out and startle a leader. Protect yourself even on the easy bits.

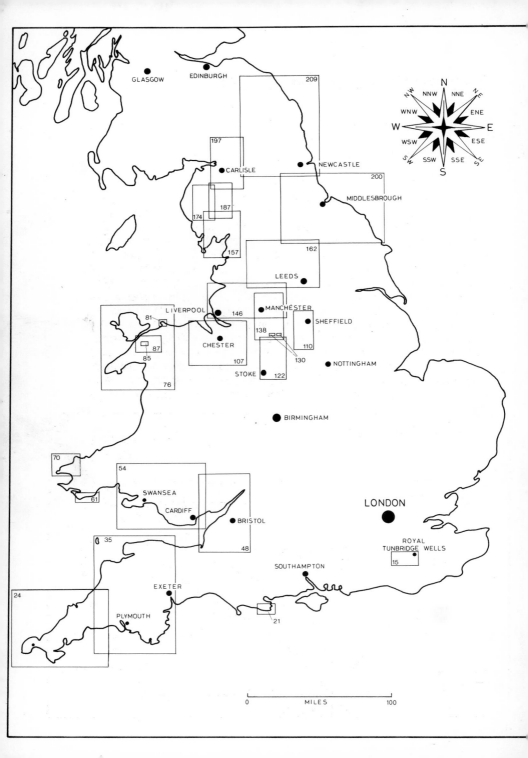

1 South East England

KENT AND SUSSEX
Sandstone

Climbing in the south east around Tunbridge Wells is always a great day's entertainment. There is much to occupy all standards of climber, and some of the best ale and pubs in Britain. The atmosphere is always friendly, and it is near enough to civilisation to persuade the completely disinterested partner to come along. It is mild here for most of the year, and even on wet days routes do not become impossible, just difficult. Often with many onlookers, a jestful atmosphere develops, and on-sight cruises of the difficult routes are not easy. The locals have the area completely wired so do not get so put off by everyone else cruising up the 5c's that you fail to leave the ground. Although short, the routes are steep with rounded holds, bulging at the top to give hard and often awkward finishes. This and the frailty of the rock mean that on-sight soloing cannot be advised. The rock is soft in comparison with other European sandstone, and over the years has suffered from frictional wear. Protection is from a

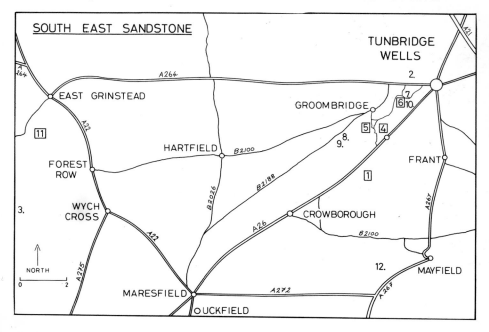

SOUTH EAST SANDSTONE

TUNBRIDGE WELLS

A264

EAST GRINSTEAD

GROOMBRIDGE

HARTFIELD

FOREST ROW

FRANT

WYCH CROSS

CROWBOROUGH

NORTH

MAYFIELD

MARESFIELD

UCKFIELD

top rope, with a sling high on a tree to prevent rock erosion and lengthen the lifespan of the rope tenfold. There is good climbing here all year round. However, the rock can often stay damp after rain for several days. An exceptionally dry summer turns the area into a climbing paradise with an amazing concentration of tough routes.

Bowles Rocks:
OS.188 GR.543 330 [1]

An open crag 20–30ft high situated in the grounds of Bowles outdoor centre. Quick drying with a southerly aspect. A pleasant and popular crag with 150 routes of all standards. Most of the routes are on walls, slabs and wide cracks which steepen for the harder routes. The best roof climbs in the area are to be found here and all can be climbed free by the gifted. Toilet facilities are provided by the centre which sometimes charges a small fee to people climbing. Weekends are often busy, especially dry ones.

Dir: 3m SSW of Tunbridge Wells. Follow the A26 (Crowborough) SW, past Eridge station for 0.7m, turn L (Bowles outdoor centre). A road leads to the centre, 0.5m, enter and park. The rocks are 100yds on. [SS]

Bulls Hollow Rocks:
OS.188 GR.569 394 [2]

The rocks, being set in a hollow enshrouded in trees, remain damp and sandy for most of the year. However, in a dry spell, climbs unrivalled in quality and interest make this an excellent crag. About 50 climbs of all standards. Adjacent to the hollow is Denny Bottom, a sandy bouldering area.

Dir: 1m W of Tunbridge Wells. Take A264 (East Grinstead). At 300yds past the Spa Hotel turn R (Denny Bottom Road). This leads to some twisting downhill bends, park. A path leads off to the R and the rocks. [SS]

Chiddinglye Wood Rocks:
Restriction
OS.187 GR.348 324 [3]

The owners of the rocks do not encourage climbing. The 20ft crag consists of a rock wall with 9 climbs, 3b–6c, and further on an isolated block offers 4 more. The climbing is on good rock, enjoyable and very secluded.

Dir: 7m SW of East Grinstead, 1m WSW of West Hoathly. From Turners Hill go S on B2028, pass the West Hoathly fork, soon after a track on the L is taken to some rock walls. From here rhododendrons and jungle hinder progress. Undeterred and after several days' travel in a SE direction the crag is reached. [SS]

Eridge Green Rocks: Restriction
OS.188 GR.555 356 [4]

Climbing here is strictly forbidden by the owners who do not hesitate in calling the men in blue. There exist – I am told – over 100 routes of all standards, 15–35ft. However, the harder routes tend to be better. The rock is excellent, clean and sometimes brittle since it is climbed on rarely.

Dir: 2.3m SW of Tunbridge Wells. A26 (Crowborough) to Eridge, a track on R past church leads to woods and the rocks. [SS]

Harrisons Rocks:
OS.188 GR.530 350 [5]

A long rambling crag with over 300 routes and countless variations. Most of the climbs are excellent, 15–35ft, and are spread over all the grades. There are many classics for which queuing is often necessary at weekends. However, the quantity of routes solves this problem. The rocks are sometimes damp and need a good, dry spell to gain their full merit, especially in the harder grades.

Dir: 2m W of Tunbridge Wells. Take the A264 (East Grinstead) from Tunbridge Wells. After 2.5m, B2188 to Groombridge, fork L at the Victoria Pub, over railway, 400yds fork R (Eridge) 70yds turn R into a lane signposted Harrisons Rocks and Birchden Wood. Park in car park and walk 10 mins or sprint 2 mins to the crag. It is hoped that the Forestry Commission will open a small lightweight campsite here in the future. [SS]

FANDANGO, 6a, Bowles Rocks. (Climber Andy Meyers, Photo David B A Jones)

High Rocks:
OS.188 GR.550 380   [6]

This is the mecca for the hard climbers in the south east of England and hosts many superb desperate routes. There are over 200 climbs here, 30–40ft, giving the longest climbs in the area. All standards of routes are to be found. However, the grades tend to be tough but fair. Easier routes are strenuous chimneys, unsuitable for beginners but excellent for VS aspirants, and often stop Extreme leaders. The harder climbs, 5a upwards, are of great distinction and require complete climbing technique. The routes are extremely varied except for the fact that all are quite steep.

Dir: 2m W of Tunbridge Wells. From TW take A264 (E. Grinstead), after 1.2m at Rusthall Common take a road L signposted High Rocks. After 0.8m High Rocks Inn and yuppie complex is reached. The rocks opposite are fenced in and an admission fee is unfortunately charged. It is common to protest before paying to enjoy the countryside and the owners should be made to feel uneasy in adopting this outrageous practice. [SS]

High Rocks Annexe: Restriction
OS.118 GR.562 385   [7]

Permission must be gained from the owner, who lives in a bungalow above and behind the crag, and is nearly always granted. A small outcrop hidden by trees, green in character but often dry when the other outcrops are greasy. About 20ft, offering 50 routes of all standards especially in the lower grades.

Dir: Opposite the N end of High Rocks across the railway. [SS]

Jockeys Wood Rocks: Restriction
OS.118 GR.516 346   [8]

Climbing permission has not been granted. A few buttresses about 25ft high offer ten 5b, 5c, 6a routes of good quality.

Dir: 4.5m SW of Tunbridge Wells. Take A264 (E. Grinstead), after 2.5m take B2188, past Groombridge. After 2m a track on the L leads down through some woods, the rocks are on the R. [SS]

Penns Rocks: Restriction
OS.118 GR.520 346   [9]

Climbing here is strongly discouraged – it is not permitted and is in full view of the owner's house. Several isolated boulders up to 25ft offer 40 routes of superb quality and interest in all grades. Worth dreaming about.

Dir: 4.5m SW of Tunbridge Wells. To Groombridge as for Jockeys Wood, after 1.8m on the B2188 a road turns sharp L up Motts Hill. After 0.3m a track leads off to Penns House. The rocks are situated at the end of the lawn. [SS]

Ramslye Farm Rocks: Restriction
OS.118 GR.568 379   [10]

Permission to climb is gained from the house opposite to the crag. Two small rock walls, 15ft, offer 15 good routes of varied standards, with some interesting bouldering problems.

Dir: 1.2m SW of Tunbridge Wells. Take A26 (Crowborough) from TW. After leaving the town up a steep hill the road levels out. A track leads off to the R where the rocks can be seen on the edge of the woods. [SS]

Stone Farm Rocks:
OS.117 GR.382 347   [11]

An outcrop of boulders reaching up to 20ft offering about 60 routes in the middle grades. A very enjoyable spot, S-facing and quick drying. Worth a visit, even if only to boulder around.

Dir: 2.3m SSW of East Grinstead. Find East Grinstead old town centre. By Clarendon House and Ship pub take the B2110 (Turners Hill). After 1.3m turn L to St Hill Green; after 0.7m T-junction turn R to West Hoathly; after 0.85m cars can be parked on the L. A track 50yds back on the L leads to the crag, 100yds. [SS]

Under Rocks:
OS.118 GR.555 264   [12]

The setting of these rocks is idyllic, the rock wonderful, for climbing here on a sunny day is unrivalled anywhere in South East England. Unfortunately the outcrop offers only a handful of climbs, most of which in essence are 5c and above. The rock is good, clean and enjoyable to climb.

SALAD DAYS, 6b, High Rocks. (Climber Matt Saunders, Photo David B A Jones)

Dir: 2m WSW of Mayfield. Take the A267 SW from Mayfield, after 2m (Butchers Cross) turn R (N) to Argos Hill. Road forks after 0.5m, park. A narrow path leads off opposite the house Twitts Ghyll. After 50yds enter the field on the L, head SW through the gate in the hedge and follow the lie of the land to a wooded hollow. Here a path leads R to the outcrop, a 25ft potholed wall and undercut bulges. [SS]

DORSET

The Agglestone:
OS.195 GR.024 828   [13]

This is a small bouldering area with quite hard problems going up to 20ft or so. Worth a short visit if rained off at Swanage. The sandstone here is quite hard and offers sound climbing.

Dir: 4m N of Swanage, 0.7m NW of Studland. Leave Studland going N and after 300yds, park and take the track that forks L, follow on to a path leading to Godlingstone Heath and the Rock, 15 mins. [SWA]

Chalk

This rock, being soft and uncertain, appeals to few climbers; even so, those initiated confess to very memorable days and thereafter quote chalk routes not as climbing but as an experience! All routes have been done by very good mountaineers and therefore climbing should not be embarked upon unless the party is very competent and experienced.

The coastguards must be informed before climbing to prevent unwanted rescue from an alarm raised by tourists or fishermen.

Beachy Head: Inf. coastguard
OS.189 GR.580 950 HT−2.50   [14]

Large sea cliffs and Etheldra's Pinnacle offer excellent, character-building climbing. Rock boots and pegs are the standard equipment.

Dir: 4m SW of Eastbourne. Take the B2103 SW from Eastbourne, after 1m a road leads off to Beachy Head. [SS]

St Margaret's: Inf. coastguard
OS.179 GR.360 430 HT−2.45   [15]

Large soft chalk cliffs offering plenty of climbing with full ice gear being the norm. The routes offer exciting climbing with plenty of interest, queuing for routes is as yet unknown.

Dir: 2m ENE from Dover. From St Margaret's Bay walk SW along the beach where the cliffs will become apparent to your R. [SS]

Isle of Wight: Restriction
OS.196 GR.294 849 HT−local   [16]

The Needles headland is owned by the National Trust who have banned climbing − check with BMC first, please. The climbing is on the pinnacles known as the Needles. Various reports recommend full ice gear and rock gear to be taken since the cliffs are somewhat softer than the Needles themselves.

Dir: At the W end of the Isle of Wight, near Southampton. Car ferries go to the island from Southampton and Portsmouth. [SS]

Old Harry Rocks:
OS.195 GR.056 825 HT−5.10   [17]

Two pinnacles, Old Harry and his Wife, give several 70ft interesting routes.

Dir: 4.5m NNE of Swanage at Handfast Point. From Studland walk E for 1m along the coastal path to the headland. [SS]

Swanage Limestone

To visit Swanage is always a pleasant experience. Lunch and perhaps a few drinks in The King's Arms at Corfe Castle, followed by a stroll along the top of the cliffs west of Swanage – delightful. However it must be admitted that the experience of climbing at Swanage is usually harrowing and sometimes positively lethal. Throughout the year several sections of the cliffs disappear into the sea leaving uncovered further masses of tottering rubble. There are more serious accidents here pro rata than at any other area in Britain. Even blocks anchoring hex 11s have been known to crumble in a fall, leaving the leader to be swallowed by the ocean below. The faithful pilgrims do climb here, however, year after year with delight and satisfaction. One should never be dissuaded from a visit, but understand that climbing on loose, crumbling, dirty, rotten, congealed white putty is not a safe pastime.

In its favour Swanage does have the best weather in England and Wales: in summer it can be very hot, giving a glare necessitating sunglasses, and the winter months offer morning sunshine to warm even the coldest days. Belays at the top with iron stakes should always be treated with great caution if found! There are serious bird restrictions here and it must be stressed that nobody tolerates infringement of these rules. If ever in doubt, keep away from Swanage during the period 1 March to 31 July. The area to the east of Black

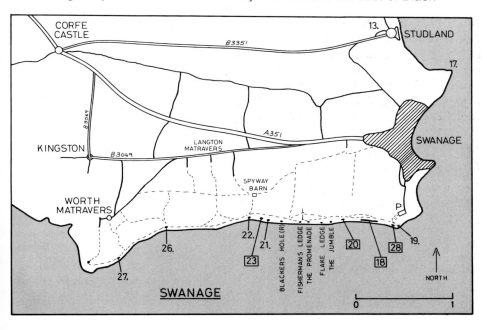

Zawn, Tilly Whim Caves, etc. has a total climbing ban for ornithological reasons and should be left well alone, especially as this has been carefully worked out and agreed by all climbing and wildlife organisations.

Boulder Ruckle: Restriction
OS.195 GR.024 768 HT–5.10   [18]

The area for 600yds W of the lighthouse has a ban 1 Mar.–1 Aug. Beyond, the next mile is unaffected. For anyone who regards himself as tough, meaty, big and definitely bouncy, this is the place to be. A Serious cliff with about 250 routes at a minimum grade of VS–HVS, abseil approach to a disappearing tidal bottom, and most routes being good Extremes. Generally around 150ft high, though pitches should be split to allow the leader plenty of spare rope to find a belay – a humorous topic here! Leaving an abseil descent in place is essential, as is a prayer book and bicycle clips.

Dir: 1.5m S of Swanage. From the town follow road signs S to car park at Durlston Head. Take footpath past lighthouse and The Ruckle, as it is known, begins and stretches for about 0.5m, a cliff with many boulders at its base (past routes!). [SWA]

The Black Zawn:
OS.195 GR.029 768 HT–5.10   [19]

This area gives many Extremes, all of which receive classic status. Approach is by abseil into an abyss, whereby good swinging is necessary to avoid ending up swimming to the cliff – yes, it is overhanging. Not an area for bad weather or bad climbers, and especially not for bad swimmers.

Dir: 1.5m S of Swanage. Approach: see Boulder Ruckle, walk to the lighthouse and take an abseil directly below into the Zawn. [SWA]

Cattle Troughs Area:
OS.195 GR.015 767 HT–5.10   [20]

This area, without any restrictions and with relatively sound putty, is popular, especially with first-time visitors (there are few second-time ones). It has 130 routes, 50–80ft, of all grades, on seven cliffs. First reached is Amphitheatre Ledge just after the stile, poor; Cattle Troughs recognised by two amphitheatres together, good climbs in the low grades and easy access;

The Jumble, good Diffs and a few harder, descent by some easy slabs; Flake Ledge, some good V Diffs and VS, easy scramble and chimney descent; Unknown Ledge, VS upwards climbs from a semi-tidal bottom, traverse in from Promenade easy; Promenade, many climbs of all standards, many Es also. Descent to the Tidal Promenade (rock) before the pylons; Fisherman's Ledge, cliff below the white pylon, mostly E1, E2, etc.

Dir: 2m WSW of Swanage. Approach: see Boulder Ruckle, carry on past stile and cliffs until white pylon. [SWA]

Cormorant Ledge: Restriction
OS.195 GR.004 768 HT–5.10   [21]

A major bird area, hence the name, necessitates no climbing 1 Mar.–1 Aug. 150ft crag offering 40 or so VS–HVS climbs. A great deal of care should be taken with the finishes, and always do in two pitches. The area to the E of this is known as Blacker's Hole, 25 routes VS to E6. Quite steep in places.

Dir: 1.9m WSW of Swanage. Approach: see Dancing Ledge, go E past Guillemot Ledge, where Cormorant in the next cliff. Abseil. [SWA]

Dancing Ledge:
OS.195 GR.997 768   [22]

A very popular crag, only 30ft high and offering a good handful of routes in the lower grades. Can get swarmed with tourists but not in the winter. Good protection and easy access make this a good spot for beginners.

Dir: 2.7m WSW of Swanage. Going back out of Swanage take the B3069 to Langton Matravers, and turn off L to Spyway Barn at Dancing Ledge signpost. Park at the farm and follow the well-worn track due S to the cliff in 0.5m [SWA]

Guillemot Ledge: Restriction
OS.195 GR.001 768 HT–5.10   [23]

Various parts have a ban 1 Mar.–1 Aug., best to avoid altogether. This cliff has about 60 routes,

VS to E3, around 150ft, which regularly change as the cliff falls into the sea. Notwithstanding this, it remains popular in the winter months since there are many large boulders at the base acting as a breakwater.

Dir: 2.5m WSW of Swanage. Approach: see Dancing Ledge. Walk back along the cliff towards Swanage, it is the first cliff on the R. Approach down a gully to some chains where a 50ft abseil gains the sea platform. A climb, Exit Chimney V Diff, can be used to escape if necessary. [SWA]

Lulworth Cove:
OS.195 GR.824 798   [24]

The climbing here is not of the best quality in the world but is nevertheless mentionable, mostly in the lower grades of varying length. Occasionally the locals make objections, so a low profile is worthwhile to enjoy the scenic beauty of this spot.

Dir: 20m W of Swanage. Drive to cove on the B3071 from Wool. [SWA]

Portland Bill:
OS.194 GR.691 702   [25]

Here the rock is definitely bad and can only be described as . . . 'interesting'! The cliffs on the W side are big and steep, and very similar to chalk, ice gear applicable. On the E side, which is bathed in morning sunshine and appears lovely, the rock is sounder but falling could be extremely hazardous to your health. There is one good cliff on the island: The Cuttings, 80ft with about 30 routes, VS to E3, solid and well protected. Being a rare island cliff it is very sheltered and provides good winter entertainment.

Dir: 7m S of Weymouth. The Cuttings, go to Easton and the Mermaid Inn. Take the L track which leads after 50yds to an open area beyond which is the crag. [SWA]

Seacombe:
OS.195 GR.985 766 HT–5.10   [26]

A pleasant area with a quarry and a zawn but better still are the walls below the quarried ledge, about 40ft high and offering good routes at all grades. About 40 routes, good family spot.

Dir: 5m WSW of Swanage. Approach: see Slippery Ledge, but follow footpath E to Seacombe Bottom. Cliff is reached in about 20 mins. [SWA]

Slippery Ledge:
OS.195 GR.975 757   [27]

A small secluded area, offering about 15 V Diffs to VSs of about 50ft, makes this a must for some. Not really affected by tides, but necessitating an abseil approach. Worth a visit.

Dir: 8m WSW of Swanage. From Swanage go W to Worth Matravers, park. Take a path S down Winspit Bottom to the cliffs, turn R (W) to reach shortly the impressive Crab Hole. Go down the gully before it to a block which is used to abseil to the foot of the cliff. Easiest way up V Diff. [SWA]

Subluminal:
OS.195 GR.029 769   [28]

The easiest crag to get to in the area and actually has some reasonable climbing on it, mainly in the lower grades. Even so treat protection with doubt. About 30 climbs, 50ft in length, from a platform unaffected by the tide and warm in winter, S-facing. An easy escape up the descent route Diff.

Dir: 1.5m S of Swanage. To Durlston Head as for Boulder Ruckle. Walk to lighthouse, directly W grassy slopes lead down to a small ridge and pedestal, with a scramble to the cliff base. [SWA]

2 Devon and Cornwall

CORNWALL WEST

The coastline west of Penzance is generally known as West Penwith and is absolutely crammed with excellent cliffs. Most of the cliffs are solid granite but there are interesting exceptions to this. The weather here is mild all year round and Easter-time is especially busy with the pubs getting very crowded. All the crags are sea cliffs yet only half are affected by the tides, making it very safe and easy to plan a climbing day. Also there are cliffs on the north and the south, allowing shelter from a cold wind in any direction. Although the rock is very solid and provides good protection, it can be brittle, which makes soloing even more risky than usual. Camping is available at various farms near St Just for very reasonable prices. For any new-route information and help in locating cliffs, the Compass West International School of Rock Climbing is the best place to go. It is situated at Sennen on the A30, has a café and is very friendly.

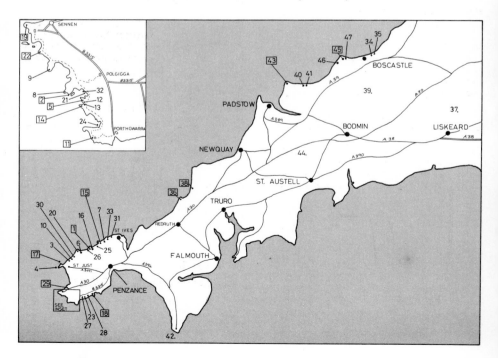

Bosigran:
OS. 203 GR.416 368 HT–3.20 [1]

The most prestigious cliffs in the area without doubt. Several cliffs reaching up to 250ft vertically, consisting of: the Landward Cliff, 17 routes low grades; Main Cliff, 50 routes (half extreme); Seaward Cliff, 20 routes all grades; Great Zawn, 25 routes with classic E4s. The routes are mainly 2-pitch and of classic status. Mostly S-facing, warm and sheltered, tides not a problem except in the Great Zawn.

Dir: 6m NE of St Just. Take the B3306 through Pendeen, past Trevowhan, continue for 1m and then park by climbing hut. From here a path leads off N to the cliffs in about 10 mins. [CWP]

Bosistow:
OS.203 GR.356 232 HT–3.15 [2]

This area consists of a Bosistow Island, which lies opposite a very forbidding wall known as Paradise Wall. Here the climbing is difficult, around the E4 grade, good solid granite but not very well protected. About 15 routes, 150–200ft. The standard of the rock stretching E deteriorates, so beware. All the routes, however, are of classic status and well worth attempting!

Dir: Approach: see Carn Les Boel, the island before the promontory is Bosistow Island. [CWP]

Botallack Head:
OS.203 GR.363 338 HT–3.20 [3]

A 150ft crag, reached easily at low tide, offers a few climbs HS and Diff on very hard slate.

Dir: 2m NNW of St Just. Take B3306, after 1m at Botallack turn L up the old mine track, for 1m where the cliffs are on the L, after passing some small zawns to a very narrow black zawn. [CWP]

Cape Cornwall:
OS.203 GR.352 314 HT–3.20 [4]

A small cliff with some Severes and VSs, only a handful of routes. There are also some more cliffs on the coastline running S to Sennen with some Diffs on, generally known to the universe as the great Progo Bay area, 1m S of the Cape. Good routes on excellent rock at most grades, but very good in the Severe and Diff standard, W-facing, sunny and good beaches. Don't forget the Moet picnic and Ambre Solaire.

Dir: 4.5m NNE of Land's End. From St Just go W, following signs to Cape Cornwall, and car park at headland, stop. An approach path leads off S to the cliff, 200yds. [CWP]

Carn Barra:
OS.203 GR.359 225 HT–3.15 [5]

An excellent crag offering 35 routes Diff–HVS and 20 E1–E5s, of around 80ft. Access is by abseil or scrambling down at low tide. The cliff as a whole, though, is non-tidal. There are three areas: Northern Platform, Central Wall and Criss Cross. A real sun trap and well worth a visit.

Dir: 2m SE of Land's End. Park car at Porthgwarra–Gwennap Head, take coastal path NW towards Land's End, after 0.5m a wall is crossed and in 160yds slopes lead down to the cliff. [CWP]

Carn Clough:
OS.203 GR.390 358 HT–3.20 [6]

A very good crag and area for beginners, many routes around Diff standard on the carn itself and in Portheras Cove.

Dir: 3.5m NNE of St Just. Take the B3306 through Pendeen, 400yds before the bend in the road at Morvah a track leads off L to Chypraze Farm. Park, and walk down to the cove, about 10 mins from the main road. [CWP]

Carnelloe Area:
OS.203 GR.442 389 [7]

A small greenstone area consisting of some slabs and offering a handful of 50–100ft Diffs, at sea-level but not really tidal, and some enjoyable traversing also at low grades.

Dir: 5.5m WSW of St Ives. Approach: see Gurnards Head, carry on for another mile to Poniou, park. Take a path leading N to Porthglaze Cove, midway between Gurnards and Zennor Heads. The crags are at the N end of the cove, on the R. [CWP]

Carn Les Boel:
OS.203 GR.357 232 HT–3.15 [8]

Situated midway between Land's End and Gwennap Head, this area is usually less crowded, a good 25 mins from either car park. The climbing, though, is very good indeed. On the promontory just N of the headland there are a handful of cracks and chimneys at Mod and Diff standard. On the S of the headland the cliffs are more impressive with 3 Severes at 150ft. Very pleasant climbs.

Dir: 1.5m SE of Land's End. Approach: see Carn Barra, take the coastal path NW for 1.5m (25 mins) to the large headland. [CWP]

Carn Sperm:
OS.203 GR.349 239 HT–3.15   [9]

The twin headland of Carn Sperm and Carn Boel provide some excellent routes. On Carn Sperm there is an upper terrace with 7 routes, 130ft, Severe standard, and on the lower cliff, which is semi-tidal, 4 Extremes. Carn Boel, lying further from Land's End, has an immaculate crack route, E3, and offers bouldering potential. In between the two headlands is a zawn offering some very fine climbing, best visited late in the day when the sun gets into the zawn. Routes up to E5, E6.

Dir: 1m SE of Land's End. Approach: see Pordenack Point, continue along the coastal path to a twin headland before Millbay. [CWP]

Carn Vellan:
OS.203 GR.364 343   [10]

A 150ft intimidating cliff of Killas slate, offering a handful of routes around HVS–E1. Also more recently there have been harder routes done to E4. The rock is often wet early on in the day, better for an afternoon visit.

Dir: 2m NNW of St Just. Approach as for Botallack Head but carry on walking for another 5 mins along the cliffs, scramble down to crag. [CWP]

Chair Ladder:
OS.203 GR.356 216 HT–3.15   [11]

This area is simply a rock climbing paradise. Routes of all grades, Mods to E6, and some very technical hard routes. Up to 200ft long, very sound rock and excellent protection. SW-facing and only 5 mins from the car park. Popular in winter as well as summer. The whole headland at Gwennap Head has over 100 routes on it, Chair Ladder having a good 80. Parts are tidal but escapes are possible almost anywhere, making it a very safe crag.

Dir: 3m SE of Land's End. Drive to Porthgwarra–Gwennap Head car park. Walk up to the coastguard station on the headland, 5 mins. The main cliff is straight ahead, however excellent cliffs run all along this part of the headland. [CWP]

Dutch Man's Zawn:
OS.203 GR.360 223 HT–3.15   [12]

A cliff for the harder climber. About 15 routes in the harder grades E2 to E6, 7a. The rock is very good and has atmosphere, I am told. 150–200ft and easiest gained at low tide.

Dir: 2.5m SE of Land's End. Approach: see Carn Barra. The zawn is on the L about 200yds before reaching Carn Barra from Porthgwarra. [CWP]

Folly Cove:
OS.203 GR.360 220 HT–3.15   [13]

Quite a good area with some very pleasant climbing in the grades HVS to E4, often quite sheltered. 100–160ft routes.

Dir: 2.5m SE of Land's End. Approach: see Fox Promontory, this is the cove just to the N of the point. [CWP]

Fox Promontory:
OS.203 GR.361 223 HT–3.15   [14]

About 25 routes of 100ft around the Severe grade. Only a couple are tide-affected, and all are on reasonable rock. There are two E2s on the nose itself for the more adventurous. Climbs all round enabling shelter or the sun to be sought.

Dir: 2.5m SE of Land's End. Park as for Carn Barra. The promontory is passed on the way to Carn Barra, about 700yds after the coastguard cottages. [CWP]

Gurnard's Head:
OS.203 GR.432 388 HT–3.20   [15]

This is a very impressive greenstone crag, popular and justly so. At 240ft it is not small and with a big sea is only fit for super spurters who bite holes in the rock for holds. The headland has a few really classic climbs, HS and E1–E3 on the Right Angle Cliff. There is also Kittiwake Zawn below the neck in the headland, offering a handful of Severe and VS climbs of about 130ft. Also if zawns are your forte, bear L before the neck in the headland and go S for 200yds to

Zawn Duel and Carn Gloose, generally hard climbing around E1, but even so some V Diffs are to be found. Mostly NW-facing, best in the late afternoon if it is chilly, but start at low tide.

Dir: 10m NNW of Penzance. From St Just go N on the B3306 through Pendeen to Porthmeor, 4m. Carry on for 200yds, park by inn at Treen, a path leads to Gurnard's Head, N-ish in about 500yds. [CWP]

Halldrine Cove:
OS.203 GR.417 372 [16]

A must for the Diff climber, only round the corner from Bosigran. A handful of 100ft climbs on excellent granite and in a pleasant situation except when a cold N wind is blowing.

Dir: 6.3m NNE of St Just. Approach: see Bosigran, the cove is behind, to the E of Bosigran. [CWP]

Kenidjack Castle Cliffs:
OS.203 GR.354 326 HT−3.20 [17]

This crag of Killas slate is superb and a must for anyone. The climbs are not very hard considering the appearance, mostly HVS and well protected on the main face, with plenty of easier Severes on the neighbouring faces. Around 150ft high and catches the afternoon sun, a real sun trap. Very solid rock but double ropes useful since gear can be spaced awkwardly.

Dir: 1m NW of St Just. Handy for the pub at lunchtime, hic! The next promontory N of Cape Cornwall. Leave St Just N by the B3306, down a steep hill for 200yds to Tregeseal, at bottom turn L down a narrow lane and park when your suspension suggests. From here walk to the headland, 10 mins. [CWP]

Lamorna–Tater Du:
OS.203 CR.439 231 [18]

A greenstone cliff of about 150ft high, with mainly middle-grade climbing. Most of the climbs are accessible at any state of the tide, about 30 routes in total. S-facing and sheltered from the cold N winds. Not overpopular but worth a visit.

Dir: 4m SW of Penzance. From Penzance take the B3315 SW for 3.7m, where a road off to the L is signposted to Lamorna, go to village and park.

Here a coastal path leads off SW and after 1m the lighthouse at Tater Du is reached. The cliff is just W of this – scramble down. [CWP]

Land's End:
OS.203 GR.342 252 HT−3.20 [19]

The most western point of England is made of hard-wearing granite, but even so the rock on this peninsula tip can vary enormously. A lot of the rock is very good and sound; in other parts it is suspect and should be treated with care and respect. The cliffs are battered by strong winds and gales, as you will be if you get stuck here; the cliffs open straight on to the Atlantic Ocean and great care should always be taken. There are often hordes of tourists around who never get into the climbing areas, thank goodness. The cliffs themselves are natural sun traps and warm even in the cold winter months. The owners of the property will allow climbers to park free of charge and use the toilets – jolly decent of them to grant this. The cliffs offer about 100 climbs and have the largest granite walls in the area, up to 300ft. There are routes here in all grades Diff to E7, with some very technically demanding routes also. Worth a visit.

Dir: Drive to the L end of England and park. Walk to the N of the hotel and the crags are below. Surprise! [CWP]

Pendeen Watch:
OS.203 GR.378 361 [20]

A group of Killas slate cliffs on Pendeen Watch headland below the lighthouse, offering a handful of 80ft routes around the Severe standard and a handful upwards to E5.

Dir: 3m NNE of St Just. From St Just take the B3306 and at the far end of Pendeen a road leads off L to the lighthouse on the headland, where parking is available. [CWP]

Pendower Cove:
OS.203 GR.361 225 HT−3.15 [21]

A large cove offering quite a few crags of all descriptions from very good to not very good. The best is perhaps Moon Buttress, which has a handful of routes in the E3 to E6 category of about 70ft. Worth doing.

Dir: 1.5m SE of Land's End. Approach: see Carn Barra, this is the cove just to the N. [CWP]

Pordenack Point:
OS.203 GR.347 242 HT–3.15 [22]

An excellent granite crag, offering 30 or so routes of all grades. One of the best in the area, and has a beautiful setting with a sunny aspect, and pro which is very good indeed. Most routes about 100ft, easy ones in cracks and harder face climbs.

Dir: 0.5m SSE of Land's End. Approach: see Land's End. Take the coastal path S to the first major point. Scramble around and down to the lower cliffs – Easy. [CWP]

Porthcurno–Treen Area:
OS.203 GR.386 223 [23]

This area is definitely for the sociable climber – a lot of smaller and broken crags above nice sandy beaches, rock pools to keep the white burgundy or champagne cool, crayfish with quails-egg salad, and maybe a short afternoon's splendid bouldering. A perfect Cornish climbing trip, warm and S-facing – bliss. This area stretches from Porthcurno to Treen, Penberth Cove and Head for about 1.5m, and then on to Porthguaron Cove which has four good, long Diffs. There are some longer routes here, up to 180ft from Severe to E2.

Dir: 3m ESE of Land's End. Take the B3315 to Treen, 3m, then a small road to the coast at Penberth, 0.3m. From here the small crags are on the coastline to the W, and Porthguaron Cove lies 800yds to the E. [CWP]

Porthloe Cove:
OS.203 GR.363 221 HT–3.15 [24]

This area is less distinct than most but does offer good climbing in the lower grades, Diffs and Severes of around 100ft. There are several buttresses in the cove, all reasonably accessible and many slabs and grooves at not too steep an angle.

Dir: 3m SE of Land's End. Approach: see Chair Ladder, but go R and descend into the first bay after Gwennap Head, which is Porthloe Cove. [CWP]

Porthmeor Point:
OS.203 GR.424 380 HT–3.20 [25]

A very good area, becoming more popular in recent years, consisting of: Wenven Cove, 5 V Diffs around 80ft just to the E of the headland; Robin's Rocks, a 150ft greenstone cliff on the point offering a few classic easy Extremes; and Windy Zawn in the cove, offering a handful of mixed routes on granite. Parts are affected by the tide and although abseil is often used for approach there are easy escape routes. Pleasant area.

Dir: 8m NE of St Just. Approach: see Gurnard's Head, but park after only a few yards, then take the footpath down to the cove. [CWP]

Rosemergy Area:
OS.203 GR.413 366 HT–3.20 [26]

This is the ridge area to the SW of Bosigran, offering plenty of good climbing. Most of the ridge routes in the vicinity go at V Diff, and the area is very well endowed in routes of all grades. The zawns offer more challenging climbing to the enthusiast. There are several towers giving good 50–150ft routes.

Dir: 5.5m NE of St Just. Approach: see Bosigran, after the town of Morvah carry on for 1m. This is 300yds before Rosemergy, park and walk L (NE) along the ridge to the cliffs. [CWP]

Saint Levan:
OS.203 GR.384 218 [27]

A crag with plenty of shorter routes around 50ft. Non-tidal and a sun trap, with routes Mod to E5,6b. Very enjoyable crag.

Dir: 4m SE of Land's End. Approach: Take the B3315 SE to Tretheway then turn R on to the small lane leading S to the coast and St Levan. The crag is on the headland to the SE from the village, 400yds. [CWP]

Saint Loy Crag:
OS.203 GR.416 228 [28]

A small, 100ft, non-tidal cliff with around 10 routes, a few V Diffs and other harder climbs to E4, E5. High in quality, but bold and quite strenuous. S-facing and warm. Worth a visit.

Dir: 6.5m SW of Penzance. Take the B3315 SW past Lamorna, turn off. Carry on for 2m to Treveren Farm on the L, park here, small fee to farmer. A footpath leads to the sea, 600yds. The cliff is a few hundred yards on the L (E). [CWP]

ATLANTIC OCEAN WALL, E5, 6a, Land's End. (Climber Mark Edwards, Photo Rowland Edwards)

Sennen Cove:
OS.203 GR.347 263 HT−3.20   [29]

Not a large cliff but a solid one. Good sturdy granite up to 80ft, a wonderful selection of lower-grade climbs: of the 120 or so climbs, 40 are below VS. There is also a very good concentration of single-pitch, hard cliffs destined to become popular, up to E8, very technical in places. A great crag for the late riser. Most of it is non-tidal, however heavy seas sweeping in from the W can make this a damp spot.

Dir: 1m NNE of Land's End. Drive to Sennen Cove and find the car park. From the village a footpath leads W up on to the cliffs to a coastguard lookout. The cliff is directly below here, as is a descent to a large platform. [CWP]

Trewellard Cliff:
OS.203 CR.368 348 HT−3.20   [30]

Several buttresses appealing to the Diff to HVS climber, offering climbs up to 130ft. Very unusual area.

Dir: 2.5m NNE of St Just. From Pendeen centre turn L to Lower Boscastle, park at end of village. Here a path leads off W down to the coast and the cliffs in about 5 mins. [CWP]

Wicca Pillar:
OS.203 GR.465 400   [31]

An interesting pillar of granite, about 50ft high, with plenty of climbing in the Diff to Severe standard nearby. Good for beginners since top-

roping is easy to set up on the harder problems.

Dir: 4.8m W of St Ives. From St Just go N on the B3306, to Zennor 10m, stay on B road, go up steep hill and round the hill for 0.8m to a track leading to Tregerthen Farm. Park and walk down track, before farm bear R over a stile and bear down hollow leading to the cove and the pillar itself. [CWP]

Zawn Kellys:
OS.203 GR.359 227 HT−3.15   [32]

A zawn with some very good, easy Extreme climbing. Rarely sees overcrowding, yet routes are very good quality, about 120ft and well protected. Friends useful here. Abseil in; there is a Diff escape, though, from sea-level.

Dir: 1.8m SE of Land's End. Approach as for Carn Barra, pass that cliff and go into the next zawn only a few hundred yards on. 20 mins from car park. [CWP]

Zennor Cliff:
OS.203 GR.449 392 HT−3.20   [33]

Most refer to this as an atmospheric crag, containing about 10 routes around VS to E1. The rock is greenstone and of a semi-reliable nature. Climbs vary from 50 to 360ft, and are from a sea-washed ledge at high tide. Abseil in.

Dir: 5m WSW of St Ives. Take the B3306 from St Just for 13m to the village of Zennor, park. A path leads off to Zennor Head and the triangulation point on the head, before reaching drop down L to Pendour Cove and the crag. [CWP]

CORNWALL EAST

This area is for the most part far less popular than the west of Cornwall. The climbing is less concentrated and in general more serious. There is some good climbing to be found, with perhaps Carn Gowla, Pentire and Tintagel being the favourites. Most of the cliffs face north and, since most people visit the south west in the colder months, they are put off from getting frozen on these cliffs. Some of the cliffs have very poor rock and should be tackled with experience, not inability.

Beeny Cliff:
OS.190 GR.108 920   [34]

A large cliff of 500ft. Not to be recommended for those who are mortal. The upper part is extremely

interesting, requiring your keenest attention. Tending very loose to worse.

Dir: 1.7m NE of Boscastle. Approach: see Bukator. [NDC]

SWIFT FLIGHT OF FANCY, E2, 5c, Sennen. (Climber Rowland Edwards, Photo Mark Edwards)

Bukator Cliff:
OS.190 GR.118 935   [35]

A very large cliff, about 600ft high and not solid at all. All the climbs are extremely something or other!

Dir: 2m NE of Boscastle. Go N on the B3263, up the steep hill, at the top just out of the trees continue for a mile, then turn L to Beeny, carry on N for 300yds, then park. A track leads off N, then a footpath to the cliffs and indeed Bukator. You do have the option of an even more interesting time by bearing W and going to Beeny Cliff, only 5 mins away. [NDC]

Carn Gowla:
OS.203 GR.698 512 HT–3.30   [36]

About 2m of coastal cliffs at St Agnes Head, mostly around 350ft high, offering plenty of multi-pitch routes on quite good rock. Not really a place for the novice, but has many HVSs and Extremes; a very notable classic, America E3 is situated on the N side of the head, the best rock. Very impressive scenery here, without the crowds, makes a real epic very possible, even probable. If the sea gets rough, pray that your leader is having a good day and you have got your jumars. Long double ropes advisable. Cliff stays damp for several days so go in a good spell. Good luck.

Dir: 10m N of Redruth. From A30 at Three Burrows take the B3277 to St Agnes and a minor road up on to the headland to parking places near the coastguard lookout. The cliffs are on the N and the W side, explore at will. [NDC]

Cheesewring Quarry
OS.201 GR.258 724   [37]

A 120ft quarry which offers plenty of amusement with several climbs at most grades, including some good hard problems and bouldering.

Dir: 7m NNE of Liskeard, on Bodmin Moor at 1,000ft. From Liskeard go N on the B3254 for 8m to Upton Cross, turn L to Minions, 2m. The quarry lies 1m to the N of here up a track. [NDC]

Cligga Head:
OS.204 GR.737 537 HT–3.30   [38]

The only granite to be found in this area, about 120ft high and offering quite a few routes, Diff–

HVS grades. NW-facing, afternoon sun and only semi-tidal. Definitely worth a visit.

Dir: 15m NW of Truro near Perranporth. From Perranporth take the B3285 S for 1m, park. On the R is the disused Cligga mine and the point beyond is Cligga Head, the climbs being on the W side. [NDC]

Devil's Jump:
OS.200 GR.103 800   [39]

Granite Tors at 750ft, offering some 70ft routes in the low grades in a very pleasant setting.

Dir: 9m N of Bodmin. Take B3266 towards Camelford, 1m after Michaelstow there is a track to Trecarne. Park and walk SE up the valley for 0.5m to the rocks. [NDC]

Doyden Point:
OS.200 GR.966 806 HT–3.45   [40]

An excellent small crag amongst the giants on the N coast. About 150ft and climbs VS upwards, only a handful though. Awkward at high tide or in heavy seas, but not hopeless.

Dir: 9m NNE of Wadebridge. Where the B3314 turns R carry straight on to Portquin and a National Trust car park. From here go W to the point, traverse into crag. [NDC]

Kellan Head:
OS.200 GR.968 808   [41]

A crag of some 230ft, offering a handful of VS slab routes with harder variations.

Dir: 9.3m NNE of Wadebridge. Approach: see Doyden Point, the other headland to the N is reached in 5 mins. [NDC]

The Lizard:
OS.203 GR.674 143   [42]

There have been reports of frenzied climbing activity here and that a visit is well in order. Who knows, but past forays have resulted in major epics from which the participants emigrated to Holland in a state of terror. There have been climbs reported at Kynance Cove, stated in the reference, which lies 2m to the NW of the point. Generally worth an investigation, preferably thorough. [NDC]

DARKINBAD THE BRIGHT DAYLAYER, E4, 6a, Pentire Head. (Climber Rowland Edwards, Photo Mark Edwards)

Pentire Head:
OS.200 GR.924 805 [43]

The great wall here is perhaps the finest piece of rock in the south west of England. The situation, being escapable and not tidal, can still be desperate if your arms are not up to it. The rock is very good, and runs to solid protection. The route up the centre is Darkinbad the Bright Daylayer E4, the classic middle-grade route of the south west. Best on a good summer's day, can be nippy with a cold N wind.

Dir: 6m N of Padstow, 12m NW of Wadebridge. Approach: see Doyden but follow signs to Polzeath. Then to Pentire Farm where near the point there is a car park. A 10-min. walk leads N to the cliff. [NDC]

Roche Rocks:
OS.200 GR.992 597 [44]

A small 60ft granite outcrop with lots of bouldering in a non-serious environment. Mainly good in the lower grades, soloing and scrambling for all the family.

Dir: 7m W of Bodmin. Turn off the A30 on to the B3274 to Roche. [NDC]

Tintagel:
OS.200 GR.048 892 HT−3.50 [45]

A definite big spurter cliff this one, the rock is best described as different. If you fall off you are not going to hit anything anyway. Not a lot of easy routes, mainly E4 upwards. A serious and committing crag, coastguards would like wallies to keep away. There are easier climbs on the smaller cliffs but they are not in the same league.

Dir: 30m W of Launceston. Get to Tintagel, follow signs to the Castle car park, fee, or park back in the town, 5 mins. From here the cliffs are on the W side. [NDC]

Trebarwith Strand:
OS.200 GR.048 864 HT−3.50 [46]

An area with some fair climbing. A 2,000ft traverse leads around the headland to Backways Cove E1, also can be reached slightly more easily by walking over the headland, here a handful of climbs S to HVS. Also by walking N some quarries with a couple of middle-grade routes can be found. Worth exploring.

Dir: From Tintagel go S on the B3263 for 2m, back sharp R down lane to cove 1.3m, Trebarwith Strand. [NDC]

Willapark:
OS.200 GR.060 897 HT−3.50 [47]

A 250ft crag on the adjacent point to Tintagel Head, with an HVS route. Best approached at low tide.

Dir: From Tintagel follow the B3263 N for 0.5m to Bossiney, park. 10-min. walk to the headland. [NDC]

DARTMOOR

This area of Devon is high moorland with most of the climbing around 1500ft high, and in the winter months it can get very cold and snow covered. In summer it provides a very pleasant climate making even very hot days bearable for climbing. The rock, with the exception of Sheep Tor, is granite and very weathered into rounded bulges of the most peculiar shapes and sizes. In general it is only ever the narrow roads that get crowded, with slow-moving caravans that cannot reverse. Protection is brilliant when found, and the advent of friends and camming devices has made this a sensible area to climb in. The area is a national park and a military battleground – bizarre indeed – so careful note should be taken of any notices, mainly in the NW, regarding DANGER! BOMBS! TANKS! SS-20s! etc. They are real.

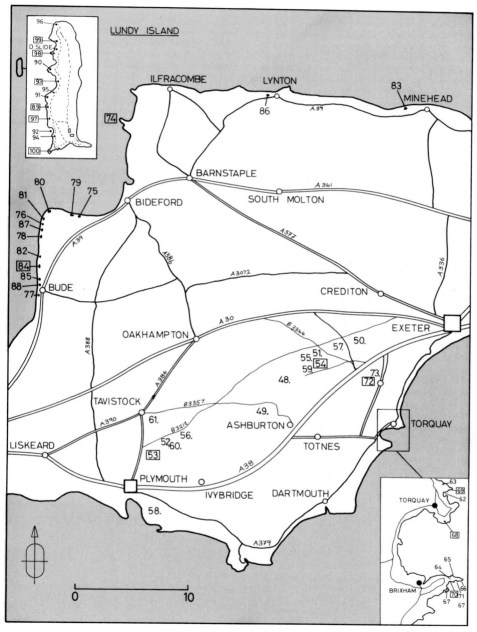

LUNDY ISLAND

96
99
D. SLIDE
98
90
93
95
91
89
97
92
94
100

ILFRACOMBE
LYNTON
86
A 39
83
MINEHEAD

74

BARNSTAPLE
A 361
SOUTH MOLTON

80   79
81   75
76
87
78
82
84
85
88
77

BIDEFORD
A 39
A 386
A 377
A 3072
A 336
CREDITON

BUDE
A 388
A 30
B 3344
EXETER
50.
57.
55 51.
59 54.
48.
73.
72.
OAKHAMPTON

TAVISTOCK
A 386
B 3357
49.
ASHBURTON
TORQUAY
A 390
61.
B 3212
56.
52 60.
53
TOTNES
LISKEARD
A 38

PLYMOUTH
IVYBRIDGE
DARTMOUTH

58.

0   10

A 379

TORQUAY
63
69
62
68
65
64
66
BRIXHAM
70 71
67   67

DEVON

Bell Tor:
OS.191 GR.730 769   [48]

Several small outcrops offering scrambling and a 60ft HVS on Widecombe Wall, between the neighbouring Honeybag and Chinkwell Tors. Tor height is 1054ft, most of the climbing is on the W side.

Dir: 6m NNW of Ashburton. From Ashburton A38, follow signs to Widecombe in the moor, take the Haytor road E after 100yds. A road on the L leads up through Bonehill, 0.7m, where the tors are up on the L. [SDD]

Bench Tor:
OS.191 GR.692 717   [49]

A handful of climbs high on the tor on its S side, Diffs upwards. An entertaining visit. Half a mile before the tor is reached there is Eagle Rock on the L bank, 60ft, with about 10 climbs Diff–HVS, down in the valley and sheltered. A good alternative.

Dir: 4.5m WNW of Ashburton. Just past on the A38 take the B3357 right towards Tavistock, after 7m arrive at Dartmeet, Clapper Bridge. A scenic stroll S along the river Dart leads to the crag in about 30 mins, a sprint E from the tor valley for a mile gets you to the Tavistock Inn, and even a campsite. [SDD]

Blackingstone Rock:
OS.191 GR.786 856   [50]

This tor and its neighbour Hel Tor give about 10 routes, Diff–VS, on N-facing slabs and faces, with tremendous views towards the river Teign. At around 1,000ft, not the place on a cold, windy day. Climbs around 100ft.

Dir: 2.5m ESE of Moretonhampstead. Take the B3212 towards Exeter up the steep, winding road. After 2m turn R towards Bridford, the road steepens after 1m and just over the top of the col the tor is seen on the R. [SDD]

Bowerman's Nose:
OS.191 GR.741 804   [51]

A large, granite pudding-block tower gives a few routes Diff upwards. At 1,200ft in a pleasant area. Worth a boulder.

Dir: 5m WNW of Bovey Tracey and near Mana-

ton. From A38, take B3344 through Bovey Tracey, 5m to Manaton, through village and after 1m a small road on the L leads up to the Nose in 0.7m. [SDD]

Combshead Tor:
OS.191 GR.587 688   [52]

A small 20ft boulder with a few V Diffs on it at 1200ft.

Dir: 7.5m SE of Tavistock. Take A386 to Yelverton, then B3212 towards Princetown, after 2m turn R to Burrator reservoir and drive to the E end, park. A track leads SE beside the woods and up to the tor in about 1.2m, 20 mins walk. [SDD]

Dewerstone:
OS.202 GR.538 638   [53]

This is perhaps the best cliff on Dartmoor, even in Devon. At around 170ft and being almost vertical, it presents superb climbs especially in the lower grades, yet not without difficulty. The climbing is good, sturdy stuff on sound, well-protected rock. The climbing itself is on a series of buttresses overlooking the river Plym, giving around 100 routes. At around 400ft above sea level, it remains sheltered and a sensible venue if the weather is dodgy. Can be seriously affected by midges though, beware.

Dir: 5m NNW of A38 at Plymouth. Take A386 towards Yelverton, after 3m turn R to Bickleigh, go through village, turn L, follow signs to Shaugh Prior. After 1.5m a bridge is crossed, park on the R. Cross back over the river and then follow path up the L side to reach the crag after 0.4m. [SDD]

Hay Tor:
OS.191 GR.758 771   [54]

This is split into High Man and Low Man, both giving superb climbing on the best tor of Dartmoor. High Man as seen from the road looks insignificant, but around the back offers some 30 routes of all grades up to 80ft high. All are well protected and require good use of jamming. The achievement of gaining the summit is somewhat tainted by the hordes of tourists streaming up in lemming-like fashion on the other side. Low Man, not visible from the road, offers the harder climbs, about 20 from Severe to E-whatever. Friends are essential to protect oneself on Low

LEVIATHAN, VS, The Dewerstone. (Climber Rob MacNair, Photo Bob Moulton)

Man for the more optimistic endeavours. At 1490ft it is not a winter crag, and in a summer emergency the inn at Haytor Vale can provide excellent wet-weather facilities.

Dir: 4m WSW of Bovey Tracey. From BT take the B3344 towards Manaton, after 0.6m fork L up a smaller lane to Haytor, which is reached after 3.4m, car park. From here walk to the tor, 10 mins. [SDD]

Hound Tor:
OS.191 GR.743 790   [55]

An area strewn with boulders provides plenty of scrambling and climbing, excellent for beginners, about 20 Diffs up to 70ft and a handful of harder climbs. At 1300ft it is very exposed and open to the N winds.

Dir: 4.5m W of Bovey Tracey. Take B3344 from BT to Manaton, from inn turn L and follow road for 2.5m to crossroads, park. Walk SE for 5 mins to tor summit. [SDD]

Leather Tor:
OS.202 GR.563 701   [56]

A handful of climbs, Diff–VS, around 30ft high, E-facing.

Dir: 3.5m ENE of Yelverton. Take B3212 towards Princetown for 3m, park. Walk SE over Sharpitor 0.6m to Leather Tor. [SDD]

Lustleigh Cleave:
OS.191 GR.762 818   [57]

A good bouldering area with many problems, a beauty spot.

Dir: 4m NW of Bovey Tracey. To Manaton B3344 from BT, turn R at village, up steep hill for 0.7m, sharp L bend, park. Walk R down track to river Bovey and follow S for 0.5m, rocks appear on the R. [SDD]

Radford Quarry: Restriction
OS.201 GR.531 505   [58]

This crag is on private land and access is variable. Although not on Dartmoor, this crag is listed here as the only other worthwhile crag in the area. A slab in a quarry, 200ft, offering a handful of solid routes, V Diff–E1.

Dir: 3m SSE of Plymouth off A379. From Plymstock follow signs to Knighton–Wembury, 0.5m before Knighton take L at fork, after 50yds a track leads off L to the quarry. [SDD]

Saddle Tor:
OS.191 GR.751 763   [59]

A small outcrop half a mile SW of Hay Tor. A handful of 30ft Severes and chimneys. [SDD]

Sheeps Tor:
OS.202 GR.565 683   [60]

A smallish cliff of around 30ft offers 20 or so routes, Diff–HS. E-facing and 1000ft up, this is more of a morning crag, nevertheless it is always pleasant to visit.

Dir: 2.5m W of Yelverton. Take the B3212 towards Princetown, after 1.5m turn R and follow signs to Sheeps Tor. Pass just through the village and park. A track off L leads up to Sheeps Tor, reached in about 15 mins. [SDD]

Vixen Tor:
OS.191 GR.542 743   [61]

Some good climbing to be found on this 100ft cliff which faces S. About 15 climbs including an Extreme – a rarity on Dartmoor. Plenty of amusement for everyone, since the summit necessitates strenuous effort to be conquered.

Dir: 4m E of Tavistock. Take the B3357 from T to Merrivale, park close to pub – what a decision – walk SW for 0.7m to reach crag. [SDD]

TORBAY

The climbing around Torbay is situated at Hope's Nose, Torquay and at Berry Head, Brixham. Both headlands are limestone and fairly solid, around 200ft high. If climbing on any of the cliffs within close vicinity of sunbathing tourists, care should be taken to avoid dislodging huge boulders. It can even get so hot in summer that swimming is by far the best pastime. In such weather, long, sea-level traverses can provide excellent amusement.

Anstey's Cove: Restriction
OS.202 GR.935 648 HT–4.36 [62]

The cliffs are straight above a very popular holiday beach and during peak days get very crowded – it is hoped climbers will refrain from climbing here during such times. About 40 routes of all grades including an E7. A pleasant spot for both the Severe climber and the E5, 6b clotted-cream team.

Dir: At Babbacombe, 1.7m NE of Torquay. From Torquay take the B3199 to Babbacombe, after 1m park in car park on the R. A path just further on the R is signposted to Anstey's Cove. [SDD]

Babbacombe Crags:
OS.202 GR.934 653 [63]

These are the cliffs which run NW from Long Quarry Point, 120–200ft high. About 10 routes in all grades.

Dir: Approach: see Long Quarry Point. [SDD]

Berry Head: Restriction.
OS.202 GR.947 565 HT–4.36 [64]

There are very strict bans on climbing here during nesting seasons – see individual crags. There are cliffs surrounding the whole of the headland reaching up to 300ft high. The climbs vary in size and standard, and some, though serious, are on good compact limestone offering thrilling climbing. High tides and rough seas can cut off many of the climbs, so care should be taken when planning a rock excursion into an angry cauldron. VS to E5.

Dir: 2m NE of Brixham. From the town Berry Head is signposted, park on Berry Head common. [SDD]

Berry Head Quarry:
OS.202 GR.945 567 [65]

A disused quarry offering a handful of routes around VS–HVS, about 200ft in length.

Dir: Approach: see Berry Head. From the car park take the road towards the point, but before the old fort fork L down the old quarry road. The cliff is on the R stretching to the point. [SDD]

Coast Guard Cliff:
OS.202 GR.947 566 HT–4.36 [66]

Some excellent climbing is to be found on the headland of Berry Head. About 20 climbs of all grades including a VS traverse around to, or back from, the quarry area. About 150ft, SE-facing, warm and sunny.

Dir: As for Berry Head. From the car park walk towards the headland, before the coastguard station a path leads down to the R and some sea-level terraces. To the headland is Coast Guard Cliff and back along the cliff is Red Wall area. [SDD]

Cradle Rock:
OS.202 GR.943 560 HT–4.36 [67]

A rather discontinuous line of cliffs leading S from Berry Head, but nevertheless worthy of inclusion, offering several routes around 120ft, middle grades to E1. The area consists of a rock buttress by a zawn, as first reached from the car park, and Cradle Rock, a worthwhile solo.

Dir: Approach: see Berry Head. From car park go back along the road for 200yds and take the footpath on the L, after 300yds a path leads down to some slabs beneath the main buttress. The coastline can be traversed, Magical Mystery Tour VS, to Cradle Rock itself and beyond at sea-level. [SDD]

Daddyhole Area:
OS.202 GR.928 628 HT−4.36 [68]

This area consists of four minor cliffs – Meadfoot Quarry, Western and Eastern Cliffs and Telegraph Hole – all around 80ft, and one major cliff, Main Cliff. This is the largest, 190ft, E-facing, and set just above the high-tide line. There is little below VS on the main cliff and indeed the harder routes are often referred to as 'serious'! On the other cliffs there are plenty of Diffs, etc. The traverse of the area is The Watchtower, a 600ft VS, possible at high tide and S-facing.

Dir: 7m SE of Torquay. From the harbour take the Babbacombe road B3199, after a few hundred yards signposts direct you rightwards to Daddyhole Plain, after 0.6m a car park is reached above Daddyhole Cove. Descent to the main cliff is made by following the ridge down to the sea then a traverse back at Severe standard. For the other cliffs, footpaths can be found leading off the coastal path. [SDD]

Long Quarry Point: Restriction
OS.202 GR.938 651 HT−4.36 [69]

Care should be taken to avoid bombing tourists with loose rocks at low tide, or swimmers at high tide. The point consists of both quarry and outer pinnacles, Diff–VS routes; slabs and a quarried wall, about 50 routes, most VS but upwards to E6, 300ft high; and Sanctuary Wall, a 150ft vertical wall with many interesting routes, some of them perilously climbable, some not! Only Sanctuary Wall is tidal and protection is varied; friends are useful as are double ropes.

Dir: 2m NE of Torquay. Take the Babbacombe B3199 road from Torquay. After 1m park on the R just beyond signs to Anstey's Cove. Take a footpath which leads to the open headland. Descent can be made easily to the cliffs except Sanctuary Wall, which is usually accessed by short abseil and to be found on the seaward side before the pinnacle. [SDD]

Old Redoubt: Restriction
OS.202 GR.947 565 HT−4.36 [70]

This is a very ornithological place and indeed the protected habitat for thousands of birds from Easter to summer. There is to be no climbing here from 1 Mar.–1 Aug. please. This is the grandest cliff in the area, a good, 300ft-high, limestone, solid(ish) crag cutting straight into the sea. The climbs are hard, min. HVS, and the only escape is the overhanging abseil into the invariably boiling cauldron of menace and doom. Nevertheless the 20 or so routes up to E5 are mostly classics and take tremendous line through massive overhangs. Protection is good, double ropes and prusik gear are essential.

Dir: 1m ENE of Brixham. Follow signs from Brixham to Berry Head, car park. Leave this on the R where a path scrambles down to the sea. A traverse in can be made 2 hrs either side of high tide, there is no other escape. [SDD]

Red Wall Area:
OS.202 GR.945 565 HT−4.36 [71]

A good small cliff, 80–120ft, with about 15 routes, V Diff–HVS. Well-protected climbs, sunny and S-facing.

Dir: Approach: see Coast Guard Cliff. [SDD]

CHUDLEIGH

Chudleigh:
OS.202 GR.864 788 [72]

A large cliff of good, solid, compact limestone, up to 120ft high. Mainly S-facing and quick to dry, thereby being popular and in places very polished. 150 climbs of all grades on steep walls and overhangs, protection being good with double ropes.

Dir: 1m SW of Chudleigh. Take the A38 SW from Exeter to B3344, turn off to Chudleigh, enter village. Turn down the road beside the police station through village, follow for a few hundred yards to a parking spot. A signposted path leads to the rocks. There is a narrow ridge which splits the N and S faces. [SDD]

Palace Quarry: Restriction
OS.202 GR.866 787 [73]

A limestone quarry with ever-changing routes as quarrying takes place, with more climbing in the area. Around 130ft with routes of all grades. A discreet approach will ensure a welcome.

Dir: 1m SW of Chudleigh. Approach: see Chudleigh. The quarry can be seen from the start of the path leading to Chudleigh Rocks. [SDD]

NORTH DEVON

The North Devon coast offers climbers complete variety and interest. There are no solid cliffs here except for the island of Lundy, which is very solid granite and simply a climbing paradise. The other cliffs tend to be large and in places very dubious. To dismiss the whole area would be understandable but regrettable, since there is some very good climbing here. The climate here is very kind, with nearly all the cliffs W-facing. Often the clouds sweep over the coast to clog up on the moors a few miles inland and leave the crags to enjoy sunshine for most of the year. Tides are quite important to get right, swimming occasionally being a necessary skill!

Baggy Point:
OS.180 GR.419 406 HT—4.15   [74]

This is the most popular of the crags on the coast and not surprisingly offers excellent climbing on solid, reliable rock. The area consists of lots of slabs stretching up to 300ft in places, about 60 routes in all grades but more of VS upwards I am afraid. The routes are occasionally sparsely protected but not really dangerous. Double full 50m ropes are useful here, and seconds should always keep an eye on the incoming tide. It is a very pleasant cliff, and on a sunny day a dream.

Dir: 15m WNW of Barnstaple. Take the A361 to Braunton then the B3231 to Croyde. Here a small road leads off to the point, park in the National Trust car park, which gets busy in the height of summer. The cliffs are a short walk from here. [NDC]

Blackchurch:
OS.190 GR.299 266 HT—4.10   [75]

A large cliff, 250ft, and a good one of its kind, but even so the rock should be treated with caution. No significant routes below Extreme, definitely not the place for the novice! Not a safe crag. Tides not really a problem.

Dir: 28m WSW of Barnstaple. Take the A39 past Bideford and 15m later at Clovelly take the B3248 R towards Hartland. After 3.1m take R turn down lane to Brownshaw Farm, park. A 15-min. walk leads to the coast and the crag on the point. [NDC]

Brownspear Point:
OS.190 GR.224 235 HT—4.10   [76]

A cliff with some climbing, some fair and some not so fair. About 200ft with a few Diffs and a few Extremes. Rock is of indifferent quality.

Dir: 2.7m WSW of Hartland. From Hartland go S on small lanes to Milford, signposted. Just before reaching Milford park at the hamlet of Lymebridge. Here a footpath leads to the coast and the picturesque spot of Speke's Mill Mouth. The cliff is the rocky point to the S. [NDC]

Compass Point:
OS.190 GR.099 064   [77]

These cliffs are of reasonable stability and offer about 15 routes in the VS to E3 grades. About 100ft high with easy access. A very amenable crag. There are reported to be lock-inns in the area!

Dir: 0.7m W of Bude. From the centre of Bude take the road that runs beside the canal, going W until it seems sensible to park. From here continue on foot to the crag, which is on the S side of the headland. [CWP]

Cornakey Cliff:
OS.190 GR.204 165 HT—3.55   [78]

This is a very serious crag! A tidal approach leads you to a very large 400ft crag, and is best described as not being conducive to life. Although the grades are around VS and HVS, this only applies if Newton is on your side. A sunny aspect with a lack of crowds is the only point in its favour. If loose rock is your game, it's Christmas.

Dir: 12m N of Bude. Follow the A39 N for 10m. Take L turn to Shop, continue for 1m, turn R to Cornakey Farm, park. Walk W for 15 mins to reach the coast and the cliff. [NDC]

Exmansworthy:
OS.190 GR.278 270   [79]

This can be best described as an adventure whereby climbing is simply secondary to a larger range of skills. There could be lots of routes here, maybe there are. Who cares? In parts there are some very good routes, of which people rave. Are you convinced?

Dir: 2m NNE of Hartland. Approach: see Blackchurch. Instead of turning R to Brownshaw Farm go straight on (lane), L, R, R to Exmansworthy Farm. Ask the farmer's permission to cross his fields and head NE to the cliffs. [NDC]

Hartland Point:
OS.190 GR.227 267   [80]

There is climbing to be found on the W side of the point around the bay 1m to the S. Typical N Devon climbing, of interest to some. The notable areas are: Cow and Calf, about 0.5m S of the point, a handful of hardish climbs; also Damehole Point 0.5m to the S again with more climbing.

Dir: 3m NW of Hartland. [NDC]

Hartland Quay:
OS.190 GR.223 247   [81]

This area offers quite a few crags for the connoisseur of the region. The area S from the quay is Screda Point, offering about 6 climbs, VS to E3, the best outing being the scramble up the knife-edged pinnacle. To the N about 15-mins walk away is Dyers Lookout. The good climbing is to be had on the smaller cliffs, about 7 cliffs around VS.

Dir: 2.7m W of Hartland. [NDC]

Henna Cliff:
OS.190 GR.199 157   [82]

If your wife gives you the Henna Cliff guide for Christmas, take the hint and accept the divorce. It is not a crag fit for anyone of sound mind – indeed to scale the 500ft of darkness is an accomplishment not of merit but of insanity. Alas, it has been done – oh, for the glory of a first ascent. The first descent could only achieve the glory of a solemn quotation chiselled in stone.

Dir: 6m N of Bude. Go N on the A39, after 5m turn L and follow signs to Morwenstow. Here a stream runs down to the cliffs where the bottom can be reached by abseil. Ice climbing gear essential. [NDC]

Hurlstone Point:
OS.181 GR.900 493 HT–4.40   [83]

Another gem of insecurity. About 10 routes in the lower grades up to 200ft.

Dir: 7m WNW of Minehead. Take the A39 to Porlock, at Allerford take a R to Bossington village and park at the National Trust car park. Follow a footpath towards the coastguard lookout on the point. The cliffs are on the E side, scramble down. [NDC]

Lower Sharpnose Point:
OS.190 GR.195 127 HT–4.00   [84]

The cliffs here are perhaps the best in the immediate area, approaching real rock – well almost. About 20 climbs up to 120ft in all grades on some very dramatic-looking fins of rock disappearing into the sky. Big nuts and friends worthwhile here. Low tide is useful but one can also abseil into a bay between the fins. There is also climbing to be found at Higher Sharpnose Point and Vicarage Cliff, 1.5 and 2m up the coastline, but it is of limited merit. Midway between is Hippa Rock with a couple of E1s.

Dir: 4.5m N of Bude. Take the A39 going N. At Stratton a small lane to the L is marked Coombe, pass through Coombe and continue for 1m to the military installation on the head. The point is directly beneath this. Walk to the crag, 10 mins. [NDC]

Menachurch Point:
OS.190 GR.201 088   [85]

A crag with about 6 VS routes around 100ft.

Dir: 2m NNW of Bude. Approach: see Wrangle Point. Take the cliff-top path going N for 20 mins to reach the point. [NDC]

Valley of the Rocks:
OS.180 GR.710 497 [86]

Some short climbs on some outcrops up to 80ft high, also good problems of all grades. Worth a visit if passing.

Dir: 1m W of Lynton. From the town there are signs to the valley. [NDC]

Welcombe:
OS.190 GR.211 185 HT–4.00 [87]

Near the village of Welcombe there are two sets of slabs. At Gull Rock to the S, approached by a 20-min. walk along the coast to the obvious point, good climbing, about 100ft with fair protection, a handful of HS routes. Nearest Welcombe are the **Foxhold Slabs**, 500yds up the beach at Welcombe Mouth, about 8 routes of 100–150ft from S to HVS. A pleasant spot, avoid high tide.

Dir: 8m N of Bude. Take the A39 N for 8m then turn off to Welcombe. Follow the road to the sea. [NDC]

Wrangle Point:
OS.190 GR.201 072 [88]

This point has a pair of slabs on it, one white and one yellow. Reports that they are both brown may be true though! A couple of routes around Severe of 150ft.

Dir: 1m NW of Bude. From Bude drive N towards Flexbury and then W to the cliff top. Walk over field to the actual cliff. [NDC]

LUNDY

The island of Lundy offers fantastic climbing in a situation unrivalled for isolation south of Scotland. The good part is that the weather here is usually 100 per cent better than that of the north. The rock is granite and in most places very good. The climbs have still not had enough traffic to make them polished and in many cases the cracks are still sandy. The routes are rarely chalked up and the hard routes here need a strong pioneering instinct to succeed. Most climbers going to the island would purchase a guidebook, I imagine, but for those not wishing to do so I will describe the island's cliffs sufficiently to enable one to climb and navigate the cliffs to the best advantage with the help of the 1:25,000 map of the island, OS. SS 44/54.

Restrictions The island is a bird-breeding colony and because of this there is never any climbing between the dates of 1 April and 31 July. In general climbers do not visit the island between these periods.

Travel To stay on the island you have to contact the Landmark Trust, Shottesbroke, Maidenhead, Berkshire, SL6 3SW. This Trust manages the island and can be contacted by post, or by phone on 062-882 5925. They are very helpful and if you state that you are wishing to climb on the island they will send you all the details you require. The method of travel to the island is by boat; there was once a helicopter service but this is now no longer. The trip takes about two hours and on a sunny day can be wonderful. At other times sea-sickness pills are recommended. Landing on the island by landing craft and tractor is an experience in itself.

Accommodation   This is the big problem with the island. There is a shortage of water and consequently the numbers have to be limited. There are several cottages and other types of house for self-catering accommodation, and a campsite. To stay at any of these, including the campsite, you must book ahead and you should do so well in advance. With a group prices can be very reasonable. Camping is also quite practical as there are no weight restrictions on the luggage you take to the island.

Survival   There is a shop on the island which supplies everything and is very good. Access and Visa facilities are available so the problem of running out of cash on the island is avoided; however the pub takes cash only. There are no banks. Remember to bring some money also for a boat trip around the island.

Climbing   It is a very civilised place to climb; all the cliffs are W-facing and warm up around lunchtime, so there are no horrible early starts unless the tides dictate. Upon arriving at the island it is a good idea to team up in a large group and to arrange a boat trip around the island. From this you can see all the cliffs properly and plan your adventures accordingly for the rest of your stay. One week is usually enough to guarantee four good days. Most of the climbs are not that long but are of a very good standard. The island is about 4 miles long and half a mile wide, and runs from north to south. The longest climbs are around 400ft and very impressive. On the whole they are single-pitch climbs. It is recommended to use double ropes and bring an abseil rope with jumars. A rescue here is awkward and to be avoided at all costs. There are over 500 routes at all grades and one can climb all day, even all week, on different crags and routes.

Alternative amusement   I recommend that you go with a friend since if the weather is bad there is absolutely nothing to do. Take a few books and games, and anything else you feel is necessary to idle away the hours.

The Areas

Battery Point:
OS.180 GR.127 448   [89]

On the tip of this area is **Flying Buttress Area**, OS.1272 4489. Some very good climbing with the classic Mod Flying Buttress and the VS Diamond Solitaire. Lots of routes in all grades, 100–150ft. [LU]

Beaufort Buttress:
OS.180 GR.130 463   [90]

This is the point to the S of St James's Stone. A pleasant spot, offering plenty of routes in the lower grades around 150ft. Worth a trip for the Severe leader. [LU]

Dead Cow Point:
OS.180 GR.127 452   [91]

The climbing here tends to be poorer but just to the N is **Bomber Buttress**, OS.1288 4534. This is

THE DEVIL'S SLIDE, Severe, Lundy. (Climber Jim Tancred, Photo Bob Moulton)

N-facing and is about 150ft, offering routes in the low E grades. [LU]

Goat Island:
OS.180 GR.131 437   [92]

This area is smaller and offers some routes in the N part around the Severe and VS grades on **Celtic Buttress**, OS.1313 4380, and **Atlantic Buttress**, OS.1302 4389. The routes are around 100–250ft. [LU]

Jenny's Cove:
OS.180 GR.132 457   [93]

A very good area, offering a whole range of different climbs from cliff to cliff. **The Egyptian Slabs**, OS.1325 4586, offer very good routes around E1. **Deep Zawn**, OS.1324 4574, offers large and serious Extremes, and classic routes for the E4 climber or E3 climber with guts. **Devil's Chimney Cliff**, OS.1320 4568, offers good 300ft routes from HVS to E3, and **The Devil's Chimney** itself offers some VS routes. [LU]

Montague Steps:
OS.180 GR.132 435 [94]

The cliffs in this area are around 100–150ft high. **Montague Buttress**, OS.1316 4360, has a good range of routes in the lower grades. **Weird Wall**, OS.1328 4352, to the S has some good routes around the E2 grade. [LU]

Needle Rock:
OS.180 GR.129 456   [95]

A nice area for the lower-grade climber, with some very good Diffs and Severes up to 80ft. [LU]

North West Point:
OS.180 GR.130 481   [96]

The most northerly part of the island, and a good hour's walk, still offers plenty of climbing, although the routes tend to be in the lower grades. This is the real place to get away from it all. S from here is **Arch Zawn**, OS.1293 4738, which offers a great deal of good climbing, 150ft on all standards to E4. This one is worth the walk. [LU]

The Old Light:
OS.180 GR.129 442   [97]

This area, running N from The Old Light, offers very good climbing. **The Old Light Cliff**, OS.1295 4428, offers about half a dozen routes, 200ft, HVS to E3 – the general standard and nature of the climbs in the area. **Alpine Buttress** and **Wolfman Jack Wall**, OS.1289 4445, offer some of the best climbs on the island at around E2, about 150ft. The next best area to the N is **St Patrick's Buttress**, OS.1283 4478, which offers superb climbs around 150ft in the VS to E3 category. [LU]

St James's Stone Area:
OS.180 GR.130 468   [98]

The biggest landmark in the area is **The Devil's Slide**, OS.1314 4688, just to the N, about 400ft long and quite smooth in places. This gives excellent climbing, HS to E1 or harder if one wishes to leave out holds. To the S of the point is **Great Falls Zawn**, OS.1320 4641, with some excellent HVS climbing on 400ft routes. [LU]

St John's Stone:
OS.180 GR.130 470   [99]

This lies about 100yds to the N of St James's Stone. The crags are very jumbled around and are better than they appear. To the S on the inlet is **The Diamond**, OS.1317 4700, offering many of the best climbs, E4 upwards, on the island. **The Fortress**, OS.1309 4703, offers excellent 150ft HVS climbs. To the N is **Long Cliff** and the buttress **Torrey Canyon**, OS.1304 4716, with lots of good routes, 150ft up to HVS, and the classic E3 Controlled Burning. [LU]

Shutter Point:
OS.180 GR.133 434   [100]

This area at the southern tip of the island offers some very good routes in the harder grades. **Focal Buttress**, OS.1338 4343, has some very fine Extremes on the large face. **The Devil's Limekiln**, OS.1338 4349, is well worth a visit for the feeling, and for looking like something out of the film *Alien*. The area in general has climbs around 300ft and is very good. Not to be missed. [LU]

3 Bristol Area

The limestone around Bristol varies from excellent to very poor. Most cliffs have good and bad sections so care should be taken in committing oneself to a pitch where the pro is not very forthcoming. All are very accessible in a very short time with the restrictions at Cheddar making it the only awkward crag. There is a lot of climbing here and although the rock is not perfect it does lend itself to interesting situations!

Avon Gorge: Access
OS.172 GR.562 743   [1]

There will be major blasting in the central section 1990–1993 which will affect access. Check with BMC for access times and areas. Almost 300 climbs make this a very popular spot. The easy grades tend to be technically easy and poorly protected, as are most climbs here anyway. VS and HVS climbs are only reasonably safe, get good gear in early. Low Extremes tend to be very good; high Extremes tend to be chop routes because of the lack of bolts and abseil inspection a must. Approaching from the motorway you first come to a big wall with a very large slab, Es only. R side is excellent, best in the gorge; L side needs optimistic pro, yellow soft rock. Very shortly there are some walls, very good easier routes and top-rope problems, a good introduction to the area. A few hundred yards on is the Main area: big 300ft cliffs with a host of routes, not many good holds and indifferent pro; hard routes, Es, on Main Wall to the L, and easier Diffs to VS on the R. The last cliff is below the Suspension Bridge, a buttress of natural limestone gives a welcome change to quarried and blasted rock. Beautiful climbing, about 12 routes HVS upwards, except for the arête VS, a classic. Abseil descent. The cliff is the fastest drying in the country – if it rains stay on the route, in 5 mins it will be bone dry. There is a heavy road beneath crag making it rather unsecluded and a muddy brown river, belay facing in with a walkman on. Double ropes are very useful here, so are bolts.

Dir: At Bristol. From the M5 turn off Junction 18, Avonmouth. Follow the A4 into Bristol along the river Avon. Crags are on the L before the Suspension Bridge. From city centre follow signs for Avonmouth, A4. [AVC]

Black Rock Quarry:
OS.182 GR.486 547   [2]

A small quarry of limited interest out of Cheddar's summer restrictions. Several routes up to about 80ft.

Dir: Approach: see Cheddar Gorge. Drive up through the gorge for 1.3m where a valley leads off to the L. Take the track for 5 mins to the quarry. [AVC]

Brean Down:
OS.182 GR.285 588 HT-5.08   [3]

A sunny crag of about 100ft high, offering 30 or so routes of good quality on sound rock at all grades from Severe upwards at the landward end and lots of easier shorter routes to the western end. A nice position over the sand flats and only interrupted for a short spell by high tide. Weston-super-Mare is a very popular summer resort – do not expect the area to be deserted, watch for falling rocks and for tourists.

Dir: 3m SW of Weston-super-Mare. From Junction 22 on M5 take B3140 signposted Burnham-on-Sea, after 400yds fork R down a small road which leads to Berrow and then Brean. Follow N to the headland, park. Walk to crag, 2 mins. [AVC]

Brockley Coombe:
OS.182 GR.474 664   [4]

Some small natural limestone outcrops, 30–50ft high. The rock here is definitely not solid. Only if desperate.

Dir: 7m SW of Bristol. Take the A370 going SW

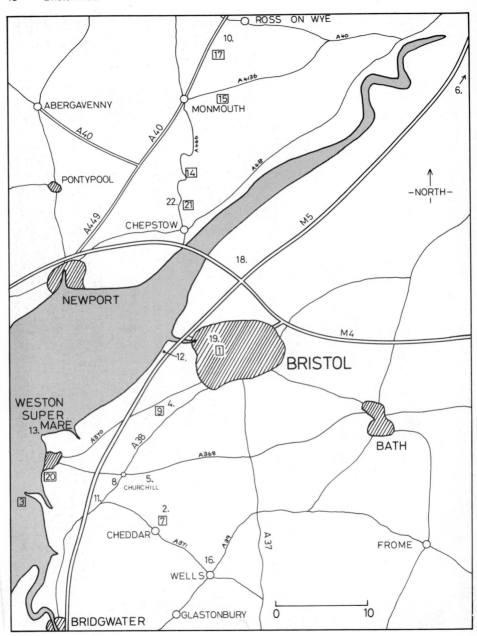

BRISTOL AREA

MIRAGE, E4, 6a, Avon Gorge. (Climber Adrian Gostick, Photo David B A Jones)

towards Congresbury. After West town and before Brockley a small lane leads off to the L and some woods to the coombe. [AVC]

Burrington Coombe:
OS.182 GR.477 585 [5]

Some small cliffs in this area give good bouldering and some short climbs of varying difficulty.

Dir: 12m E of Weston-super-Mare. Take the A38 from Bristol to Churchill. Take the A368 E towards West Harptree, after 2m turn R on the B3134. Arrive at the coombe after 1m. [AVC]

Castle Rock:
OS.150 GR.984 262 [6]

This small 30ft limestone outcrop offers a good 20 routes to entertain climbers of almost any standard. Good for bouldering.

Dir: 5m NE of Cheltenham. Take the A46 N from Cheltenham to Cleeve Hill and The Rising Sun pub. The rocks are 5 mins walk along and up the hill. [No guide]

Cheddar Gorge: Restriction:
OS.182 GR.472 542 [7]

Not a bird restriction but a tourist restriction. No climbing here I am afraid from Easter, mid-March, until October. It is common sense really, the cliff is directly above the road and unsuspecting tourists. Climbing at the top end of the gorge is usually tolerated, but on hot, crowded days the police will act to prevent climbing – a pity since the crag faces N and is cool even in summer. Lots of woollies needed here. Its 400 routes up to 410ft long on interesting and sometimes vegetated rock provide excellent entertainment: lots of Extremes, ample supply of V Diffs and Severes, many classic VS and HVS lines. Descents take a long time, even longer in the dark, occasionally very short though. Cheddar is a major tourist attraction, caves, cliffs, etc., and of course the wonderful cheese, which goes so well with beer.

Dir: 0.7m NE of Cheddar. Follow the signs to the gorge. [AVC]

Churchill Rocks:
OS.182 GR.445 592 [8]

A small outcrop of some walls and a slab with some good climbs around V Diff, Severe. Interesting.

Dir: 10m E of Weston-super-Mare. Take the A38 S from Bristol to Churchill, 20m, carry on for 0.4m to a wall above the road on the R. [AVC]

Goblin Combe:
OS.182 GR.483 653 [9]

Quite a pleasant crag of limestone about 80ft high, offering about 40 climbs below HVS and as many above. A steep and overhanging crag giving plenty of entertainment to the rock athlete. The rock is variable but does enjoy sunshine.

Dir: 8m WSW of Bristol. Take A370 SW to Cleeve. Take the lane on the L before The Rising Sun pub, towards Wrington, park after 300yds. A track and then a footpath lead E to the crag in about 15 mins. [AVC]

Huntsham Crags:
OS.162 GR.559 167 [10]

Some N-facing buttresses, quite small at around 20ft, offering lots of entertainment in the lower grades. The rock is a mixture of conglomerate and sandstone and cannot be described as completely reliable.

Dir: 10m NE of Monmouth. Take the A40 N from Monmouth. [WYE]

North Quarry:
OS.182 GR.386 563 [11]

A quarry of blackstone slabs, 50–150ft, can be seen easily from the M5, 5m after Junction 21. A good 15 routes in the Extreme grades, mostly E2 upwards. Not a bad crag but N-facing. The climbing is on the R wall of the quarry.

Dir: 3m W of Axbridge. Turn off the A38 to the R at the small village of Cross and go towards Compton Bishop. Continue on the small road at the base of the hill without going into CB. Before the motorway bear round to the R and the quarry will be seen in about 200yds on the R. [AVC]

Portishead Quarry:
OS.172 GR.450 747 [12]

A limestone quarry with about 30 routes at 150–70ft. There are climbs of all standards but most are in the low Extreme grades. The rock is never beyond suspicion. Worth a visit.

Dir: 1m SSW of Portishead. Leave the M5 at Junction 19 and take the A369 to Portishead. At the roundabout after 2m take the B3124 to Clevedon and after 1m the quarry can be seen to the R. [AVC]

Sand Point:
OS.182 GR.318 659 HT−5.10 [13]

A good stretch of small and compact limestone cliffs on this headland offers scope for climbing up to 50ft. A very good long traverse around VS has been done and is said to be worth repeating.

Dir: 3m N of Weston-super-Mare. From the town drive N along Sand Bay to a car park at its N end. 5-min. walk to the point. [AVC]

Shorncliff:
OS.162 GR.542 993 [14]

A natural limestone cliff about 100ft high in most places. Of the 150 routes here only 15 are below VS, with about 100 in the VS–HVS grade. The rock and the protection are not that bad, tops are jungle-like and abseil descent is common, double ropes essential. W-facing and in a lovely setting, good if the weather gets chilly. The cliff can often take a while to dry out, though, best in the spring with no leaves on the trees.

Dir: 8m N of Chepstow. Take the A466 N from Chepstow, after 7m reach Tintern Abbey on the R. Just further on is a road to the R going over a bridge, park. Then cross over and follow a track up E to a large forestry track running N–S after 1m. Turn L and go for 1m (S) until the crag can be seen on the R. [WYE]

Spion Kop Quarry: Restriction:
OS.162 GR.597 108 [15]

The usual bird restrictions here – no climbing 1 Mar.–1 Aug. The quarry is a nature reserve and access is possible but delicate. There are areas specified on which not to climb; enquire first or just stick to the chalked-up lines. About 50 routes across the grades on this 90ft cliff.

Dir: 6m ESE of Monmouth. From Coleford go NE on the B4028 for junction. Go straight through the village and the quarry is in the wood on the R. [WYE]

Split Rock Quarry:
OS.182 GR.539 471 [16]

The rumours that holds keep coming off in people's hands at this limestone quarry are most probably true. 50–80ft routes, mainly in the harder grades.

Dir: 2m NW of Wells. From the centre of town on the A371 there is a road signposted to Wookey Hole. Take this and after 1.5m turn R on to an untarmacked road which leads to the crag. [AVC]

Symonds Yat:
OS.162 GR.563 157 [17]

Not a bad crag, quite a lot of climbing to be done here, but few if any memorable routes. A friendly place, though, offering plenty of enjoyment to the beginner and less-confident climber. Almost 500 climbs never exceeding 100ft and of all grades, the harder ones tending to be on small, not totally reliable, holds. Top-roping easy, and often sensible since bolts are not breeding very quickly here. After rain bring the wellies, and in summer nettles can make shorts a silly idea.

Dir: 5m NE of Monmouth. From Monmouth take the A4136 E towards Gloucester, after 4m at the village of Coleford turn L on the B4432. After 3m Symonds Yat is reached. There are very organised Forestry Commission car parks and tea shacks, and a good pub for lunch down on the river below. Also a campsite. [WYE]

Tockington Quarry:
OS.172 [18]

A good, small quarry of sound limestone, about 40ft high and offering plenty of routes in the lower grades. There are harder routes as well.

Dir: 2m SSW of Thornbury. From Alveston take the A38 SW to the village of Tockington and the quarry after 1m. [No guide]

Trym Valley Gorge:
OS.172 GR.559 783 [19]

A crag with some character, the rock here is never above suspicion. 40–120ft of natural limestone with usually quite hard routes. There is often substantial vegetation on the crag in the summer months.

SPLIT FLIES, E2, 5c, Wintour's Leap. (Climber Jeff Odds, Photo David B A Jones)

Dir: In Bristol, NW corner. From Junction 18 of the M5 take the A4 in towards Bristol. After 2m at the set of traffic lights turn L and carry on for 0.7m. Here a footpath goes up the valley to the L and Blaise Castle. The crag is situated about 600yds up the valley. [AVC]

Uphill Quarry:
OS.182 GR.315 584 [20]

This limestone crag has a pleasant W-facing aspect with about 30 climbs at 120ft in the Severe and above grades. The cliff, though, lends itself to harder climbing in the E grades.

Dir: 1m S of Weston-super-Mare. From the town take the A370 S along the front, at the end of the straight the road bends to the L. Carry straight on up the smaller road and after 100yds fork R, which leads to the top of the hill and cliff in about 400yds. [AVC]

Wintour's Leap:
OS.162 GR.542 958 [21]

Nobody could ever dispute that this cliff is a pile of rubbish. The idea that it does have some good climbs is just a rumour put about by those who have suffered a day at this overgrown cliff and wish others to do so. It is a crag of merit only when you become accustomed to climbing through undergrowth on positively unattractive rock, and when memories of Pembroke and High Tor are lost in a drunken stupor. It rises vertically in places for 300ft and gives over 300 long routes, of which only 25 are below VS. A very popular crag with beginners, don't know why though. The easy routes are quite unprotected and unattractive anyway. Hard routes get all the stars for quality, some of which are deserved, most of which are definitely not. Bring a bolt kit with you, or some dynamite if you want to do everyone a favour. The cliff is W-facing and in winter can give some amusing days if sunny. Dries very quickly. A few big spurter E6s.

Dir: 2m NNE of Chepstow. Take the B4228 N from Chepstow to the Rising Sun pub after the village of Woodcroft. Park hereabouts, being careful not to obstruct any driveway. Opposite the very friendly shop a track leads up to a wire fence; this is skirted to the R and one can walk down a ramp into the quarry. Directly beneath this is Fly Wall, the only descent rock in the area; to the R is Go Wall which was not quarried. Surprise, surprise, the quarrymen knew crap rock when they saw it. [WYE]

Wyndcliffe:
OS.162 GR.527 974 [22]

Two limestone buttresses situated high up in the trees above the A466, out of sight and sound to the road beneath. A beautiful spot to come and enjoy the morning sunshine on a winter's day. Actually to climb would ruin the whole experience. There are 60 listed routes above HS, but only about 10 are worth doing and even those are shaky enough. If you stick to the trade route VSs you can enjoy the spot, otherwise enjoy the epic abseil descent from the 130ft crag.

Dir: 2.5m N of Chepstow — actually in Wales, bring your passport. Take A466 N out of Chepstow from the Chepstow Racecourse roundabout. Follow this road for 2m, ignore the sign to Wyndcliffe and follow the road around to the R. Continue for 0.5m to a Forestry Commission car park, take the small lane forking L and up to a small car park in 50yds. A path off R leads up to the crag in 10 mins through the woods. [WYE]

4 South Wales

SOUTH EAST WALES

The climbing in South East Wales has long remained undiscovered – needless to say that it is not over-brilliant. Even so, if one is willing to put up with second- best, then a huge amount of enjoyment can be obtained from a visit to the area. The rock in most parts is limestone of poorish quality; occasionally there are other rock types but even these leave much to be desired. The best climbing in the area is at Ogmore but one also has to contend with large tides and quite difficult routes. For bouldering the region comes into its own; the larger, tottering cliffs often have good bases on which to boulder around. Always bring your boots to South East Wales; ropes are for the more enthusiastic. Come here expecting little and you will go away pleased.

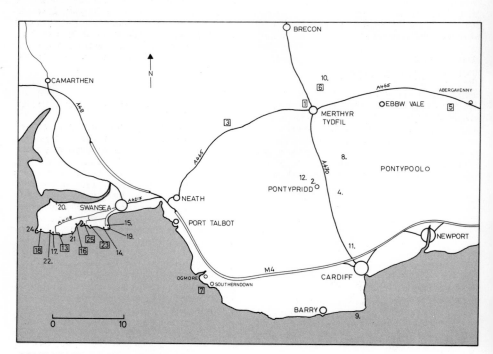

SOUTH EAST WALES AND GOWER

Cefn Coed:
OS.160 GR.035 083   [1]

A quarried limestone crag about 100ft. Quite a bit of vegetation but nevertheless about 50 routes on good-quality rock. Pro makes climbing in the Severe to E3 grades very enjoyable and safe. SE-facing and 'down in the valley, boyo', staying reasonable in the colder months.

Dir: 1.5m NW of Merthyr Tydfil. Follow the A470 NW from MT, after 1m turn on to the A465 going to Abergavenny. Almost immediately park in a lay-by on the R just past the big bridge. Cross over the road going right along a fence to a descent after 50 or so yds. [GSW]

The Darren:
OS.170 GR.067 912   [2]

A small sandstone outcrop up to 70ft, offering a handful of climbs in the 4c to 5c area. Worth looking at.

Dir: 0.5m NW of Pontypridd. From town take the B4273 Ynysybwl road for 0.8m to a lane leading off L under the railway. Here one can walk up the hill for 400yds, where a path leads back L for 600yds to the crag. [GSW]

Dinas Rock:
OS.160 GR.913 080   [3]

Some good crags but in the main more of interest to the expert, offering some 30 routes, over half being good Es. A very pleasant surrounding, however, makes this crag always worth a visit. Nice in spring without leaves on the trees and coolish in summer. Climbs around 120ft on solid to loosening limestone, bolts in places but not many. A few good roof climbs.

Dir: 7m WNW of Aberdare. Follow A465 to Glyn Neath, take A4109 for a few feet, then take the B4242 for 1m to Pont Nedd Fechan. Here bear R down a lane for 0.6m to a parking spot. A path up the river leads to more crags. [GSW]

Llanbradach:
OS.171 GR.146 895   [4]

A sandstone crag with one 5b climb at 150ft.

Dir: 2m NNW of Caerphilly. Take the A469 to Llanbradach, just before reaching the village the cliff is visible on the L. [GSW]

Llangattock:
OS.161 GR.215 147   [5]

A long limestone escarpment with several outcrops offering climbs of up to 100ft. A fine setting, but open to the vicious N winds! About 100 routes of all grades, but more suited to the HVS and Extreme-grade climber.

Dir: 6m W of Abergavenny. Take the A465 Merthyr road going W to Gilwern, here turn R on to the A4077 to Llangattock in about 3m, then turn L into the village over the narrow bridge. Take the lane bearing R up the hill to the crags in 3 miles. [GSW]

Morlais:
OS.160 GR.047 098   [6]

A quarried escarpment consisting of three tiers of up to 100ft high. Plenty of scope for any climber on this solid but not very interesting limestone. About 70 climbs of average standard with a few good technical pitches.

Dir: 2m N of Merthyr Tydfil. On the A465 above MT a small road leads off to Vaynor. Take this road, going over the A465 and past the golf course on the R, for 0.6m to a small lane on the L and a track on the R. Park here and follow the track on the R N for 400yds to the quarries. [GSW]

Ogmore:
OS.170 GR.875 738 HT–4.35   [7]

Climbing at Ogmore should be a great experience, especially if you get the tides wrong. Here the tides are very fast and the rocks very sharp and jagged to fall on, however the climbing makes it worthwhile. There are a lot of routes here for the expert and headcase, but also plenty of scope in the other grades. In parts it is wild, just overhanging, and in others even steeper. The rock is surprisingly sound except for some of the top belays. Friends are very useful and double ropes essential on the harder routes, as are prusik loops for the second of insufficient ability. Few of the climbs are escapable at high tide and if a high sea is running the dangers will become obvious! About 150 climbs of up to 150ft and SW-facing.

Dir: 5m SW of Bridgend. Take the B4524 to Southerndown, then a small lane to Dunraven Bay car park, here the cliffs run NW for about 1m.

One can also park just near Southerndown by the cliffs and walk down via the W end. Walk along the beach, do not leave bags at the bottom as the incoming sea will swallow them very quickly. [GSW]

Penallta:
OS.171 GR.138 952 [8]

This is a small, sandstone outcrop which provides some excellent bouldering and easier small routes. Up to 50ft in parts, warrants soloing or top-roping in a pleasant and often sunny situation. Nothing above 5c, plenty of good Severes though.

Dir: 7m NNW of Caerphilly. Take the A469 N to Ystrad Mynach, then take a small road through the village due N towards Gelligaer for about 0.3m. Turn L into a housing estate and park at the far end. The crag is NW from here, about 5 mins. [GSW]

Sully Island:
OS.171 GR.167 670 HT–5.02 [9]

A good small, bouldering area, but only accessible at low tide.

Dir: 4m E of Barry on the coast. From Barry towards Cardiff on the A4055 for 2m, turn R on to the B4267 for 1.7m through Sully. Turn R to reach the coast and Sully Island in 600yds. [GSW]

Taf Fechan:
OS.160 GR.062 105 [10]

A small, quarried outcrop with rock of generally poor nature, offering about 20 routes in the lower grades up to 120ft.

Dir: 3m NNE of Merthyr Tydfil. From turning off and over the A465 due N of MT, take R branch to Pontsticill, after 0.4m at T-junction turn L for 1m and park. The crags are up on the right. [GSW]

Taffs Well Quarry:
OS.171 GR.128 827 [11]

A large and definitely dangerous dodgy dump. Some love it, though, so it is worth including. The rock is very frail and offers negligible protection, and a companion to drop a top rope is desirable. Up to 250ft high, extremely hazardous, with climbs requiring the ability of an Extreme leader. Nearest hospital, being optimistic, Cardiff.

Dir: 5m NW of Cardiff. Take the A470 out of Cardiff and turn off at Tongwynlais. Quarry is on the E side of the A470. [GSW]

White Rock:
OS.170 GR.061 912 [12]

A very popular sandstone bouldering area, up to 20ft walls with numerous problems. Worth a short visit.

Dir: 1.2m WNW of Pontypridd. Follow the A4058, after 1.1m take a small road under the railway, first L, first R up the hill a bit, rocks are on the R. [GSW]

GOWER PENINSULA

The Gower is a friendly place to climb. There are no daunting cliffs like Pembroke; the average length of a climb is around 60ft. Tides do play a part on some of the cliffs but since there are nearly always Diffs around you are very unlikely ever to get cut off. The cliffs are mostly SW-facing and quite mild in winter. Sunny afternoons in January can often mean T-shirts here, whereas on the hills at Brecon they have a foot of snow. A single rope is often adequate, but even so there are sharp edges to much of the limestone and double ropes can never be dismissed as a waste of time. As a peninsula, the area sees little rain compared with the cliffs inland, and in any case dries very quickly. If you think you can do everything at the Gower try doing a level round at Pennard Golf Course – it makes Right Wall seem easy.

Boiler Slab:
OS.159 GR.452 849   [13]

A great cliff for those without enormous arms. About 10 routes, Diff to VS, about 60ft. Very pleasant and the best in the immediate area. There are many other small buttresses, offering small climbs on quite good rock. S-facing. Worth a ramble around.

Dir: 14m WSW of Swansea. Take the A4118 all the way to Port Eynon, just before reaching the few houses turn R to Overton and park. Go to the cliffs and along for 5 mins to the crag. [GSW]

Caswell Slabs:
OS.159 GR. 591 876 HT–4.00   [14]

The only drawback with this crag is that high tide makes it very awkward and hardly worth the effort. At low tide it offers about 30 routes of 70ft at the Severe standard, some easy and some hard. Some very good slab routes on the Great Slab and the Yellow Pinnacle and Yellow Flecked Slab. Nice spot, 3 mins from the car park, S-facing.

Dir: 5m SW of Swansea. From the Mumbles take the B4593 for 1.3m to Caswell. The climbing is near the point on the W side of the bay. [GSW]

Conservative Club Crag:
OS.159 GR. 621 878   [15]

A 70ft crag set back from the road behind the Conservative Club. A few routes around HVS and E2. A wall with overhangs at the top.

Dir: 4.5m SW of Swansea. Enter Mumbles and carry on down the front on the B4433, go past the Antelope Hotel for 150yds and the crag is behind the row of houses. Walk on down 50yds to the Conservative Club, a path leads off from behind to the R and the crag is 2 mins. [GSW]

Great Tor:
OS.159 GR.530 876 HT–4.00   [16]

Although Great Tor offers the best climbing, there are in fact three tors: Great, West and Little Tor. About 100 routes around the Severe grade, 60ft in length. Very pleasant climbing on reasonably angled rock with good protection. Often sunny and sheltered. Low tide makes life easier but only affects some of the climbs.

Dir: 13m WSW of Swansea. Take the A4118 from Swansea to the village of Penmaen after 9.5m. Car park by the village shop. Here a footpath leads off to the coast and Great Tor is on the headland to the R with the detached flake. [GSW]

Juniper Wall:
OS.159 GR.441 855   [17]

About 15 climbs around VS with a few Extremes and a few desperates. 150ft of steep but well-protected rock. A good spot but beware as some of the bird life on this crag is quite large and, if annoyed, very unfriendly.

Dir: Approach: see Paviland Wall. From the inlet, turn L and scramble down to the foot of the cliff. [GSW]

Mewslade Bay:
OS.159 GR.415 872 HT–4.00   [18]

Try not to get this confused with Mewsford at Pembroke or your partner along the coast will have a very interesting day's soloing. One of the few areas in the country where the rock can be really good and awful within yards. Generally the lower tiers coming up from the sea are very good, solid and enjoyable. The upper reaches are dramatic, exposed and often frighteningly loose. This area stretches from Fall Bay nearest to Worms Head, along the S-facing coast for 1,000yds to Thurba Head, just past the inlet leading up to the footpath from Pitton. There are about 400 climbs, VS and below here, 60ft, which offer good enjoyment. Midway from either end is Boulder Cove which has Yellow Wall and Jacky's Tor, about 20 Extremes, 100ft, of interest. This area, though, is tidal, inhabited by birds 1 Mar.– 31 Sept., and generally difficult.

Dir: 16m WSW of Swansea. Approach: see Rhossili. From the car park you can either walk to the headland and then walk around the coast to the bay, 1.6m total, or cut across the fields by footpath. On a first visit the former is recommended because you can start at one end and explore thoroughly; most return by the 0.5m path across the fields. The approach to the S end is from Pitton, 0.6m before Rhossili on the B4247. Here a footpath leads SW to the R of the stream, running down to the bay in 10 mins. At the bay the climbing is to the R except for a few hard climbs on Thurba Head to the L. [GSW]

RADICAL HOLIDAY, VS, 4a, Great Tor. (Climber David Jones, Photo Joe Healey)

Middle Head:
OS.159 GR.632 872 HT–4.00   [19]

This small island, separated at high tide, offers some good easy slab routes for beginners. Very close to the shore but giving some interest if caught unaware. About 50ft Diffs to Severe. Catches the evening sunshine, pleasant.

Dir: 4m SW of Swansea. Drive to the point at The Mumbles, park. A footpath leads towards the islands on the point. [GSW]

North Hill Tor:
OS.159 GR.453 938   [20]

Some 120ft slabs give good climbing at Diff–V Diff. A handful of routes with a few harder problems, also a shorter VS slab. N-facing, not very pleasant in winter but sheltered from the SW winds.

Dir: 15m W of Swansea. From Swansea A4118, B4271 to Llanrhidian. From here take the small road towards Cheriton, after 2.8m turn R to Landimore and park at the end of the road after 500yds. Walk W along a path between the hill and the marsh, beneath Tor Gro (a few slab VS climbs) and on to North Hill Tor, about 14 mins. (GSW]

Oxwich Point:
OS.159 GR.500 852   [21]

Another useful crag not affected by tides and (even more useful) tourists or anybody else. The cliff is only small, about 40ft, and offers a handful of routes around Severe. The rock is good but never totally reliable.

Dir: 11m WSW of Swansea. Take the A4118 towards Port Enyon. 1m after Nicholaston take road on the L to Oxwich, carry on through Oxwich Green. Take a footpath leading S to the coast and the crag on the point, 10 mins. [GSW]

Paviland Wall:
OS.159 GR.438 859   [22]

Quite hard climbing on this 150ft cliff, about 12 climbs around HVS. Good steep climbing often through good overhangs, quite airy in the upper reaches.

Dir: 14m WSW of Swansea. Take the A4118 to almost the W end of the Gower, turn R on to the B4247, after 1m park at Pilton Green. Beside a white(?) house a footpath leads SSW to the coast in 15 mins. Upon reaching the inlet the cliff is located just down and to the R. [GSW]

Pennard:
OS.159 GR.565 866   [23]

The cliffs here are situated well above the waterline and comprise some excellent buttresses. The bird life can sometimes force you off-route. There are about 30 routes Diff to VS, and about 20 Extremes of very good quality. S-facing and quick drying. Worth a visit.

Dir: 12m WSW of Swansea. Approach: see Three Cliffs. From car park go L (E) along the coast until after 10 mins some impressive 100ft buttresses are reached. [GSW]

Rhossili: Restriction
OS.159 GR.405 878 HT–4.40   [24]

The big island at the end is the Worms Head. There is a complete ban on climbing since it is a very precious bird sanctuary and a national nature reserve. This crag is NW-facing and often dampish. It always seems to be high tide anyway. It does need a good low tide to make access around the base of this cliff worthwhile. About 15 climbs VS and below, 40ft. About 10 Extremes, 80ft, which have rusty old bolts and are not very well naturally protected – bring a bolt kit if you can be bothered.

Dir: 15m WSW of Swansea. Take the A4118 towards Port Enyon, turn on to the B4247 after 12m. Road leads to village, go to National Trust car park. Walk down the track leading to the head, after 10 mins the cliffs come very close to the track. The cliffs are down to the R, scramble down to a grass bank, then to a flat terrace and a little cove. [GSW]

Three Cliffs:
OS.159 GR.542 875 HT–4.00   [25]

This cliff has all the ingredients of great mountaineering: a proper start at sea-level, some arduous climbing, nervous moments and a proper sharp pointed peak – well almost. The only disappointment is that it is only 70ft high, but as the sides are only 45° it gives climbs of 100ft in places. About 20 climbs, Diff to HS. The sea washes around and is most enjoyed at low tide. A nice, sandy beach, good for sandcastles.

Dir: 13m WSW of Swansea. Take the A4067 coast road out of Swansea then before the Mumbles turn R on to the B4436. After 3.5m at Pennard, where the road turns sharp R, carry straight on to Southgate, keep following the road to the National Trust car park at the end. From here walk E and down to the bay with the cliffs – 15 mins. The bay also has the cliffs of Shire Combe. Climb at will, it is all safe and pleasant. [GSW]

SOUTH PEMBROKE

This area is the best introduction to sea-cliff climbing in Britain. About half of the cliffs are tidal and unless a heavy sea is running there are very few areas which present really serious situations. There are a few cliffs, however, with no easy ways out, and they will be obvious to the intrepid adventurer. Nearly all the rock is good enough to climb safely on and protect, but many of the climbs – even VSs – are steep and therefore could require self-rescue techniques in the event of a fall. The limestone has incredible friction and wears through rock boots at a very expensive rate; often old boots are perfectly adequate. The army own a lot of the coastline and use it occasionally, but it is rarely a problem since there are so many areas – we don't argue since chalk bags are no match for the Royal Artillery. An abseil rope is well worth having, as is a towel to protect it from the sharp edges at the top. Although a good selection of gear is necessary, large nuts will be found particularly useful, as will friends 2, 2.5 and 3. A very pleasant area where climbers are made welcome by the locals. There are parts with strict bird restrictions and very delicate negotiations have resulted in being able to climb on these cliffs out of nesting season – our thanks to those involved. There are routes here for everyone, classics in every grade, with over 1,000 routes in the area. There are four different places to park:

Lydstep From Tenby take the A4139 SW through Penally and into Lydstep, go on for 100yds past Lydstep Home Farm, a turning L at West Lodge takes you down a lane with a white gate. After 0.3m turn R to a car park up on the headland.

Stackpole From Pembroke take the B4319 Castlemartin Road leading S, after 3m pass through St Petrox and at the bottom of the hill turn L to Freshwater East and Stackpole. Pass through Stackpole and turn L at signpost to Stackpole Quay.

St Govan's Head From Pembroke take the B4319 Castlemartin Road leading S, after 3.8m fork L to Bosherston, go through village with excellent café, campsite opposite church, and continue to head-land through firing range, arriving at St Govan's car park on Trevallen Downs.

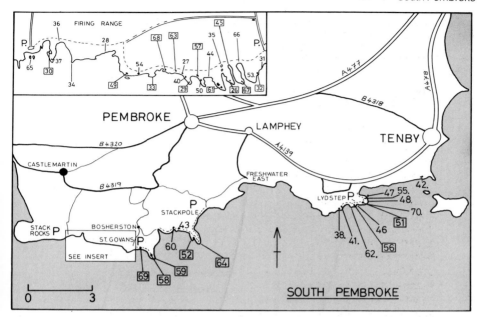

SOUTH PEMBROKE

Stack Rocks From Pembroke take the B4310 Castlemartin Road leading S, instead of forking L to Bosherston follow the road R from here for 2.3m just through Merrion, a road L leads to a car park after 2m at the Elegug Stacks.

Bosherston Head:
OS.158 GR.961 928 HT–4.30 [26]

A superb head offering very good climbing in all grades from Diff to E5. Of the 30 or so 100ft routes, most are hard but some good VSs do exist on the headland. Most of the climbs are non-tidal but a low tide can be useful, or an abseil to the R of the huge overhanging wall.

Dir: From the St Govan's car park, enter the firing range, following the track past 2 fords, the head on the L is Bosherston. By continuing on to the next head, Saddle Head, one can view the Bosherston Head properly and spot the descents and indeed the big blank wall. [PE]

Buckspool Down:
OS.158 GR.953 936 [27]

An area little affected by the tide, or even rough seas. A very broken area of cliffs, 100–150ft, running between Space Buttress and The Fort-ress. About 30 very good VS and HVS climbs here. Abseil entry at will, escape route HS.

Dir: Approach: see The Castle and Fortress. The line of broken cliffs leading NW. [PE]

Bullslaughter Bay:
OS.158 GR.940 942 HT–4.30 [28]

This area has lots of slabs and walls on the poorest rock in the area, in some cases frighten-ing. 200yds on from Crocksydam Point are the Crystal Slabs, 200ft, offering mainly VS climbs on shaley 160ft rock. Just E of these is Mosaic Wall which is good, a vertical and in places holdless wall, but with good cracks offering an HVS and two E3s, 150ft. Then on to the serious Thunder Wall, two E2s, and into the bay itself where several HVS routes can be found.

Dir: From Stack Rocks car park, walk E past The Cauldron, then Flimston Bay, to Bullslaughter Bay in 25 mins. [PE]

The Castle:
OS.158 GR.954 934   [29]

A gem of an area, little affected by tides or bird restrictions. Not over large, around 100ft, but offering some superb climbs on a hollowed-out headland. About 10 VS–HVS routes on the W face, 6 very good routes on the S face, around E3. The E face gives about 20 wonderful routes but not easy, E1 to E5. A groove in the S face, abseil groove, Severe leads to the foot of the cliff and access to most climbs.

Dir: From St Govan's car park, walk into the range, follow the track past the wire enclosure of Saddle Head, past the next blunt headland and on to The Castle, which is recognised by a large through cave. About 1m, 15 mins. [PE]

The Cauldron: Restriction
OS.158 GR.929 945 HT–4.30   [30]

A bird-nesting area, out of bounds 1 Mar.–1 Aug. This 180ft hole in the cliffs gives awe-inspiring climbing. Can be a bit miserable on a poor day but often has a powerful, eerie character. Abseil approach to the bottom. About 10 climbs, VS upwards, recommended only to competent leaders.

Dir: From the car park at Stack Rocks, walk E along the cliffs for about 400yds to a big cauldron-type hole. [PE]

Chapel Cove: Climbing Safety Ban
OS.158 GR.967 929   [31]

This cliff is directly below the car park at St Govan's, S of Bosherston, where a path leads down to a chapel. This is a mega tourist spot and in agreement with the National Trust and for the safety of the sightseers from falling rocks, climbers do not climb here. [PE]

Chapel Point:
OS.158 GR.966 928 HT–4.30   [32]

This headland offers about 20 difficult climbs, E1 to E5, all on fairly good rock and quite technical for the area. All around 110ft and cut off at high tide. Good routes, with the classic Ultravixens E1, 5b in the L-centre of the face.

Dir: From St Govan's car park, go directly down to the chapel. Then to the R there is an arch on this point, pass behind and the cliff is on the R. To the L of the cliff there is the E face of Newton Head, with about 5 Extremes on it. [PE]

Crickmail Point:
OS.158 GR.947 938 HT–4.30   [33]

This is a very good crag, sometimes known as B-team Buttress, has about 30 routes, 70–160ft, on good, sound rock. Nearly all of it is non-tidal. A superb area for the VS leader and the E2 aspirant. Access is by an abseil down some slabs on the W side. An easy escape route, Severe, makes this a very friendly spot.

Dir: Approach: see The Castle. This point is about 0.5m further on and is the last major buttress before the headland curves round at Mewsford. Recognised as a big buttress sitting on a 15° ramp with an angle strata line half-way up, E face. [PE]

Crocksydam Point:
OS.158 GR.935 943   [34]

A good, solid buttress, offering a handful of 90ft climbs from Severe to E1. Every route is worth doing.

Dir: From Stack Rocks car park as for Flimston Bay, this is the southernmost point of the bay. Descend on the W side of the point, scramble. 10 mins from car park. [PE]

The Devil's Barn:
OS.158 GR.959 929 HT–4.30   [35]

A large double zawn offers 3 routes, E1, E2, E3. Fair 120ft routes. Abseil into the zawn from a post. Situated between Bosherston Head and Saddle Head. Affected by high tide. [PE]

Flimston Bay:
OS.158 GR.933 945   [36]

Some very good slab climbing in the lower grades. About 30 climbs, 150ft, Diff through to VS. Tides not a problem but easiest approach is often by abseil. Well worth a visit for the less adventurous.

Dir: From Stack Rocks car park, walk E along the cliffs for 500yds, past The Cauldron. The first bay is Flimston Bay. [PE]

Flimston Ridge: Restriction
OS.158 GR.931 944 [37]

A bird area, no climbing 1 Mar.–1 Aug. A nice area for novices with tides not being a problem, a handful of Diffs. Back towards The Cauldron the cliff is less hospitable and gives two E2s and several harder routes.

Dir: Approach: see The Cauldron. The ridge runs directly S from here, descend by scrambling and go round to the W face. [PE]

Forbidden Head:
OS.158 GR.083 973 HT–4.30 [38]

A good headland, about 100ft high, offering about 15 routes in the mid-Extremes with 5 classic E4–5s. As with most cliffs in this area, low tide is essential for access to the routes, which can be reached by abseil from E end or by scrambling into W end. They are separated by an easy 110ft wall with a few VS climbs. The routes at the far W end can also be reached by a scramble at low tide.

Dir: From Lydstep car park, as for Frontier Zawn. The next headland from the concrete bunker is Forbidden Head. 10 mins. [PE]

The Fortress: Restriction
OS.158 GR.955 935 [40]

No climbing here 1 Mar.–1 Aug. A large under-cut wall with several E2 climbs on the L and HVS routes on the R following cracks between the caves. Not really affected by the tides. W-facing routes, 150ft.

Dir: As for The Castle. The wall running N from The Castle is The Fortress. [PE]

Frontier Zawn
OS.158 GR.084 974 HT–4.30 [41]

A mixed area of climbing, some very good routes, some poor, others very awkward for access and belays. Minimum grade here HVS to escape or a very good swim at low tide; rough sea, no chance. An amazing E4 in No Man's Zawn on the mirror-smooth wall just at the southern end of the zawn, needs absolute low tide. Second climbs for 20ft and takes belay, if the leader is unsuccessful and you cannot swim, you are in big trouble!

Dir: From Lydstep car park, follow the footpath leading W down to the caverns, up the next hill, and after a big rest round to a headland with a concrete bunker on it. Fix abseil rope to centre column via low hole and attach krab near edge, ropes will have to be pulled through. Leave ab rope trailing along cliff top to use as a top belay if successful. [PE]

Giltar:
OS.158 GR.120 983 HT–4.30 [42]

This is a superb area for beginners, on easy-angled slabs offering hundreds of routes and variations around the Diff grade, in most places not exceeding 100ft. Low tide makes access easier even though abseil approach is never very serious. The land is in an army firing area so if there are lots of big bangs going on stay in the pub! A great area for family scrambling around.

Dir: 2m SW of Tenby. Take the A4139 SW from Tenby for 1.7m where on the L a signposted path leads to the sea, cliffs to the E. [PE]

Gun Cliff:
OS.158 GR.988 944 HT–4.30 [43]

A rather broken cliff, but interesting scenery. About 20 routes up to 120ft. The climbs here are either HVS or E3. Some very good routes on the main cliff. Next door is the zawn of Ramming Hole with an HVS and an E2, 120ft, the harder being the better. A good cliff in the nesting season when Mowing Word and Stackpole are out of bounds.

Dir: From Stackpole car park, go S up the long hill path and over to Dunraven Beach, cross this and up the other side. From here cut across the headland to avoid the peninsula, with Mowing Word Cliffs on the L the coast is reached. Carry on until a large narrow zawn, Ramming Hole, is reached, Gun Cliff is to the L (E) of this. Descent is by scrambling down the ramp to some abseil rings or a Diff descent. Access to Ramming Hole is by abseil. [PE]

Hollow Caves Bay:
OS.158 GR.957 932 [44]

Not a lot of climbing to be found in the bay but some routes noted in the zawns at the back end. All routes in the low Extreme grades, around 120ft.

Dir: Approach: see Saddle Head. This is the next bay, 10 mins from St Govan's car park. [PE]

Huntsman's Leap:
OS.158 GR.962 929 HT–4.30   [45]

This is a superb area for the hard climber. Both walls of the ford offer superb Extreme climbing, with the easiest escape from the ford being E1. The E side offers big slab climbing, E1 to E5, the W side offers steep routes, E4 to E5. About 40 climbs to 140ft in total.

Dir: From St Govan's car park, take the track through the range past the first ford, Stennis, to the second, Huntsman's. [PE]

Lydstep Cavern Bays:
OS.158 GR.087 974 HT–4.30   [46]

Some very good, easy or hard traversing to be had in this beautiful area, stretching from Recess Face, past Lydstep Caverns through to Mother Carey's Kitchen. Mostly around Severe standard, encompassing a slabby buttress with a few VSs on it also. In calm seas a treat; in rough seas a harrowing experience with good drowning potential.

Dir: From the car park at Lydstep, take the footpath immediately out at the W end, R, and after 30yds take the fork leading down to the caverns. To avoid tourists descend as for Recess Face. [PE]

Lydstep Pinnacle:
OS.158 GR.094 977 HT–4.30   [47]

A pinnacle offering a few routes, about 140ft, at HVS standard. Only one of the routes is tidal. Explore at will.

Dir: Approach: see Prow Bay. [PE]

Lydstep Point:
OS.158 GR.094 974 HT–4.30   [48]

This small point offers some good routes, only a handful but worthy of ascent, VS to E1. Abseil to the large block, then at low tide one can scramble to The Rip, E1, just. The other climbs are reached by scrambling down the W bank.

Dir: From the car park at Lydstep, go W to reach the SE point. [PE]

Mewsford Point:
OS.158 GR.942 938 HT–4.30   [49]

This area is perhaps the finest open crag in the firing range. Plenty of climbing here at all grades on routes up to 200ft long. The W face has about 10 climbs of Severe to VS. The SW and S faces offer about 25 middle Extremes, of which most receive classic status.

Dir: Midway between St Govan's and Stack Rocks, quicker from the Stack Rocks car park. Go past The Cauldron and Two bays, and then round to the point recognised by the coastguard lookout and a huge tilted rock platform at the base of the cliff which becomes isolated at high tide. Approach to the W face is by abseil 70ft down the W side. For the S faces it gets complicated. An extra rope is needed to lengthen the 180ft drop from the flagpole. [PE]

Misty Wall:
OS.158 GR.955 932   [50]

A good area with very good rock and about 15 routes of mostly classic status. All around 80ft, S-facing and in the E1 to E5 category.

Dir: From the car park at St Govan's, take the track into the range. After 5 mins pass the wire enclosure, go around the next bay to the low headland of Quarry Point. Along the next bay soon is a large S-facing wall, Misty Wall, scramble down to ledges at sea-level. To the N are the Rusty Walls. [PE]

Mother Carey's Kitchen:
OS.158 GR.090 975 HT–4.30   [51]

Without doubt the finest crag at Lydstep, even though there are no easy routes. The easy route out is Severe, which is useful since the first sight of the cliff from below makes a nervous leader terrified. There are about 35 routes here, spread from VS upwards, and each route is a classic, though some are better than others. To the E end is the Space Face which is quite steep – you can't miss it – the routes on here are wild! Retreat from anywhere on it is down into the sea, and the top pitches of any of the routes are interesting enough to make most leaders shake uncontrollably. Needless to say, seconds should be experienced in how to cope with major epics, especially if a high sea is running and darkness is near.

FITZCARALDO, E5, 6a, Huntsman's Leap. (Climber Dave Viggars, Photo David B A Jones)

Dir: From the car park at Lydstep, take the path S for 100yds where a narrow path leads off E to the Kitchen in about 300yds. Descent is by abseil, 140ft to a small platform at high tide, a boulder beach is uncovered at low tide. All climbs are accessed from here. [PE]

Mowing Word: Restriction
OS.158 GR.992 943 HT–4.30 [52]

Here there is a strict seasonal bird restriction, no climbing 1 Mar.–1 Aug. A very large nesting site for auks. This is the place to climb. Wow! A sunny day here in late August is the way to enjoy life: do a route, drink a bottle of champagne, then leap off the top of the cliff into the sea, the norm here. The climbing is just so good, 150ft, pleasant VS–HVS routes, interesting E1s, exciting E2s, and nothing really any harder. Don't let anyone kid you, they are *easy*. Big holds and lots of gear. Abseil in at the centre of the cliff down a groove to a small pedestal, or half-way where one can traverse on to any of the routes. At low tide one can traverse easily along the cliff. It is W-facing, sunny and best inspected from the sea – on the way down, splash! There is also more climbing on the S face, a bit more difficult though. Around on the E face there is a host of VS climbs. About 150 climbs in the area. This cliff also qualifies for the silliest name in Britain.

Dir: Approach: see Stackpole Head. [PE]

Newton Head:
OS.158 GR.965 928 [53]

Lots of good climbing in the lower grades, an upper tier for some good bouldering and the lower tiers offering some excellent routes, V Diff, Severe and HVS, all around 80ft. For the East Face see Chapel Point.

Dir: From St Govan's car park, go W over the stile and on for about 100yds, turn L before the first ford and walk to the headland, where one can descend on the R. [PE]

Panzer Walls:
OS.158 GR.946 938 [54]

An area of grey walls to the E of Mewsford Arches, offering about 10 middle-grade routes at 120ft. The cliffs in between have the usual nesting restrictions in the spring. To the E is Battleship Buttress offering a handful of E1s.

Dir: Approach: see Mewsford. [PE]

Prow Bay:
OS.158 GR.094 977 HT–4.30 [55]

This has about 12 climbs at roughly 110ft, mainly around HVS with one Severe. Low tide necessary. There is also a traverse from the southern point to the bay, an interesting VS expedition, calm seas preferable.

Dir: From the car park at Lydstep, take the path S then E along the cliffs, past the Kitchen and along to the point, then go N to the pinnacle, with Prow Bay just before. [PE]

Recess Face:
OS.158 GR.086 976 HT–4.30 [56]

Some very reasonable E1 and E2 climbing here. About 15 routes up to 130ft on good rock. The face continues into Skomar East Face but is treated as one. The L end is very tidal, the R hardly affected.

Dir: From Lydstep car park, go W along the coast path, down to the caverns, up the headland and the face will appear. Scramble down the ridge before the bay. [PE]

Rusty Walls:
OS.158 GR.966 933 [57]

Some good climbing here, routes around 100ft, VS to E4 standard, the N end offering the harder lines. Approach by abseil, a walk around to the next point, The Castle, offers a good view of the wall.

Dir: Approach: see Misty Wall, 15 mins from St Govan's car park. [PE]

St Govan's Head:
OS.158 GR.973 927 HT–4.30 [58]

A fantastic cliff with merits in all areas, but unfortunately there is very little here for climbing below VS. Above this there are about 100 climbs, equally spread up to E4 with a few harder climbs. The cliffs generally run to big holds and steepness, with protection being very good. There are stakes over the top for most climbs and a good abseil point by a square detached boulder, or alternatively a Diff chimney. The W end is non-tidal, as indeed are most of the climbs, but low tide is necessary to traverse to the E end.

Dir: From St Govan's car park, walk E along the

cliffs for 10 mins towards the headland, an abseil point will be obvious. [PE]

St Govan's East:
OS.158 GR.976 926 HT–4.30   [59]

A very good cliff, offering about 25 routes above HS. Being tidal at either end, it is reached by an abseil in the middle which is unaffected by tide. Some classics around the E3 grade, all around 100ft.

Dir: From St Govan's car park, walk to the headland, 12 mins, the cliff is below the coast-guard lookout facing SE. [PE]

Saddle Bay:
OS.158 GR.984 943 HT–4.30   [60]

This is not to be confused with Saddle Head, about 2m away. This area has some good climbs around the Severe standard for the explorer. There are some routes out on Church Rock about 500 yds offshore, wait for low tide to reach it. Moving into and around the bay, Chance Encounter Zawn is reached, an area with a handful of Severes, 80ft.

Dir: Instead of going to St Govan's from Boshers-ton, take the road to Broad Haven. Star Rock is by the car park, cross the beach to Saddle Point and round to Saddle Bay. [PE]

Saddle Head:
OS.158 GR.959 928 HT–4.30   [61]

This is the cliff for beginners, an upper tier with lots of Diffs and Severes, around 60ft. The tip of the point offers some good HVSs and E1s. The main cliff, with its low-tide platform, offers some VS climbs in a setting equal to E4 territory on most sea cliffs. A wonderful crag enjoying the afternoon sun. To the N some very good HVS routes approached by abseil down a hole about 100yds N of the wire enclosure on the top of the cliff.

Dir: From the St Govan's car park, go W into the range and follow the track past 2 fords and on to the headland with the wire enclosure on top of it. This is Saddle Head. [PE]

Skomar Towers:
OS.158 GR.085 974 HT–4.30   [62]

A bit of a holiday resort this one. Some really good HS and VS routes here in a very peaceful setting away from the crowds. You can climb anywhere and traverse at sea-level with interest. There is a good E1 up through the hole, otherwise it is all fairly straightforward. About 150ft with 10 climbs, S-facing. At HT you can climb from a non-tidal platform.

Dir: From the Lydstep car park, go W along the headland down to the cavern bay and up to the concrete bunker as for Frontier Zawn. Go right out on to the headland and down the W side where a Diff goes diagonally down, or abseil. [PE]

Space Buttress:
OS.158 GR.953 937 HT–4.30   [63]

A very impressive buttress, about 160ft, with some very good climbs, VS–HVS upwards, on some good overhanging rock. About 10 climbs in total, mostly 2-pitch and very exhilarating. Well worth a visit.

Dir: Approach: see The Castle. Carry on for about 300yds to a large buttress with two sets of overhangs and angled strata. The abseil approach is down the face E, as seen on approach, to boulders above high tide. [PE]

Stackpole Head: Restriction
OS.158 GR.995 942 HT–4.30   [64]

There is a bird restriction here, 1 Mar.–15 Aug., except for the W face, 1 Mar.–1 Aug. The most climbing, and indeed the best, is on the W face. Most of the climbs are around 140ft, VS and above. The climbing is very good indeed, especially in the E2 and E3 grade, not really any harder anywhere. An easy day for superstars, desperation for beginners. The base is accessible 2 hrs either side of low tide, and from a descent ridge to the N of the W face.

Dir: From the car park at Stackpole, take the cliff-top path S over the headland, across the beach (stopping for a swim of course if it's sunny), up the other side and right out along to the long peninsula. This is Stackpole Head. Immediately to the W of this is the promontory of Mowing Word, obviously reached by cutting across the headland. [PE]

Stack Rocks: Restriction
OS.158 GR.926 945 HT–4.30 [65]

A bird area, no climbing 1 Mar.–1 Aug. Here there are two very spectacular sea stacks, offering a couple of VS routes either by swimming or low tide. To the W is the Green Bridge of Wales and cliffs of dubious nature, climb at your peril.

Dir: Get out of your car at Stack Rocks car park, walk to cliff. [PE]

Stennis Ford:
OS.158 GR.964 929 HT–4.30 [66]

A daunting chasm, offering a handful of Extreme routes on the W face, E2 to E4. Around 150ft high and only just tidal, it is nearly serious with the easiest escape being E1. Good, solid rock and first-class routes.

Dir: From the car park at St Govan's, go W along the track into the range, the first ford reached after 100yds is Stennis Ford. [PE]

Stennis Head:
OS.158 GR.963 928 [67]

An excellent cliff, every route a classic. Non-tidal, catches the sun, and destined to become the most polished crag in Pembroke. There are two faces, W and E. The W is reached by scrambling down to a slanting terrace below the crag, going around to a large dome-type face. The E is reached by scrambling down some slabs and then traversing L, interesting in a high sea. The W side has all the classics, a V Diff, at the L end and all the routes getting progressively higher as the cliff attains its full 130ft. The E side, mornings, offers HVS climbs with a few harder ones in some good positions. Can get quite busy at times.

Dir: From the St Govan's car park, go W into the range area, past the first ford, then go L out on to the headland, E or W to the respective descents. [PE]

Triple Overhang Area:
OS.158 GR.949 937 HT–4.30 [68]

Though not listed as a restriction, the area just to the E of Triple Overhang Buttress is a bird-nesting area and is out of bounds 1 Mar.–1 Aug. Common sense hopefully will prevail and any routes with birds nesting on can easily be avoided. This is the area between Space Buttress and Crickmail Point, and includes Blockhouse Buttress, Ripper Cliff, Triple Overhang Buttress and Seaside Gully area. The area as a whole is very good with plenty of climbing, VS upwards, 100–160ft routes. Some of the areas tidal, others not. The most spectacular is indeed Triple Overhang Buttress, about 200yds E of Crickmail Point, with a series of overhangs, the top one being large to say the least.

Dir: Approach: see Crickmail Point. [PE]

Trevallen Cliff:
OS.158 GR.969 929 [69]

Not a cliff for beginners. An excellent crag, offering perhaps the best selection of hard Extremes in the area, over 30 of the 70 routes are E4 and upwards. Some classic routes, all 100ft single-pitch desperates, or paths depending on your forearms. Some good E2s as well, with an HVS being the escape route at high tide.

Dir: From St Govan's car park, go E towards St Govan's Head, after 50yds leave the track to walk along the cliff top. After 70yds an abseil point will become obvious, abseil in here to a non-tidal platform. [PE]

White Tower:
OS.158 GR.092 975 [70]

This amazing landform is completely hidden from land, a white sheet of rock with some very difficult climbs and perhaps the most spectacular route in South Wales, The Great White, E6, 6c, taking its centre. Abseil inspection for protection is advisable. About 90ft with a handful of climbs E4 upwards. There are also some VS routes to the E on the face of the tower and a traverse of the nearby zawn at VS also. From here to the far E point is fair and offers many lines, the best being around VS and definitely worth a visit for the VS climber, most around 100ft, S-facing and unaffected by the tide. Cliffs are known as Pinnacle Buttress, Bridge Zawn and South Face.

Dir: Approach: see Mother Carey's Kitchen, the next promontory is the White Tower. Scramble down to the tip on either side, easier on the W side. [PE]

*WALK ON THE WILD SIDE, E3, 5c, Stennis Head. (Climber David Jones,
Photo Unknown)*

NORTH PEMBROKE

This area has long remained very undisturbed and quiet, and will probably remain so despite recent development. The cliffs do not have the sunny aspect of the S coastline and indeed the rock is not so friendly. The climbing, though, is very good and there is plenty here to occupy one's interest. Good but not brilliant.

Abercastle Area:
OS.157 GR.845 343 HT–5.25 [71]

A nice area for the low-grade climber, offering some good Severes. Two cliffs: Craig Ddu, offering two VS climbs, 110ft and good; and the interesting headland of Ynysdeullyn, with two islands and a sea stack approachable at low tide. This offers about 15 climbs, V Diff to VS, slabby routes.

Dir: 7m SW of Goodwick, 2m NW of Mathry. From Mathry take the small road to Abercastle and car park. From here walk along the cliffs NW to the headland, Craig Ddu is reached after about 700yds, and Ynysdeullyn is situated on the headland. [PE]

Aber-Mawr Area:
OS.157 GR.875 345 [72]

A very good area for the inexperienced climber looking for V Diffs to VSs. Most of the routes are on slabs, some steepening to walls. Morfa Slabs, 180ft, offer 2 VS routes and are situated midway between the beach at Aber-Mawr and the square-cut promontory of Penmorfa, which offers a handful of low-grade routes. The next headland W is Trwynllwwnog, which offers some VS pitches.

Dir: 5m SW of Goodwick. From the A487 4.5m SW of Goodwick take the road to Granston, through the village, over a crossroad, shortly R then down a steep hill. Turn L before crossing

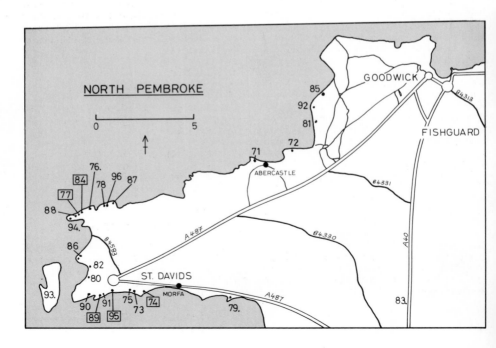

the river and this leads to a car park by the beach at Aber-Mawr. Walk W to Morfa Slabs and other crags. [PE]

Caerbwdi Bay:
OS.157 GR.764 242   [73]

This bay has two sets of slabs on its W side, both around 100ft, the more southernmost of these being Belly Buttress. BB is semi-tidal and an abseil rope is very useful for the descent to the sea-washed platform at the bottom and the generally low-grade routes. The more NE crag is Cathedral Slabs, which has generally harder climbs.

Dir: 1.2m SE of St David's. Approach: see Craig Caerfai, carry on around the headland and into the next bay and the crags. [PE]

Carreg-Y-Barcud:
OS.157 GR.774 242 HT—4.55   [74]

This is easily the best crag in the area, just S of St David's and not to be missed. About 30 or even 40 routes of all grades to E4. The crag is of a slabby character and of quick-drying sandstone, offering good protection except for a few of the harder routes — which makes them more interesting! The cliff rarely exceeds 100ft but manages to pack in quite a lot. Most of the routes are not affected by the tide, but a calm sea and receding tide makes access a lot easier.

Dir: 1.5m ESE of St David's. Take the A487 W from the town and after 1.2m turn R to Trelerw, where there is a car park. The cliff is almost directly to the S and only a few minutes walk away. There are belay stakes in places to give relatively easy abseil access. [PE]

Craig Caerfai:
OS.157 GR.762 240 HT—4.55   [75]

A 130ft crag, offering about 10 climbs, Diff to E1, scattered quite evenly. The cliff base is easily approached but semi-tidal.

Dir: 1m SSE of St David's. Follow the road to Caeferi Bay from the town and park in the car park. From here take the coastal path SE and just before the headland is reached there is an inlet with the crag. [PE]

Craig Carn Porth Llong:
OS.157 GR.727 285   [76]

A large cliff offering routes up to 250ft in the middle grades, about 10 routes including some Diffs and Severes.

Dir: 2m NW of St David's. From the car park at Whitesands Bay, B4583, take the coastal path to the NW coast and the cliff is almost directly beneath the highest point on the ridge, which should be almost straight ahead. Recognised by a narrow zawn and a promontory of black rock. [PE]

Craig Coetan:
OS.157 GR.724 282   [77]

An excellent crag, especially for the low-grade climber. About 25 climbs, of which 20 are below VS on this red, slabby cliff. About 200ft high, yet with a terrace running up it half-way to give an upper and lower tier. Good rock makes this crag very enjoyable.

Dir: 2.2m NW of St David's. From the car park at Whitesands Bay, B4583, take the coastal path N past the 2 bays and straight over to the cliffs past the burial chamber. The cliff, easily seen from the path, is recognised as a big slabby lump. Descent is made by scrambling down the gully, Diff, or abseil. [PE]

Craig Hebog:
OS.157 GR.732 287   [78]

A good crag with about 20 routes, mainly in the Diff and Severe grades, with a few obvious VSs, 100–150ft. NW-facing.

Dir: 2m NW of St David's. As for Craig Carn Porth Llong, then carry on up the coast for 400yds to the first substantial buttress, the second is Trwyn Llwyd. [PE]

Dinas Fach:
OS.157 GR.826 227 HT—4.50   [79]

A good crag for the VS leader, having a good 5 VSs about 100ft long. W-facing and on a nice, scenic headland out of the way, a relaxing spot. The rock towards the top of the climbs, however, is not above suspicion.

Dir: 2m SE of Solva. From Solva take the A487 E for 1.5m to park on the R at Pointz Castle. From here a footpath leads SW to the coastal path and the thin promontory of Dinas Fach. The crag is situated on the W side and is reached by scrambling down to ledges, semi-tidal. [PE]

Green and Purple Slabs:
OS.157 GR.724 248 [80]

Here lie some 100ft slabs, offering a handful of lower-grade routes. Non-tidal and worth bringing an abseil rope.

Dir: 2m W of St David's. Approach: see Llenrac Slabs. Take the coast path S from here to find the slabs, after about 300yds Green Slab and then in another 100yds Purple Slab. [PE]

Llechdafad:
OS.157 GR.880 358 [81]

This steep crag of about 150ft offers about 16 routes, VS up to E3, with over half being Extreme. Not really affected by the tide because of a large platform beneath it. Most of the climbs can be viewed from the promontory to the S. W-facing and often sunny, a good spot. 500yds to the S of this crag is Carreg-Golchfa, a small 110ft promontory offering 3 slabby routes of V Diff and Severe standard.

Dir: 4m WSW of Goodwick. Approach: see Pwlldawnau. Instead of going N go S on the coastal path for 0.5m to a stile. Platform reached by abseil from the centre of the crag. [PE]

Llenrac Slabs:
OS.157 GR.720 255 [82]

Some nice slabs, offering about 20 or so routes ranging from Diff to VS. All around 100ft and non-tidal. Often abseil is the easiest descent, bring a spare rope. A nice situation, near to the car park and W-facing, semi-sheltered by Ramsey Island.

Dir: 2m W of St David's. From the town take the road going W towards Rhosson through until the coast and a lifeboat station, park. The slabs are situated on the coast N of here, reached in about 5 mins. [PE]

Maiden Castle:
OS.157 GR.954 248 [83]

Small rocks up to 30ft, with plenty of interest in the bouldering fields of S. Wales. There is also more climbing to be had further on up the hill at Wolf Rock, several Diffs, perfect for beginners, about 50ft.

Dir: 6m N of Haverfordwest. Take the A40 to Treffgarne and instead of turning off to the village carry on for 1m, stop and park. Walk to the rocks, which are up on the hillside to the L, a few hundred yards. [PE]

Mur Cenhinen:
OS.157 GR.725 283 [84]

A very good crag, which is unseen from the land. Excellent rock and climbing, about 20 routes, 80–200ft. Most of the climbing here is VS–HVS with a few Extremes. Being NW-facing can be very chilly in the morning. The climbing becomes less well protected towards the S end of the crag, as the routes tend to get more difficult.

Dir: 2m NNW of St David's. Approach: see Craig Coetan. Some of the climbs are accessed by traversing around the headland, for the others a ramp leads down from a gully at the N end of the cliff. [PE]

North Penbwchdy: Restriction
OS.157 GR.880 376 HT–5.25 [85]

There is a bird-nesting ban on climbing, 1 Feb.–1 Aug. This area of coastline has cliffs of dolerite and shale reaching up to 300ft in places. Nearly all of the documented climbs are HVS upwards and of a serious nature, involving awkward access and tidal difficulties. There is good climbing to be found, but as the area is so rarely visited routes tend to grow rather a lot of flora. The cliffs stretch along the NW coastline, the best perhaps being Shipwreck Wall, offering a handful of routes around E1.

Dir: 4m W of Goodwick. From Goodwick take a small road NW, then up a steep hill signposted Llawanda. After 0.5m fork L and follow signs to Trefasser after 3.5m. Turn R and go down to the youth hostel, park just before in car park, Phll Deri. Here the coastal path leads SW along the clifftop. The first substantial cliff reached after 15 mins is Shipwreck Wall. [PE]

Pencarnan Slabs Area:
OS.157 GR.721 260 HT–5.00 [86]

This area offers many good climbs mainly as slabs in the Diff to Severe range of about 80ft. Nearly all the routes are non-tidal. A good area.

Dir: 2m WNW of St David's. From the car park at Whitesands Bay, B4583, take the coastal path S along the bay following it around to the S headland, about 1m. Here the coast runs SW for about 600yds and the slabs can be found. 15 mins. [PE]

Penllechwen:
OS.157 GR.741 291   [87]

This crag of 80–180ft offers plenty of climbing in the Diff to VS grades. Not that good in the winter months since it is N-facing and tends to get rather slippery.

Dir: 2m NNE of St David's. From the car park at Whitesands Bay, B4583, take the coastal path N and then follow the coastline up until the top NE corner of the headland to the crag, 35 mins. [PE]

Penmaen Coetan:
OS.157 GR.723 282   [88]

A small crag, 80ft, offering some worthwhile easy climbs and a few VSs. W-facing and on good rock. This is a must.

Dir: As for Craig Coetan. This is situated on the point just to the W of the crag, on the western side. [PE]

Porth-Clais:
OS.157 GR.743 238 HT–4.55   [89]

A crag with about 20 routes to 70ft and all around the Severe standard, some harder and others easier. Access is made easier at low tide or with the use of an abseil rope at high tide. A very good crag.

Dir: 1m SW of St David's. From the town take a road SW to Porth-Clais and park at the head of an inlet. Walk down to the E side of the inlet above the quay to the point and the crag, 5 mins. [PE]

Porth Henllys:
OS.157 GR.722 231   [90]

Some good climbing to be found on this part of the coastline in the lower grades. Most around 100ft in length and S-facing.

Dir: 2m SW of St David's. Approach: see Porth-Clais. From head of inlet take the coastal path on the S side of the inlet. Follow this around the long

point after 0.7m and into the next bay, where the climbing lies on the far side, about 25 mins. [PE]

Porth-Y-Ffynnon:
OS.157 GR.745 240   [91]

The climbing to be found here is mainly on some 80ft slabs, all of which are S-facing and very accommodating. Grades range from Diff to HVS, with most climbs except the hard ones being well protected. A good spot.

Dir: 1, SSW of St David's. Approach: see Porth-Clais, but continue around into the next bay where the slabs are situated, 10 mins. [PE]

Pwlldawnau:
OS.157 GR.878 371 HT–5.25   [92]

The cliffs here never reach higher than 200ft and the climbing tends to be around HVS or E3. A series of small bays just S of the headland of Penbwchdy gives several crags. The crags are impressive, with Rainbow Zawn and People's Cliff being most noteworthy. Approach to most is by abseil from stakes already in place, but it is rumoured that a full complement of friends is useful for belays.

Dir: 4m W of Goodwich. From Goodwich take the A487 SW for 5m just past the R turning to St Nicholas, turn R to Granston. After 1m over crossroads, then R down and up and on for 1m to Velindre, park. Take the footpath W to the coast and bay of Pwllcrochan, turn R and walk N for about 0.7m, cliffs will appear on the R. [PE]

Ramsey Island:
OS.157 GR.695 235   [93]

There is climbing here, quite a bit I am told. The island, however, is a bird sanctuary and if climbing is permitted I would think a restriction of climbing to after 15 Aug. probable. The situation is vague since in the past some climbing under scrutiny has taken place. With so much climbing in Pembroke there is obviously no need for any confrontation, details of access should be available from the BMC. In this case, if in doubt do not bother.

Dir: 3m WSW of St David's. [PE]

St David's Head:
OS.157 GR.722 278   [94]

Although to most people the whole area around St David's is classified as the head, for climbing purposes this term applies only to the cliffs right on the end of the W point. Here there is a small 50ft crag offering 10 or so routes, Diffs and Severes mainly. The rock is good even if the routes are not as spectacular as on the larger cliffs, and approach is made easily from the far W end of the peninsula.

Dir: From the car park at Whitesands Bay, B4583, take the coastal path N. Go past two sandy bays and then carry on around on to the head. [PE]

St Non's Bay:
OS.157 GR.753 242   [95]

Some walls and some slabs offer some nice climbing in this bay, about 30 routes up to 80ft mainly Diffs and Severes. Non-tidal and W-facing.

Dir: 0.7m S of St David's. Take a road S out of the town to St Non's Chapel and Well, park. The coastal path leads off to the E and the cliffs in the bay, 5 mins. [PE]

Trwyn Llwyd:
OS.157 GR.733 287   [96]

This crag has some notable lines around VS, HVS and E3, about 250ft and non-tidal. Only a handful of routes, but well worth a visit. About 150yds away to the NE there is a handful of slab routes around the Severe standard, about 150ft. Indeed the coastline from here to the E head has many smaller crags offering plenty in the way of Diffs and Severes, the most notable being Porth Llwch situated about 200yds further on.

Dir: 2m NW of St David's. Approach: see Craig Hebog, 20 mins from car park. [PE]

5 North Wales

ANGLESEY

To any British climber Anglesey means only one thing – Gogarth. A forbidding name when spoken slowly and deliberately. Gogarth is really the only crag on Anglesey. However its many cliffs are so different in character to one another that it seems the wealth of climbing is endless. There must be at least 500 routes here, of which perhaps only 50 are under Extreme. Not a crag for the beginner in any way and even excellent climbers have come to grief here. An accident at Gogarth is a major epic definitely to be avoided, and injury on the main cliff itself causes problems almost insolvable except by the very skilful and talented. Tides at Gogarth play an important part on some of the cliffs, as do rough seas. The rock is quartzite, different in many ways from typical rock – it nearly always gives huge holds, even on E5s, and often has a soapy texture making chalk very useful for most people. Protection is generally either very good or non-existent, indicated in crag descriptions. The rock is covered in a coat of green fur and looks uninviting. However this is usually in the area between the routes and scrapes off easily. Best time of year is a nice calm day in summer when everyone is in the mountains and you can swim around the main cliff and get a fantastic view. Most, though, come here when it is raining in Snowdonia since Anglesey, being on the tip of a peninsula, often stays dry. The climbs are often multi-pitch, and good-standard seconds are almost essential since the rock overhangs; if the second falls off and swings into midair, the epic begins! There are nesting restrictions in some parts, but these areas are few and anyway present in only a small area of climbable rock.

The crags can be reached from many directions but the South Stack car park is perhaps the best because it has a café and as it is a popular tourist spot you are less likely to have your car burnt out. Crags are described in access from this car park.

South Stack   Enter Holyhead by road, or boat from Ireland, and take the small road out of the town leading W and signposted to South Stack, reached in about 3m. Park in the car park.

Castell Helen:
OS.114 GR.205 820 HT–3.35   [1]

A superb cliff for the climber who does not want to be frightened. Lovely rock in a very pleasant position makes this easily the most popular cliff in the area. About 20 routes, VS to E2, and the very interesting Obelisk E5, well protected on solid rock which is not too steep. The base is semi-tidal, a bit of a crush on a ledge at high tide,

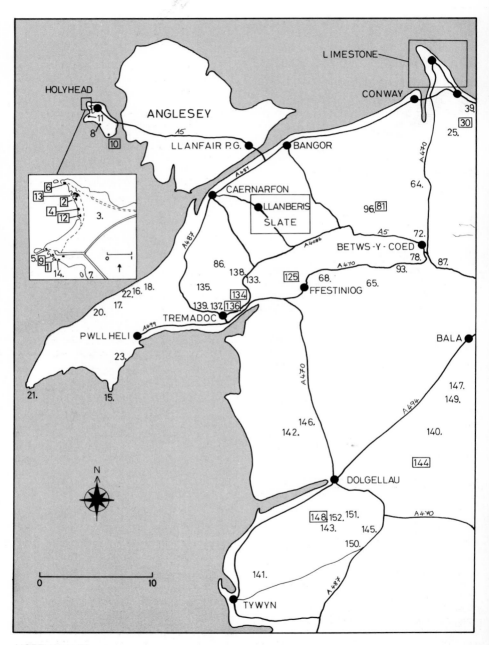

NORTH WALES

entertaining in a heavy sea though. Abseil rope useful here for top abseil. A big cliff with most routes about 250ft.

Dir: 2.6m WSW of Holyhead. From the car park at S Stack walk S to Helen's cottage then R. Dropping down and to the L there is a short rock wall, well worn with a peg belay abseil, often backed up and rope left in place. Abseil down and use to further abseil to the foot of the cliff. [GO]

Easter Island Gully:
OS.114 GR.215 838 HT–3.35   [2]

The entrance to some very impressive rock scenery and the R-hand end of the main cliff. A good VS to E3 area, about 30 routes, 100–200ft. Definitely worth a visit if only for the abseil in.

Dir: 2.5m WNW of Holyhead. Approach: see North Stack and Wen Zawn. The gully is directly behind, S of the seaward ridge of the slab by about 70 yds. Descend by scrambling down a horror gully to a block with an abseil point. 100ft abseil rope required and often left in place! [GO]

Holyhead Mountain:
OS.114 GR.220 827   [3]

There are some very useful crags here offering plenty of climbing in the lower grades, V Diff–VS, and a handful of easy Extremes, 70–120ft. Being away from the sea and not so intimidating, they offer a good day's climbing for a mixed party whose cream team are fully occupied on the main cliff, scenery is a bit bland though. About 60 climbs in total scattered all around the mountain.

Dir: 1.6m W of Holyhead. Approach: see Main Cliff, but bear up towards the crags seen on the mountain. [GO]

Main Cliff:
OS.114 GR.215 835 HT–3.35   [4]

This cliff can only be described as fantastic and is worth a visit if you are fit and have big arms. It dominates the whole coastline and offers huge routes up to 400ft of really challenging climbing. Most of the routes are classics and receive the afternoon sun. All are at least 2-pitches and an abseil from the belay will often deposit you in the sea. The rock is mostly sound, but large bits have been known to break off with climbers

attached! Friends are useful here, as well as small nuts. The tide affects the bottoms quite a lot, 2 hrs either side of HT prevents access to the main section; one can climb over the small pinnacle at high tide to gain access on a calm day. About 70 routes, with many E4–E5 climbs and a few easy E6s.

Dir: 2m W of Holyhead. From S Stack take the footpath NE towards a small mountain and some radio masts, after 1.5m the cliffs should become visible on the L. Descent down a gully is by some boulders, usually lots of rucksacks. Descend and cross beneath the upper tier, awkward in the wet, then descend the steep bank to rocks and down to sea-level. If you look up and don't see a fantastic 350ft cliff in front of you, you're lost! [GO]

Mousetrap Zawn: Restriction
OS.114 GR.205 822 HT–3.35   [5]

There is a bird restriction here, no climbing 1 Mar.–1 Aug. This crag is actually climbed quite frequently, which is quite bizarre since the rock is certainly awful in comparison with most of Gogarth. Anyway, go for it. 300–400ft routes from a tidal base, about 20 in total. Nothing technical here – rock not very strong, it comes away in big chunks. Large nuts useful as well as big protection.

Dir: 2.7m W of Holyhead. Directly opposite the S Stack lighthouse. Approach at low tide from the bottom of the steps, at high tide abseil in from the Red Wall ridge to the R, looking at the cliff from the lighthouse. The wall is recognised by the geological folding formation of the rock. The area just to the R of this is the Red Wall area. [GO]

North Stack:
OS.114 GR.215 840 HT–3.35   [6]

This is a cliff for the very bold leaders, with ability! The North Stack Wall does not see many falls, good job too. About 20 routes up to 150ft on fairly predictable rock (that does not mean solid). It supports well enough, whether or not protection holds is questionable, nobody usually tests gear here. The routes are all easy E3 to not-so-easy E6. There are E7s and beyond for the levitation experts with plenty of guts. Abseil approach from poles (watch the tar at the bottom, bring a rag) or some metal rings set well back.

Dir: 2.5. ENE of Holyhead. From S Stack go past the Main Cliff, in a NE direction to the N stack, where there is a wall and coastguard station above. Standing on top of the wall there is the huge Parliament Cave to the L, with several aid routes on it. Before this bay is reached there is a large zawn with a huge white slab about 200yds away. These are called Wen Zawn and Wen Slab. [GO]

Penlas Rock: Restriction
OS.114 GR.207 816 HT–3.35 [7]

This is an important nesting area and not climbed 1 Mar.–1 Aug. About 10 routes of VS, 130–200ft. Not great routes on variable rock, a crag really only for use if you want to avoid the crowds.

Dir: 2.3m WSW of Holyhead. Follow access path not to incur the wrath of the local farmer. From S Stack car park follow the coastal path S to the rock, which is round and covered in grass, about 600yds. [GO]

Porth Dafarch:
OS.114 GR.233 799 [8]

A super little crag with a handful of climbs in the easy Extreme grade, about 40ft. Quite steep, good for the arms.

Dir: 2m SW of Holyhead. Approaching Holyhead on the A5 at Dyffryn turn L on to the B4545 to Trearddur. Just after the beach turn L up the coast road, after 1.7m a sandy bay is reached, park. The cliff is on the L headland of the bay. [GO]

Red Wall: Restriction
OS.114 GR.205 822 [9]

There is a bird restriction here, no climbing 1 Mar.–1 Aug. This area consists of two walls, Red Wall and Left Hand Red Wall. Both are serious places to climb and not without difficulty. There are about 50 Extremes here and about half of them are very hard indeed. Most are about 300ft, involving a belay half-way up, even the second has to be a headcase. There are stories of seconds refusing to visit the crag because of the belays on some of the routes! A lot of the routes receive three-star classic status, which must make them very memorable indeed. The route Red Wall itself gets E1 5a – need I say more?

Dir: 2.6m W of Holyhead. Descend immediately behind the café to an abseil point between the two walls. [GO]

Rhoscolyn:
OS.114 GR.257 756 [10]

A good crag with lots of climbing, some of the climbs are definitely better than others. About 50 routes up to 150ft on fairly sound rock, S-facing. Worth a visit.

Dir: 6m S of Holyhead. Take the B4545 S through Trearddur then turn off R to Rhoscolyn. At the church go up a small track to the coastguard lookout. Here a path leads NE to the crag on the headland in about 10 mins. [GO]

Smurf Zawn: Restriction
OS.114 GR.210 814 HT–3.35 [11]

There have been reports of an angry farmer, who is not small or unarmed, wishing that climbers would keep away. Check with the BMC first or seek up-to-date info. A good little zawn with an impressive R wall, offering a handful of routes around the easy Extremes up to 170ft. Approach at low tide is easiest by descending the arête to the N.

Dir: 2.4m WSW of Holyhead. Approach: see Penlas Rock, carry on down the coast for about 400yds. [GO]

Upper Tier:
OS.114 GR.216 833 [12]

This cliff is unaffected by tides and a good introduction to the area. However the routes here are nowhere as impressive or as good as others in the area. Lots of slabby climbs – steep slabs admittedly, but slabs nevertheless. About 70 routes, HVS upwards to E6, on reasonable rock. Often the routes not on the walls present the most amusement, but the walls can provide an absorbing time for the second.

Dir: 2m W of Holyhead. Approach: see Main Cliff. [GO]

Wen Zawn:
OS.114 GR.215 839 HT–3.35 [13]

A great area, one of the finest in Wales. This zawn on a sunny afternoon warms to T-shirt temperature even in the coldest of winter days.

There are many climbs here at all grades VS upwards, about 30 routes up to 200ft. There are some quite challenging lines through some spectacular overhangs. Approach is by abseil to the tidal bottom or by scrambling down the seaward edge of Wen Slab. The slab can be climbed in almost any weather, including 60ft waves – trendy.

Dir: 2.5m WNW of Holyhead. Approach: see North Stack. [GO]

Yellow Wall:
OS.114 GR.205 819 HT–3.35   [14]

About 10 routes in this impressive zawn area. Routes are all E2 upwards, around 250ft, and can entail some amusing activities if the leader or second should fall off – it is quite overhanging. In a heavy sea, spray tends to make the area quite damp and difficult to climb.

Dir: 2.6m WSW of Holyhead. Approach at low tide is by scrambling down a grassy bank to the L of Helen's Cottage, just below the car park, and then scrambling along a tunnel. The area can be seen perfectly from Castell Helen cliff.

LLEYN PENINSULA

This is an area little known to climbers and the only reports to come back are horror stories and the like. It is either very good or very bad. Explore at will and live to tell the tale. The area does have a certain charm in parts that are isolated from the holiday resort of Pwllheli. The crags are isolated indeed. The weather here is often very good since there are no real mountains to attract the clouds, hence the holiday resort. The area has to some extent not been explored very well except for some of the unstable sea cliffs, and no doubt quarries or other small edges might interest development.

Cilan Head: Restriction
OS.123 GR.291 235   [15]

There is a bird ban on climbing here, 1 Feb–1 Aug. This cliff has had many tales told of its past in many a bar. Route descriptions include 'traverse the shattered band to a tottering pillar and continue to a doubtful stance'. Need I carry on? About 250ft and needing the skill of an extreme headcase.

Dir: 4m SSW of Abersoch. Go S to Sarn Bach where there are signs to Cilan, park in the car park at the end of the road. A path leads to the coast and the cliffs. [LPI, GO]

Craig Gyfrinach:
OS.123 GR.367 456   [16]

About 10 routes in different grades of around 200ft on these hillside crags overlooking Trefor. There are three cliffs in a cwm.

Dir: 5m N of Pwllheli. From Llanaelhaearn on the A499 take a small road over the hills to Trefor,

after 1.7m park. The cliffs are up on the R at the top of the valley, 3-min. sprint. [LPI, GO]

Craig Y Llam: Restriction
OS.123 GR.333 436   [17]

There is a voluntary climbing ban here, 1 Feb.–1 Aug. Quite a large crag with two routes, one 700ft VS, the other 800ft E2. Meant to be good, solid rock offering little protection. In desperate need of a bolt kit, at least for belays anyway.

Dir: 6m NNW of Pwllheli. From Nefyn take the B4417 towards Llithfaen, after 3.2m turn L and go down to some old quarries. From here scramble down to the sea and L (W) along to the crags. [LPI, GO]

Gurn Ddu Quarry:
OS.123 GR.395 467   [18]

A quarry of about 230ft, with about six routes, Severe to HVS. The rock is granite and is generally good but quarried.

Dir: 7.5m NNE of Pwllheli. From Trefor N, A499, follow a track leading off up the hill about 100yds further on. Then take the footpath, which leads to the quarry after 10 mins and a heart attack – it is a steep hill. [LPI, GO]

Nefyn:
OS.123 GR.324 410 [20]

There is, I am told, some very good climbing to be found here, about 15 routes of VS and above, 220ft. There are two venues, Gwylwyr Quarry and Carreg Lefain, both within a minute of each other.

Dir: 6m NW of Pwllheli. A497 to Nefyn, take the B4417 NE towards Llithfaen, after 1m park. The crags are up on the hillside to the R, 5 mins. [LPI, GO]

Pen Y Cil and Parwyd:
OS.123 GR.158 240 [21]

These two crags are of unstable character and worth a visit if you wish to get away from it all on the remote southernmost tip of the peninsula. An epic here would leave you stranded, perhaps for months. Pen Y Cil is about 200ft and Parwyd around 450ft, big, very loose, and not surprisingly Serious!

Dir: On the S tip of the peninsula. Go to Uwchmynydd (a mouthful for starters). From here take a small lane L going S a few yards after the church, continue to a T-jctn, L then R to a farm at Solfach. The cliff is directly ahead in about 400yds. [LPI, GO]

Trwyn-Y-Gorlech:
OS.123 GR.355 457 [22]

Some large quarries by the sea, offering quite a few routes and with the introduction of bolts a good few more. A few Diffs and Severes up to 800ft.

Dir: 6m N of Pwllheli. From Trefor take the coastal path SW for about a mile to the obvious cliffs. [LPI, GO]

Tyn Towyn Quarries:
OS.123 GR.330 304 [23]

Five quarries up to 250ft, offering about 30 routes mainly in the VS and HVS grades.

Dir: 5m SW of Pwhlleli. Take the A499 SW past Llanbrdrog. The quarries are situated on the S side of the big hill S of the town. Carry on for 0.5m, then a lane leads around to a spot for parking. Walk to Quarry No. 1, 2, etc. [LPI, GO]

SNOWDONIA NORTH

Limestone

The limestone in this area is situated to the north of the national park, mostly on the coast but still with a few inland crags. The majority of routes are in the Extreme grades. However this should never deter other climbers since there are routes below E1 worth doing; see crags for details. The most important fact is that, being in the rain shadow for SW weather systems, it does not rain here very much. But if the weather system is from the north it is going to be wet and windy, so seek any crags in the Snowdonia South area. The rock itself is very good and quite reliable, protection being mostly nuts. Bolts are used where necessary but because of the close proximity to the sea they must be treated with caution, as should bits of tat and krabs left in place for abseil descent. There are no slabs here, and those used to climbing on the volcanic rock of Snowdonia will find it very steep and tiring on forearms and calfs. All the climbs are essentially single-pitch with easy access and descent, the exception being the larger cliffs on the Little Orme.

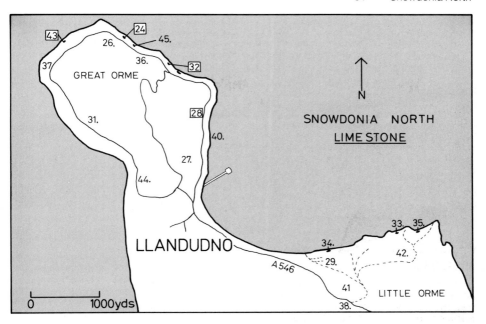

Castell Y Gwynt
OS.115 GR.758 846 [24]

This is the big cliff of the Orme, with no less than 12 three-star routes on it. Sorry, punters, average grade E5. There are, though, two fine E2s and an E3, superb routes. About 120ft cliff but many run to 200ft of climbing, with often a good 4 hrs of flying time involved. The obvious line is Central Pillar E6, going straight up the middle, one of the more difficult routes to flash on the Ormes. N-facing and can get cold on the hanging belays. Also the smell of the bird excrement is unbelievably disgusting. Come here with a very good cold.

Dir: 2m NW of Llandudno. Take the marine drive, toll, which runs up the E side of the Great Orme until the lighthouse. Just past the lighthouse entrance go over the wall and down a grassy gully, the crag will appear on the R. It is big and impressive. [NWL]

Castle Inn Quarry:
OS.116 GR.891 770 [25]

A small quarry offering a handful of routes, E2 to E4, about 80ft and behind a pub. A good day to be had here.

Dir: 1m SE of Colwyn Bay. Approach: see for Craig Y Forwyn. Carry on up the road for 1m to the village of Llysfaen, straight on in the village to the Castle Inn and the crag. [NWL]

Craig Arwahan: Restriction
OS.115 GR.758 843 [26]

This crag, being above the road, has a ban, no climbing at Easter, bank holidays, 1 July–10 Sept. A 60ft crag, offering a good selection of about a dozen routes across the grades. The crag has an easy descent at the rear.

Dir: 1.7m NW of Llandudno. Take the marine drive, toll, on to the Orme and continue until the entrance to the lighthouse. The crag is on the L. [NWL]

Craig Dinas:
OS.115 GR.779 832 [27]

A small, 120ft crag with about 5 routes on it, HVS to 6c.

Dir: On the outskirts of Llandudno. Park just before the toll gate on the Great Orme. Here a footpath leads up to the Happy Valley Gardens and the cliff beyond. [NWL]

Craig Pen Trwyn: Restriction
OS.115 GR.781 837 [28]

The restriction to climbing here is because of the road beneath the crag and danger to cars. It is a busy road and the local council sensibly insists that climbing must take place only in quiet periods. Hence climbing above the road is banned 9 a.m.–5 p.m. at Easter, bank holidays, and 1 July–10 Sept. There are also rare plants and flowers on the cliff, so care should be taken and overactive gardening instincts restrained. The climbing is good and hard, about 50–120ft, over 250 routes from E1 to E7, with 76 E4s. The classics are all E5 upwards, a lot of E2s and E3s. Some are not so well protected, be careful, all the harder routes are tough. To do all the routes here in a week is known as going well.

Dir: 0.5m NNE of Llandudno. From the town turn R at the Empire Hotel then L at the Grand Hotel to the Great Orme. Go through the toll gate and after 200yds round a bend the crag is seen. The big main section has lots of E6s, then the walls stretch around the corner to some yellow and black walls. [NWL]

Craig Y Don:
OS.116 GR.812 824 HT–3.00 [29]

A good introduction to the climbing on the Little Ormes. About 20 routes, HVS–E5 on the upper and middle tiers, 130ft. On the lower tier which is tidal, there are about 10 routes, around 200ft, E1–E5. The best routes are on the upper tier and in the E3–E5 range, however the route Hydro at E1 takes the obvious easy way up the centre of the buttress.

Dir: 1.3m E of Llandudno. Park as for Little Ormes. Take the footpath for 150yds, then bear L on a path which leads down to the L side of the head and the crag will be on the R. For the lower tier approach by abseil. Go beneath the middle tier then drop down to a flat ledge. Here one can abseil to a small ledge at the foot of the cliff. Looking at the cliff, to the R is the lower tier, to the L and along is Diamond Buttress. At very low tide one can also reach the cliff from scrambling along the beach. [NWL]

Craig Y Forwyn: Restriction
OS.116 GR.907 767 [30]

This crag is on private land and access is very much a problem. The main reason is that it is the best crag outside Snowdonia for most people, hence hordes of climbers would descend on wet days, making thoroughfare on the road difficult and causing annoyance to the farmer. Negotiations are nearly resolved, please check with the BMC and, if unable to, ask the farmer for permission to visit the crag. The climbing here is good and well protected. about 150 routes in all grades, with 20 on the Two Tier Buttress, mainly Es. E-facing but quite well sheltered. Often referred to as 'Craggy Forearm', a crag for people with big, butch biceps.

Dir: 3m ESE from Colwyn Bay. Take the A55 coast road E from Colwyn Bay., After 2m take the turn off to Llanddulas on to the B5443 (may be called the A547), after 0.2m turn R up the valley by the river, continue for 0.6m. The crag is on the R. Two Tier Buttress is 500yds back along the road from here. [NWL]

Creigiau Cochion: Restriction
OS.115 GR.762 831 [31]

There is climbing here, but not of fantastic merit and since the council are worried about its close proximity to the road it is perhaps best left alone. About 50–100ft crags.

Dir: 1.3m WNW of Llandudno. Take the marine drive around the Orme, 1m after the lighthouse Creigiau Cochion is some cliffs on the L. [NWL]

Crinkle Crags:
OS.115 GR.765 843 [32]

Crinkle Crags are 60ft, non-tidal cliffs by the sea, offering about 40 routes. There are Diffs and Severes here, also VSs. Needless to say there are many Extremes. Some of the crags are reached by scrambling down and others from bolt belay abseils. The cliffs here are known as Surprise Zawn, Crinkle Crags, Fluted Wall. By continuing along the road to the next bend Wonderwall and Peninsular Wall are reached. Abseil approach and hard routes, with escape route VS.

Dir: 1.5m NNW of Llandudno. Approach: see Hamburger Buttress. [NWL]

Detritus Wall: Restriction
OS.116 GR.815 826 [33]

A bird ban, no climbing 1 Mar.–15 Aug. A couple of easy Extremes run up the L side. the main

500ft wall has some very impressive routes in the Extreme category, all being very committing.

Dir: 1.5m E of Llandudno. Approach: see Meadow Walls. [NWL]

Diamond Buttress: Restriction
OS.116 GR.813 825 [34]

A bird ban here, no climbing 1 Mar.–1 Aug. A large, black wall offers 500ft routes, HVS plus aid? There is also the classic Gemstone E2, the obvious ramp L to R but often damp.

Dir: 1.3m E of Llandudno. Approach: see Craig y Don. [NWL]

Great Zawn: Restriction
OS.116 GR.817 827 [35]

There is a bird restriction on the L side of the cliff (looking in) but does not affect most of the climbs. No climbing 1 Mar.–15 Aug. The climbing here is very good and on good, solid rock in an impressive position. About 15 routes in the lower Extreme grades, 150–500ft, with an HVS escape route, best to leave abseil in position. Most of the routes are classics, the only drawback being that the cliff is N-facing.

Dir: 1.7m E of Llandudno. Approach: see Meadow Walls. [NWL]

Hamburger Buttress: Restriction
OS.115 GR.766 842 [36]

Because of the danger to passing cars there is a climbing ban at the following times: Easter, bank holidays, 1 July–10 Sept. A handful of routes around E4, 60ft, most worth doing.

Dir: 1.5m NNW of Llandudno. Take the marine drive on to the Orme, go for about 1.5m. About 0.5m from the lighthouse at the N end of the Orme, the crag is just above the road. Beneath the road are the areas around Crinkle Crags. [NWL]

Hornby Crags: Restriction
OS.115 GR.753 842 [37]

This area is home for lots of nesting birds, no climbing 1 Mar.–1 Aug. The crags offer some varied climbing on perhaps the worst rock in the area. Still there are some worthwhile routes here. About 16 routes around VS, HVS. Further on is the Observatory Buttress at the same level, with about 15 routes, HVS to E4-ish. About 100ft in most places, N-facing and remote.

Dir: 2.3m NW of Llandudno. Approach: see St Tudno's Buttress, walk L to the coastguard post and take the gully down to the R and the crag. [NWL]

Little Ormes: Access
OS.116 GR.814 822 [38]

The parking here is where you can, and as close to the footpath as possible; moreover it is a bloody steep hill to have to walk up. The A546 links Llandudno and Colwyn Bay, running close to the sea. This road cuts over the shoulder of the Little Ormes. Almost on the top of the shoulder there is a footpath which leads on to the Ormes. [NWL]

Llanddulas Cave:
OS.116 GR.915 779 [39]

A small wall and a cave, offering about 10 routes, E2 to E4.

Dir: 3m E of Colwyn Bay. Turn off the A55 coast road on to the B5443 (or A547) to Llanddulas, after 0.5m the cave is on the hill to the R. Approach by a path up through the trees. [NWL]

Lower Pen Trwyn:
OS.115 GR.782 833 HT–3.00 [40]

A crag regarded by some, but not others, as the best on the Orme. The routes here are good but not easy, anything really worth doing around E5, with one E7 exception. Also a good, 500ft HVS traverse. About 70ft with 30 or so routes. The cliff is very awkward at high tide but has no other restrictions.

Dir: 0.5m N of Llandudno. Go past the toll on the Ormes road and park at the first big caves on the L. Go over the wall and down the gully to the boulder beach below, quite a walk. [NWL]

The Manor Crag:
OS.116 GR.813 823 [41]

A tiered crag with about 15 small-problem routes, 5b–6b.

Dir: 1.5m E of Llandudno. Park as for the Little Ormes. Take the footpath, the crag is immediately on the L, all the climbs are on the upper tier. [NWL]

Meadow Walls:
OS.116 GR.817 825 [42]

A good little spot offering some tough little spurts. About 4 routes, E3–E5, with the easiest, Hole of Creation going straight up the middle. 60ft, N-facing.

Dir: 1.5m E of Llandudno. Park as for Little Ormes. Take the footpath and keep bearing R, after 400yds the meadow is reached. By going down the R side and looking back up the hillside the crag can be seen. By carrying down to the obvious rock peninsula, you arrive at the abseil point to the Detritus Wall which is on the L. By walking to the R for about 80yds you arrive at an abseil point which goes down to the slab at the bottom of the amphitheatre of the Great Zawn, full rope length. [NWL]

St Tudno's Buttress:
OS.115 GR.754 843 [43]

A crag in an impressive position, with good rock and routes. About 30 routes around E2–E3, with a few Severes to HVSs, 30–160ft. One of the most useful places to climb, no restrictions and generally away from the tourists. This is the home of the famous Gritstone Gorilla, it is rumoured!

Dir: 2.3m NW of Llandudno. Take the marine drive around the Great Orme, just past the lighthouse there is a tea shack, park here. About 50yds on there is a scree gully, descend this and to the R is the crag. To the L is Observatory Buttress. By descending even further to some steps and carrying on to the R **Craig Pen Gogarth** is reached. This has some impressive overhangs, explore at will. This crag has a bird ban, though, 1 Mar.–1 Aug. [NWL]

Toll Gate Crags: Restriction
OS.115 GR.770 823 [44]

A few 100ft buttresses, offering several routes in the Diff and VS grades. The rock is not of the best quality, and care should be taken at all times.

Dir: 0.5m WNW of Llandudno. On the most southern part of the Great Orme Head itself, above Toll Gate Lodge. [NWL]

Unnamed Crag: Restriction
OS.115 GR.758 844 [45]

This is a bird-nesting crag, no climbing 1 Mar.–31 July. A 50ft section with about 6 routes around E3, and a 200ft section with about 10 routes VS–HVS and one E2.

Dir: 2m NW of Llandudno. Take the marine drive, toll road on to the Orme. Upon reaching the lighthouse at the point go over the wall (not in the car) and down the gully, which runs to a path leading down past a cave to ledges beneath the crag at sea-level. [NWL]

Slate

At the time of writing all the slate climbing is situated around Llanberis, but since there are very many slate quarries in N Wales there may well be many more areas developed in future. To those uninitiated in climbing slate, do not miss out – give it a try and scare yourself silly. With the introduction of sticky rubber, climbers can now at least get some friction on slate and start to enjoy the routes. Bolts have also made a large difference and any well-protected route becomes an instant classic. There are many unprotected climbs on slate and these should be treated with respect since some of them are very hard indeed. Most of the climbs have been done by short-arses so there is no need to worry about reach, just the size of holds.

The quarries themselves are not really that scenic at all, but they do offer a real contrast in scenery from the mountains. Their very big

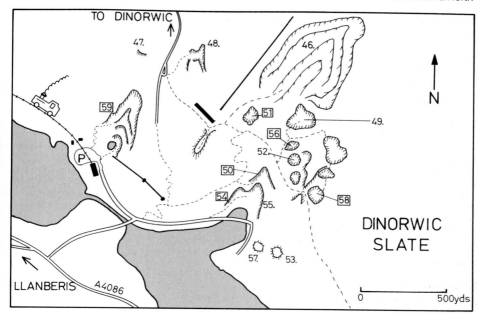

bonus is that they dry almost instantly, which in N. Wales is perhaps the single most important factor with any crag. Also those who intensely dislike walking will be happy at the one-minute walking time for the lower quarries. You can see some of the quarries from the café in Llanberis and with binoculars spy on illegal tactics – not that there are many runners to pull on.

There are really no worthwhile routes below VS here; in the main E1 is the starting grade, with the most routes being around E4 and E5. There are a whole handful of E7s to keep most of us down to earth when going really well, and one E8 for the optimistic. Abseil inspection and, indeed, top-rope practice is advised for anything above E4–E5. The routes can be very dangerous, a full complement of RPs and HBs are essential. There are very sharp edges also, so watch the ropes – double are often the most practical. Friends are useful for belays, as are bolts.

Access restrictions are sometimes a problem since the areas at the bottom of the quarries are frequented by drenched tourists who are unnoticed by climbers and falling rocks. Climbing above roads or footpaths is therefore banned, and the sheer size of the quarries makes this very easy to accept.

For access descriptions follow the map above and always park in the car park shown. This is a sensitive issue.

Australia:
OS.115 GR.598 610   [46]

This area consists of several walls and areas: Looning the Tube, Railtrack Slab, The Rognon, Gorbals Level and Skyline Buttress Level. All are around 60–80ft and offer a handful of truly unmemorable climbs. The climbs are mostly around E3, except for the Skyline which has easier climbs on it. [LLP]

Blast Shelter Crag:
OS.115 GR.590 611   [47]

A small 60ft slab in a small bay opposite The Rippled Slab, offering an E1 and a VS. Nothing stunning. [LLP]

Bus Stop Quarry:
OS.115 GR.592 612   [48]

This quarry contains 2 areas: Dinorwic Needles, about 80ft with about 10 routes, HVs, E2, E5; and The Rippled Slab, a great 100ft slab with a handful of hardish routes, interesting run-outs. [LLP]

California Wall:
OS.115 GR.596 605   [49]

A great area, not the best but offering about 4 classics in the E5 grade. A 100–200ft wall offering itself mainly to 6a and 6b moves, Central Sadness E5 being the classic, taking a line just L of centre, split by a bolt belay. [LLP]

Colossus Wall:
OS.115 GR.593 602   [50]

A magnificent wall, 150ft, offering classic routes, E3 to E5. Not to be missed, and because of the bolt protection extremely popular. The route Colossus E3 5c is probably the safest route in the quarries, with more bolts than holds. [LLP]

Dali's Hole Area:
OS.115 GR.595 606   [51]

Believe it or not, a surreal hole amidst the creative world of quarrymen. About 25 routes in the E1 to E4 grades, 60ft. [LLP]

Never Never Land Area:
OS.115 GR.596 604   [52]

About 15 routes of all difficulties, VS to E7, the route Never Never Land E5 6a being the classic and exciting as well, 150ft. [LLP]

Peppermint Tower:
OS.115 GR.593 598   [53]

A small tower around from Rainbow Walls. About 120ft with 2 climbs on it, HVS and E5. [LLP]

Rainbow Slab: Restriction
OS.115 GR.593 601   [54]

Please do not climb on the tier below Rainbow Slab, it could easily result in a total ban here. Keeping a low profile is always useful. The slab is situated on your L as you approach, about 150ft high and 200ft across. The best-looking slab in the area, offering about 15 routes in the more interesting and exciting grades. Abseil inspection thoroughly advised, with the exception of complete headcases. [LLP]

Rainbow Walls:
OS.115 GR.595 602

These walls are situated opposite the Rainbow Slab and are in tiers. Climbing above level 3 is banned – it is too long a walk anyway. About 40 climbs of 80ft across the grades. [LLP]

Serengeti Area:
OS.115 GR.596 604   [56]

Mostly 70ft climbs, a right mixture from VS to E7. Areas known as: Peter Pan Wall; Seamstress Slab with The Medium and Windows of Perception, difficult climbs; Yellow Wall with Loved by a Sneer, quite difficult and rumoured to have imaginary protection; and Heaven Walls, a larger, 150ft crag with exposure. [LLP]

Trango Tower:
[57]

Climbing here is strictly banned. [LLP]

Twll Mawr – The Big Hole:
OS.115 GR.598 601   [58]

What a crag! This quarry is definitely worth a visit. The West Wall has some of the most amazing routes in Llanberis, if not the universe. The Quarryman, 300ft of E8, offers a challenge to anyone fully conversant with the powers of levitation. Pitches of 6c, 6b, 7a and 7b make onsight cruises of this route somewhat optimistic. The North Wall of the quarry offers some 700ft routes of VS, E1 and E3. [LLP]

Vivian Quarry: Restriction
OS.115 GR.587 605 [59]

Please use the car park and do not climb above the tourist footpath. The most popular area in the quarries and the easiest for access, many classic lines of all difficulties. About 70 routes, 80–150ft, E1 to E7, the classics tending to be in the harder grades. Home of the ever-popular Comes the Staircase, now regarded as HVS, 5c by most. Dries very quickly, also close for a sprint to the car in the unlikely event of rain. [LLP].

SNOWDONIA

This area offers the greatest climbing in Wales if not the world. There are climbs of all standards, types and lengths. The cliffs are scattered from the valley floors to the summits and offer climbing of unrivalled interest. Most of the crags are easily identified and accessed since, although the valleys are deep, they virtually all have roads in. In poorer weather the high crags can become very hostile, and sufficient warm clothing and food should be carried. In such conditions a map and compass can prove very useful in getting back to the car very quickly, but by walking downhill one always arrives at a road after 2 hours. The crags really need good weather and any north facing ones need a good day to dry out after rain. Protection is usually very good and double ropes are very useful to cut down on drag since most of the

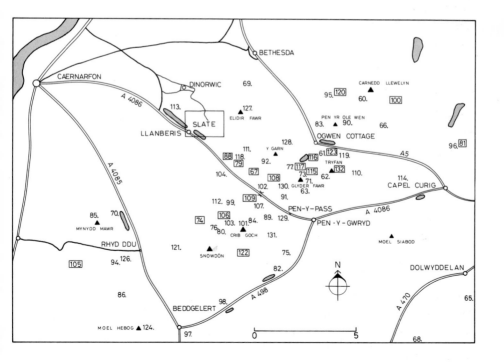

routes wander around. There are no bolts in the mountains and they are not welcome here. Winter is a dead loss here; so is summer often – if it is a warm, sunny day, wake up, you are dreaming. If it is raining go to the areas Snowdonia South or North, or even further afield. Listed here are all the main crags – there are millions of rock outcrops in Snowdonia and their inclusion here would necessitate sixteen volumes and defeat the object of a single guidebook.

Black Ladders:
OS.115 GR.670 632   [60]

This cliff is really best as a winter ice-climbing playground, even then there is rarely enough ice to make it worthwhile. For rock climbing it is very broken and situated in a N-facing cwm, making it dark and damp. It does offer about 20 climbs in the lower grades, around 200–700ft.

Dir: 4m SE of Bethesda between Carnedd Dafydd and Carnedd Llewelyn. From Bethesda go up to the village of Gerlan, past the post office and down the lane for 0.5m, park. Here a footpath leads SE to the valley with Carnedd Dafydd at the end. After crossing the boggy area a good track is followed in the valley and a crag, Llech Ddu, will appear on the R nearly at the end of the valley. Pass this to the cliffs at the head of the valley rising up to the ridge. 1–1½hrs walk in. [CDU]

Bochlwyd Buttress:
OS.115 GR.657 597   [61]

A very good crag with 100–200ft routes on it, about 10 in total but very many variations possible, Diffs to HVSs. Excellent holds, very assuring for the beginner or young leader. NW-facing but gets the evening sun. A gem.

Dir: 5.4m WNW of Capel Curig. Go down the A5 to a car park half-way along Llyn Ogwen. From here a path leads up the hillside to the crag in about 15mins, just to the L of a cascading stream. [OGW]

Bristly Ridge:
OS.115 GR.662 587   [62]

A marvellous ridge and most probably the best in Snowdonia. This goes at a good Moderate and is well worth doing, making any traverse of the Glyders an E to W proposition. The face to the E of the ridge offers some very good harder climbs of 400ft or so, V Diff to Severe.

Dir: 5m W of Capel Curig. From the bend in the A5 at Ogwen a path leads SE. After 1.3m the col between Tryfan and Glyder Fach is reached. The ridge going S is Bristly Ridge. [OGW]

Bryn Du:
OS.115 GR.639 569   [63]

A fine crag high up at 2,250ft, offering a handful of VS routes and a couple of Diffs. Worth a visit in nice weather.

Dir: 5.3m SE of Llanberis. Park at Pen y Pass, expensive, and then take the path up L behind the youth hostel to the small ridge leading up to Glyder Fawr. The crag is reached in about 40 mins, 1.3m, quite steep though. [LLP]

Cae Coch Quarry:
OS.115 GR.775 653   [64]

A quarry in the Conway valley, apparently offering 8 fair routes on average rock, however worth visiting. The climbs are 150–250ft, but all in the VS category.

Dir: 3.5m NNW of Llanrwst. Take the B5106 N on the W side of the Conway valley, pass through Trefriew, on for 1.2m, park. A path leads off L (NW) through the trees to the quarry after about 5 mins. [SNE]

Carreg Alltrem:
OS.115 GR.739 507   [65]

There is no quick way here from Llanberis, hence it remains one of the most beautiful spots in Snowdonia. There are 15 or so routes up to 150ft, worth splitting pitches, belay trees are set well back. Routes, just hard not very difficult to HVS. The rock is excellent and runs to very sensibly sized holds.

Dir: 6m SW of Betws Y Coed. Take the A470 Blaenau Ffestiniog road and at Dolwyddelan turn L down the small road and over the railway.

Turn R and go up the valley, lots of gates. The crag is about 0.5m up the valley, on the L (E) side. [TGM]

Carreg Mianog:
OS.115 GR.687 619   [66]

A small crag of around 100ft overlooking the Ogwen valley. About 15 routes up to HVS on some good, sound rock. In places it is quite steep, and some of the routes are definitely better than others.

Dir: 3.5m NW of Capel Curig. Approach: as for Craig Yr Ysfa to the reservoir road. Walk up the road for 1m, the crag is on the L about 800yds across and up, 20 mins [CDU]

Carreg Wasted:
OS.115 GR.626 570   [67]

The poorest of all the crags in the pass but nevertheless has some very good climbing and the classic Severe, Crackstone Rib, a gem. About 250ft with 30 climbs at all grades, the rock is never above suspicion and the central route, Erosion Groove, is aptly named.

Dir: 3.8m SE of Llanberis. Go up to the pass to some turnings off to the R, some climbing huts and a campsite. The crag is 500ft up on the L, rather rambling in appearance. [LLP]

Carreg Y Fran:
OS.124 GR.732 449   [68]

A somewhat broken crag, offering a few buttresses worth climbing on. About 20 climbs of 70 to 140ft, Diffs to HVS, with the exception of one E4. Quite a remote and peaceful spot.

Dir: 3m NE of Ffestiniog. Upon entering the town from Blaenau on the A470 take a small road on the L, after 50yds go under the railway, and continue up Cwm Teigl. This turns to a track which after 2m leads to the crag on the R. [TGM]

Carnedd Y Filiast:
OS.115 GR.623 627   [69]

Some good, long routes in the Mod to Hard Severe grades, about 15 routes, each 1,000ft. The routes are renowned to be poorly protected, tent pegs for belays can be essential. The rock improves with height ascended, as does the satisfaction of being a real mountaineer.

Dir: 3m SSW of Bethesda. Go S on the A5 from Bethesda for 1.8m, take the small road off to the R over a bridge, then L and up the valley for 0.9m just past a cottage, park. The cwm above to the R has all the climbing, first encountered is a small, red slab, then the cliffs above. [OGW]

Castell Cidwm:
OS.115 GR.550 554   [70]

A very awe-inspiring cliff, with about 10 routes of VS upwards with reasonable protection. The cliff seems a lot bigger than its 180ft, especially when encountering the steep right-hand section, mainly E3 to E6. SE-facing with a very picturesque outlook.

Dir: 6m SE of Caernarfon. Drive down the A4085 from Caernarfon to Betws Garmon. 1m later, just past Salem, cross the bridge on the R over the river and walk up to the lake, wet in parts. After 10 mins the crag previously hidden will appear up a gully. [CWC]

Castell Y Gwynt:
OS.115 GR.732 599   [71]

A high crag at the top of the central pass to the Crafnant valley, steep but turning slabby on the R. About 5 routes to 120ft, HS and VS.

Dir: 1.5m NNE of Capel Curig. Approach: see Craig Y Dwr. [SNE]

Clogwyn Cyrau:
OS.115 GR.789 571   [72]

Some very good small cliffs overlooking Betws Y Coed. Quite solid rock and good pro make this an ideal beginner's crag, often popular with teaching groups from the centres. About 30 routes, Diff to Vs, around 100ft. S-facing and good in winter, dries quickly as it is quite exposed.

Dir: Above Betws Y Coed. Park in the village. Cross the bridge on the B5106, turn L past the car park, first R up the short hill and into the forest, where a nature trail leads up to the crags. [SNE]

Clogwyn Du:
OS.115 GR.646 582   [73]

A dark, forbidding N-facing crag, high up in the Glyders. This crag really does need good ather. The views are fantastic to say the least. About 10 routes, Diff to E1, routes around 300ft.

Dir: 5m W of Capel Curig. The cliff drops away on the N side of the ridge between Glyder Fawr and Y Gribin. Map and compass essential. [OGW]

Clogwyn Du'r Arddu:
OS.115 GR.600 550   [74]

To some this is the climbing mecca, although for most of the year it is cold, wet, windy and thoroughly unpleasant. To others it is simply just too far from the car park. It has about 150 routes of VS and above, virtually all multi-pitch and around 250ft. The lower-grade routes are very good and it is well worth a visit if you are going at VS or HVS. There are plenty of easy Extremes yet very few mid-Extremes. The hard routes on the big walls and slabs are often unprotected and abseil inspection is advisable.

Dir: 4m SSE of Llanberis. In the town take the small road just S of the mountain railway, passing under the railway after 0.6m, to some lay-bys after 1.3m, park. Walk up following the railway, at a small shack after 1.5m the path forks off R to a small lake beneath the crag. You can't miss it. [CGY]

Clogwyn Y Bustach:
OS.115 GR.652 535   [75]

A crag always remembered, if only for the same reasons as the classic Diff, Lockwoods Chimney, in the guidebook description: 'It is customary to do this climb by moonlight in the worst possible conditions; the climbing party should preferably be large and of large men.' The climbing is not brilliant, but the 15 or so routes of Diff to HVS offer typical mountain-climbing experiences.

Dir: 7.5m SW of Capel Curig. Approach: see Clogwyn Y Wenallt. [TGM]

Clogwyn Y Ddysgl:
OS.115 GR.615 554   [76]

This large cliff, high up on the mountain at around 3,000ft, is really a summer crag. About 25 climbs in the lower grades, with a few E3s for good measure. In damp wintry conditions the Diffs can turn into E3s. 200–400ft.

Dir: 4.6m SE of Llanberis. Approach: see Clogwyn Y Person. [LLP]

Clogwyn Y Geifr:
OS.115 GR.639 589   [77]

To most people this is known as the Devil's Kitchen. It is a crag of mixed quality and receives very mixed opinion. It is often very wet and then offers completely disgusting climbs; at other times it can dry out to give some thrilling experiences. Most of the routes have a serious nature to them, only the VS leader will feel at home here – well maybe. About 40 routes reaching up to 250ft. The actual Kitchen can be climbed, a somewhat damp experience. The ridge to the R, Castell Y Gefir, offers some Diffs of marginal merit.

Dir: 6m W of Capel Curig. Approach: see Idwal Slabs, continue up to the amphitheatre. [OGW]

Clogwyn Y Gigfran:
OS.115 GR.793 542   [78]

A 150ft crag of indifferent quality in pleasant surroundings. About 8 climbs in the harder Severe grades.

Dir: 1.8m SSW of Betws Y Coed. Take the A470 S, after 0.3m the road twists sharply, carry on around the bend R, then find a parking spot in about 300yds. There is a small path on the R leading up into the woods, where the crag is easily found! [TGM]

Clogwyn Y Grochan:
OS.115 GR.621 572   [79]

A superb, steep cliff, offering some really excellent climbs on really solid rock with good protection, one of the best cliffs in the pass. About 250ft high with a steepish central section. The climbing here is often very technical with lots of side pulls and layaways. About 50 climbs with some very good E3s as well as the classic HVS Brant Direct, a must for the aspirant leader. Good climbs in all grades VS and upwards.

Dir: 3.6m SE of Llanberis. Approach: see Craig Ddu, this is the next crag up 'the pass'. There are several lay-bys beneath the crag. [LLP]

GREAT WALL, E3, 6a, Clogwyn Du'r Arddu. (Climber Ed Drummond, Photo Ken Wilson)

Clogwyn Y Person:
OS.115 GR.617 555 [80]

This cliff, known as the 'Cliff of the Parson', has some very good Moderates and Diffs on it, climbs around 200ft. The rock is not wonderful, but the holds are good and the position is superb.

Dir: 5m SE of Llanberis. A mountain crag. From the bridge at The Cromlech Boulders a footpath leads due S to a small lake, Llyn Glas. Here the screes run up to the ridge of Clogwyn Y Person and, to the R, Clogwyn Y Ddysgl. 1hr. [LLP]

Clogwyn Yr Eryr:
OS.115 GR.733 604 [81]

The best crag in the Llanrwst area. There is plenty of climbing here for everyone. The Forestry Buttress is the first encountered, about 20 routes up to HVS, between 100 and 200ft, offering some very good little pitches. Next along is Two Tier Buttress with 7 routes around VS. These cliffs, though, are completely diminished in stature by the South Buttress. This is *the* crag, it is big, butch and hunky. Its 20 or so routes average out at E3, but more impressive is that they average 2 stars each – that's going it, I tell you. The routes are around 160ft and 2-pitch, Snowdrop E3 and Carousel Waltz E5 being the gems. A morning crag for the sun. It can seep quite a lot so a good dry spell is useful; however, some of the harder routes on the arêtes dry very quickly.

Dir: 5m W of Llanrwst. Take the B5106 to Trefriw, turn L and go up the road to Llyn Crafnant. After 2.3m reach the lake, carry on to the end and park the other side of a gate. Walk across the valley floor and follow a track into the forest. Turn L to a hairpin bend, then R and head towards a boulder field which leads up to Forestry Buttress. The South Buttress is on the L. [NWS, SNE]

Clogwyn Y Wenallt:
OS.115 GR.647 528 [82]

A superb little crag offering some excellent VS–HVS climbs. 15 routes in total, VS to E5, on good, steep and well-protected rock, up to 150ft high.

Dir: 8m WSW of Capel Curig. From CC take the A4086 then at the top of the pass carry straight on, the A498, down the twisting road to the lake at the bottom. Park here and follow the footpath

to the head of the lake, where a footbridge is used to cross the river and reach the crag. By walking further upstream for 500yds the crag Clogwyn Y Bustach can be reached, high on the hillside. [TGM]

Craig Braich Ty Du:
OS.115 GR.650 610 [83]

This is a series of crags all around the 200ft mark, offering many routes of all grades but especially in the Diff–Severe standard. The easiest to get to is virtually at the bridge at the bottom of the mountain, worth a quick trip if waiting for the rest of the party to come down from the hills or if there is little daylight left. There are about 10 crags in total, of reasonable size, stretching up and across the W face of Pen Yr Ole Wen, the mountain due N of Ogwen Cottage. Nice sunny aspect, great place.

Dir: 5m SSE of Bethesda. Park at the W end of Llyn Ogwen, if you can find a place, A5. Cross the road and go over the river, the first buttress is up on the R, 100yds. The other buttresses are scattered all over the hillside to the L. [CDU]

Craig Cwm Beudy Mawr:
OS.115 GR.628 556 [84]

The translation of this is absolutely brilliant: Crag of the Cwm of the Big Cowshed – excellent. A good 250ft crag, offering a handful of routes in the Diff and Severe grades. No ascent of any route can be valid without continuing to the summit of Crib Goch, thereby preserving the spirit of the mountains.

Dir: 5m SE of Llanberis. Crib Goch is the mountain overlooking the top of the Llanberis Pass. This crag lies about 400yds short of the summit on the N side. [LLP]

Craig Cwm Du:
OS.115 GR.537 551 [85]

The place to go on bank holidays if you are a Diff or Severe climber and want to get away from the crowds. Here lies not the best of cliffs in Snowdonia but rock worth climbing and giving mixed routes of up to 500ft. About 20 lines of distinction, with various eliminates for the enthusiastic. For the even more enthusiastic, follow on up to the summit of Mynydd Mawr, then, by walking S for 600yds to the top of Craig Y Bera, drop down to the L and climb back up the 500ft buttress (several routes, Diff to Severe), continuing back at leisure to Mynydd Mawr summit for the second time.

Dir: 6m SE of Caernarfon on the N slopes of Mynydd Mawr. Going SE on the A4085, at Betws Garmon the cliffs will be visible ahead to the R, high up in a cwm. A footpath crosses the river and goes up and around the forest to the cwm. [CSC]

Craig Cwm Trwsgl: Restriction
OS.115 GR.550 494   [86]

There are parts of this cliff which have birds nesting and it is hoped that any climbers using the crag will be careful not to cause unwarranted disturbance. The climbing is generally good on the smoother parts that lend themselves to the harder routes, only a handful in total up to 300ft, VS to E3. W-facing but up at 1,400ft, very cool in winter.

Dir: 5m SW of Snowdon in the next range. Approach from Porthmadog area. Take the A487 W from Tremadog, after 2.5m turn R and make for the end of the Cwm Pennant valley, through Llanfihanger-y-Pennant. Here Craig Y Issalt is up on the hillside to the R, 5 mins. At the head of the valley the crag can be seen up to the R (NE). [CSC]

Craig Dinas:
OS.116 GR.808 538   [87]

This super little crag is a godsend in the colder months. Around 150ft high, offering about 10 routes, Severe to HVS, on very satisfying rock. SW-facing and 100yds from a pub.

Dir: 2m SSE of Betws Y Coed. On the A5 going S up the hill from Betws, the Silver Fountain Hotel is reached. The crag is above and to the N of this, 5 mins. [SNE]

Craig Ddu:
OS.115 GR.618 573   [88]

This cliff is about 250ft and for most of the year is a waterfall and seepage crag. There are good climbs to be found in a very dry summer. The crag is steeper than expected and in the rain even the easy-looking slabs are horror experiences. About 25 routes in all grades.

Dir: 3.5m SE of Llanberis. Take the A4086 SE

through Nant Peris, this is the first substantial crag on the L after leaving the village. [LLP]

Craig Fach:
OS.115 GR.634 554   [89]

A crag of sombre appearance offering some challenging climbs when dry. About 15 routes in the E4 and Diff–Severe standard, 60–120ft. The centre of the buttress is quite steep with a slight overhang, giving interesting climbing.

Dir: 4.7m SE of Llanberis. From Pen Y Pass car park take the Pyg track towards Snowdon for about 1m, after 12 mins look to the L and you will find the crag below the path. [LLP]

Craig Lloer:
OS.115 GR.661 619   [90]

A crag without difficult climbs, about 12 routes of 280ft, mainly Diffs and Severes. The setting here on a nice summer's day is fantastic, quite secluded and, with the lovely lake down below, perfect for an after-climb swim. However the weather in Wales usually takes care of this *en route*.

Dir: 5m WNW of Capel Curig. Take the A5 Bangor road to the E end of Llyn Ogwen, park in the car park. Cross the bridge and go past the climbing hut to a vague path going up the mountain, a far more pleasant way to Carnedd Dafydd, up to the small lake. The cliff is up on the L. Has been done in 15 mins! [CDU]

Craig Nant Pen Y Pass:
OS.115 GR.637 562   [91]

This crag is the most obvious from the road going up through the pass, about half-way from The Cromlech Boulders and the top of the pass. About 6 climbs of easy and hard grades, 100ft. There are many small outcrops worthy of entertainment here but not worthy of inclusion.

Dir: 5.6m SE of Llanberis. Park in the lay-by and the crag is on the N side of the road and river. [LLP]

Craig Nant Peris:
OS.115 GR.626 574   [92]

A broken crag about 200ft but offering an excellent opportunity to combine some Diff climbing with an ascent of Glyder Fawr. A

of climbs, none really above V Diff, but ~000ft and a superb position, a good-weather crag though.

Dir: 4.4m ESE of Llanberis. Directly above Carreg Wasted in the Llanberis Pass, the ridge of Esgair Felen, about 1 hour. [LLP]

Craig Rhiw Goch:
OS.115 GR.767 541   [93]

A small crag situated above the Lledr river, excellent for trout fishing – whatever you do, do not disturb the fish. A handful of 100ft climbs, S to HVS, and three E2s.

Dir: 2.5m WS of Betws Y Coed. Go S on the A470. After 1.7m the road goes under a bridge, carry on for 0.6m and find somewhere to park! The crag is situated below the road and above the river further upstream. [TGM]

Craig Trum Y Ddysgl:
OS.115 GR.543 520   [94]

A large 400ft cliff offering two Diffs of reasonable merit, but quite broken and with vegetation.

Dir: 4.7m NW of Beddgelert. To Rhyd Ddu then the B4418 towards Pen Y Groes. After 2.4m there is a parking spot, yes park here. The cwm to the SE here has a very obvious large cliff. [CSC]

Craig Y Cwm Glas Bach:
OS.115 GR.660 638   [95]

An average crag of some merit, about 10 routes up to HVS in quite vegetated territory. Around 200ft.

Dir: 2.5m SE of Bethesda. Approach: see Black Ladders, the crag is up and to the R of Llech Ddu. [CDU]

Craig Y Dwr:
OS.115 GR.732 602   [96]

A crag 100–300ft and offering 15 or so routes, all around VS except for one hard Extreme, the famous Crash Landing.

Dir: 5.5m W of Llanrwst. To the head of the valley as for Clogwyn Yr Eryr, this crag rises unmistakably above the top of the valley due W of the farm, 15 mins. [NWS], [SNE]

Craig Y Llan:
OS.115 GR.594 477   [97]

Not the greatest crag in the world, but nevertheless offering a good couple of routes, a Diff and a V Diff, both around 250ft. The crag leads to a ridge which if continued makes an enjoyable walk.

Dir: 0.4m S of Beddgelert. Park in the village. Cross the river at the top of the village and follow the path down the E side of the river going S. After 700yds the crag should become visible up on the L. [TGM]

Craig Y Llyn:
OS.115 GR.619 502   [98]

Not a crag if you are going badly, the protection here is not as forthcoming as one often wishes! Protection aside, it is a very good crag, reaching up to 200ft, and has some very interesting routes, VS to E5. In the main expect the harder routes to be more satisfying. About 20 routes, SE-facing and quite low, fairly good on winter mornings. The crag, if damp, is not a sensible place to climb.

Dir: 3m NE of Beddgelert. Take the A498 from Beddgelert towards Betws. After 2m there will be a small lake on the R, park at the far end. The crag can be seen above the road to the L. [TGM]

Craig Y Rhaeadr:
OS.115 GR.622 562   [99]

A very wet and mostly horrible crag, fit only for frogmen. When it dries out there is some very enjoyable climbing to be had. It is said to have an unusual atmosphere! About 30 routes at all grades up to 400ft.

Dir: 4.2m SE of Llanberis. Approach: see Dinas Mot, the cliff is up and to the R, unmistakable, reddish and very wet. [LLP]

Craig Yr Ysfa:
OS.115 GR.694 637   [100]

The climb at Craig Yr Ysfa is one of the stepping stones in any mountain climber's lifetime. The best Diff in Wales, for position anyway, is here – Amphitheatre Buttress, 970ft. This indeed splits the whole crag into two parts, the R side catching more of the early morning sun and having the best routes on it. There are some 70 routes here mainly in the lower grades, and a few easy Extremes. The routes vary from 200–1,000ft. At 2,000ft and NE-facing, it can get bitter any time other than summer, the routes are long and warm clothing should not be left at the foot of the crag but carried *en route*.

Dir: 4.5m NNW of Capel Curig. Go along the A5 for 2m from CC park in a small car park opposite an entrance on the R to a water-board road. Follow this road N up to the Llugwy reservoir, then up the well-constructed footpath to the col. Here drop down the other side and the crag will be on the L. 1 hr. [CDU]

Crib Goch:
OS.115 GR.625 553   [101]

There are on the N side of this very picturesque mountain some excellent 300ft mountain routes of around V Diff to Severe, ending up on the summit. Map and compass territory, big boots, etc.

Dir: 5.7m SE of Llanberis. [LLP]

The Cromlech Boulders:
OS.115 GR.630 566   [102]

These boulders were once up at the Cromlech, only to fall out and leave a magnificent cliff and some very good bouldering on the valley floor. About six boulders which present numerous problems.

Dir: 4m SE of Llanberis. Approach: see Dinas Cromlech. [LLP]

Cwm Glas:
OS.115 GR.615 558   [103]

In the cwm lie several crags with mainly easier routes, Intermediate Slabs about 200ft with some Diffs on the E side of the cwm; Cyrn Las Fach about 270ft with a few Diffs to the W of Cyrn Las at the same level.

Dir: 4.4m SE of Llanberis. Approach: see Cyrn Las. [LLP]

Cwm Glas Facet:
OS.115 GR.618 568   [104]

This crag is one of those odd ones with some good Diffs and Severes of mountain tradition and also a couple of E6s, short, desperate 60ft

problems. Easier routes take in the whole crag, about 300ft of climbing giving good if somewhat overgrown pitches. About 12 routes in total. Up on the R skyline there is the ridge of Llechog, with some very good V Diffs and Severes, about 300ft, to entertain those who love good Welsh mountain routes.

Dir: 4m SE of Llanberis. Go up the pass from Llanberis and after leaving Nant Peris park in the lay-by near a bridge over the river. Cross over the bridge and follow the ridge up the hillside shortly to come across the crag. [LLP]

Cwm Silyn:
OS.115 GR.518 502   [105]

A superb area offering so much climbing in the lower grades that to recommend any particular climb would be unjustifiable. There are climbs also around E1–E3, but more frightening than particularly difficult. There are several crags, all of which though are dwarfed in quality by **Craig Yr Ogof**. This cliff, the most obvious on arrival at the twin lakes of the Cwm, has two areas: the front nose, which in the correct sunlight looks like a giant's head; and the right wall, consisting of some good slabs. The climbs on the slabs have sparse protection but nowhere are unduly difficult. About 40 climbs on the 400ft cliff split equally between Diffs and Extremes. There is a botanist's cliff, **Clogwyn Y Cysgod**, away to the R with some routes on, the harder routes, HVS, tending to be the best. The large cliff, **Craig Fawr**, away to the L, although looking impressive, offers little in the way of good, non-vegetated, continuous routes.

Dir: 7m SSE of Caernarfon. Approach from Penygroes L on the A487. Turn L, and after 0.7m turn R up a small lane, continue for 1m. Then walk on the track, continuing E around the mountain. After 2m some small lakes twinned together are reached, lovely for swimming on a hot summer's day. The cliffs should be obvious. [CSC]

Cyrn Las:
OS.115 GR.614 561   [106]

A fantastic high mountain crag. Over 400ft routes of absolute quality and distinction make this a must for everyone. 30 routes of all standards, nearly all classics. NE-facing at about 2,000ft, sometimes a very cool spot. Hot summer only.

Dir: 4m SE of Llanberis. Park at The Cromlech Boulders in the Llanberis Pass. From here go S up to the lake Llyn Glas, then head up R to the big cliff, which is dome-like in appearance. [LLP]

Dinas Bach:
OS.115 GR.632 560   [107]

A fine little crag, 60–150ft. Some excellent rock gives very good climbing on this crag, about 15 routes of all standards.

Dir: 4.4m SE of Llanberis. Approach: see Dinas Mot, the crag is situated about 300yds above the road and 400yds up from the bridge. [LLP]

Dinas Cromlech:
OS.115 GR.629 569   [108]

The undisputed greatest crag in England and Wales. Translated, it means the Fortress of the Cromlech. This cliff offers single-pitch 140ft Extremes of the finest quality. The easier routes on the wings of the cliff are just as good but without the position of the routes on the walls. The showpiece is the open-corner Cenotaph Corner E1, which takes the line direct. The L arête, Corridors of Power E4; the crack in Left Wall E2; the Right Wall E5; and the crack on the R arête, Cemetery Gates HVS, are the classics and are brilliant routes. There are plenty of routes filling in the gaps, mostly E5. The experience of soloing any of the routes in the corner is unforgettable and thrilling, and I can fully recommend it. About 200yds E of the Cromlech is a 30ft monolith of rock known as The Thumb, offering 4 routes, HS to E3, 6a.

Dir: 4m SE of Llanberis. Go up the pass to the bridge by the boulders, park. Walk up to the crag in about 5 mins. [LLP]

Dinas Mot:
OS.115 GR.627 563   [109]

One of the great crags of the pass. On the S side it rarely catches the sun and is best kept for those very hot, sunny summer days. There are several buttresses with different types of climbing, slabs, roofs and walls. About 300 to 500ft high, with about 100 routes of all grades.

Dir: 4.4m SE of Llanberis. Take the A4086 SE to The Cromlech Boulders, park. The cliff is on the R only a few hundred yards away. [LLP]

Drws Nodded:
OS.115 GR.672 586   [110]

A small 150ft cliff, quite steep with a handful of easy climbs and an E5 roof-pitch to entertain those who like hanging upside down.

Dir: 3.5m W of Capel Curig. Go W along the A5 and park somewhere with Cwm Tryfan to the L. At the top of the cwm on the L is the crag, walk up 40 mins. Over the ridge back E is another short cliff, Craig Nant Yr Ogof, offering about 4 easy routes leading up towards the summit. [OGW]

Drws Y Gwynt:
OS.115 GR.621 574   [111]

A little 150ft crag with good, sound rock and routes of all grades, about 20 climbs. Worth a visit.

Dir: 3.3m SE of Llanberis. Approach: see Clogwyn Y Grochan. The crag lies above and to the L of the Grochan. Quite a hike up though. [LLP]

Equator Walls:
OS.115 GR.610 561   [112]

Some very good slabby walls, brownish in appearance and with three 160ft routes, two E5s and an E1. The climbing is very good and, if you have 6b fingers, well worth the walk up.

Dir: 3.8m SE of Llanberis. Approach: see Cyrn Las, these walls lie to the R of the W Buttress of Cyrn Las. [LLP]

Fachwen Boulders:
OS.115 GR.563 624   [113]

Some excellent boulders in the Llyn Padarn County Park, offering a good finger-testing and smearing area. Dries out quite quickly.

Dir: 2.5m NW of Llanberis. Take the A4086 NW out of Llanberis, after 2m turn R on to the B4547, then turn immediately R and follow Fachwen signs. Spot crags and climb. [LLP]

Gallt Yr Ogof:
OS.115 GR.693 595   [114]

A good crag for beginners, offering about 30 routes below E1 of around 80–200ft. Not far from the road, yet reasonably unpopular.

Dir: 2m WNW of Capel Curig. Take the A5 towards Bangor for 2.5m, the crag can be seen on the hillside to the L. Another 0.5m further on there is a place to park and a bridge to cross the river. Walk back and up to the crag. [OGW]

Glyder Fach – Main Cliff:
OS.115 GR.656 586   [115]

A real mountain crag, offering perhaps the best selection of routes below E1 in the area. About 40 to 50 routes on good rock which dries quickly after rain, essential here. The rock is never too steep but always manages to tire the arms sufficiently during a day's cragging.

Dir: 5.5m W of Capel Curig. Up the A5 to Ogwen, park. Here there is a path leading up SE past a small lake after 0.7m, the cliffs will be seen high up in the cwm. In bad weather this place gets very confusing, map and compass advisable. [OGW]

The Gribin Facet:
OS.115 GR.650 596   [116]

A little gem of a crag, offering a very good introduction to the harder Severes for the Severe leader. About 30 routes, Diff to HVS, with a couple of good Extremes on the steel wall. About 150ft.

Dir: 5.5m W of Capel Curig. From parking on the A5 at Ogwen, take the footpath up towards Llyn Idwal. After 600yds it levels out, the crag is due S at this point about 800yds and up a bit. Often a wet approach. [OGW]

Idwal Slabs:
OS.115 GR.645 591   [117]

The largest concentration of routes in the area, about 60 routes in total, offering fun for all the family. This crag is good but suffers from terrible overcrowding, especially with groups from centres. However, the attraction of such fine routes will tempt everyone at some stage. The crag is a combination of the main slabs, with about 6 classic Diff–Severe lines. Suicide Wall around to the L is aptly named, covered with Extremes and very dangerous. To the R is Holly Tree Wall with some fine middle-grade routes. Above the main slabs there are continuation walls with some very good middle-grade routes, but a Diff route can always be taken to the very top of the cliff. By continuing on up Glyder Fawr

Upper Cliff is reached, with its 20 or so routes, 300ft in all grades. An expedition to the summit from the bottom of the slabs is a great mountain day.

Dir: 6m W of Capel Curig. Park on the A5 at Ogwen. Take the marked trail up to Llyn Idwal, the slabs are at the far end of the lake, 20 mins. [OGW]

Little Buttress:
OS.115 GR.619 573   [118]

A small crag in the pass, 30–120ft, offering a handful of routes, Severe to E5, 6c. A small buttress capped by a steep yellow wall with hollies.

Dir: About 100yds L of Clogwyn Y Grochan. [LLP]

Little Tryfan:
OS.115 GR.672 601   [119]

Some great slabs for beginners to practise on. About 200ft, offering about 20 routes of easy grades, but allowing for more difficult eliminates. Can get busy with teaching groups.

Dir: 4.5m WNW of Capel Curig. On the A5 from CC, the slabs are on the L just as you reach the end of Llyn Ogwen. [OGW]

Llech Ddu:
OS.115 GR.666 636   [120]

This crag is a large and powerful-looking buttress tucked away in the confines of the Carneddu. It has some good hard routes on it, however they do need to be dry and even in a good summer two dry days are the minimum requirement. The 40 or so climbs vary from 200 to 400ft in length, mostly Diffs or Extremes. There are others, but they are few.

Dir: 2.5m from Bethesda. Approach: see Black Ladders, 1 hr. [CDU]

Llechog:
OS.115 GR.597 537   [121]

This cliff is 350ft high in places and commands a fine view. The 15 or so routes, all in the Diff–Severe standard with a few exceptions, are broken in character, but do offer some worthwhile pitches on good, sound rock. At 2,500ft and NE-facing, necessitates fine weather or very strong character.

Dir: 1m WSW of Snowdon. From Rhyd Ddu on the A4085 take the old mining track going E. After 1m turn L at a footpath crossroads and follow the footpath up the ridge, past some ruins in about 1.5m, and up a steep hill for a mile to arrive at the Llechog Ridge. Drop down to the crag. [CSC]

Lliwedd:
OS.115 GR.623 534   [122]

This is the most traditional crag of all Wales, the subject of the first ever authoritative Welsh guidebook in 1909. It is a magnificent crag and a day spent on Lliwedd is always remembered, not for the moves but for the atmosphere. It is not a hard man's crag at all, but do not think you can simply stroll up the routes. About 1,000ft from bottom to top, it offers many 10-pitch climbs. There are terraces on which to crack open a good bottle of Bordeaux and have a jolly good lunch. The rock can get very greasy, which can see you disappearing downwards into the gloom from which you came. About 100 routes, Diff leaders could well find themselves in deep water, Severe standard is best for the exploration of this NE-facing cliff.

Dir: SE ridge of Snowdon. From the top of the Llanberis Pass at Pen Y Pass, take the miners' track towards Snowdon and turn L at the large lake. Lliwedd is the big cliff to the L-hand end of the lake. [LLW]

Milestone Buttress:
OS.115 GR.663 601   [123]

A very good crag for the lower grades and only a few minutes from the road. 30 routes of Diff to HVS, about 200ft long. The rock is very clean, as are the routes, very well worn and polished. Can get crowded with very slow-moving parties.

Dir: 5.5m W of Capel Curig. On the A5 just as you reach the end of Llyn Ogwen there is a car park. The crag is the obvious one just above the road on the S side. A wall leads up to the crag. [OGW]

Moel Hebog:
OS.115 GR.565 469   [124]

This very dramatic and pleasing mountain falls short of expectations on rock-climbing terrain.

There are climbs to be found, but only amongst flora and fauna and magic mushrooms. One can wander around to explore the area for enjoyment and seek cliffs at will.

Dir: 2m SSW of Beddgelert. The distinct majestic peak to the W. [CSC]

The Moelwyns:
OS.115 & 124 GR.675 450   [125]

This area offers about 100 routes mainly in the lower grades, all of which are absolutely superb on very good rock. There is also some very good bouldering to be had at the foot of the cliffs in the valley floor. To list every crag would be meaningless since all are quite similar and none holds any hidden nasties. You can easily and safely explore the crags here. Centres tend to use the area quite often but there are plenty of routes to go round. When approaching up the track from Tanygrisiau, the first crag to be seen up on the R is **Craig Y Clipiau**, the hard crag of the valley with 10 Extremes on. Following the road around to the L, the crag almost directly above is **Craig Yr Wrysgan**, 20 excellent routes especially in the lower grades. Crossing an incline is a scruffy crag before the waterfall, which is of little interest. Next is **Clogwyn Yr Oen**, with about 25 very good routes. About 300ft high, the largest crag in this area, it has the best Severes around. Following the scree and the stone wall, the last reasonable crag is **Clogwyn Y Bustach**, a short 100ft crag offering about 10 routes around E1 and a few Diffs.

Dir: 1m WSW of Blaenau Ffestiniog. From the A470 take the small road just S of the bridge W over the railway, follow this to Tanygrisiau where the road curves round to the R. Shortly park and continue up the track by foot. The cliffs will be visible ahead. [TGM]

Nantlle Y Garn:
OS.115 GR.551 526   [126]

Only two routes here but each is worth doing. Both around 400ft, one S the other VS, finishing at the summit. E-facing, worth waiting for good weather to enjoy what should be a splendid day's outing.

Dir: 4.7m NNE of Beddgelert. Park at Rhyd Ddu on the A4085. From here walk due W to the ridges leading up to Y Garn, both ridges to the R giving interesting climbing. [CSC]

DOUBLE CRISS, VS, 4b, Craig Y Clipiau. (Climber Nick Escourt, Photo Ken Wilson)

The Pillar of Elidir:
OS.115 GR.615 616 [127]

As remote crags go, this is pretty remote. About 15 stern routes, Severe to E1, about 150ft. Also some good 200ft VS slab routes.

Dir: 3.5m SSW of Bethesda. On the NE slope of Elidir Fawr. Take map and compass. [OGW]

Pinnacle Crag of Cwm Cywion:
OS.115 GR.634 603 [128]

A cliff of 200ft with a fine pinnacle and a handful of routes. Diff to HVS. A quiet crag.

Dir: 4.5m S of Bethesda. From Ogwen at the bend in the A5 take the trail up to Llyn Ogwen. Go across the bottom of the lake and head off R to the far ridge. Go up this for about 20 mins, then around R into the cwm where you should see the crag high up on your R. The summit above is Y Garn. A very quiet spot. [OGW]

Pyg Track Crags:
OS.115 GR.645 554 [129]

Upon leaving the Pen Y Pass café and youth hostel on the Pyg track towards Snowdon, there are numerous rocks, slabs and buttresses up the hillside. A good area to explore at will.

Dir: 6m SE of Llanberis. [LLP]

Scimitar Ridge:
OS.115 GR.635 564 [130]

A small ridge offering about 10 routes in the VS, E1, E3 and E5 grades on its R side. The rock is fair and some of the routes well worth doing. The ridge itself is a pleasant Severe.

Dir: 5m SE of Llanberis. About 600yds E of The Cromlech. (LLP)

The Teryn Bluffs:
OS.115 GR.638 545 [131]

Here are some very good cliffs for the lower grade climber with about 30 routes in the Diff and Severe grades, around 200ft. There are harder climbs which are more like eliminates. The higher cliff, **Craig Aderyn**, has a very good slab giving about 5 routes.

Dir: 6m SE of Llanberis. Park at the Pen Y Pass car park and take the miners' track towards Snowdon. Walk for about 1m past a small lake, here the crag can be seen up to the L on the ridge above the pipeline. 30 mins. [TGM]

Tryfan East Face:
OS.115 GR.664 594 [132]

The E face of Tryfan is one of the biggest and best cliffs for that real mountaineering challenge. The routes start from half-way up the face and reach 600ft to the summit. Only artificial lines exceed VS in difficulty, and mostly one can climb below Severe with tactful route finding. There are many Snowdonian classics on the cliff and on a good summer's day the route tickers will be out in force. About 50 routes in total. The W face offers climbing of a more broken character, mainly Diff in standard.

Dir: 5.5m W of Capel Curig. The big mountain first encountered S of the A5. [OGW]

SNOWDONIA SOUTH

Although the climbing listed in this area is very close to the Snowdonia area, it is separated because the weather pattern here is very different, and to anyone concerned with rock climbing it will seem like another area. The crags are situated close together and are often referred to as Tremadog, also the name of the nearest town.

The climbing here is fantastic, routes of all types and difficulties. The rock offers the best natural protection in the country and there is no excuse if you hurt yourself. The friction is very good and holds, when found, very positive. Double ropes are useful since the routes often wander around, taking the easiest way up the steep cliffs.

HITLER'S BUTTOCK, E5, 6a, Bwlch Y Moch. (Climber Andy Pollitt, Photo Steve Ashton)

Carreg Hyll-Drem:
OS.124 GR.614 432   [133]

A very impressive 200ft crag of unrelenting steepness situated right above the road, about 20 routes around E3. The bottom half stays completely dry in wet weather. Not a crag for weak arms, but a definite must for the super spurter.

Dir: 5m NE of Porthmadog. Take the A498 NE to Prenteg, the B4410 to Garreg, then L on to the A4085. The crag is reached in 1.5m, if you miss it you are blind. [TGM]

Craig Bwlch Y Moch:
OS.124 GR.577 406   [134]

This is the finest crag in southern Snowdonia, offering some of the most classic routes in the country. A long crag with several buttresses of overhanging rock gives about 80 routes of all standards from Diff to E6. The showpiece is the Vector Buttress, which overhangs so much it must fall down one day – this would be a terrific loss and I can only recommend you do all the routes on it before it disappears. They are all E1 upwards though, and include the classics Void E3, Cream E4, Sultans of Swing E4, and the famous Strawberries and Dream Topping E6. The VS climbs here do not give in easily. All routes are at least 2-pitch, around 200ft. Gets crowded here on rainy days in the mountains, the only other option being the pub. Yes, no option – hic!

Dir: 1.5m NE of Porthmadog. From Tremadog take the A498 E towards Snowdonia, after 1m park at an old petrol station. Looking at the crags, Bwlch Y Moch is on the R and Craig Pant Ifan is high up on the L. To reach, walk back down the road for 100yds to a stile and a scree slope running up to the crag. There are facilities to camp here also.

Craig Issalt:
OS.124 & 115 GR.533 450   [135]

A crag of different parts. Some very vegetated, best left to the plants, the slabs to the R-hand end offering some very worthwhile Severes of about 80ft. There is some very good bouldering in the area if fed up with cruising the desperates at Tremadog, or want to train in secrecy!

Dir: 5m NW of Porthmadog. Approach: see Craig Cwm Trwsgl, Snowdonia main section [TGM]

Craig Pant Ifan:
OS.124 GR.569 406   [136]

The other great cliff at Tremadog, not quite so popular since it requires a 5-min. walk. Desperate exhaustion – whew! After arriving at the crag and taking a breather, it appears you are in the trees; that is because you are, but about 30ft up the route's sudden exposure is felt, making it a very enjoyable place to climb. The majority of routes here go up slabs, some smoother than others, and through overhangs, some tiny, others not so tiny. About 80 climbs of all grades, with a lot being around E1–E2. A few good desperates including Psyche 'n' Burn, grade 6ish.

Dir: 1.5m NNE of Porthmaog. Approach: see Craig Bwlch Y Moch. [TGM]

Craig Y Castell:
OS.124 GR.557 403   [136]

This is the smallest of the three great cliffs at Tremadog, a 180ft crag offering about 25 routes, a good many in the lower grades. The climbing is excellent and not to be missed.

Dir: 1m NNW of Porthmadog. From the square of Tremadog walk E to W along the A498 for about 50yds. Follow a lane up for a short while until a path leads back to the L and goes on to the crag. [TGM]

Craig Y Gelli:
OS.124 GR.591 436   [138]

A small crag, 150ft, with about 10 routes, HS to E1. Some interesting climbing to be found on good rock.

Dir: 4m NNE of Porthmadog. Go N on the A498, past the B4410, carry on for 1.5m, park. The crag should be visible up to your R above the road. [TGM]

Craig Y Gesail:
OS.124 GR.545 411   [139]

Not as impressive as the other crags in the Tremadog area, but good, sound rock nevertheless, and enjoyable to climb on except in mid-summer when the midges really get going.

About 20 routes, all below E2 and mainly around VS.

Dir: 2.6m NW of Porthmadog. Take the A487 W from Tremadog and after 1.3m Penmorfa is reached. Take a small road on the R and then do a sharp turn R again, continue for 500yds where the crag can be seen to the N. Park and walk to the crag. [TGD]

DOLGELLAU

This area consists of mountain crags around Cader Idris, the Rhinogs, Craig Cywarch and the Arans. Being south of Snowdonia, with access and facilities being poorer, the crags are less frequented and can often be a pleasant relief from the crowds in the holidays. The actual climbing is very similar to the mountain crags of Snowdonia, but the cliffs themselves fall short of their counterparts in merit. The area is very beautiful and is one of the few really unspoilt parts of Britain. The climbing is best in the lower grades, below Extreme, and protection is sufficiently sparse on the steeper faces for resort to bolts. There are two options: to leave the lines for top-roping and bold leading, or to climb elsewhere, and by doing so preserve the natural flavour of this unspoilt area. Some pegs have been placed by mechanised rock vandals in the past, and it is hoped that this act of sheer desecration will never happen again.

This area is not within the boundary of a national park and consequently climbers should be that bit more careful when approaching crags, and keep to footpaths where possible.

Aran Fawddwy:
OS.124 GR.863 224   [140]

Not a large area but with two 600ft routes, either worth including in a day's scramble, both V Diff yet not sustained. One rises up from the S end of the lake and the other from a gully on the N spur.

Dir: 9m SSE of Bala. Best approached by taking the B4403 from Bala, then the small road S via Bwlch Groes, and then walking up the valley on the R to arrive at Creiglyn Dyfi, the small lake to the E of Aran Fawddwy. Take map and compass, map 125 is very useful also. [MW]

Bird Rock: Restriction:
OS.124 GR.643 069   [141]

The area of the E face, looking at the rock on the L, is a bird sanctuary and climbing is banned, 1 Mar.–31 July. Quite a good outcrop offering three parts on which to dice with death. The Bastion is the lowest and most formidable crag, about 140ft high with Extremes, HVS and VS routes up the side, and easier routes to the R. Above and set back is the Central Buttress with a handful of easier routes. The E face, high up, has some much easier and accommodating climbs. About 30 routes in all, NW-facing. There is also a more sheltered Far Southern Buttress around to the R of The Bastion, with a handful of 130ft Severes. Care should be taken in accessing this crag, keeping close to walls.

Dir: 6m SSE of Barmouth. From Dolgellau take the A487 S for 7m, turn R on to the B4405, to Abergynolwyn, then R again on to a small road. Follow this road up the steep hill and around for 2.8m, the crag is easily recognised L. [MW]

Craig Bodlyn:
OS.124 GR.650 237   [142]

A crag for the hard men, well almost. There are no routes here below VS, but little to attract a good extreme leader. About 10 routes in the middle grades of 300ft on rock and mixed vegetation.

Dir: 7m NNE of Barmouth. Not a short walk this one. Take the A496 N from Barmouth, 800yds after Tal-y-bont take the small road on the R (dead straight) for as far as you can. The track continues up to the lake of Llyn Bodlyn, the crag overlooks the lake, facing N. [MW]

Craig Cau:
OS.124 GR.712 122   [143]

A large and rambling 900ft crag. Although there is some very good climbing to be found here, much scrambling over poor territory has to be accomplished as well. There are about 30 established routes from Diff to E3, friends are useful, as is a trowel for digging out belays.

Dir: 5m SSW of Dolgellau. Parking as for Idris Gate Crag. Follow the footpath to the R as it winds alongside the stream to the lake of Llyn Cau. The crag is then ahead, facing N and, if lucky, dry. [MW]

Craig Cywarch:
OS.124 GR.842 187   [144]

There is some very good climbing to be had here in the lower grades, about 30 different crags, all within a mile. The climbing is mainly in the lower grades because of the angle and nature of the rock. There are at least 300 routes in the area, of which only 30 or so are above VS, climbs vary in length up to 300ft. The aspect is SE, but even so many climbs hold the sunshine till lunchtime. The crags are at about 2,000ft and can often stay rather cool. One should not expect dry, clean, big sweeps of rock here. Climbers interested in flora and fauna will feel at home.

Dir: 14m SSW of Bala. From Dinas Mawaddwy on the A470 take the minor road NE towards Aber-Cywarch, after 1m and crossing over a bridge turn L up the Cwm Cywarch road. The crags are at the end of the valley on the L. [MW]

Craig Rhwyddfor:
OS.124 GR.734 122   [145]

A steep 100ft crag within striking distance of the road, offering a handful of climbs, VS upwards, E-facing.

Dir: 4.6m S of Dolgellau. Going S on the A487 a campsite is reached just before the B4405. The crag overlooks the site up on the hilltop to the N. [MW]

Craig Y Cae:
OS.124 GR.708 235   [146]

A 180ft crag reminiscent of the hanging gardens of Babylon. A handful of routes weave their way up through the overhangs, varying grades on rock which is never above suspicion. A lawn-mower would be useful here.

Dir: 5m NNW of Dolgellau. Take the A470 N for 5m, pass the Ty'n-y-groes Hotel, take the turning about 50yds further on the L. Here a track leads up through the forest, with severe loss of calories, 15 mins. [MW]

Craig Y Gefir:
OS.124 GR.873 268   [147]

A small granite crag of about 100ft, but the cleanest in the area. A handful of easy routes, very good for beginners with good sound holds, and one tough little crack climb, Grit. N-facing with a fab view. Worth a look.

Dir: 7m SW of Bala. Take the B4403 down to Llanuwchllyn, 70yds after the Talardd turn-off there is a track leading S. Follow this, then the footpath up the ridge to the crag in 2m. [MW]

Cyfrwy:
OS.124 GR.703 135   [148]

The largest stretch of crags in the area, about 0.5m long and offering about 50 climbs, 150–400ft, of all standards and very different quality. The rock often needs careful attention and one never feels really at home here. A high crag at 2,000ft, not the place for a winter picnic.

Dir: 5m SW of Dolgellau. Approach: see Twr Du. Follow the Fox's Path up to the second lake, the crag is obvious, 40 mins. [MW]

Gist Ddu:
OS.124 GR.872 255   [149]

An impressive central buttress gives rise to some good climbing. The crag is around 250ft in height with most of the climbs following the vertical grooves and arêtes. About 20 routes of all grades with good rock and only vegetated in parts. As a rough guide, the harder routes are on the R-hand side following the big corners. E-facing and quite high up, good weather needed here. Lovely views though, making it well worth a visit.

Dir: 7m SE of Bala. Take the B4403 SE and at Llanuwchllyn turn L on the small road to Talardd. Turn R over the bridge, on for a while, park. Walk up the R side of the valley, 5 mins, the crag should be visible. Keep R, then traverse along to avoid really wet, boggy ground. 20 mins. [MW]

Idris Gate Crag:
OS.124 GR.724 115 [150]

A crag not without vegetation. The best way down from the crag is a vegetated gully on the L side called Crack of Gloom – enough said. About 10 climbs up to 200ft in the lower grades, but access quite straightforward, as is retreat from the elements.

Dir: 4.7m S of Dolgellau. Take the A487 S, turn off after about 7m onto the B4405, park after 100yds. Here a footpath leads off up to the forest where the crag is easily located, 10 mins. [MW]

Mynydd Moel:
OS.124 GR.728 138 [151]

A good, steep crag offering little in the way of routes below VS. About 200ft with a handful of very good routes in a fine position, finishing at the top, 2500ft.

Dir: 3m S of Dolgellau. After getting lost in Dolgellau find a road going S to Bwlch Coch, via Wenallt, up several steep hills. At the end of the road a footpath leads to Llyn Aran, a small lake and the source of the Afon Aran, which runs due N into Dolgellau. The crag is situated at the top of the screes above the lake. [MW]

Twr Du:
OS.124 GR.719 135 [152]

A fair crag, although being broken it has some good climbing with interest. Large at 400ft and worth using double ropes since routes tend to wander. About 10 routes in the lower grades.

Dir: 4m SSW of Dolgellau. Take the minor road SW out of Dolgellau towards Islawr-dref, park after 2.8m at the Gwernan Lake Hotel. Take the Fox's Path S from here for 1.7m to a lake, Llyn Gafr. The crag is about 1,000yds to the SE here, up and to the L. [MW]

SHREWSBURY

Nesscliffe: Restriction
OS.126 GR.384 193 [153]

The access here is uncertain and to the best of my knowledge climbing is banned, closer inspection may reveal a large outcrop of fair-quality sandstone. Top-roping is advisable here since the rock is not that strong. There are some large corner cracks which offer good long pitches, and some amazing rock architecture.

Dir: 8m NW of Shrewsbury. Take the A5 NW, at the village of Nesscliffe park near the pub, excellent huge meals and very good beer. A lane opposite leads to the rocks. [No guide at present]

CHESTER AREA

The area around Chester is full of different types of crags, the sandstone of the north coast outcrops and the limestone escarpments stretching down towards Llangollen in the south. All offer good climbing at every grade, with every crag having its own personal character.

Craig Arthur:
OS.117 GR.224 471 [154]

You cannot miss this crag, it is big. Its 170ft at the top of the valley feel like 1,700ft, and quite *out there*, man. Some of the best routes in the area are to be found here, also some of the hardest.

There are some 40 routes here, with little below E1, mostly E3 upwards. A pity since the position is sensational. The rock in parts is questionable, as is the distance between some of the runners!

Dir: 5m NNE of Llangollen. Approach: see World's End, the large set of high cliffs overlook-

top end of the valley. Go to the hairpin bel... at Craig Y Forwen, where a path contours round to the crag, about 1m, and saves the awful hike up, which angers the farmers anyway. [CL]

Craig Y Forwen World's End
OS.117 GR.234 478   [155]

Here are some superb climbs for everyone in an almost alpine setting, friendly Diffs and Severes rising up to exposed E5s. The cliff is split into three tiers, but it is the top tier that provides the best climbing and most excitement. There are about 200 lines, giving about 80 climbs below E1. The cliff faces SW and is reasonably sheltered in its small cwm. Worth a visit.

Dir: 6m NNE of Llangollen. Approach: see World's End, Eglwyseg valley N. This is the first crag encountered on a sharp bend when dropping down into the trees. About 400yds long, rising up highest on the L end. [CL]

Devil's Gorge:
OS.116 GR.189 643   [156]

An impressive gorge of around 120ft giving about 15 routes of standard above Severe.

Dir: 4.5m W of Mold. Take the A494 for 4m and park by the hamlet of Loggerheads. Here a footpath runs NE along the bank of the river Alyn, follow this to the crag. about 35 mins of really scenic walking. [CL]

Dinbren Crags:
OS.117 GR.221 445   [157]

A very accessible crag, offering some really good climbs and quality moves, also within very close range of the car. A must for the lazy cragrat. Two walls at 90° to one another. About 80 routes mainly in the harder grades, however there are about 10 Severes and Diffs. For dessert you can also sample the tier below and to the R, guaranteed to finish you off.

Dir: 2m NNE of Llangollen. Approach: see World's End, S. At the T-junction turn R and park after 800yds. Here just past Dinbren Farm a path leads off around the woods to the crags very shortly. [CL]

Frodsham:
OS.117 GR.512 753   [158]

The OS map actually says sandstone. This crag consists of a series of small boulders set in the trees, about 8 in total of which all are good and offer plenty of fun. The climbing is generally very strenuous and in the higher grades, even so there is still plenty for the enthusiastic struggler. There must be over 100 problems and countless variations. In summer it is a gem; in winter it can stay rather damp as the trees enshroud the crag somewhat. To say the crag exceeds 15ft anywhere is garbage, it may feel 30ft high, though, when you are performing strange contortions on the lip of an overhang.

Dir: 2m SSW of Frodsham, which is 15m SE of Liverpool. Go W on the A56 leaving Frodsham, turn L on to the B5393. After 1.4m the road turns R, carry straight on for 700yds. Here a path leads off L into the woods and the rocks. [HEL]

Handbridge Outcrop:
OS.117 GR.406 656   [159]

Some good bouldering to be had in the middle of Chester. The crag is sandstone, NE-facing on the S bank of the river Dee, and the climbing is quite powerful.

Dir: Chester town centre. In a park seen from the Old Handbridge. [CL]

Helsby:
OS.117 GR.492 755   [160]

A large crag with over 100 routes on it, 20–40ft. The sandstone has excellent climbing properties but is too weak for protection. People do lead routes and fall off and live, but to top-rope a route here is very acceptable, it is a fun crag anyway. There are some very good problems which will test your ability to levitate. Routes at all grades. Faces W and gets the sun well, however it is very exposed, and being covered in green dust, or slime when wet, it is not the best winter crag.

Dir: 7m NE of Chester. The crag is directly above the town of Helsby and is reached by an exhausting scramble from the village. [HE]

Maeshafn: Restriction
OS.117 GR.214 615   [161]

There is no right of access here and it is with kind

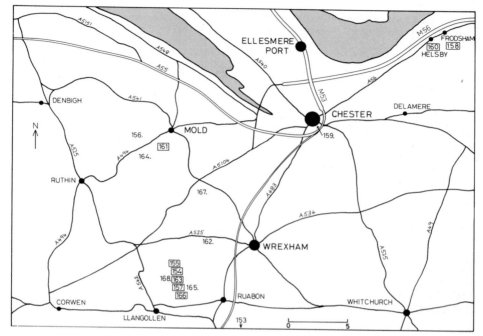

CHESTER AREA

permission of the owner that small groups of climbers are allowed to use the quarry. The owner is Mr Thomas of Bryngwyn Farm from whom permission must be sought to climb. The farm is at the entrance to the drive leading to the rocks. Even though this crag is a quarry, it has the mood of a natural limestone escarpment with views over the surrounding countryside, a hole in the ground. It faces W and at 1,000ft catches little bad weather compared with other areas to the S and W. The climbs vary from 40–80ft with about 80 in total in all grades. The rock in the main is clean and sound since the quarry ceased production in the last century.

Dir: 2m SW of Mold. From Mold take the A494 SW for 2m, going through Gwernymyndd take the sharp L going up a steep hill. After 0.6m reach a T-junction and pub, turn R – hic! – and the farm is 500yds down the lane and the crag close by. [CL]

Minera:
OS.117 GR.268 511   [162]

A small outcrop of little merit except for a few corners and cracks.

Dir: 5m W of Wrexham. Approach: see World's End, this is the small crag above the turning at Minera to World's End. [CL]

Pinfold Crags:
OS.117 GR.222 453   [163]

This crag offers over 100 routes, of which most deserve a visit. High up and generally N, this can be a very hostile place. The rock is mostly good and offers good protection. Mainly routes in the middle and Extreme grades.

Dir: 2.6m NNE of Llangollen. Approach: see World's End, S. At the T-junction turn L and after 0.5m park near Rock Farm. Here a footpath leads off E and up to the crag, about 700yds. [CL]

Pot Hole Quarry: Access note
OS.116 GR.192 597 [164]

The quarry is owned by a nearby farm and the farmer has given kind consent to climbing here as long as approach is made by the recognised footpath and no litter is left. A small quarry of up to 70ft with about 30 routes of all grades. Some of the routes are top-roped to avoid bolting and others can be led quite safely. The rock is very good and there are some interesting climbs.

Dir: 5.4m SW of Mold. Go SW on the A494 for 5m to the village of Llanferes and within 700yds of sighting the river Alyn on the L there is a footpath leading to a footbridge. Carry on to a parking spot, return and take the footpath which leads upstream to a stile then a track, which leads to the quarry after 100yds. [CL]

Trefor Rocks Quarry:
OS.117 GR.234 433 [165]

A 100ft quarry with a handful of routes, VS upwards. Protection in places can be variable!

Dir: 2m ENE of Llangollen. Approach: see Dinbren Crags, carry on down the road for 1.3m and park in the lay-by beneath the quarry. Cars must not be taken up or parked on the track leading up to the quarry. [CL]

Twilight Crags:
OS.117 GR.223 463 [166]

These are two crags facing each other, only about 60ft high but offering about 70 really good routes on excellent limestone. To the N is the Tower Buttress, the one getting the most sun and best outlook. There is also some good bouldering to be had on the tier above these crags. A very good area.

Dir: 1.7m NE of Llangollen. From the hairpin at World's End go down the valley for 1.3m and park. From Plas yn Eglwyseg take the marked footpath to the crags which are due E from here through some woods, keeping close to the stream. [CL]

Waun Y Llyn Country Park:
OS.117 GR.284 580 [167]

A couple of small quarries. The sandstone is of fair quality and does give some interesting boulder problems.

Dir: 5m NNW of Wrexham. Take the A541 N through Caergwrle, immediately turn L to Horeb, after 1m at a T-junction turn R to the village and the country park. Alternatively, turn L, go down the lane for 0.5m and park. There are some conglomerate boulders, Hope Mountain Boulders, offering a few problems in a hollow down to the L. [CL]

World's End:
OS.117 GR.220 472 [168]

Approach N: From Wrexham take the A525 towards Ruthin from the ring road, after 3m turn L on to the B5426 to Minera. After 1m take a small road signposted to World's End which goes back R up a hill, if after 2m you are in the middle of nowhere you are on the right road. Continue for another 4m praying that your car does not break down, the road then drops into the Eglwyseg valley and the crags.

Approach S: From Llangollen on the A5 cross the bridge in the centre of the town and turn L on to the A592. After 1m turn R up to the Eglwyseg valley and World's End, after 600yds take the L turn to the valley. A T-junction is reached after 0.6m, turn L to the N end or R to the S end. [CL]

6 Peak District

This is the heart of climbing in England and Wales, offering superb variety with a reasonable weather pattern. There are more climbs here than the whole of the rest of the country put together. There are two main styles of climbing which are split up by rock type into gritstone and limestone. The centre of the southern peak is all limestone, and is surrounded to the north, west and east by gritstone. About one-third of the limestone is quarried, only a small amount of the gritstone has been worked. To a newcomer, visiting the grit edges around Stanage would be the best introduction to the area. The limestone is less friendly; Stoney Middleton is the testing ground, and if you can cruise routes on sight there you will have little problem elsewhere. As bolts are not used on gritstone and since many of the good belays are slightly set back, a 30ft length of rope is very useful. Top-roping the unprotected routes is a very sensible idea and should be encouraged to avoid the bolting and scarring of these nature outcrops. On limestone anything goes.

PEAK EAST

The crags in the east are essentially in the rain shadow of the rest of the peak. It is the driest area but nevertheless still has a lot of rain. Climbing is possible all year round, but in winter the high grit edges do get a fair bit of snow – gritting one's teeth and thinking of England is the usual way to cope with the situation. The dales do have very accommodating pubs in which to thaw out and get that well-known burning feeling in the fingers.

Agden Rocher:
OS.110 GR.263 934   [1]

About 100 routes on quite suspect gritstone, mostly in the lower grades. SW-facing and overlooking Agden reservoir, warm and sunny, a midge haven. Maybe worth a visit?

Dir: 7m NW of Sheffield. Take the B6077 from Sheffield, then turn off R to High Bradfield, bear R and park after 0.4m. Here a footpath leads off L and through a small wood, the crag is reached in about 5 mins. [STA]

Bamford Edge: Restriction:
OS.110 GR.208 850   [2]

The edge and surrounding moor are owned by Mr J. Archdale. There is grouse shooting here, one can only advise of the hazards of climbing in the shooting season, here 1 Apr.–30 Sept. At other times the keeper should be contacted first before climbing, Mr F. Darwent, tel. (0433) 51459. The gritstone here is very good and offers about 100 routes in all grades, most below Extreme. SW-facing and with a superb view.

Dir: 3m NNW of Hathersage. Take the A625 then the A6013 through Bamford, carry on for 0.8m. Take a sharp turn up to the R, park after 1m. A path L leads to the crag in 15 mins. [STA]

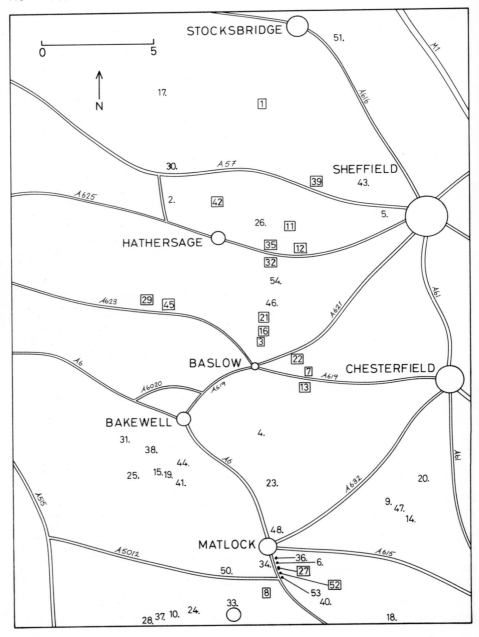

PEAK EAST

Baslow Edge:
OS.119 GR.260 745 [3]

A very good edge for beginners, one of the smaller and friendlier outcrops. Nowhere is the rock really steep and the holds unusable. About 100 climbs below E1, plenty of Diffs. W-facing and rarely crowded, the Diff climber's retreat.

Dir: 5m NE of Bakewell. Approach: see Curbar Edge. [DG]

Beeley Quarry: Restriction:
OS.119 GR.267 666 [4]

The owners of the quarry do not wish it to be used for climbing. I personally can see no problem here. An unsafe and generally overgrown tip with about 30 routes up to 70ft in the lower grades.

Dir: 3m ESE of Bakewell. Take the A6 S to Rowsley, turn L to Beeley on the B6012, continue for 500yds. Here a track by the millstone on the side of the road leads eventually to the crag. [DG]

Bell Hagg:
OS.110 GR.300 867 [5]

A short crag but about 600yds long. There are about 50 routes around 30ft on good gritstone, but mainly strenuous on overhanging or steep rock. Some very good bouldering to be had. N-facing and tends to stay damp after rain.

Dir: 3.5m W of Sheffield. Leave on the A57, just after the golf course take the small road leading off to the L up a steep hill. After 500yds the road turns sharp L, park near here. Take the footpath L, which leads to the crag. [STA]

Bend Tor:
OS.119 GR.296 595 [6]

An unsatisfactory limestone crag with a handful of routes around HVS and a worthwhile E4.

Dir: Just S of Matlock. Approach: see Pic Tor. [PSO]

Birchen Edge:
OS.119 GR.280 728 [7]

The great crag for bumblies in Derbyshire. Be proud to be a bumblie. Have a great full set for breakfast, do a few climbs, adjourn for lunch, pheasant pie and a few pints, then take in a few more Diffs in the afternoon. This crag fills all those criteria: about 40ft at the highest, VS at the hardest and 400yds from the pub. About 150 climbs and SW-facing.

Dir: 5m NE of Bakewell. Take the A619 to Baslow and on towards Chesterfield, past roundabout, then up hill for 1m. Turn L into car park next to the pub. A footpath leads N to the edge. [DG]

Black Rocks:
OS.119 GR.294 557 [8]

Some excellent gritstone rocks up to 60ft, offering routes of all standards. The rocks appear small at first, but upon soloing a route on sight they take on a more interesting perspective. About 60 routes with countless variations and very good bouldering. Although NW-facing, they seem to remain sheltered and warm for most of the year.

Dir: 3m S of Matlock. Take the A6 S to Cromford, here take the B5035 S up the hill. After 0.7m turn L to the rocks and a car park. By carrying on along the footpath beneath the crag to the W, the High Peak Trail, one reaches the **Alport Stone** and **Bauston Tor** within 400yds. Both offer a handful of routes. [DG]

Bradley Quarry:
OS.119 GR.338 626 [9]

A small gritstone quarry, 40ft with about 40 routes in the Diff to HVS standard. Quite steep but with adequate holds.

Dir: 3m NE of Matlock. Go NE on the A632 from Matlock, past the golf course up the hill, on the top take a R turn (slight fork). Park after 600yds, just after another lane joins from the L. Take the footpath leading straight on to some woods, but turn L at the woods to reach the quarry. If you turn R at the woods you will arrive at **Bradley Tor** in about 5 mins. Some small bouldering on natural grit. [DG]

Brassington Tor:
OS.119 GR.235 543 [10]

A small limestone outcrop above the village, offering a handful of climbs.

Dir: 5.3m SW of Matlock. Take the A5012 from

Cromford to Grangemill, turn L to Longcliffe on the B5056, then turn L to Brassington. The tor is above and to the E of the village, and is reached by a footpath. [PSO]

Burbage North:
OS.110 GR.265 828 [11]

A fine gritstone outcrop with most probably the best rock in the area. Fantastic bouldering for any grade. About 150 routes in all grades up to 30ft but very good for the lower-grade climber. SW-facing and, although 1400ft high, tends to be much more sheltered than Stanage. Very quick and handy, worth a visit.

Dir: 2m ENE of Hathersage. Take the A625 E from Hathersage, after 1m and The Millstone pub a road leads off L, leading up to a junction after 1.8m. Higgar Tor will be seen to the R, best approached from above. At the junction the crag can be seen over to the R. Park above and walk, 1 min. [DG]

Burbage South:
OS.110 GR.266 812 [12]

A NW-facing crag which consists of an edge and a quarry, both solid gritstone. About 120 routes in total covering all grades, with some very interesting Extremes. The Cioch Block in the quarry is a very spectacular piece of rock. About 20–50ft in height with some of the best bouldering in Derbyshire, even 40ft boulder problems. Excellent crag.

Dir: 2.4m E of Hathersage. Take the A625 E, after 2.5m the road bends sharp R, park on the L just past here. A footpath and a track lead off L to the quarry and then the edge. [DG]

Chatsworth Edge:
OS.119 GR.275 720 [13]

A crag not often visited since it faces virtually N and is very close to the main A619. Nevertheless it has about 70 climbs covering most grades, though the best climbing is in the lower grades. About 40ft. Watch the mosquitoes in late summer, they breed here.

Dir: 5m ENE of Bakewell. Approach: see Birchen Edge, the crag is on the S side of the valley about 600yds before the pub. [DG]

Cocking Tor:
OS.119 GR.344 617 [14]

A small gritstone tor offering some good bouldering, high in parts.

Dir: 3m ENE of Matlock. Approach: see Turning Stone Edge. [DG]

Cratcliffe Tor:
OS.119 GR.228 623 [15]

A small crag with some classic routes, but disappointing as a whole. The grit is good but becomes lichenous in winter and in summer heats up to a furnace. Not a lot here for the beginner, 40 routes, 20–50ft. There is also some bouldering to be had on Robin Hood's Stride.

Dir: 5m S of Bakewell. Take the A6 S for 2m, turn R on to the B5056, stay on this – not easy – for 2.3m. The crag will appear on the R, drive on for 400yds and park. Follow a footpath leading off up to some woods, then go R towards the crag – not going near the house as this will threaten access to the crag. Robin Hood's Stride is up to the L of the crag, the footpath leads to it. [DG]

Curbar Edge:
OS.119 GR.255 755 [16]

A marvellous edge, offering over 200 routes varying a lot in size and difficulty, 30–70ft. The easy routes are fewer than at most crags, the harder tend to be long and sometimes very unprotected. The coldest grit edge in Derbyshire, even though SW-facing.

Dir: 5m NE of Bakewell. Take the A619 to Baslow, then the A623 (Manchester) road for 1m, turning R up the lane to Curbar village. Arrive and go up the hill, Curbar Edge is on the L, Baslow Edge on the R. [DG]

Derwent Edge:
OS.110 GR.197 898 [17]

A marvellous gritstone edge, offering good sound climbing in the Diff to HVS grades. The edge consists of **Dovestones Tor**, the largest of the outcrops, with about 40 routes. Other outcrops are **The Wheelstones**, **White Tor** and **Back Tor**. All of these have good bouldering. None of the outcrops exceed 40ft in height. W-facing but quite high up at 1,650ft, chilly on a cold day. In a very typical peak setting.

ULYSSES OR BUST, E5, 6b, Curbar Edge. (Climber John Allen, Photo Bernard Newman)

Dir: 6m NNW of Hathersage. Take the A6013 to the Ladybower reservoir and the junction with the A57, turn R past the pub and up the hill for 0.9m. Park here at Cutthroat Bridge. Take the footpath leading off up the valley with a stream to the N, after 300yds turn L on to another footpath to reach the ridge after 1m. The crags run N from here over 3m: **Hurkling Stones**, **Wheelstones**, **White Tor**, **Salt Cellar**, **Dovestones Tor**, **Cakes of Bread**, **Back Tor** and eventually the esoteric **Howshaw Tor!** [STA]

Duke's Quarry: Restriction:
OS.119 GR.334 545   [18]

There is no known permission to climb here. A quarry with some fair climbs, the best of which are cracks. About 60ft and W-facing. It is often overgrown and the 50 or so routes can include several moves encountering severe undergrowth. A crag for the enthusiastic botanist.

Dir: 4.5m SE of Matlock. Take the A6 S for 5m to the B5035, turn off L to Crich, over the river and railway, and immediately turn L to Holloway, park after 200yds. Here a path leads off to the R and the quarry, 1 min. A few hundred yards further up the road to the R is **Wildgoose Quarry**. A place of little merit, although offering climbing for the enthusiast. [DG]

Eagle Tor:
OS.119 GR.235 627   [19]

A small gritstone bouldering area worth a few hours on a summer's evening.

Dir: 5m S of Bakewell. Approach: see Cratcliffe Tor. [DG]

Eastwood Rocks: Restriction:
OS.119 GR.360 633   [20]

The farmer who owns the crag does not wish it to be used for climbing purposes, those caught will be forcibly removed it is said. A small grit crag offering a good mixture of climbing. Cracks, slabs and steep slabs, a few little gems, rarely exceeding 30ft high. If ever the access position should change it would be a good introductory crag, with nearly all the climbs below E1.

Dir: 5m ENE of Matlock. Take the A632 up out of Matlock, after 4m turn R to Ashover on the B6036. Turn L down the village street, follow it round, then bear L up the steep hill where the rocks will be visible on the R. [DG]

Froggatt Edge:
OS.119 GR.250 763   [21]

A great crag. About 30–60ft high, offering over 150 routes of all grades. Famous most of all for its unprotected slab routes. The edge is about 0.5m long and is broken for the first 300yds, it then becomes more continuous. Nearly all routes can be well protected and, if not, top-roping is very easy to arrange. W-facing and very quick to dry.

Dir: 6m NNE of Bakewell. Take the B6001 to Calver, over the junction then take the B6054. After 1m pass The Chequers pub, carry on for 1m to some bends in the road and a large (often white) gate, park. Enter on to footpath at gate and after 0.5m pass through another gate. The crag begins 200yds on, where the track bends at a boulder. [DG]

Gardoms Edge:
OS.119 GR.271 732   [22]

One of the less-frequented crags, which is understandable since it does stay damp for quite a while after rain. Nevertheless the 180 or so routes offer really good climbing on sound gritstone, 30–60ft, and cover all grades very well except the high Es. W-facing but surrounded by trees.

Dir: 5m NE of Bakewell. Take the A619 to Baslow, then the A621 towards Sheffield, past the roundabout and up the hill. The crag is on the R. Park wherever and go route-stomping [DG]

Hall Moor Quarry: Restriction:
OS.119 GR.277 635   [23]

It appears that the owner of the quarry does not wish for climbers to cause any concern or be seen, act accordingly please. A fair quarry up to 60ft and offering about 15 routes, V Diff to E5. Stays rather damp and needs a good, dry spell, most pleasant on a sunny morning.

Dir: 3m NNE of Matlock. Go N on the A6 to Darley Dale, turn R on to the B5057, first L for 200yds, bear round to the L for 170yds, park. Here a footpath leads off up into the woods and the quarry. [DG]

Harborough Rocks: Restriction
OS.119 GR.242 552   [24]

The farmer who owns the rocks does not want to be invaded, and it is hoped that large groups will stay away. Small groups of countryside enthusiasts are very welcome. An excellent area of climbing on good pocketed limestone, unfortunately only 30ft high but nevertheless very worthwhile. Very good for beginners, with the 50 or so routes spread from Diff to VS. Good spot.

Dir: 5m SW of Matlock. Take the A5012 from Cromford to Grangemill. Here turn L to Longcliffe on the B5056. At Longcliffe turn L down a small lane, after 0.6m turn L again and continue past some small lakes for 0.7m. Here a path leads off L to the rocks. [PSO]

Harthill Quarry:
OS.119 GR.217 615   [25]

A gritstone quarry with about 20 routes, 70ft, above VS. Dangerously loose at the top.

Dir: 5m S from Bakewell. Approach: see Cratcliffe Tor. Carry on up the road, turn R to Elton, go through the village to the end and turn R to Alport. Follow this for about 600yds to a bend; a track leads off to the L and the quarry. [DG]

Higgar Tor:
OS.110 GR.255 819   [26]

The steepest gritstone outcrop in England. About 35 routes in all grades but mostly VS and above, a couple of gem E5s which will tear your hands to pieces. Up to 40ft in places on steep and rough rock, S-facing. Friendly place, great crag.

Dir: 1.7m E of Hathersage. Approach: see Burbage North. Nearby to the SE, 5 mins walk, is **Carl Walk**, a 30ft outcrop with about 20 routes mainly around Diff – worth a visit if defeated by terror at the sheer sight of Higgar. [DG]

High Tor:
OS.119 GR.298 590   [27]

The most impressive cliff in Derbyshire, any route here is a classic 3-star route. The limestone is just the friendly side of vertical in most places, but the holds are smooth pockets which, while giving excellent finger holds, fail miserably in supporting the feet and in consequence the rest of the body. At 200ft-plus and a good 500ft above the valley, exposure is certainly felt.

Facing W, it gets very difficult on hot summer days and being so exposed it can get very cold. There is one climb at VS and some very good classics at HVS, including the obvious easy way up the centre. The grades then move very swiftly up to E2 and beyond. E5, 6a is the best grade for the 15 strolls up the centre of the crag. Of the 80 routes here nearly all are worth doing more than once.

Dir: Between Matlock and Matlock Bath. Take the A6 S from Matlock until the very impressive crag is seen on the L, park near the second footbridge. Cross the river to the High Tor Grounds, walk up to the crag in 5 mins. [PSO]

Hipley Hill: Access:
OS.119 GR.210 541   [28]

Access here is granted as long as the fences are respected and not damaged, please be careful. A nice collection of 60ft climbs on natural limestone, Severes to E2, about 10 routes.

Dir: 6m WSW of Matlock. From Cromford take the A5012 to Grangemill, turn L on to the B5056, continue for 3.2m to some bends in the road. The cliff is on the L. [PSO]

Horseshoe Quarry:
OS.119 GR.208 761   [29]

As far as grotty-looking quarries go, this one is not bad. About 70 distinctive routes which are all Extreme and tend to be around E4. Anything worth climbing has lots of bolts. For the routes with less than adequate gear as viewed from below, abseil inspection seems very advisable.

Dir: 4m N of Bakewell. Go N to Baslow, A619 then B6001. Turn L on to A623 to Stoney Middleton, pass through village and continue up the dale, past the Eyam turn off and on for 0.5m. On the R is a track leading to a quarry, park without blocking the track. The quarry is quite large and one can climb almost anywhere. [PST]

Ladybower Quarry:
OS.110 GR.208 867   [30]

An uninteresting jumble of gritstone walls in an unused quarry. Along with Birch Quarry 50yds up the road about 25 routes in the lower technical grades. With the very close proximity of the pub and all day licensing hours there is little need ever to visit this grottsville place.

BASTILLE, E5, 6b, High Tor. (Climber Andy Parkin, Photo Mike Browell)

Dir: 4m NW of Hathersage. Take the A6013 to the junction with the A57, turn R and the quarries are 200yds past the Ladybower Inn. [STA]

Lathkill Dale:
OS.119 GR.184 655   [31]

A small limestone crag. About 10 climbs, Diff to VS, up to 70ft.

Dir: 3.6m SW of Bakewell. Take the B5055 Monyash road from Bakewell, after 2.4m turn L to Haddon Grove and park in about 600yds, where a signposted track leads to the dale. The crag is in the valley opposite the weir on the river. [PSO]

Lawrencefield:
OS.119 GR.249 797   [32]

A very good gritstone crag which is sheltered from the elements – everybody knows this so on windy unpleasant days do not expect to have the crag to yourself. About 80 routes across the grades, up to 70ft, about 10 different bays, with the pool bay and wall dominating the outcrop. There are some fine Extremes on the back wall, none very hard. To the sides are some excellent VS and HVS routes, also some easier slabs. Very good in winter, a sun trap. Keep for the rainy day.

Dir: 2m SE from Hathersage. Take the A625 E from the town up the hill, go round the bend L at the top to a car park in 100yds. From here cross the road to a footpath going S, which leads to the top of the crag in about 5 mins. Descent is to the R as walking in. [DG]

Lime Kiln Quarry:
OS.119   [33]

A 70ft limestone crag, offering a handful of routes in the mid-Extremes. The routes are in full view of the Lime Kiln pub and climbers are asked to act responsibly.

Dir: In Wirksworth, behind the pub. [PSO]

Lorry Park Quarry: Restriction:
OS.119 GR.293 588   [34]

Climbing here is totally forbidden. There are about 6 routes, E2–E4, 60–90ft.

Dir: 0.2m S of Matlock. Take the A6 from Matlock, the quarry is shortly on the R. [PSO]

Millstone Edge:
OS.110 GR.248 804   [35]

Not really a crag for the beginner, although only half of the 160 routes are hard. For the Extreme climber this is the 3-star gritstone attraction, the classics are London Wall, Edge Lane, Scrittos Republic and Masters Edge. All on-sight possibilities for the levitation expert. The easy embankment Extremes with the keyhole cave area make this a great crag for the low-grade Extreme leader. The routes are all quarried lines and reach up to 130ft. The best quarried gritstone in England, a must for the visitor.

Dir: 1.4m SE of Hathersage. Take the A625 E from the town up the hill, park in the lay-by just before the road bends sharp L at the top. A track leads off back to the L and the crag after 400yds. [DG]

Pic Tor:
OS.119 GR.299 598   [36]

Some good 60ft routes here around the low Extremes. About 15 routes in total, including a VS, 2 HVSs, an E1, 3 E2s, 4 E3s and 2 E4s. A sheltered crag and quite pleasant. NW-facing, pocketed limestone.

Dir: At Matlock. From the town centre take the A6 S towards Matlock Bath, after 300yds go under a railway bridge, park in the car park on the L. Walk back up the road and take the footbridge on the R over the river, turn L following the path under the railway to the crag in 2 mins. By turning R after the footbridge, Bend Tor is reached after 300yds. [PSO]

Rainster Rocks: Access:
OS.119 GR.219 548   [37]

The land is privately owned and permission to climb must be obtained from J. K. Breakwell, Tinkers Inn, Wyaston Road, Ashbourne, Derbyshire, tel. Ashbourne (0335) 42824. The rocks here are scattered all around and to list individual outcrops would detract from the fun of exploration. Around 40ft high, offering over 100 routes in the lower grades. Worth a visit.

Dir: 5m SW of Matlock. Take the A5012 from Cromford to Grangemill, then the B5056 to Longcliffe. Carry on for 1.2m, turn L and continue for 0.6m, park. Take the footpath N to the rocks, 10mins. [PSO]

Rheinstor: Access:
OS.119 GR.218 644 [38]

The crag is on private land. If visiting take care not to damage any plants, etc., which would probably result in a climbing ban. A small crag, heavily overgrown in places. A handful of routes especially in the lower grades. Limestone, painful holds.

Dir: 3m S of Bakewell. Take the A6 S for 2m, turn R on the B5056 for 0.7m, turn R to Youlgreave. Before entering the village turn L to Bradford and go to the bottom of the hill. Here a path leads along the river and to the crag. [PSO]

Rivelin:
OS.110 GR.280 873 [39]

At Rivelin there is an edge with about 100 routes and a quarry with 50 routes, gritstone. The natural edge offers the best climbing and is famous for its Needle, a 60ft pinnacle which can be ascended by the VS climber. Most of the climbs are in the lower grades and the less popular routes tend to get overgrown. A bit green and prone to slippery epics, also midge and mosquito territory.

Dir: 4.5m W of Sheffield. Leave Sheffield by the A57. After a few miles the A6101 joins from the R, 0.7m further on a path leads off to the R to the crag in 5 mins. [STA]

Robin Hood Quarries: Restriction:
OS.116 GR.334 549 [40]

There is no existing permission to climb here. 4 quarries of mixed merit and little distinction, about 70 routes in total, mainly in the lower grades around 30–40ft. Can be damp and miserable here, nevertheless it does exist, I am afraid.

Dir: 4.2m SE of Matlock. Take the A6 S for 0.5m, turn off L on to the B5035. After 100yds over the railway and the river turn L on to the Holloway road. After 400yds a path leads off R to the quarries. [DG]

Rowtor Rocks:
OS.119 GR.235 622 [41]

Some jolly good bouldering on these much-bouldered boulders.

Dir: 5m S of Bakewell. Take the A6 S for 2m, turn R on the B5056 for 2.6m, turn L and go up the hill to Birchover. The rocks are very close to The Druids Inn – now see how much cragging gets done! [DG]

Stanage Edge:
OS.110 GR.247 832 leading N [42]

The most famous gritstone edge in England. Over 700 listed routes in every grade and of all types, nearly all SW-facing and commanding a fine view over the Hope valley. The climbs reach up to 80ft in places, but are mostly around 50–60ft. The rock is hard and coarse to the weak hands, dries very quickly but is very exposed at 1,500ft. Any bad weather can be seen coming from the W and rapid descent to the car is often a wise decision. Midges in late summer. Excellent bouldering. A must for anyone, very busy at weekends.

Dir: 2.5m N of Hathersage. Drive up through Hathersage, take the small road off L as the road bends to the R, past The Scotsman's Pack pub (food) and to a junction after a windy 1.6m. Park here and walk up to the crag. For access further along the crag, drive down to the tree plantation where there is a car park and footpath, or drive even further. [STA]

Stannington Ruffs:
OS.110 GR.305 892 [43]

This crag cannot be recommended for so many reasons that to explain would waste valuable space. 60 climbs, loose, low grade.

Dir: 3m WNW of Sheffield. Approach Stannington on the B6076, take the small road on the R opposite the church, leading to some woods after 0.5m and the crag. [STA]

Stanton Moor Quarries:
OS.119 GR.252 636 [44]

Some old quarry workings, offering about a dozen routes, HVS to E2, at about 150ft.

Dir: 5m NW of Matlock. Take the A6 to Darley Dale, turn L on to the B5057 to Darley bridge, take the small road to Stanton Lees on the R, pass through on the R and carry on for 400yds. The quarry entrance is on the L. [DG]

Stoney Middleton:
OS.119 GR.228 757   [45]

This is without doubt one of the greatest crags in Britain. Just over 200 routes of which 150 are Extremes, however the VS and HVS climbs that do exist are very good indeed. About 100–200ft and S-facing. To flash any route at Stoney on sight is one of the rarest achievements in British climbing. Just about everybody has fallen off the test pieces here. Satisfied that you have cracked a particular grade, come to Stoney and come back to planet Earth. The classic test pieces are Scoop Wall, Soapsuds E1, Wall of Bubbles Direct, Cabbage Crack E2, Pickpocket, Our Father E3, Bitter Fingers, Kink, Millionaire Touch E4, Scarab, Menopause, Circe E5, Little Plum, Helmut Schmidt E6. They will get you somewhere, Millionaire Touch got me. You can often see yourself in the limestone here, but sticky boots solve the problem and make all the routes quite easy these days.

Dir: 4.5m N of Bakewell. Take the A621 up hill, the B6001 to Calver, then L on to the A623 to Stoney Middleton. Drive through the village to a petrol station on the R, park in the lay-by opposite. The crag is on the R side of the valley, the other side is a working quarry. The cliff is in many buttresses which go on for about 1,000yds and end in a small quarry with an electricity station. By crossing the road the crag does continue, known as Cucklet Delf to the R and Stoney West, nothing to rave about.

Tegness Pinnacle Quarry:
OS.119 GR.255 780   [46]

A good little quarry with no worthwhile routes. The pinnacle, however, offers 5 classic routes, around 25ft, Diffs to HVS. Good spot, a must for anyone, and quite possible in the rain, admittedly with added interest.

Dir: 3.5m SE of Hathersage. Take the A625 E, after 3.3m turn R on to the B6055 to Fox House Inn, then shortly R again on to the B6054. Shortly pass the Grouse Inn and then park in the car park on the R. From here a footpath leads off R through the woods to the crag. By carrying on further N, one comes to **North Quarry** and then **Padley Quarry**. Both are overgrown and of exploratory interest only. [DG]

Turning Stone Edge:
OS.119 GR.342 621   [47]

A fine edge of natural grit in a very pleasant setting. About 30 climbs, Diff to E2, 40ft high, good for the HS and VS climber.

Dir: 3m ENE of Matlock. Take the A632 up out of Matlock, at the top of the hill take the R turn to Butterley. After 1.1m there is a track on the L leading to a quarry and just further on is Cocking Tor, where the edge, about 100yds long, can be seen. [DG]

The Upper Matlock Quarries:
OS.119 GR.298 610   [48]

Some gritstone quarries with about 20 routes in the lower grades, Severe to HVS and about 40ft high. Mostly unpleasant.

Dir: NE side of Matlock. By the recreation ground at Cavendish Road in Matlock. [DG]

Via Gellia Buttress:
OS.119 GR.277 571   [49]

A small, 100ft limestone buttress, offering a handful of 100ft routes VS–HVS, and an E2.

Dir: 3m SW of Matlock. Take the A6 S for 2m, turn R up the A5012 and carry on for 1.5m. A track leads off L up the hillside to the crag. [PSO]

Via Gellia Quarry:
OS.119 GR.265 567   [50]

A 60ft limestone quarry, offering a handful of VS routes.

Dir: 4m SW of Matlock. From Cromford take the A5012 towards Grangemill, after 2.3m stop at the lay-by. Here a track leads off the road N towards the quarry in about 5 mins. [PSO]

Wharncliffe Crags: Restriction
OS.110 GR.300 972   [51]

The crags are on private ground and access is limited to Monday, Thursday, Saturday and bank holidays. The most northerly of the gritstone eastern edges offers 30–50ft climbs of variable quality, about 150 routes in all grades with only 20 or so of notable merit. The rock is often green and although facing SW, is best in the hot summer. Worth a visit if desperate.

DOUBLE SCOTCH, E1, 5b, Stoney Middleton. (Climber Fred Bloggs, Photo David B A Jones)

Dir: 1m ESE of Stocksbridge. The crag is above the A616 leading S from Deepcar to Sheffield. Turn L at Deepcar on to the B6088, then take the first R and park just over the river. From here take the footpath on the L under 2 railways and then R along to the crag, which runs for 1m SW from here. [STA]

Wildcat Crags:
OS.119 GR.297 575   [52]

The limestone alternative to High Tor for those without superhuman forearms. Unfortunately the quality here is very poor compared with High Tor, even so there are some very good routes. This 120ft crag offers plenty of VS–HVS routes, only 45 of the 200 routes are Extremes. The rock is very dubious in places, beware of falling off. The crag is long and rambling and not often very crowded.

Dir: 0.3m S of Matlock Bath. The access to the crag has always been awkward as part (Southern) is privately owned. Park in one of the car parks at Matlock Bath. From the Pavilion a footpath runs down along the river to a footbridge in about 300yds. Use this to access the other bank, where crags lie upstream and downstream. [PSO]

Willersley Castle Rocks: Access
OS.119 GR.298 570   [53]

The rocks are privately owned, it is hoped that sensible behaviour by climbers will allow the continued use of this crag. A small crag offering 50 worthwhile routes and 25 not so worthwhile, 100ft in places with climbs well spread from VS upwards. Can stay damp after rain, but is very useful when High Tor is getting battered by icy winds.

Dir: 2m S of Matlock. Take the A6 S from Matlock through Matlock Bath. At the A5012 turn-off take the small road forking away on the L, car park in 100yds. Return back to the junction by foot and the entrance to the crag is on the R, between the crossing and the bus stop. [PSO]

Yarncliffe Quarry:
OS.119 GR.255 794   [54]

A small quarry of reasonable merit, about 30 routes, Diff to E4. The gritstone in most places is good and there are some excellent slabs for the low-grade climber. Can stay damp but quite a good bet in cold, windy weather. **Yarncliffe Edge** is also close by and offers 30 or so more climbs, best in spring or autumn.

Dir: 2.4m SE of Hathersage. Take the A625 E up out of Hathersage, after 3.2m turn R on to the B 6521. After 0.9m a drive leads off up to the quarry on the L through a gate, park. To reach Yarncliffe Edge follow the footpath going S, which contours around the hillside, for about 5 mins. [DG]

PEAK SOUTH

This area covers all crags in the south east corner of the peak, and is generally less popular with the exception of The Roaches and Chee Tor, two of the finest crags in Derbyshire. Dovedale is invaded by walkers – battle your way along the footpaths. The western grit edges get hit by snow in winter and are very exposed; they are also the wettest crags in the area. The climbing is good though.

Aldery Cliff:
OS.119 GR.097 663   [55]

An old limestone quarry with about 40 climbs, mainly around the VS grade, 50–100ft high and mostly solid in places. There tends to be vegetation here in summer and it is E-facing. None of the routes is particularly brilliant to say the least, a cliff for the enthusiast. The crag is on private land and use is subject to sensible behaviour.

Dir: 5m SSE of Buxton. Take the A515 SE, after 3m fork L on to the B5053 to Earl Sterndale. Here go L into the village and take the road to Crowdecote. The crag appears shortly on the R. [PST]

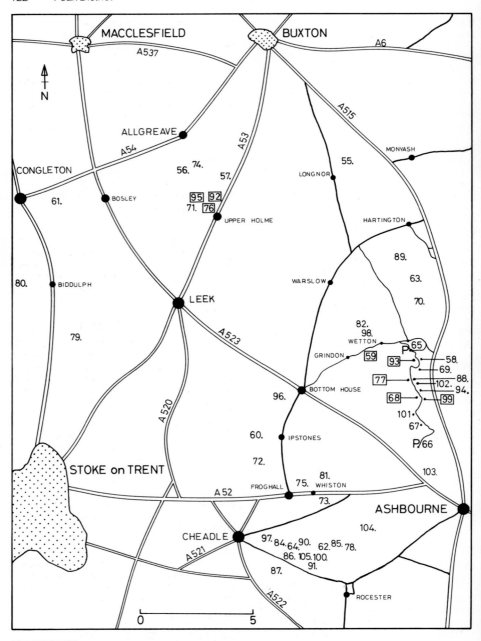

MACCLESFIELD

BUXTON

A6

A537

N

A515

ALLGREAVE

MONYASH

A54

56. 74.

55.

57.

LONGNOR

CONGLETON

61.

BOSLEY

A53

95 92

71. 76

UPPER HOLME

HARTINGTON

89.

63.

WARSLOW

70.

80.

BIDDULPH

LEEK

82.
98.

WETTON

79.

A523

GRINDON

59

P 65

58.

93

69.

77

88.
102.
94.

A520

96.

BOTTOM HOUSE

68

99

101.

67.

P/66

60.

IPSTONES

STOKE on TRENT

72.

103.

A52

FROGHALL

75.

81.
WHISTON

ASHBOURNE

73.

104.

CHEADLE

97. 84. 64. 90. 62. 85. 78.

A521

86. 105. 100.

87.

91.

A522

ROCESTER

0   5

PEAK SOUTH

Back Forest Crags:
OS.118 GR.987 653 [56]

These crags offer good gritstone problems, up to 20ft high in all grades. There are about 100 problems of all sorts in about 30 routes. At around 1,000ft they are quite exposed and best kept for a summer's evening, a dry spell makes the approach walk a lot more pleasant. Great fun for all the family.

Dir: 5.5m N of Leek. Take the small road running N from Meerbrook for 2.8m to the viewpoint. Here the crags can be seen to the L for about 1.6m. The crag known as **The Hanging Stone** is at the L-hand end overlooking Danebridge. [SG]

Baldstones:
OS.119 GR.019 644 [57]

The outcrop is neighboured by **Newstones** to the S and **Gib Tor** to the N. All are dealt with as one, as the climbing on each is so similar and they are only a minute apart. From 20–50ft high, about 50 routes and a good ton of boulder problems, all grades from Diff upwards. E-facing gritstone with good holds, about 1,400ft and cold on a cool day. Definitely worth a visit for the bouldering, also weird rock formations for those with weird tendencies and lurid imagination.

Dir: 5.5m NNE of Leek. Take the A53 NE for 5m, 1.5m past Upper Hulme a road leads off L to Newstone Farm in 0.5m. From here the rocks are seen on the ridge N, walk in 5 mins. [SG]

Baley Buttress:
OS.119 GR.142 538 [58]

About 10 routes, V Diff to E3, with a couple of excellent limestone HVSs. About 150ft and S-facing.

Dir: 5m NNW of Ashbourne. Approach: see Dovedale North. [PSO]

Beeston Tor:
OS.119 GR.106 541 [59]

One of the best limestone crags in the Peak District. The rock often runs to good pockets and good protection. About 40 routes, VS upwards, mostly HVS and E3, around 200ft high with most climbs running to 2 pitches. The stinging nettles in summer mean a big stick and long trousers for the approach, remember you still have to descend the L side of the crag in the undergrowth. Gets the morning and early afternoon sun, worth a visit at any time.

Dir: 6.5m NW of Ashbourne. Take the A515 N, turn off to Alstonfield and carry on to Wetton, then towards Grindon. After 1m and winding down a steep hill to a narrow bridge, the crag will be seen on the L. Take the track on the L to a farm where one can park for a small fee. Walk to the crag, 5 mins. [PSO]

Belmont Hall Crags:
OS.119 GR.007 504 [60]

Some 50ft gritstone outcrops, offering about 15 routes at all grades. Excellent climbing, worth a visit.

Dir: 4.5m SSE of Leek. Take the A523 then the B5053 to Ipstones. Enter the village, take the first R towards Basford, carry on for 0.6m, park. Before the sharp bend a path leads off to the L and the crag in about 2 mins. [SG]

Bosley Cloud:
OS.118 GR.905 637 [61]

Some good climbing to be found here, but it is NE-facing and can get rather lichenous. Most of the climbs are around VS with a few easier and others harder, about 20 routes in total up to 50ft on natural gritstone. There is a quarry at the N end of the hill with some routes as well as some suspect rock. Quite good views reward the hike up to the crags. Having found the crags easily near the summit trig point, one should not miss the two outcrops on the W side farther round, **Secret Slab** and **The Catstone**. Both offer good routes, especially 6a problems on the Secret Slab, worth a top rope.

Dir: 3m E of Congleton. Take the A527 SE for 1m through Hightown, bear L at the golf course at Mossley Hall on to a small road which leads to Timbersbrook. From the village the big hill known as The Cloud will be seen to the N. Take the steep lane up out of the village to the N, after 300yds the buttress of The Catstone is on the R, 0.5m further round is Secret Slab, and around to the N side the crags come into view. [SG]

Castle Crag:
OS.119 GR.073 425 [62]

Some good climbing to be found here, and on

Alton Cliff, about 500yds to the L. Anything worthwhile is VS and above. About 50ft and 15 climbs in total, nearly all around HVS, 5b, a couple of 5cs at Alton Cliff. Mostly walls with undercut bases, good for the arms. Worth a trip for the HVS leader.

Dir: 4m E of Cheadle at Alton. From the village go down to the river and castle, the crag is directly below. A track leads to the crag from the Talbot Inn. The crag is on private ground so please act courteously. [SG]

Celestial Twins:
OS.119 GR.133 582 [63]

An open crag with some good climbing. About 20 limestone climbs, around HVS to E3, a few harder and easier climbs. The left of the Celestial Twins offers all the climbing, 60ft high and W-facing. Worth a visit.

Dir: 9m SW of Bakewell. Take the B5054 to Hartington, carry on W through the village and for 1.5m, turn L at signpost for Beresford Dale. After 0.6m turn L, 200yds on L again, at 0.6m the road ends with limited parking. Here cross the river by footbridge and walk downstream for 400yds to the crag, which is easily recognisable. [PSO]

Dimmings Dale:
OS.119 GR.055 433 [64]

There are no access problems here since no one can find any of the crags in the dale, but winter can help to locate the crags. A very beautiful spot with some worthwhile climbs, most around 5b but a fair amount of 4a, 4b climbing. About 30 climbs in total, most of which are rewarding. Worth a visit to avoid the crowds.

Dir: 2.5m E of Cheadle. Take the B5417 E from Cheadle, after 2m and entering forested areas take the next R down a small road. After 400yds the road bears round L to a junction, park. Walk straight on down a track, which shortly enters Dimmings Dale. The crags are hidden in the trees. Explore at will. [SG]

Dovedale North: Access
[65]

Leave Ashbourne on the A515, go N for 6 miles, then turn off L to Alstonfield. After 0.5m take the fork L for light vehicles and after 400yds pass through Milldale to the car park. Dovedale valley to the S is signposted. For crags see map. [PSO]

Dovedale South: Access
[66]

Leave Ashbourne N on the A515, after 0.6m turn L down a small road to Thorpe and follow the road L toward Ilam. At the bottom of a valley 500yds out of Thorpe turn R to Dovedale car park, signposted. A footpath leads up the valley all the way to Milldale. For crags see map. [PSO]

Dovedale Castle:
OS.119 GR.147 515 [67]

About 10 routes from S to HVS, with one good route, an E4. NE-facing and a wade to get to it. For the enthusiast.

Dir: 3.5m NNW of Ashbourne. Approach: see Dovedale South [PSO]

Dovedale Church:
OS.119 GR.144 522 [68]

A group of limestone pinnacles, offering about 25 routes of all standards. The best routes are E3 upwards, however there are exceptions so make the trip. A summer crag this one, approach can be very overgrown and includes wading the river, not fun in winter – you could always walk across the ice. About 100ft high with the best routes on the wall facing the river. Best descent is by abseil.

Dir: 4m NNW of Ashbourne. Approach: see Dovedale South [PSO]

Dove Holes:
OS.119 GR.142 535 [69]

A very good tourist spot at any time of the year. Nothing easy here, min. grade E3 going up to E-whatever if your fingers and stonemasonry skills are sufficient. Abseil descent for all routes. Only a handful of free routes at present.

Dir: 5m NNW of Ashbourne. Approach: see Dovedale N. [PSO]

Drabber Tor:
OS.119 GR.139 750 [70]

A 70ft limestone crag, offering about 10 routes, VS to E2, on good rock. Not a crag visited often since you need to trek a good 1.5m and wade across the river to get to it. To be reserved for the sweltering hot summer days.

Dir: 10m SW of Bakewell. Go S on the A515, turn off to Alstonfield. After 0.5m the road dips down to the valley of Milldale, park. Walk upstream N for 1.5m and the crag will be seen on the L. [PSO]

Five Clouds:
OS.119 GR.001 625 [71]

A great alternative to The Roaches when every university freshers' meet descends upon the upper crag. About 50 climbs up to 50ft in all grades, with plenty of bouldering. Good solid gritstone, SW-facing but still very unsheltered. Excellent views, worth a visit.

Dir: 4m NNE of Leek. Approach: see The Roaches. [SG]

Flintmill Buttress:
OS.119 GR.004 483 [72]

A steep crag, offering about 10 or more climbs in the VS–HVS grade. N-facing and stays rather damp. For the enthusiast.

Dir: 5m S of Leek. Take the A520 S then the A52 E to Kingsley. At the village turn L and go to Hazelcross, then N on to river Hazels. The crag is here beside the river. [SG]

Garston Rocks: Restriction
OS.119 GR.051 476 [73]

Seek permission to climb from the farm first and please do not block the lane with your car. A good gritstone crag, offering about 20 routes, 30–40ft, and lots of good bouldering just past the farm. Climbs mostly in the lower grades, yet problems to test anyone. Better in the summer or a dry spell. Worth a visit.

Dir: 7m SSE of Leek. Approach: see Oldridge Pinnacle, but instead of parking turn R down a lane for 400yds, then turn L and go 200yds to the farm. The crag can be seen from the road. [SG]

Gradbach Hill:
OS.119 GR.001 653 [74]

A W facing, lonely outcrop, ideal for getting away from it all. About 20 climbs in the lower grades, with one 5c. Still plenty of bouldering, though, on this sound grit outcrop. Worth a visit.

Dir: 5.5m almost N of Leek. Take the A53 towards Buxton. 2m after Upper Hulme a road leads off L towards Newstones Farm and eventually Allgrave. After 400yds fork R, carry on for 1m, pass a triangular junction and the crag is up on the hill to the L. Over on the opposite side of the road, about 500yds away to the R, are **Flash Bottom Rocks**, offering some good Diffs and a few harder problems. Easily visible as two buttresses. Worth noting. [SG]

Harston Rocks:
OS.119 GR.032 477 [75]

A softish gritstone crag, offering about 50 routes, 30ft, in all grades. The routes tend to stay green with the exception of Harston Rock itself, which offers a handful of routes, VS to E3, around 60ft. The crag is hidden in trees and is best in early spring. Harston Rock itself is a gem and well worth a visit.

Dir: 6m SSE of Leek. Drive to Kingsley, then Froghall, carry on up the A52 and park just past the sharp R bend up the hill. Here a track leads off to the L to a farm and the rocks after passing over two stiles. Beware of the dog! [SG]

Hen Cloud:
OS.119 GR.008 616 [76]

A very impressive crag with some excellent climbing on it. There are 100 or so climbs, Diff to E3. Some climbs reach 100ft in length and most routes are well worth doing, however none ever seems easy. There are some very difficult walls for which a top rope is highly recommended, bolts are strongly discouraged here. Bring a 30ft length of rope to help top rope as the belays are set back. The gritstone is tough on the hands, SW-facing but very exposed, always bring a jacket. Great views.

Dir: 3.5m NNE from Leek. Take the A53 NE to Upper Hulme, turn off L and follow the road around to beneath the crag. It is the first big outcrop, 0.6m from the main road. For The Roaches and Five Clouds carry on 400yds to a parking spot. [SG]

Ilam Rock:
OS.119 GR.142 532   [77]

A superb 70ft spire of limestone sticking out of the river bed. Only a few routes though. The summit can be gained by a Severe from the gully behind and grass ledges with interest. There are 6 Extremes, from E1 facing the river to the very impressive overhanging wall, Eye of the Tiger E6, guaranteed flying time. Definitely worth a visit.

Dir: 4.5m NNW of Ashbourne. Approach: see Dovedale North. [PSO]

Ina's Rock:
OS.119 GR.087 429   [78]

A sandstone crag, 30–80ft high. The climbs are steepish to say the least, about a dozen in number and Severe to E2. However, the harder routes tend to be cleaner and better, good at HVS.

Dir: 5m W of Cheadle. Park at Alton, then take the path by the river Churnet, downstream to the E for 10 mins, and cross to the N bank by Gig Cottage. Here a path runs up and to the R and along to the rock. The crag is on private property, act accordingly. From the cottage one can easily reach Park Banks Crags up to the L. [SG]

Knypersley Rocks:
OS.118 GR.900 557   [79]

A good solid gritstone crag, but set in the trees and gets green and unpleasant quite often. A score of routes in the very easy grades, around 30ft. A pleasant spot, worth a visit for the low-grade climber.

Dir: 1.5m SE of Biddulph. From the town of Biddulph on the A527, turn L into Rock End Road at the crossroads just past the church with the spire. Follow this for 1.2m to Rock End, a track leads off to the R and down, park in about 300yds. Take the public footpath to the crags up on the L. The track leading off L from the road leads to some small outcrops on private land which also provide good climbing. Seek permission first, though, from the house at the L end of the outcrop. The outcrop is known as **Rock End**. [SG]

Mow Cop:
OS.118 GR.858 576   [80]

A unique rock formation, **The Old Man of Mow**, offering about half a dozen routes around 60ft, in the HVS category with the exception of Spiral Route at HS, the classic route of the crag. Descent is by abseil. There are some quarries nearby with about 30 routes in the middle grades, of which very few have real merit. The crags are known as **The Folly Cliff**, **Hawks Hole Quarry** and **Millstone Quarry**. They are situated beneath the castle, Folly Cliff being the most northern.

Dir: 2m W of Biddulph. Drive to Mow Cop and the top of the hill. [SG]

Oldridge Pinnacle: Restriction:
OS.119 GR.043 480   [81]

The crag is on private ground. Please ask the farmer before climbing on the pinnacle, a long-standing tradition. Access is usually granted. The pinnacle is steep and offers about 10 good 40ft climbs, all VS and above with the exception of the SE crack at Severe. Worth a visit.

Dir: 6.5m SSE of Leek. Go to Kingsley and then on to Whiston on the A52. Carry on for 0.6m after the pub in the village on the L, park. Take a track leading to Oldridge Farm and the pinnacle. [SG]

Ossam's Crag:
OS.119 GR.096 554   [82]

This is a 150ft limestone crag, for the green-fingered not the white-fingered. There are some fair routes here, and on the neighbouring crag known as **The Chimney**, about 15 in total from Severe to E5. A crag to get away from the crowds.

Dir: 7.5m NW of Ashbourne. Approach: see Thor's Cave. [PSO]

Ousal Dale:
OS.119 GR.058 436   [84]

Some good climbing for the lower-grade climber in this valley. About a dozen routes in total on three separate buttresses. About 30ft high.

Dir: 3m E of Cheadle. From Alton take the road W along the river, upstream for 0.7m to Lords Bridge and park. Here a footpath leads up to a pool in the dale. Where the path forks go R and in 200yds **Cottage Rocks** will be seen, carry on for another 200yds to reach **Lone Buttress**, hardish routes, and then another 300yds to reach **Ousal Crag**. [SG]

Park Banks Crags:
OS.119 GR.082 429 [85]

A few separate crags of reasonable sandstone in the trees. About 30 climbs, 30–60ft, Diff to E5. Worth a visit for anyone, especially for Brad's Chimney, V Diff – and a classic at that, aye.

Dir: 4.5m E of Cheadle. Approach: see Ina's Rock. [SG]

Peakstone Inn Amphitheatre:
OS.119 GR.055 428 [86]

A somewhat green, damp and vegetated crag, however in extremely close vicinity to an ale-slurping spot – guzzle, hic! About 20–50ft with climbs in the lower grades up to 5a.

Dir: 3m E of Cheadle. Take the B5032 towards Alton and after 2.6m the Peakstone Inn will be seen on the L. The crag is behind the pub. Also a good spot for access to Wright's Rock. Take the public footpath to the R side of the amphitheatre and the rock will soon come into view over on the R. [SG]

Peakstone Rock:
OS.119 GR.052 422 [87]

A small group of rocks up to 30ft high with some suspect rock. About 10 climbs around VS, most though tend to be technically quite hard and strength is somewhat useful. In fact, brute force is even better, good place for hulks.

Dir: 2.5m E of Cheadle. Take the B5032 E for 2m. Pass the small road leading to Bradley in the Moors on the R and shortly after there is a track on the R leading to a farm. Walk up the track and seek permission at the bungalow, has always been granted. The crag is off to the R. [SG]

Pickering Tors:
OS.119 GR.143 531 [88]

These tors consist of four separate crags. From L to R as viewed are Pickering Tor, Pickering Wall, Overhanging Buttress and then the classic Watchblock Buttress with Wall of Straws E5 and

Adjudicator Wall E3. All are W-facing and in a very pleasant setting, offering very good limestone climbing. About 30 routes in total, mostly 60–100ft in the middle to upper grades, some easier routes but more for interest than enjoyment. Worth a visit.

Dir: 4.5m NNW of Ashbourne. Approach: see Dovedale North. [PSO]

Pike Crag:
OS.119 GR.129 590 [89]

About 10 climbs in the VS to E2 category, fairly solid limestone up to 60ft. The crag is quite steep but generally runs to good protection. A pleasant spot.

Dir: Approach: see Celestial Twins. Take the footpath on the L going upstream for 400yds to pike pool, which has a curious pinnacle rising from it. Just beyond this is a footbridge leading right across the river. The crag is just up the grassy bank. [PSO]

Rainroach Rock:
OS.119 GR.063 430 [90]

A steep, large and impressive piece of rock. About half a dozen routes, HV Diff to E1. Do not get put off by the vegetation on the ledges – it's really natural, man.

Dir: 3m W of Cheadle. Take the road running along the river W from Alton to a sharp R bend after 0.4m. A track leads near to the crag, which is up and almost straight on. [SG]

Rakesdale:
OS.119 GR.066 424 [91]

Some climbing in this dale on various outcrops. Routes of most grades around 30ft. Explore at will.

Dir: 3m W of Cheadle. On the B5032 coming towards Alton just as you reach the edge of the town there is a small road on the L leading to the town. Take this, then park at a track leading off to the L almost immediately. A footpath carries on down this to the dale and the crags. [SG]

Ramshaw Rocks:
OS.119 GR.019 622 [92]

A truly great crag for the connoisseur of gritstone. About 120 routes in all grades up to 50ft. There is plenty here for all, good bouldering, big and small. The crag faces E and is quite exposed – in winter an hour can easily be enough, on hot summer days it can offer delightful bouldering in the shade. Strength can be useful since in parts it is steep, but tact and skill will soon win through as the hulks get exhausted. Very near the road, good bet if the weather might turn. At about 1,400ft, though, and prone to wet, horrible weather.

Dir: 4m NNE of Leek. Take the A53 towards Buxton, the crags are on the L 0.7m after Upper Hume. [SG]

Ravens Tor:
OS.119 GR.141 539 [93]

A very good, steep limestone crag, offering perhaps the best middle-grade climbing in the Dovedale valley. About 25 routes, VS to E5, with a few very easy routes! E-facing and chilly on a winter's day. Worth a visit though.

Dir: 5m NNW of Ashbourne. Approach: see Dovedale North. [PSO]

Reynard's Cave:
OS.119 GR.146 525 [94]

A natural arch offering about 5 Hard Extreme routes and a VS. The L wall is taken by The Lime Arch, a very good E3, worth doing. W-facing and quite sheltered in the winter.

Dir: 4.5m NNW of Ashbourne. Approach: see Dovedale North. [PSO]

The Roaches:
OS.119 GR.003 627 [95]

The most popular gritstone crag in the area. The crag offers plenty for everyone to enjoy, slabs, cracks, roofs. There are 300 routes and as many boulder problems. Every grade imaginable, the harder slabs mostly being top-roped. The big roof is taken by The Sloth up the crack in the middle at a good HVS. There are two tiers, but the bottom one tends to get green very quickly and also stay damp. SW-facing and up to 100ft high, open to the elements. Wonderful aspect but often wet and windy. Always worth a visit though.

Dir: 4m NNE of Leek. Take the A53 Buxton road for 3m to Upper Hulme, turn off L up past the Rock Inn – gulp – and follow the road round past the first outcrop, Hen Cloud, to a car park after 0.5m. From here The Roaches can be seen to the R, a bit of a walk. The Five Clouds are the series of outcrops beneath the ridge of The Roaches. [SG]

Sharpcliffe Rocks: Restriction:
OS.119 GR.015 520 [96]

The rocks are privately owned and a discreet approach is necessary. About 30 routes in the lower grades and with about 10 Extremes as well. Conglomerate rock which is never beyond suspicion, varying from 20 to 50ft. Not a bad crag.

Dir: 4m SSE of Leek. Take the A523 S for 4m, then turn R on to the B5053. After 1.3m turn R, continue for 0.5m, park. Continue up the road to Sharpcliffe Hall, the rocks are over on the R, about 5 mins. [SG]

Stony Dale Quarry:
OS.119 GR.048 438 [97]

About 10 routes on gritstone, mainly corners and arêtes. 20–60ft with routes of all grades V Diff to E4. After a dry spell worth a visit.

Dir: 3m W of Cheadle. Take the B5417 to Oakamoor, at the bottom of the hill at the village turn R and go along the river, then after 400yds bear up R. The crag is up on the L (S) side of the dale. [SG]

Thor's Cave:
OS.119 GR.098 549 [98]

Some futuristic climbing here on this very impressive limestone cave. About 20 routes, VS upwards, most worth doing, around 150ft and pleasant. This is also a very popular tourist attraction. Worth a visit.

Dir: 7m NW of Ashbourne. Take the A515, turn off to Alstonfield and then go through to Wetton. From here take the Butterton road, park at the bottom of the hill by the river. Cross the river and take the footpath down it. Ossam's Crag is reached in about 5 mins, Thor's Cave in about 10 mins across on the other bank. There is a footbridge to reach the cave. [PSO]

Tissington Spires
OS.119 GR.146 521 [99]

A very good group of crags offering about 60 routes in total, of which half are definitely worth doing. VS upwards for nearly everything, lots of good E1s and a good handful of middle-grade Extremes. W-facing but with awkward trees and undergrowth. At the S end is the John Peel Wall, with the best selection of routes on the crag, and the classic HVS John Peel, following the rightward curving scar. Definitely worth a visit.

Dir: 4m NNW of Ashbourne. Approach: see Dovedale South [PSO]

Toothill Rock:
OS.119 GR.068 425 [100]

A rather vegetated crag with no great merit, about 10 climbs, S to HVS, 30–60ft. Some climbs are cleanish, though, and worth doing.

Dir: 3m W of Cheadle. From the castle in Alton go upstream on the S bank for 500yds. Here a path leads uphill and to the rock. [SG]

The Twelve Apostles:
OS.119 GR.144 517 [101]

A large tower about 70ft high, offering three routes, VS to E2. Not over-inspiring, NE-facing.

Dir: 4m NNW of Ashbourne. Approach: see Dovedale South [PSO]

Vista Buttress:
OS.119 GR.145 528 [102]

A small 40ft outcrop, offering a couple of routes at VS and S.

Dir: 4.5m NNW of Ashbourne. Approach: see Dovedale North [PSO]

Waterhouse's Quarry:
OS.110 GR.092 502 [103]

A quarry with some climbing on what is thought to be limestone or shale. Some reported 40ft slab routes around 5c.

Dir: 7m WNW of Ashbourne. Take the A52 Leek road. After 6.5m the road is met by a river on the R, turn R down a small track and park. The quarry should be above and on the L. [SG]

Wootton Lodge Crags:
OS.119 GR.095 435 [104]

Steep and generally hard climbing on these two buttresses with undercut bases. About 50ft high and VS to E4. There is a small buttress, however, with a couple of Severes on it just up to the L of the crag. Not a bad outcrop but a bit limited.

Dir: 5m E of Cheadle. From Alton go E on the B5032 for 4m to Ellastone. Just after the B5033 turn-off take a small road on the L for 0.8m. Take the L turn where the road bends sharp R, and park on the L in about 400yds at a small parking spot opposite the entrance to Wootton Lodge. A track leads off L to the crags, leading from the R side of the cave. [SG]

Wright's Rock:
OS.119 GR.058 430 [105]

A good crag in a nice position with good firm rock – firm for this area, that is. The crag is about 40ft and steep, about 10 climbs at all grades to 6a, some good easy routes around Diff. There is also more climbing to be found on **Painter's Rock**, which is about 300yds further on at the same level. Top-roping seems sensible in light of the rock's frailty. In general worth a visit.

Dir: 3m E of Cheadle. Approach: see Peakstone Inn Amphitheatre. [PSO]

CENTRAL SECTION

This section of the Peak consists entirely of limestone and is the haven for Extreme climbing in the Peak. There are good–quality easy routes, but the Extremes outnumber them by about 50 to 1. Some of the rock is quarried and some is natural. There are many suspect holds in the area, and one should come well-equipped with plenty of protection in the way of wires and stoppers on rope. Friends are useful in extreme situations, but medium-sized stoppers on rope in

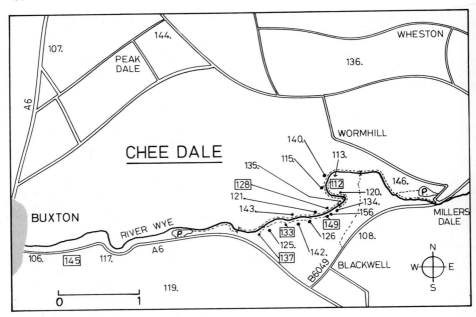

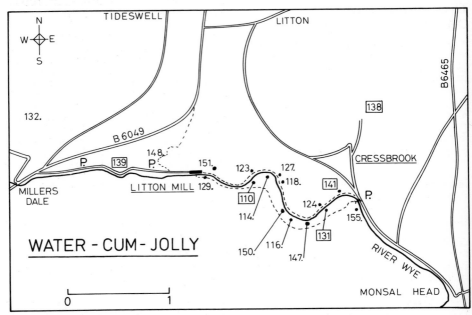

PEAK CENTRAL

the horizontal breaks are the best protection. Bolts have been used and will no doubt become a lot more popular in the future. There are many threads and slings *in situ* to make abseil descent easy; with a few more the trees at the top of the crags will last even longer. Most of the crags are shaded by trees and in late autumn are not in very good condition. The big, steep crags begin to seep water from the back in late Oct.–Nov. and unfortunately can often take to mid-June to dry out. For locating the crags of Cheedale and Water Cum Jolly see the map opposite. There is a café at Stoney Middleton where climbers often meet and are usually helpful in advising on crags and routes.

Ashwood Dale:
OS.119 GR. 076 727 [106]

About 15 routes, nearly all around VS with a couple of E1s of some merit. The cliffs unfortunately are very close to the road so they hardly present an opportunity to enjoy the countryside – perhaps in a petrol strike they will become popular. Worth a visit for the lower-grade climber.

Dir: 1m E of Buxton. Take the A6 and the crags will be seen very shortly on the L. [PST]

Bibbington Quarry:
OS.119 GR.076 769 [107]

About 20 routes here in the grades Diff to HVS. Some loose rock at the top, a spare rope can be useful in order to secure a belay there. Not bad, but nothing to rave about.

Dir: 2.5m N of Buxton. Take the A6 for 2.5m, the quarry is on the R. [PST]

Blackwell Dale:
OS.119 GR.133 729 [108]

A 50ft crag offering a few routes, about 6 on the ravine around VS and about 10 on the upper rocks with a few classic E6s. Also a few E4s worth doing. 6b fingers very useful here. Worth a visit.

Dir: 4.5m E of Buxton. Take the A6 for 4m, then turn L on to the B6049 and carry on for 0.7m to a parking space on the R. The crag is above, the ravine is down on the other side. [PCH]

Cave Dale:
OS.110 GR.150 827 [109]

A very quiet dale away from the mainstream climbing activity, often used as an alibi having spent all afternoon in the pub. There are about 50 listed routes – who cares, most look unclimbed and feel very unclimbed. Diffs, Severes and VSs, no real horrors, just vegetation and loosish rock. Most pleasant on an early, warm spring day.

Dir: 5m E of Hathersage. Take the A625 to Castleton, park in the village. Take a footpath heading directly S beneath the ruins of Peveril Castle to the dale and the crags. See Peak North map. [PST]

Central Buttress – Water Cum Jolly:
OS.119 GR.163 729 [110]

The most impressive cliff in these parts, sombre-looking with lots of dubious holds. Some leave this cliff never to return. The climbs are generally hard in the areas of obvious steepness. The routes come up to expectation and are very out-there in the upper reaches. A bold approach is necessary here, as is full competence in arranging protection. There are also some worthwhile easier routes in the R wing, VS to E1. The main cliff itself has about 25 routes at 150ft and generally 2-pitch around the E5 grade. The L wing offers about 10 exciting E3s. In general, a cool and creepy place to climb, best on a hot summer's day – have an epic in peace. Definitely worth a visit or two!

Dir: 6m E of Buxton. Approach: see Water Cum Jolly – Litton Mill. [PCH]

Cheedale:
OS.119 GR.104 726 downstream to GR.138 732 [111]

All the crags in this area of the river Wye have been listed separately, refer to the local map for individual location. A wonderful setting, usually quieter than its counterpart Water Cum Jolly downstream. Access can be made from either end, however there is a café at the E end as well as a very large car park. The crags are nearly all 15 mins away, but the walk is very pleasant. [PCH]

Chee Tor:
OS.119 GR.123 734 [112]

One of the best crags in Derbyshire, offering plenty of climbing in every grade HVS to E7. About 80 routes of 80ft. Most of the climbs stop at the break and it is usual to climb back down. Routes are generally easier than they look and can be done very quickly, it is easy to amass a total of 30 or 40 E points in a day. The rock is natural and offers good protection. Bolts are sometimes on the harder routes, if not the break offers an easy traverse and a top rope can be rigged quite easily, as well as abseil inspection. Catches the sun in the morning in winter and all day in summer, if it has been raining avoid at all costs – the rock is dry but the bottom will be a mud bath. You will find some very esoteric giant rhubarb here in late summer, a botanical feast.

Dir: 4m E of Buxton. See Cheedale map. [PCH]

Chee Tor East:
OS.119 GR.124 535 [113]

A 60ft crag just downstream from Chee Tor itself. Good climbing on about 6 routes, all around E4, 6a. It faces N, though, and is rather dark and cool. Ideal for the hot summer's day, reach by wading across the river.

Dir: 4m E of Buxton. See Cheedale map. [PCH]

Church Buttress:
OS.119 GR.165 730 [114]

This crag, on the bend in the river after Central Buttress, offers about 15 routes of limited merit in the middle grades.

Dir: 6m E of Buxton. Approach: see Water Cum Jolly – Litton Mill. [PCH]

The Cornice – Cheedale:
OS.119 GR.123 733 [115]

At one time an aid climber's domain, now has given more up to free climbing. Even so the L-hand end is nearly always wet and is perhaps best left to underhand activities. Bolts have been introduced well here and well-protected routes have become popular. There are about 40 routes here in the grades E4 and above and guidebook writers tend to go bananas with star ratings for every route. About 60ft in height and one of the most popular areas for hard routes. To the R end there are a few easier Extremes for those without 6a/b fingers. All are worth doing. Definitely worth a visit.

Dir: 4m E of Buxton. See Cheedale map. [PCH]

The Cornice – Water Cum Jolly:
OS.119 GR.167 726 [116]

This area offers some excellent 60ft E6 climbs for the strong. On the L-hand end there are some Severes and a few mid-grade Extremes. The hard routes take the obvious challenge of the main wall, which becomes quite steep at the top. Definitely worth a visit for the E6 climber. Also stays in the shade in the hot summer afternoons.

Dir: 2.5m NW of Bakewell. Approach: see Water Cum Jolly – Cressbrook. [PCH]

Cow Dale:
OS.119 GR.084 721 [117]

Not a large crag but worth a visit by the climber with 6a arms. A steep 60ft buttress with four routes, E1, 3, 4, 5. Quite safe and enjoyable.

Dir: 1m E of Buxton. Approach: see Staden Quarries, the crag is seen above the A6. [PST]

Cupid Buttress:
OS.119 GR.167 730 [118]

A good buttress offering a handful of routes for the HVS and E1 climber. The buttress is just to the R of Matto Grosso Walls with its base lower down. About 60ft high and W-facing. Worth a visit. To the R is an area known as **Psyche's Buttress**, which offers a handful of 30–60ft climbs in the lower grades around Severe and Diff. Not a lot to rave about though.

Dir: 6m E of Buxton. Approach: see Water Cum Jolly – Litton Mill. [PCH]

Deepdale:
OS.119 GR.097 712 [119]

There are buttresses all the way up Deepdale and to mention any but **Secret Garden Buttress** would definitely waste space. All the climbing here is in the lower grades as the rock tends to support small holds for a very short time only. There are about 10 different crags up the dale where a very pleasant walk can be had. Buttresses range from 20 to 70ft. Secret Garden Buttress has about 15 routes, Diff to HVS. Worth a visit with caution. A very pleasant spot getting the morning sun, wander at leisure.

Dir: 2.5m ESE of Buxton. Take the A6 and after passing under 4 railway bridges park in a car park immediately on the L. Cross to the S side of the road and walk to the quarry. Take the footpath going S for about 100yds. Be careful not to carry on to the dale you see in front but go up and R on a track, past a mud lake, and then into the real Deepdale which lies to the R. The SGB is about 1m away up the dale. [PST]

Dog's Dinner Buttress:
OS.119 GR.125 732   [120]

An indifferent buttress, offering some reasonably scary climbing. In need of lots of bolts. Several 5a pitches and a couple of E4s, all about 60ft. Being dangerous, and with Chee Tor nearby, sees very little traffic.

Dir: 4m E of Buxton. See Cheedale map. [PCH]

The Embankment:
OS.119 GR.119 728   [121]

Some of the rock here is suspect, whatever anybody tells you. About 10 routes, 60ft high and mostly in the E3 to E5 grades. A few top-roping bolts would be needed to make this a popular spot, even so it is sheltered and S-facing.

Dir: 4m E of Buxton. See Cheedale map. [PCH]

Grin Low:
OS.119 GR.046 723   [122]

A small 70ft crag offering 3 HVSs and a V Diff. Of limited interest.

Dir: 0.5m SSW of Buxton. Take the A53 S from Buxton, turn L at the country park and follow the road all the way to the car park at the end. Here walk to a pool in a quarry where a slab is beside a tower. Climb if you feel attracted, if not go to the pub. See Peak North Map. [PST]

Jackdaw Point:
OS.119 GR.164 732   [123]

The first largish buttress on the area known as **The Upper Circle**, 40–60ft high, mostly Extreme climbing. About 15 routes, VS to E1, with a few desperates as well for good measure. Little of great merit here.

Dir: 6m E of Buxton. Approach: see Water Cum Jolly – Litton Mill. [PCH]

Lammergeyer Area:
OS.119 GR.169 728   [124]

A reasonable area considering the undergrowth. About 50ft high, offering half a dozen E5s. Worth a visit if all the routes on Rubicon and Moat done. Catches the morning sun in winter quite nicely. To the R about half-way to Rubicon is **Ivy Buttress** with a handful of Extremes, mostly hard ones. To the L on the bend of the river are **Strip Search** and **The Keep**, both areas offering 30–60ft routes of no great merit in the middle grades.

Dir: 4.5m NW of Bakewell. Approach: see Water Cum Jolly – Cressbrook. [PCH]

The Lifts:
OS.119 GR.117 728   [125]

A series of three tiers which, linked together, give some long and interesting expeditions of some 200ft. Most of the 25 routes are in the HVS –E1 category. To the L is a pinnacle known as **The Obelisk**, offering a handful of 30ft V Diffs and Severes.

Dir: 3.5m E of Buxton. See Cheedale Map. [PCH]

The Long Wall:
OS.119 GR.122 728   [126]

A fair crag with some good, hard routes around the 6b grade. About 15 routes up to 70ft – a couple of HVSs, about 5 E2s and other E4–E5s.

Dir: 4m E of Buxton. See Cheedale map. [PCH]

Matto Grosso:
OS.119 GR.167 731   [127]

A good little area in the Upper Circle, offering the classic two routes Mandrake and Deception at E4, and a handful of other hardish routes to keep you occupied. About 70ft and the best rock in the area. The area to the L is generally known as **Christmas Cracks**, an area with about 20 routes in the low E grades and not taken seriously.

Dir: 6m E of Buxton. Approach: see Water Cum Jolly – Litton Mill. [PCH]

Max Buttress:
OS.119 GR.122 730   [128]

A very popular crag with the E5–6b limestone addict. About 25 routes, of which 15 are either E5 or 6a. There are a couple of easy Extremes but this is not the crag on which to teach beginners. About 50ft and sunny aspect. Most of the routes are called Max something-or-other and are worth doing.

Dir: 4m E of Buxton. See Cheedale map. [PCH]

Mill Buttress:
OS.119 GR.160 729   [129]

A rather dark and oppressive crag on the S bank of the river Wye overlooking the old Mill. There are about 30 routes from VS to E1. I will refrain from commenting on its worthiness for a visit.

Dir: 6m E of Buxton. Approach: see Water Cum Jolly – Litton Mill. [PCH]

Miller's Dale:
OS.119 GR.150 732   [130]

The climbing in Miller's Dale is most famous on Raven Tor, listed separately. The pub here, The Angler's Rest, is very good on a horrible, wet day if rained off. There are some small outcrops on the S bank which remain dark and in the shade. Those who seek such cliffs will be left to their own devices – may they climb in peace.

Dir: 6m E of Buxton. [PCH]

Moat Buttress:
OS.119 GR.169 728   [131]

A very impressive buttress with about 30 routes in the top Extreme grade, E5, 6b being the standard of most climbs, some easy and others hard. The lake has disappeared beneath the crag and might reappear at some time, if so large stepping stones could well be the answer. About 100ft high and a must for the hard climber, one of the best crags in the area. N-facing and a bit chilly on winter's days, especially for the second belaying next to water, good duvets essential. If the routes prove too hard, take punishment on the **Black Buttress** to the L of the crag, easy Extreme climbing with no merit at all.

Dir: 2.4m NW of Bakewell. Approach: see Water Cum Jolly – Cressbrook. [PCH]

Monk's Dale:
OS.119 GR.135 737   [132]

A small 30ft crag up this quiet dale offers only three climbs at HVS, E2, E3. Quiet and secluded.

Dir: 6m E of Buxton. Go to Miller's Dale on the B6049 and turn off to The Angler's Rest pub. From behind the pub a public footpath runs N up the dale, follow this for about 10 mins and the crag is seen on the L. [PCH]

Moving Buttress:
OS.119 GR.118 727   [133]

Quite a lot of climbing here. About 40 routes of various difficulties from Severe to 6c, but mostly in the lower grades with a good deal of VS climbs. Little around E1–E3, either easy or hard. Some of the climbs worth a visit, especially for the HVS leader.

Dir: 3.5m E of Buxton. See Cheedale map. [PCH]

Nettle Buttress:
OS.119 GR.124 731   [134]

A good crag offering plenty in the way of hard routes. About 20 routes at all Extreme grades with a couple of desperates, too hard to wander on to by mistake. A good, small crag, about 60ft high. Stays in the shade a long time in summer.

Dir: 4m E of Buxton. See Cheedale map. [PCH]

The Nook:
OS.119 GR.124 731   [135]

The crag in the dale for the Arnolds. Quite a few have been here over the years and with so much strength to spare have pulled off many of the holds, making the routes now rather difficult. Big roofs give about 10 climbs, 30ft, in the Extreme grades. Santiano E4, the original route, is the best excursion into the horizontal.

Dir: 4m E of Buxton. See Cheedale map. [PCH]

Peter Dale:
OS.119 GR.128 753 [136]

About 10 routes here, Diff to E3, on a small 40ft outcrop. A pleasant setting, not bad on a cold winter's day since it is S-facing.

Dir: 4.5m ENE of Buxton. From Tideswell take the small road to Wheston, carry straight on down into the bottom of the dale. Park here and walk down the dale for about 0.5m to a bend where the crag lies. [PST]

Plum Buttress:
OS.119 GR.115 726 [137]

One of the most impressive pieces of rock in Derbyshire. Some classic routes here, Big Plum E5 up the middle and Sirplum E1 up the R-hand side. About 15 routes, at 200ft in all grades E1 upwards with the addition of one classic VS. The climbing is very out-there, and leaders with leg-wobble problems should have at least three Shredded Wheat for breakfast. NW-facing and exposed, ideal for a summer's evening to round the day off in the setting sun. Should exhaust you completely.

Dir: 3.5m E of Buxton. See Cheedale map. [PCH]

Ravensdale:
OS.119 GR.173 737 [138]

A 150ft limestone crag where the view and situation far exceed the actual climbing. There are about 70 routes, of which 30 are worth doing. These, however, are very good, though some-what loose in places. A good crag in general, and a very good crag for the VS to E1 leader. There are easy routes as well, but only a few hard ones.

Dir: 6m NW of Bakewell. Take the A6 to Ashford in the Water, turn R on to the B6001, after 1.4m turn L down a hill to Monsal Dale and Cress-brook. After 1m take R fork up the hill, after 300yds a road leads off R to Ravensdale cottages in 500yds, park. The crag is seen on the hill to the R, a footpath leads across the dale and up to the crag. [PST]

Raven Tor:
OS.119 GR.151 732 [139]

If you are a very good climber forget this one, it is reserved for the super-élite climbers. At E6 it is the best crag in Derbyshire, about 30 routes reaching up to 200ft. The crag is very impressive and quite steep, most find it tiring to the fingers and the arms. The protection is generally very good, it has to be since this cliff easily clocks up the most flying time in Derbyshire. The home of Revelations, Indecent Exposure, Body Machine, The Prow, and the really easy Sardine E5, 6b. Most use this as the descent route. Best of luck to visiting climbers of reputation, on sight here is very difficult.

Dir: 6m E of Buxton. From Miller's Dale take the small road running downstream beside the river to the crag unmistakable on the L after about 0.6m. [PCH]

Rhubarb Buttress:
OS.119 GR.123 735 [140]

Very similar in nature to The Cornice with about 20 routes, either 5c or 6b. Only 60ft high, but the hard routes pack in a lot of excitement.

Dir: 4m E of Buxton. See Cheedale map. [PCH]

Rubicon Wall:
OS.119 GR.172 729 [141]

A very popular spot for walkers and climbers. The climbs are about 60ft in length and in all grades E3 upwards, with the exception of a couple of VSs. The main wall offers 15 routes of E5 and above with most routes involving the use of smallish holds, i.e. 6c. There is a big over-hanging section at the R-hand end, offering some classic steep pitches, Rubicon E3 is the obvious line and an interesting solo. To the L end are a host of E3s, none of which are really easy, and the classic Honeymoon Blues E5 from the hanging thread. A must for the hard climber. It used to be scenic, but now with so much traffic it looks quite drab – a pity.

Dir: 4.5m NW of Bakewell. Approach: see Water Cum Jolly – Cressbrook. [PCH]

Runyon's Corner:
OS.119 GR.120 728 [142]

The crag on the river for the VS leader with a machete. About 20 routes, about 60ft, of which most are VS and well vegetated. Nevertheless good fun can be had here by the enthusiastic.

Dir: 4m E of Buxton. See Cheedale map. [PCH]

The Sidings:
OS.119 GR.117 728 [143]

A fairly good crag that is sheltered and catches the sun in winter. About 15 routes in the VS to E2 category. Also a couple of very hard desperates in the centre of the crag. Worth a visit.

Dir: 4m E of Buxton. See Cheedale map. [PCH]

Smalldale Quarry:
OS.119 GR.097 771 [144]

A large and steep quarry with questionable rock. About 100ft high and offering some 20 routes spread equally from VS up to E5.

Dir: 3m NE of Buxton. Leave Buxton N on the A6 and after 1.4m turn off R to Peak Dale. Smalldale is about 400yds further on and the quarry is on the R. [PST]

Staden Quarry: Restriction
OS.119 GR.080 723 [145]

Permission to climb must first be obtained since the quarries are privately owned. An access arrangement to this effect has been agreed by the BMC. About 60 routes in the upper quarry and 15 in the lower quarry, up to about 60ft on steepish limestone. Some like it here, others definitely do not. Routes at VS upwards to E2, a few desperates for the levitation experts as well.

Dir: 1m E of Buxton. Take the A6 E under two railway bridges, then in 200yds follow a narrow track on the R up to Cowdale Hall. Visit and seek permission from Mr Morton to climb in the quarries. [PST]

Strawberry Rocks:
OS.119 GR.131 734 [146]

A crag of questionable quality. About 20 routes, VS to E4, some solid, others not.

Dir: 4m E of Buxton. Park as for Cheedale E end. Walk along the disused railway track and branch off R before crossing over the river, the crag is reached very shortly. There is also an area here known as **Strawberry Quarry**, not to be recommended. [PCH]

Swamp Wall:
OS.119 GR.168 726 [147]

Not one of the best areas to climb in Derbyshire. About 10 routes, 100ft, around HVS. Vegetated, loose and insect-prone. For the masochistic.

Dir: 2.5m NW of Bakewell. Approach: see Water Cum Jolly – Cressbrook. [PCH]

Tideswell Dale:
OS.119 GR.154 736 [148]

There are about 5 crags in this dale on either side. All offer climbing of reasonable quality, but hardly worth a trip to Derbyshire. Most of the climbs are around 40ft with the exception of **Buffoon Buttress**, which is around 60ft and has about 10 climbs at around E1.

Dir: 6m E of Buxton. From Tideswell go S on the B6049 to Miller's Dale, turn sharp L and go down the small road past The Angler's Rest for 0.8m and past Raven Tor. Here a dale runs up N past a youth hostel. In about 200yds **The Enclosure** is on the L and **Alpha Buttress** is on the R. The dale turns R after this and in about 200yds there is **Buffoon Buttress** on the R. About 100yds further up on the L is **Beltonville Buttress** (easier routes) and a footpath leads off on the R to **Freda's Buttress**. [PCH]

Two Tier Buttress – Cheedale:
OS.119 GR.122 728 [149]

A very good crag in a beautiful setting for the Hard Extreme climber. About 40 routes here in the 6b, c category and ranging from E3 to E6, a few easier ways up the cliff but poor lines. About 100ft in parts, though often the climbing is in short, very hard sections. The best routes are the hard ones, the cliff has seen many casualties and many more near-misses. If it is polished it is also usually well protected, improving with bolts.

Dir: 4m E of Buxton. See Cheedale map. [PCH]

Two Tier Buttress – Water Cum Jolly:
OS.119 GR.165 729 [150]

An obviously named cliff with half a dozen routes around VS to keep the bumbler happy and content for many an hour. The climbs are of little distinction, but an alternative on a hot summer's afternoon.

Dir: 6m E of Buxton. Approach: see Water Cum Jolly – Litton Mill. [PCH]

Vision Buttress:
OS.119 GR.162 731   [151]

Only two routes here but one is The Vision, E6 and a classic, well protected by bolts and hence popular. About 60ft, S-facing and pleasant. Worth a visit.

Dir: 6m E of Buxton. Approach: see Water Cum Jolly – Litton Mill. [PCH]

Water Cum Jolly:
OS.119 GR.164 730   [152]

This must be the best name in Britain for a climbing area. The climbing here is quite different to that of Cheedale, though still natural limestone. There are a few crags with similar names so W-C-J is placed after them. For the uninitiated, Central Buttress is referred to as Water Cum Jolly and all the other crags are referred to by name. Confused? You will be. The three areas of note are Central Buttress, Rubicon Wall and Moat Buttress. All offer very hard climbing and stay dryish in the rain. [PCH]

Water Cum Jolly – Litton Mill:
[153]

Dir: 6m E of Buxton is Miller's Dale. Go down the small road to Litton Mill in 1.4m, where footpaths lead downstream. One can cross here for crags on the S side, but then locating the crags becomes difficult. It is more practical on a first visit to wade the river if you like what you see! [PCH]

Water Cum Jolly – Cressbrook:
[154]

Dir: 2.3m NW of Bakewell. Take the A6 to Ashford in the Water. Here take the B6465 towards Wardlow, after 1.3m at Monsal Head turn L down a steep road by a pub to Cressbrook

Dale. After 0.8m park by an old, large, falling-down house. Here a footpath leads off through a stone-cutting yard to the river and the crags run W from here. [PCH]

Waterfall Crag:
OS.119 GR.172 725   [155]

Not the driest of crags. About 40ft, offering a handful of routes in the middle to harder Extremes. Very easy access.

Dir: 2.2m NW of Bakewell. Approach: see Water Cum Jolly – Cressbrook. [PCH]

Waterline Buttress:
OS.119 GR.123 729   [156]

A small 60ft buttress down to the L of Two Tier Buttress, offering a handful of routes in the E3– E5 grade. Above the crag is the Upper Tier, which has about 6 more E5 desperates of around 40ft. A good area for the E5, 6b climber, top-roping very advisable though.

Dir: 4m E of Buxton. See Cheedale map. [PCH]

Winnats Pass: Restriction:
OS.110 GR.138 827   [157]

The pass is owned by the National Trust which does not wish climbing to take place. A sensible suggestion: I have witnessed a rock descend from the side of the pass and crash into the road, which is used by cars. However, if the road is ever closed to cars there should not be a problem. There are some very enjoyable ridge climbs at Diff, and high up on the L are a couple of bolt-protected E5s, classics of their kind in a superb position. The crags are somewhat disappointing, though, when reached. Lots of stinging nettles at the bases.

Dir: 5m E of Hathersage. Drive to Castleton on the A625 – lovely pubs – then take the small road to Speedwell Cavern and Winnats Pass. See Peak North map. [PST]

PEAK NORTH

This is essentially the area north of Buxton. The national park is at its highest here, reaching over 2,000ft. The cliffs, however, are at their lowest and rarely do pitches exceed 80ft. The climbing is entirely gritstone, of which half faces north and is often damp and inhospitable.

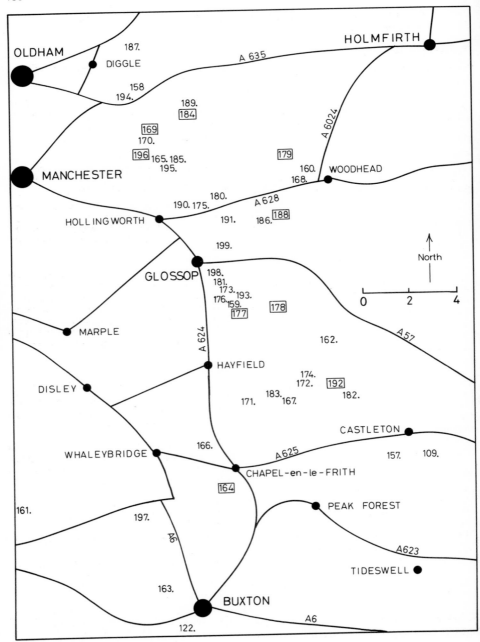

PEAK NORTH

In the good summer months there is plenty of scope for enjoyment, particularly in the grades below Extreme.

Alderman Rocks:
OS.110 GR.015 045   [158]

Some pleasant climbing to be found on this natural gritstone edge. About a dozen or so routes at 30–70ft in the lower grades, with a classic VS. Plenty of scrambling around, with a southerly aspect. This crag is good for beginners.

Dir: 6m E of Oldham. Take the A635 from Mossley to Dovestone reservoir, just past Greenfield, car park on the R. Walk up the road for 400yds, then take the public footpath on the L which leads up the hill L and to the crag. By following the footpath around to overlook Uppermill, one finds **The Druid Stones**, a small buttress offering a few climbs, and the quarries known as **Pots and Pans**. These offer a dozen or so routes in the lower grades, pleasant walking and scrambling generally. By continuing up the A635 for a mile past the car park one arrives at Upperwood quarries on the L. [CV]

The Amphitheatre – Kinder:
OS.110 GR.081 889   [159]

A pleasant crag with about 40 routes, 30–90ft in all grades, a good selection of Diff and VS climbs. Catches the sun, but in windy weather the waterfall makes everything quite damp. Not a bad crag if one is selective.

Dir: 3.5m SE of Glossop. Approach: see Kinder Downfall. [KB]

Bareholme Crag:
OS.110 GR.062 010   [160]

A superb small gritstone crag, ideal for beginners and those who enjoy climbing only to the standard of Severe. About 30 routes, 20–40ft, in the lower grades around Just Hard Very Difficult Almost. W-facing and in a very pleasant situation. One can spy with binoculars the tigers at Laddow romping up the Severes.

Dir: 4.5m NNE of Glossop. Approach: see Laddow. [KB]

Beeston Quarry:
OS.118 GR.934 778   [161]

The access situation here has always been unclear, proceed with tact and caution. The quarry is about 60ft in height and offers about 30 routes at all grades.

Dir: In the centre of Bollington. From the B5091 take the small road on the L just after passing under the aqueduct. The road turns sharply up the steep hill, Beeston Brow, and in about 100yds the quarry is in the woods to the R. [KB]

Blackden Edge:
OS.110 GR.127 588   [162]

Climbing to be found on a 30ft gritstone pinnacle with a handful of routes around the Severe grade. The buttress is situated just below the rocky escarpment of Blackden Edge. At 2,000ft and N-facing.

Dir: 7m ESE of Glossop. Take the A57 over Snake Pass, through the trees to Snake Inn. At 1.2m further on is a footpath leading off up to the R over a footbridge. Follow this up Blackden Brook for a few mins, or carry on up the valley to the top then traverse back L along the edge to the outcrop – 25 mins, but easier. [KB]

The Buxton Boss:
OS.119 GR.041 757   [163]

A small rock pinnacle about 35ft high with a few scrambles on it. Worth a visit on a nice day to get away from the beaten track.

Dir: 2m NW of Buxton. Take the A5002 for about 1m, park. Take a small track which leads up to a public footpath across the moor, the pinnacle is reached in about 15 mins. [KB]

Castle Naze:
OS.119 GR.054 785   [164]

A gritstone outcrop with about 40 routes up to VS. An excellent spot, but at about 1,500ft and open to strong W winds. Best on a nice summer's day. The crag is on private ground and climbers are asked to act responsibly. Worth a visit, especially for beginners.

Dir: 1.5m SSW of Chapel en le Frith. Take the A6 W for about 1m then turn off L to Combs. At the village turn L and go up the hill for about 0.6m, the crag is seen up on the R. [KB]

Charnel Stones:
OS.110 GR.027 027 [165]

Some good rocks at 1,500ft, offering a score of climbs in all grades to HVS, 20–70ft and W-facing. Afternoon spot.

Dir: 5.5m E of Oldham. Approach: see Wimberry Rocks. [CV]

Cracken Edge Quarries:
OS.110 GR.037 837 [166]

A 40ft quarry situated high up on the hillside and facing E, a bitter place in winter. About 20 climbs in the easy grades. In general of questionable merit.

Dir: 2.5m NW of Chapel en le Frith. Leave the town N on the A624 then shortly turn off on to the B6062 to the village of Chinley. Where the road bends L take the small road on the R, which almost immediately turns L. Follow this up the steep hill for 0.5m, park. Here a footpath runs N along the ridge of the hill and to the rocks in about 10 mins. [KB]

Crowden Clough Face:
OS.110 GR.096 873 [167]

Some excellent gritstone here offers a dozen routes up to HVS on SE-facing cliffs, up to 80ft and very enjoyable. 2,000ft high with superb views. There is also some climbing to be had on **Crowden Tower**, to the L of the crag, about 40ft and a handful of Diff–Severe climbs. The jump across the top always provides entertainment. Worth a visit.

Dir: 4.5m NNE of Chapel en le Frith. Take the A625 E for 3m to the turn off L to Edale. After 1.3m up the hill there is a small road on the L to Upper Booth. Take this under the railway to the end at a parking spot. From here follow the R of the two valleys in front. The path leads up by the river through the trees then goes up Crowden Brook. The cliffs are at the head of the valley on the L, reached in about 25 mins. [KB]

Crowden Great Quarry:
OS.110 GR.075 998 [168]

As far as Peak District quarries go, this is not one of the better ones, and in view of the other climbing in the area it is best avoided. It is, however, quite large and may appeal to a certain breed of climber! About 50 routes across the grades up to 100ft.

Dir: 4m NE of Glossop. From Tintwistle take the A629 4m E to the tiny hamlet of Crowden. The quarry is up behind the youth hostel about 200yds away. The smaller quarry further down the hillside is called **Brockholes Quarry**, with a handful of routes. [KB]

Dovestones Edge:
OS.110 GR.025 040 [169]

A very good edge, offering about 70 climbs on good rough gritstone. All grades to E2, with lots of Diffs as well as VSs. NW aspect at 1,400ft makes this a crag for the better days and can offer unrivalled quality on a late summer's evening at sunset. Worth a visit.

Dir: 6m E of Oldham. Take the A635 out of Greenfield to a car park on the R after 1m. From here go down and cross the reservoir, and bear round to the R for 200yds. The crag is straight ahead up the hillside which can be reached direct. By carrying on around the hill at the bottom for 400yds, one can approach the crag by way of Dovestones Quarries. These may be of interest, only 5 more mins. [CV]

Dovestones Quarries:
OS.110 GR.024 037 [170]

Steep, dirty, loose, lichenous quarried faces offering about 100 interesting routes, 40–160ft, in all grades, particularly the more serious, little in the easier grades. Worth a passing glance.

Dir: 6m E of Oldham. Approach: see Dovestones Edge. [CV]

Edale Rocks:
OS.110 GR.079 867 [171]

A couple of outcrops of weathered gritstone, rising to about 30ft. A dozen routes mostly in the lower grades around Diff, but there are some more taxing problems for the enthusiastic. SE-facing and at 1,800ft, a crag for a fine summer's morning. There are also a handful of easy climbs on **Edale Cross Rocks**, which are about 300yds to the S. These climbs are even shorter, but worth a visit for the lower-grade climber.

Dir: 4m NNE of Chapel en le Frith. Take the A625 for 3m to a small road leading off L towards

Edale. After 1.3m up the steep hill there is a small road off to the L to Upper Booth, take this under the railway to a parking spot at the end. There are two valleys leading off, take the L one, which is also the alternative start to the Pennine Way. After 0.6m, 10 mins. walk, you can take the footpath going up L in a zigzag to Edale Cross Rocks at the top. For The Pagoda direct, go up the R side of the valley from here to the crag, which comes into view after about 15 mins. The best trip is to go to Edale Cross Rocks first, then around to Edale Rocks, lunch at The Noe Stool, and finish up at The Pagoda. A great summer day for the Severe leader. [KB]

Fox Holes:
OS.110 GR.108 870 [172]

A good score of climbs in the Diff–V Diff grades on very good gritstone, 20–40ft with just a couple of hard climbs for the VS tigers. About 2,000ft up and facing NE, chilly. Worth a visit on a good day, especially for the V Diff leader.

Dir: 5.5m NE of Chapel en le Frith. Approach: see Upper Tor, 35 mins. [KB]

Great Buttress:
OS.110 GR.083 887 [173]

This 80ft gritstone buttress offers a score of routes in all grades to Extreme. Most are very good and well worth doing, there are some classic VS routes. The cliff enjoys a westerly aspect and commands what must be the best position on Kinder. A must.

Dir: 3.5m SE of Glossop. Approach: see Kinder Downfall. [KB]

Grinds Brook Towers:
OS.110 GR.107 873 [174]

Some towers either side of the brook at the top R-hand side of Grinds Brook. About 20–40ft in height, offering little in the way of real climbing, but worthy scrambling and Diff climbing.

Dir: 5.5m NE of Chapel en le Frith. See Upper Tor. 35 mins. [KB]

John Henry Quarry:
OS.110 GR.027 976 [175]

A vegetation-free quarry with 25 routes of lower grades. Quite solid, 40–80ft high, gritstone.

Dir: 2.5m N of Glossop. From Hollingworth take the A628 to Tintwhistle. Go through the village parallel to the main road, just before joining the main road again is the quarry on the L. [KB]

Kinder Buttress:
OS.110 GR.078 888 [176]

An excellent 100ft crag to the L of The Amphitheatre. Gritstone and offering a dozen routes from Severe upwards. Worth climbing on.

Dir: 3.4m SE of Glossop. Approach: see Kinder Downfall. [KB]

Kinder Downfall:
OS.110 GR.082 889 [177]

This area offers plenty of climbing in the lower grades, but at 2,000ft is predominantly a summer crag. The popular walk, the Pennine Way, nearby makes it rather busy with walkers and one should always be aware of the possibility of rocks kicked or even thrown over the edge.

Dir: 3.5m SE of Glossop. Take the A625 S to the village of Hayfield, turn off L into the village and follow the small road around L to Kinder reservoir after 1m. The crags are about 1.5m behind and slightly to the R of the back of the reservoir. From here the best approach is from the L. Take a footpath up the valley from the back L-hand corner of the reservoir. This goes up William Clough to a col at the top in about 30 mins. The first crag to the R is Mill Hill Rocks, then in about 600yds is Upper Western Buttress. Carrying on around one reaches Kinder Downfall, about 1m from the col. Here Amphitheatre Crag is just to the R looking out, and Western Buttress further R still. Carrying on is Great Buttress almost directly below. [KB]

Kinder Northern Edges:
OS.110 GR.093 898 [178]

This area is dealt with as one for the purposes of this guide, since it represents one continuous edge offering very similar climbing. About 3m in total length, with about 200 routes in the lower grades on mostly good gritstone. The cliffs face N in most places and attract a lot of lichen and any bad weather that is going – 2,000ft high and always in a cool airstream. Not a lot in favour really: buy someone the guide to it for Christmas and you will get it back next year. The routes, though, are quite good and if a high settles over the Peak in summer with many nice days a trip up here can be very enjoyable. It is not a crowded area. Climbs are 20–70ft and on the whole quite strenuous. The well-known parts of the edge are called **Ashop Edge**, R-hand side, and **Chinese Wall** to the L-hand end, with **Misty Buttresses** at the turn in the crag. An early start would give the benefit of having the morning sun at the latter.

Dir: 4m SE of Glossop. Take the A57 Snake Pass road E for 4m to the Snake Inn. About 400yds further on the R is a footpath over a footbridge, which runs up Fair Brook to the crags in about 40 mins. [KB]

Laddow Rocks:
OS.110 GR.056 014   [179]

A great gritstone crag of tradition in a splendid situation and often very quiet. About 70 routes to HVS, of which nearly all are worth doing. The climbs in parts reach over 100ft but in most cases 60ft is the usual route length. The cliff faces E and morning is the best time in which to appreciate the climbing Laddow offers. At about 1,500ft it can get very hostile in the winter.

Dir: 4.5m NNE of Glossop. From Tintwhistle take the A628 E 3.5m to the tiny hamlet of Crowden. A valley here leads off to the L. Take this by public footpath on the L-hand side of the stream, in fact the Pennine Way. This goes up the L of the two valleys, after 600yds a crag will be seen on the L. This is **Black Tor**, which offers 8 reasonable routes of 50ft. After 1m is **Rake's Rocks** on the L, which is generally loose and vegetated although it sports a dozen or so routes. After 2m from the main road you reach Laddow, unmistakably, on the L. A good pair of waterproof walking boots is useful for this walk. Directly across the valley at this point is **Bareholme Crag**. 35 mins.

Lad's Leap:
OS.110 GR.052 997   [180]

About a dozen routes on this natural gritstone outcrop, 30–90ft and of the lower grades around Diff–Severe. SW-facing at 1500ft, and sheltered from the N winds. A nice relaxing spot.

Dir: 3.5m NNE of Glossop. From Tintwhistle on the A628 go E up the valley to the plantation on the L after 1m, park at the end of this on the L. The crag is high above, directly at the top of the valley to the N. [KB]

Mill Hill Rocks:
OS.110 GR.068 898   [181]

Quite good climbing to be found on this W-facing cliff. About 25 routes, 30–70ft, up to VS but mainly in the Diff and Severe grades. The climbing is similar to that of Western Buttress.

Dir: 3.5m SE of Glossop. Approach: see Kinder Downfall. [KB]

Nether Tor:
OS.110 GR.124 876   [182]

Very good climbing on this S-facing gritstone crag up at 2,000ft. A good score and ten routes in the lower grades, 30–80ft. Always worth a visit.

Dir: 5.5m NE of Chapel en le Frith. Approach: see Upper Tor, 25 mins. [KB]

The Pagoda:
OS.110 GR.091 868   [183]

A fine outcrop of good, solid gritstone in a lovely, S-facing setting, offering the best climbing in the immediate area. A handful of 50ft routes, Severe to VS, take the obvious lines. In between this outcrop and Edale Rocks on the W side of the valley is **The Noe Stool**, an interesting, mushroom-shaped rock offering plenty of fun and scrambling. All at about 2,000ft, needs a good, sunny day. Not to be missed.

Dir: 4m NNE of Chapel en le Frith. Approach: see Edale Rocks. [KB]

Ravenstones:
OS.110 GR.036 048   [184]

Some very good gritstone offers excellent climbing here. Over 100 routes in the lower grades up to VS. Very good for the beginners, well-protected climbs, 30–60ft, in a nice position. At 1,500ft and N-facing, worth a visit on a nice summer's day, vile in winter.

Dir: 7m E of Oldham. Take the A635 through Greenfield for 1m to the car park at Dovestones reservoir. Walk up past the two smaller reservoirs into the top valley. Ravenstones are up to the R and Standing Stones are to the L, both reached in about 40 mins. from the car park. [CV]

Robinson's Rocks:
OS.110 GR.029 019   [185]

About 15 climbs of 30ft in the lower grades, with plenty of Diffs, V Diffs. Southerly aspect, at 1,500ft in pleasant surroundings. Worth a visit, especially for beginners.

Dir: 5.3m ESE of Oldham. Approach: see Wimberry Rocks. [CV]

Rollick Stones:
OS.110 GR.081 985   [186]

A broken crag with about 30 routes, especially in the lower grades. Gritstone, 1,500ft and N-facing. Of limited interest.

Dir: 3m NE of Glossop. Approach: see Shining Clough. [KB]

Running Hill Pits:
OS.110 GR.018 075   [187]

Some gloomy quarries, about 8 in total, offering some 50 routes in all grades and of limited merit. NW-facing.

Dir: 6m ENE of Oldham. From Uppermill take a small road to Diggle, cross over the railway and go up the valley which leads to Diggle reservoir. The crags are up on the R and are reached in about 15 mins. [CV]

Shining Clough:
OS.110 GR.098 986   [188]

The major outcrop of the Longendale area. A gritstone crag, 20–80ft, offering about 80 good routes in all grades to the Extremes. Extensive and very good climbing to be found here. The crag is steep, in most parts, N-facing and at 1,600ft. Worth a summer visit.

Dir: 3.5m NE of Glossop. Take the B6105 NE out of Glossop for 4m until 200yds before it joins the A628 at Crowden, park before the road does a sharp L. From here take the track on the R leading up the hillside to the edge. Shining Clough is at the far L-hand end, alternatively bear to the R-hand end of the edge to the Rollick Stones. [KB]

Standing Stones:
OS.110 GR.040 053   [189]

A very isolated position, but with the wind coming from the N the main road can be clearly heard. Gritstone and mostly around 50ft, offering 30 or so routes in the middle grades, Severe upwards. A few Diffs but an excellent crag for the Hard Severe leader. SE-facing and pleasant, but peat soil often washes down on to the crag making many of the routes dirtyish.

Dir: 7m E of Oldham. Approach: Ravenstones, 40 mins walk. [CV]

Tintwhistle Knarr Quarry: Restriction
OS.110 GR.043 992   [190]

It is believed that access to this quarry is forbidden. The climbing here, though, is reported to be very good indeed, especially in the central section. Faces S at about 1,250ft. There are some two score routes listed here in the lower grades of VS and HVS, 30–80ft on very high-quality gritstone. More of a place for the VS climber upwards.

Dir: 3.5m N of Glossop. From the village of Tintwhistle carry on up the A628 for 1m to a forest plantation on the L. Here a track leads up the L-hand side to the top, the crag is about 700yds over on the R. [KB]

Torside Clough:
OS.110 GR.065 972   [191]

A NE-facing and somewhat green crag offering about 40 routes in all grades, weather permitting. Natural gritstone with sharp edges and generally sound in nature. For the sunny morning after a dry spell.

Dir: 2m NE of Glossop. Take the B6105 NE out of Glossop, after 1.5m the road makes a few tight bends, carry on for 0.8m to a sharp L bend just after the reservoir dam. Here a track leads straight on to a house. Take the public footpath up to the R, which leads up the ridge and to the crag in about 20 mins. [KB]

Upper Tor:
OS.110 GR.113 876   [192]

A brilliant gritstone crag, offering about 30 climbs Diff to Extreme, 50–70ft. There are lots of climbs in the Hard Severe grade, even so most routes are worth doing. At 2,000ft, but S-facing with a nice, sheltered aspect and gets any sun that is going. The best crag on South Kinder, worth a visit. To the far L-hand end of the crag is the cliff known as **Far Upper Tor**, about 10 climbs around the Severe grade but on rock of a lesser merit.

Dir: 5.5m NE of Chapel en le Frith. Take the A625 and after about 3m turn L up the small road to Edale. Park in the car park – as the start of the Pennine Way it gets fairly busy here with walkers. Walk up the road and the valley directly to the N (Pennine Way). About 500yds after the trees on the L the crag is directly up to the R. For Fox Holes and Grinds Brook Towers carry on up to the end of the valley, the crags are to the L and R respectively. For Nether Tor the path splits at the end of the trees coming up from Edale, take the valley to the R here to the top, the crags are just on the L. To the R and around the spur are three pinnacles, **The Sentinels**, offering Diffs, leading to **Ringing Rodger Buttress**. [KB]

Upper Western Buttress:
OS.110 GR.073 892   [193]

Some broken buttresses, offering reasonable climbing on rock which is suspect in places. All S-facing, about a dozen climbs, 20–100ft. The centre section provides the most interest with the central chimney, Extinguisher Chimney, worth doing at VS. There is a crag below, **Lower Western Buttress**, which offers a handful of 40ft Diffs on very good rock, worth the excursion.

Dir: 3.5m SE of Glossop. Approach: see Kinder Downfall. [KB]

Upperwood Quarries:
OS.110 GR.022 060   [194]

About 30 routes, VS upwards, in this gritstone quarry. Worth a visit.

Dir: 7m E of Oldham. Approach: see Alderman Edge. [CV]

Wilderness Rocks:
OS.110 GR.025 016   [195]

A crag with about 30 unpleasant routes in the easier grades, 50ft, but mostly lichen- and peat-covered. Worth a visit for the masochist and the ardent gloom-doom climber.

Dir: 5.5m ESE of Oldham. Approach: see Wimberry Rocks. [CV]

Wimberry Rocks:
OS.110 GR.016 024   [196]

Most probably regarded as the best outcrop in the Chew valley–Dovestones reservoir area. N-facing crag, offering about 50 routes in all grades, 20–70ft, on very good, firm gritstone. The best routes are the hard ones, but this should not deter the V Diff leader who can also enjoy this crag. Best on a fine summer's day when the rays are too strong.

Dir: 5.5m ESE of Oldham. From Greenfield on the A625 turn R just past the George and Dragon Hotel to a car park after 0.7m at the end of the reservoir, and a mountain rescue post. A path leads off to the L, then after a few hundred yards head straight up the hill to the rocks at the top, 20 mins. By not going up the hill but carrying on to the L and through the trees, one enters Chew Brook. A track leads up this, eventually to the Chew reservoir. 1m up on the R are Wilderness Rocks, 0.5m on the L are Charnel Rocks, and 1m up on the L are Robinson's Rocks, all reached within 30 mins. [CV]

Windgather Rocks:
OS.118 GR.995 784   [197]

An excellent outcrop for beginners, offering about 30 routes in the lower grades, 20–30ft. Excellent natural gritstone and W-facing, about 1,200ft up with a very good view.

Dir: 2m SSW of Whaley Bridge. Take the A5002 to Kettleshulme, turn off L up the hill for 0.6m to a junction, carry straight on to a car park in about 500yds on the L. The rocks can be seen to the L, keep to the path. [KB]

The Worm Stones:
OS.110 GR.042 916   [198]

For the keen gritstoner. Some small buttresses, offering about 20 routes in the lower grades and some more difficult problems for the connoisseur. E-facing and at about 1,000ft, requires a warm day.

Dir: 1.5m SSE of Glossop. Take the A624 S. About 400yds before the hamlet of Chunal take the turning off to the L for about 200yds. A footpath leads off S up the moor, 10 mins. [KB]

HORROR ARETE, 6a, Bridestones. (Climber Joe Healey, Photo David B A Jones)

Yellowslacks:
OS.110 GR.075 957 [199]

A S-facing gritstone outcrop but at 1,500ft, offering about 20 routes, 20–40ft. Climbs are generally in the lower grades with a few VSs as well.

Dir: 2m ENE of Glossop. Take the A57 out of Glossop. After 1m, where the road turns sharp R follow the track leading off to the L around the hill to a valley straight ahead. The crag is at the top of the valley and is reached in about 30 mins. Up and to the R in the valley before Yellowslacks is the old, NW-facing quarried area known as **Shelf Benches**, OS.073 947, which offers about 20 routes up to 40ft. [KB]

7 Lancashire

LANCASHIRE SOUTH

The climbing in this area is nearly all to be found in disused gritstone quarries, some small, others large, but generally 40–50ft. The best crags are often quite crowded on good weekends, especially in the early spring when people are keen to get out on the rock after the winter. They offer a superb platform on which to learn climbing skills and develop finger strength at an early age, and they are the home ground of most top English climbers. The quarries also offer endless bouldering on summer evenings. Not the most scenic area in Britain but nevertheless not to be missed. As the county boundaries do not conform very well with climbing areas, some of the crags included here are in Merseyside and Yorkshire.

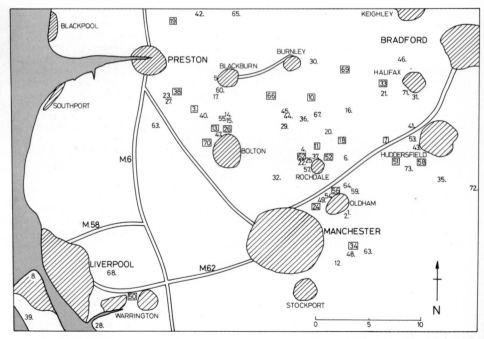

Abraham's Chair Quarry:
OS.109 GR.986 027   [1]

A small gritstone quarry, offering a handful of routes around Severe.

Dir: 4.5m ESE of Oldham. From Mossley, leave the town on the NE side on the B6175. Take a small turning to the R just past the school, for about 200yds up the hill, then sharp L around the hill for 300yds to the quarry. [LNW]

Alt Hill:
OS.109 GR.946 027 [2]

There is a quarry and an outcrop here, of which the latter offers better climbing. Nothing to rave about though. About 10 gritstone climbs, 30ft, S–VS.

Dir: 1.5m SE of Oldham. Leave Oldham SE on the B6194, to the town of Alt after 1m. Turn R before going down the hill over the river, follow this twisting road down for 0.7m to Park Bridge junction. Here a footpath leads back up the valley to the quarry and the crag in about 300yds. [LNW]

Anglezarke Quarry:
OS.109 GR.621 162 [3]

Although the rock here is actually called flag-stone it is for most purposes gritstone in charac-ter. A very good crag with some very good routes, about 130 in total up to 70ft, with plenty of problems. The rock is good but does deteriorate towards the top rather too often. There are climbs here to suit everyone, worth a visit.

Dir: 7m WNW of Bolton. From Horwich round-about on the A673 at the N end of town follow the road for a few yards N, then turn off R up the small road to Rivington. After 2.1m at the T-junction turn R and follow the small road up and round, which comes back down to the reservoir after about 1.8m. Carry on to a sharp R bend up a hill, the crag is just on the R. About 300yds further on is Leicester Mill Quarry on the L. [LNW]

Ashworth Moor Quarry:
OS.109 GR.824 159 [4]

A good, solid quarry, 15–30ft, with about 20 climbs in all grades. Ideal for an evening's visit.

Dir: 5m NW of Rochdale. Take the A680 NW to a small dip with a lake 0.5m past the Ashworth Moor reservoir. Here a footpath on the L leads off S to an old, disused mill after 600yds. The quarry is just up the hill from here. [LNW]

Billinge Hill Quarry:
OS.103 GR.658 283 [5]

A small quarry up to 30ft, offering some climbing and bouldering.

Dir: 1.5m W of Blackburn town centre. Take the A677 out of the town centre, after 1m turn L to Billinge Hill, a wooded hill with a country park to the S. Walk into the woods to a pond and the quarry. [LNW]

Blackstone Edge:
OS.109 GR.973 167 [6]

A small gritstone outcrop, 30–40ft, offering about 20 climbs, V Diff to 6a. The rock is good and sound but often dirty. Some good boulder-ing to be had in the area.

Dir: 5m ENE of Rochdale. Take the A58 from Littleborough E for 2m to the White Horse Inn. From here walk S, the opposite side of the road on the Pennine Way, to the crag in 15 mins. [YG]

Booth Dean Clough:
OS.110 GR.016 161 [7]

A very good gritstone quarry with about 50 routes, 30–60ft. Nearly all the climbs are in the VS–HVS range but there are a good handful of easier climbs. The tops tend to be loosish and care should be taken accordingly. Being so close to a reservoir, climbers should take par-ticular care not to pollute the area or leave litter. S-facing and good on a winter's day.

Dir: 8m W of Huddersfield. From Junction 22 on the M62 take the A672 E for 2m to the start of Booth Wood reservoir, park in a lay-by. A path leads down to the reservoir and the crag. [LNW]

The Breck:
OS.108 GR.298 918 [8]

A very good bouldering area near the centre of Liverpool. There are about 50 routes, of which most are around 5c. Good sandstone and worth a visit.

Dir: On the Wallasey side of Liverpool. Awkward to find, very close to the Ship Inn. Take the A551, the long dual carriageway running W to E in Wallasey, to the roundabout at the R-hand end. From here turn R on to the A road, after 0.3m take the R fork, a B road. The crag is about 100yds on the L. [LNW]

Bride Stones:
OS.103 GR.928 269 [10]

One of the best bouldering areas to be found.

Problems at all grades, 15ft, in a very peaceful setting. Quite exposed and quick drying, best on a good summer's evening.

Dir: 4.5m NE of Bacup. From the roundabout at Todmorden take the A646 towards Burnley, after 2.8m turn R at Cornholme on to a small road which leads up to Shore and the road going across the moor after 1m. Here turn R and go for 1m to The Sportsman's Inn. The rocks are over on the R, reached by a track. [YG]

Britannia Quarries:
OS.109 & 103 GR.881 200   [11]

Some very extensive quarries, offering plenty of climbing in an area thought to be in danger of further quarrying a while back. Over 100 routes in all grades, mostly in VS and above, with a handful of easier climbs.

Dir: 4m N of Rochdale. Take the A671 to Whitworth. At the town centre turn L on to Tong Lane, past the Cock and Magpie, to a track which becomes rougher. This leads to the quarry in 0.8m at the top of the hill. [LNW]

Broadbottom Crags:
OS.109 GR.997 937   [12]

Here are some gritstone quarries up to 30ft in height, offering about 30 routes in total at all grades up to the mid-Extremes. Some good bouldering to be found here, as well as variety of climbing. Not a bad spot.

Dir: 3m ESE of Hyde. From the end of the M67 take the A57 for signs to Broadbottom, reaching the station in about 1m. To get to **Broadbottom Quarry**, follow the road under the railway and around to the small bridge, the crag is on the other side of the river to the L. For **Squirrel Quarry** and **River Crag**, before the railway bridge turn L up Gorsey Brow, then R into Hague Road, which leads to the quarry in the trees on the L, with the crag to the R. [LNW]

Brownstones Quarry:
OS.108 GR.681 125   [13]

A very good bouldering area with around 130 short routes up to 20ft. Good gritstone that dries out quite quickly. Worth a visit, good on winter's days too cold for all the other crags.

Dir: 3m NW of Bolton. From the ring road, A58, at the top of Bolton, go W on the B6626, after 0.6m turn R at the pub and up the hill. Follow this road round R for 0.7m to some woods, 200yds past these on the L is the quarry. [LNW]

Cadshaw Rocks:
OS.109 GR.708 182   [14]

A very good natural gritstone outcrop, offering about 50 routes in the easier grades around Diff to Severe. There are a couple of hard routes, but little in general to test the VS leader. 30–35ft in most places with ample protection. Worth a visit.

Dir: 5.5m N of Bolton. Approach: see Cadshaw Quarry. [LNW]

Cadshaw Quarry:
OS.109 GR.708 180   [15]

Some gritstone quarries, offering up to 50 routes in all grades, 30–70ft, with few routes of difficulty exceeding 5b. Some of the routes are vegetated, but this does not affect the majority of climbs.

Dir: 5.5m N of Bolton. Take the A666 N out of Bolton, pass Delph reservoir on the L, the road then bears round R after the long straight. About 1m from here are the few houses of Cadshaw, turn R and park in a few yards where a footpath signposted to Egerton leads off to the R. The quarries and Cadshaw Rocks are a few minutes' walk around the hill. [LNW]

Castle Quarry: Restriction
OS.103 GR.953 246   [16]

The crag is on private ground and permission to climb must be gained before going to the crag from Mr Driver, Bank Side Farm, the second house on the R up the lane beyond the crag entrance. A very steep quarry with about a dozen routes to E3, but very little below VS unfortunately. Plenty of scope apparently.

Dir: 8m NNE of Rochdale. Take the A6033 to Todmorden, from the roundabout in the town centre go E on the Hebden road, A6033, for 1.3m. Turn right to Hough Road and cross over the canal. The quarry is about 60yds to the R. 1m further down on the L is **Withnell Quarry**, which offers a handful of climbs below VS on a buttress. [LNW]

Central Quarry:
OS.103 GR.641 217 [17]

A small gritstone quarry, 30–80ft offering about 10 routes around VS. Worth a visit for a few hours in the evening.

Dir: 4.5m SW of Blackburn. Take the A674 SW for a few miles to a roundabout, then turn L on to the A675 and follow this for 1.6m to Abbey Village. Turn R at signpost for Withnell and continue for 0.3m to the quarry, which is on the L. [LNW]

Cow's Mouth Quarry:
OS.109 GR.962 195 [18]

A fair quarry with about 60 routes mainly in the Severe and above grades, a good lot of climbing around the VS grade. Some good hard problems also to entertain most people. Mostly around 30ft but higher in places. Excellent for bouldering.

Dir: 5m NE of Rochdale. From Littleborough take the A58 E for 1.8m to the White Horse Inn and a car park. From here the Pennine Way track goes N past the crag, about 1m. [LNW]

Craig Y Longridge:
OS.103 GR.619 384 [19]

An excellent crag, offering superb bouldering on good to poor gritstone. The rock deteriorates towards the top and it is usual not to complete the routes. The crag is quite steep and offers zilch below 5a, about 50 routes 5a to 6a. A must if you are in the area.

Dir: 7m NE of Preston. Drive to Longridge, from the town centre take the road leading NE towards the golf course on Jeffrey Hill. After 0.7m fork R, 0.3m later there is an iron gate and a track that leads to the quarry. [LNW]

Cross Stone Quarry:
OS.103 GR.951 248 [20]

A small gritstone quarry, 40ft, offering up to 20 routes mainly around VS. A couple of easier and harder routes also.

Dir: 8m NNE of Rochdale. From the roundabout in Todmorden take the A646 E for 1m, turn L and go over the railway, turn R up the hill to reach the crag. [LNW]

Crow's Nest Wood Quarry:
OS.103 GR.996 266 [21]

A good, sound quarry, offering about 20 routes in the grades Severe to E2 but mostly around VS–HVS. 40–70ft with generally good protection. Sheltered by trees, takes time to dry out after heavy rain. Worth a visit.

Dir: Just S of Hebden Bridge. From the A646 go S to the railway station and a hairpin bend. Follow the second footpath by a factory, leads to the quarry in 5 mins. [LNW]

Deeply Dale:
OS.109 GR.824 149 [22]

A very good, small quarried area, offering about 30 routes, 20–40ft. There are a few easy climbs but in general 4b–4c is the minimum standard. There are a handful of E3, 6a climbs as a result of previous aid climbs. Nearly all the climbs are worth doing.

Dir: 4.5m WNW of Rochdale. Take the A680 NW from the town to Ashworth Moor reservoir, 4.7m, then the small road off to the L across the front of the reservoir for 0.5m to a track on the R. Here a footpath leads down to Deeply Dale. [LNW]

Denham Quarry:
OS.102 GR.592 228 [23]

A popular crag, offering 80 or so routes in all grades to E3. Good gritstone, 30–90ft, and plenty of good climbs. Home of the famous VS, Mohammed the Mad Monk of Moorside Home for Mental Misfits, a classic. Well worth a visit.

Dir: 5m SSE of Preston. From Junction 29 on the M6 take the A6 S to the second roundabout, turn L on to the B5256, past a roundabout and over the M61. After 0.3m turn R – the crag is in 5 mins.

Den Lane Quarry:
OS.109 GR.994 059 [24]

Quite a large gritstone quarry, but a bit mouldy. About 100 routes, Diffs to mid-Extremes, 30–50ft. Some routes are good, others not so.

Dir: 5m E of Oldham. Take the A669 to Greenfield, pass the station on the R as the road bears round N. Take a L turn here on to a small road running N parallel with the railway, the quarry is reached on the R in 0.8m. [CV]

Docky Dam:
OS.109 GR.854 151   [25]

A good quarry with half a dozen routes in the VS–HVS grades, 25–55ft. Steep and strenuous routes at their grade, and can be in reasonable condition when other crags are not. Sheltered.

Dir: 2.5m WNW of Rochdale. Take the A680 for 2.5m to Norden. At the Bridge Inn turn R up Greenbooth Lane, then immediately L, follow round for 300yds to a lay-by at a small lake. Take the footpath to the R of the lake to the crag in the woods. [LNW]

Egerton Quarry:
OS.109 GR.719 143   [26]

Quite a large area of climbing with about 100 routes in all grades up to 50ft. Some climbs are better than others and should be sought out, others should be avoided at all costs. Fairly predictable gritstone.

Dir: 3m N of Bolton. Leave Bolton on the A666 and go to Egerton, where the quarry can be seen up to the R. Turn R down the B6472, then the first L leads up to the area. [LNW]

Flying Shed Quarry:
OS.102 GR.583 217   [27]

A reasonable quarry with a score of routes of 25–60ft in grades Diff to E3. The HVS climbs are particularly worthwhile. Worth a visit.

Dir: 6m SSE of Preston. Take the A6 S to Whittle-le-Woods. The crag is in the town up on the L, 400yds away from the main road. [LNW]

Frogsmouth Quarry:
OS.108 GR.507 815   [28]

About 50 climbs in this sandstone quarry, mostly 5a–5c, 20–60ft high and quite steep. The rock is not of a sound nature and it is advisable to bring a top rope.

Dir: At Runcorn. The crag is situated on the hill which is on the W side of Runcorn near The Traveller's Rest pub. From the dual carriageway going around Runcorn, take the exit on the NW corner, go over the road and then up the hill to a T-junction at the top. Take the second R only a few yards, leads to the quarry in about 300yds on the R. [LNW]

Gauxholme Crag: Restriction
OS.103 GR.927 231   [29]

Please remember to seek permission to climb at the cottage to the L of the crag. A very small crag of 80ft with a couple of climbs at VS and Extreme.

Dir: 4m W of Bacup. From the roundabout at Todmorden take the A6033 S for 0.7m, turn L on to the A681. About 200yds up the road, the crag is behind a stone wall on the R. [LNW]

Gorple: Restriction
OS.103 GR.931 315   [30]

The crag is on private land on which shooting takes place, climbing here during firing enhances the possibility of a serious accident. The crag offers plenty of climbing and bouldering. Worthy of a visit on a fine summer's day.

Dir: 4.5m E of Burnley. Approach: see Widdop. [YG]

Greetland Quarry:
OS.104 GR.094 215   [31]

A small quarry, offering about 50 short climbs on good solid gritstone. Worth a detour if in the area.

Dir: 2m S from Halifax. Go to the junction of the B roads at Greetland, take the B6113 for 200yds and the crag is on the L. [YG]

Harcles Hill Quarry:
OS.109 GR.779 169   [32]

About 25 routes from Mod to E4. Some of the finishes are loose and in consequence a top belay hung down some feet is a sensible precaution. Climbs up to 40ft with good scope for bouldering.

Dir: 4m NNW of Bury. Take the B6214 out of Bury, cross the A676 after 3m. Carry on for 0.9m to the Shoulder of Mutton pub on the R, turn L up a track, Moor Road, which leads to the quarry via a L fork. [LNW]

Heptonstall Quarry:
OS.103 GR.985 277   [33]

A fine quarry with about 50 routes in all grades. The central quarry wall has very few easy routes but includes the classic Forked Lightning Crack 5c. The main quarry is of a hard sandstone, the outcrops to the L and R are of gritstone and offer the easier routes. The crag offers plenty of hard climbing to amuse, 80–120ft climbs in general.

Dir: 8m ENE of Bacup. Go to Hebden Bridge, from the A646 take the turning up to Heptonstall, 0.7m. A path leads off S from behind the church to the top of the crag, 2 mins. [YG]

Hobson Moor Quarry:
OS.109 GR.988 967   [34]

The best quarry in the Stalybridge area, a good 40 routes up to 50ft on fairly good gritstone. All grades of climb to E4, but best around VS–HVS. Worth a visit for the middle-grade climber.

Dir: 1m SE of Stalybridge. Take the A6018 SE to the roundabout at Roe Cross, 0.5m before Mottram in Longendale. Here take the small lane on the L, which forks L uphill for about 400yds, and the quarry will be seen on the L. [LNW]

Holmfirth Edge:
OS.110 GR.148 086   [35]

A reasonable outcrop of quarried gritstone, offering some good but short climbs. Faces NW.

Dir: 5m S of Huddersfield. Drive to Holmfirth, turn on to the B6106 going S, then immediately turn L up a small road leading steeply uphill. After 50yds turn sharp L on to a road which leads uphill and to the crag in 500yds. [YG]

Horsehold Scout:
OS.103 GR.982 269   [36]

A couple of natural gritstone buttresses, offering a score of routes in the lower grades, V Diff to VS. N-facing and liable to hold lichen, better after a good dry spell. 70ft high in places but because of the situation they feel very exposed. Not bad for the lower-grade leader.

Dir: 7m E of Bacup. From Todmorden take the A646 towards Hebden Bridge. After 3.7m a railway crosses above the road, just before this the crags can be seen across the canal. Take the first R over the canal, a footpath leads to the crags. [LNW]

Houses o' th' Hill Quarry:
OS.109 GR.876 175   [37]

A good gritstone quarry, offering about 30 routes in the VS–HVS category and a handful of Diffs for good measure. The crag is quite sheltered and is one of the better locations to climb.

Dir: 2.5m NNW of Rochdale. Take the A671 to the junction of the B6377, carry on up the A671 for 1.3m and turn L on to Hall St. Go past the school to a T-junction, turn R and continue to quarry after 300yds. [LNW]

Hoghton Quarry: Restriction
OS.102 GR.626 265   [38]

The crag is owned by the Hoghton Estate, which does not wish climbing to take place outside the months February to June because of unsettling the game birds. The best crag in the area SE of Preston. A large gritstone crag, 50–120ft high and very impressive in places, offering over 100 routes in all grades with plenty of good Extremes. The crag is surrounded by trees and can get green quite quickly. Best in early spring. Fun for everyone, well worth a visit.

Dir: 6m SE of Preston. Take the A675 from Preston, via the A6. Pass under the M6 and continue for 2.9m to The Boar's Head pub, after which turn L, continue for 0.6m over a railway bridge. Immediately to the R a track leads along the railway to a crossing and the crag is in the trees to the L. [LNW]

Irby Quarry:
OS.108 GR.252 858   [39]

A sandstone quarry up to 50ft high, offering good climbing in the lower grades and very useful for beginners. Top-roping very sensible.

Dir: 1.5m NNW of Heswall. Take the A540 NW from Heswall for 3m, turn R on to the B5140 towards Frankby. After 0.7m at a junction by a pub turn R on to a smaller road to Irby Hill. The crag will be seen on the R after 400yds, a public footpath leads to the quarry. [LNW]

Leicester Mill Quarry:
OS.109 GR.619 164   [40]

A good gritstone quarry with about 70 routes in all grades V Diff to HVS and a handful of

Extremes at each E grade to E3. Some of the routes are definitely better than others.

Dir: 8m NW of Bolton. Approach: see Anglezarke Quarry. [LNW]

Lindley Moor Quarry:
OS.110 GR.102 188   [41]

A good, small 30ft gritstone quarry with some fine climbs on it. Good bouldering to be found here also. Worth a visit.

Dir: 3m WNW of Huddersfield. From the M62 at Junction 23 take the A643 NE for 0.7m and then turn L under the motorway. The crag is just here on the bend. [YG]

Little Bowland Quarry:
OS.103 GR.642 439   [42]

A limestone quarry offering about 10 routes which classify as large boulder problems, 4b to 6a. Worth a detour if passing.

Dir: 10m NE of Preston. From Longridge drive to Chipping Village, enter from the S ('town') end, and drive up to the centre. Turn R at the church, fork L after 100yds and take the road which passes to the S of Leagram Hall Farm. Stay on this road for 1.4m, at a few houses and a R-hand bend in the road a footpath leads off to the R and the crag. [LNW]

Longwood Quarry:
OS.110 GR.104 174   [43]

A small 35ft gritstone quarry with a few routes of limited merit.

Dir: 2.5m from Huddersfield. From the centre ring road take the A640 to the second round-about. Carry on for 1.2m, turn L to a T-junction, in 200 yds. Turn L and the crag is reached in about 200yds. [YG]

Lumbutts Quarries:
OS.103 GR.955 223   [44]

A series of about 6 quarries on open moorland, giving plenty of short climbs. Of the 40 or so routes most are around HVS and 40ft, a good place for the VS climber. NE-facing, a very pleasant setting but can stay wet for a long time after rain.

Dir: 6m E of Bacup. From the roundabout at Todmorden take the A646 for 1m, turn off R to Lumbutts, follow this road for 0.8m to a T-junction. Turn R and park in a few hundred yards at a L fork, triangle junction. Here take the track on the L and then the public footpath, which leads up to the ridge on the R and the quarries. [LNW]

Mytholm Steep Quarry:
OS.103 GR.979 277   [45]

A quarry with about 10 routes, Diff to E2, 40–80ft. Quite impressive and worth a visit. Also nearby is Mytholm Edge, which is well worth a visit for its problems.

Dir: 7m ENE of Bacup. From the roundabout at Todmorden take the A646 towards Hebden Bridge. After 4.2m, 0.6m before the junction with the A6033, turn L into Church Lane, signposted Mytholm. Go up the steep hill to some hairpin bends after 400yds, the quarry is just on the R past the bend. The edge is back further down in the trees. [LNW]

Ogden Clough:
OS.104 GR.055 318   [46]

A small gritstone crag, offering some excellent bouldering.

Dir: 5m NNW of Halifax. Take the A629, from the bends in the road at Illingworth carry on for 1.7m to a staggered crossroads, turn L and take the road to the R of Ogden reservoir, park at the end. Walk to the crag, about 500 yds to the N, almost straight on. [YG]

Ousell's Nest:
OS.109 GR.731 142   [47]

About 20 routes on this very pleasant gritstone crag in grades VS to E4, a Diff and a Severe also. All routes just under 40ft. At the foot of the crag there is a pool of water which tends to disappear during the later summer months, so July–Aug. the best time for easy access.

Dir: 3m N of Bolton. Take the A676 to Bradshaw, turn L on to the B6472. After 0.7m pass under the railway and turn R on to the B6391 to a car park below Prospect Hill Cottages on the L in 0.8m. Here a footpath leads off R into the quarry. [LNW]

Outlands Head:
OS.109 GR.984 962 [48]

A gritstone quarry in not particularly beautiful surroundings, but with fine views. However there is some very good climbing, mainly in the grades up to VS, on a large 70ft slab. Worth a visit for the VS aspirant leader.

Dir: 2m SE of Stalybridge. Take the A6018 to the roundabout at Roe Cross. Here turn back R and then immediately L on to a small road for 500yds to a track which leads to the quarry. [LNW]

Pack Horse Quarry:
OS.109 GR.995 084 [49]

A couple of small gritstone quarries, offering a dozen or so routes in the lower grades to E1, 20–40ft. Not bad.

Dir: 5m ENE of Oldham. Take the A62 to Delph, 400yds after passing over the river a footpath leads off up the hill to the quarries. [LNW]

Pex Hill:
OS.108 GR.501 887 [50]

One of the great bouldering areas in the country. There are over 125 routes in all grades up to 7a on really good, compact sandstone. Height varies from 10ft to 50ft. Most of the routes are nearly always chalked up – not that it matters since the holds are obvious, it is getting between them that can prove awkward. A top rope is very useful for the longer routes, which are rarely soloed. No overhangs to shelter in, only steep walls on which to boulder. Enjoys quite reasonable weather. Beware of car thieves, the area is not known for its honesty. Always worth a visit.

Dir: 6m from the outskirts of Liverpool. Leave the M62 at Junction 7, S on the A569, after 0.7m turn R on to the A5080. After 400yds take the turning on the R with some green posts, leads to the quarry in about 200yds. [LNW, HEL]

Pule Hill:
OS.110 GR.032 105 [51]

This good gritstone area consists of an edge and a quarry, about 100 routes covering all grades well to E1, 20–60ft. The crag is W-facing and one of the most popular in the area.

Dir: 8m WSW of Huddersfield. Take the A62 to

Marsden, 1m outside the town the road follows the valley around to the L. The crag is 0.8m up the valley on the L side, park at a lay-by then follow a path to the crag. [LNW]

Reddyshore Scout:
OS.109 GR.942 197 [52]

One of the best gritstone quarries in the area, offering about 40 routes, 40–60ft, in all grades with plenty of classic climbs. Worth a visit.

Dir: 4.5m NE of Rochdale. Take the A6033 through Littleborough and on for 1m. Turn off L to Calderbrook, bear L, and then turn R at a T-junction. Take this for 0.6m to a footpath which leads off L to the crag in 200yds. (LNW)

Robin Hood Rocks
OS.104 GR.011 243 [53]

A good, small crag in a nice setting, offering 30 routes up to 40ft in the easier grades. The crag is split into two parts, the R offering more of the climbs. Worth a visit, especially for the VS climber who can cope well with 4c climbs.

Dir: 5.5m W of Halifax. From Mytholmroyd take the B6138 S for 1.5m. On the R is a sign and a footpath that lead the way to Robin Hood Rocks in 5 mins. [YG]

Rough Knarr:
OS.109 GR.981 071 [54]

A small, E-facing gritstone quarry, offering about a dozen routes in the lower grades. Worth visiting of an afternoon or evening, or on a sunny winter's morning.

Dir: 3m ENE of Oldham. From the centre of Delph take the small road from the junction of the A6052 and the B6197 past the library for 0.5m to the crag on the R just above the road. [LNW]

Round Barn Quarry:
OS.109 GR.728 193 [55]

A reasonable, lowish crag with few climbs exceeding 30ft. About 70 climbs, especially in the lower grades Diff to Severe, a few harder problems to keep the harder climber happy. Most of the climbs in the quarry are worth doing, but little is climbed on the lower tier.

Dir: 6.5m N of Bolton. Take the A676 for 3m from

the ring road going N. Turn L to Edgeworth, carry on till 4.2m from the main road and 1m N of Entwhistle station, just short of The Crown and Thistle pub. Here a footpath leads up the hill to the quarry on the R. [LNW]

Shaw Quarry:
OS.109 GR.952 102   [56]

A good gritstone quarry, offering about 50 routes in grades VS to E4, 20–50ft. Bring a top rope along for some or even all of the routes. There is a lot around 5b to occupy the 5b–5c climber who enjoys the safety of a top rope. Well worth a visit.

Dir: 3m NNE of Oldham. From Shaw go N out of the town and take the B6197 on the R for 400yds, past the Park Hotel. Here a track leads off to the L past some cottages, round and up to the quarry. [LNW]

Shore Quarry: Restriction
OS.109 GR.922 171   [57]

The crag is on private ground and only small parties may use the crag. Please respect the owner's walls, fences and privacy. A small gritstone quarry with a couple of routes, HS to HVS, about 30ft.

Dir: 2m NE of Rochdale. Take the A6033 out of Rochdale for 2.7m then, 0.7m after the Wardle turn-off, turn L to Clough. Take this road for 400yds to a crossroads, turn L on to Shore Road and continue up this to the King William pub, 700yds. From here a public footpath leads off round two houses up the grassy hill to the quarry. [LNW]

Shooter's Nab:
OS.110 GR.065 109   [58]

A very large quarry on the N edge of Binn Moor. The gritstone edge is about 1,000 yds long and offers a good 70 routes, 20–60ft in all grades to E4, a few classic HVSs. N-facing and at 1,300ft. In parts quite impressive, worth a visit.

Dir: 6m SE of Huddersfield. Take the A62 to Marsden, turn sharp L on to the B6107. After 300yds there is a track which leads off S up the hillside and to the crag in about 20 mins. [LNW, CHV]

Standedge Quarry:
OS.110 GR.012 103   [59]

A gritstone quarry, 20–40ft and SW-facing, offering a handful of climbs in the lower grades. The crag is loose in the lower parts and one should climb cautiously here.

Dir: 6m ENE of Oldham. Take the A62 to Delph and Bleak Hey Nook in 2m. Turn L on to the small road which leads off and around to the R, the crag is clearly visible up on the moor. [LNW]

Stanworth Quarry:
OS.102 GR.638 241   [60]

Some quite extensive quarries, 30ft gritstone still active as dumps for shale, etc. – the state of climbing is liable to change at any time. There have been 100 routes here from time to time, of all grades but mostly VS upwards. Hopefully the BMC will have secured the long life of the better of the climbable faces.

Dir: 3m SW of Blackburn. Take the A674 W to the roundabout with the A675, turn L and go S for 0.4m to a track on the L. This leads to the quarries after 400yds. [LNW]

Stronstrey Bank Quarry:
OS.109 GR.619 186   [61]

Some good climbing to be found here on this gritstone quarry and a few surrounding buttresses. About 40 routes in total, mainly in the lower grades up to VS. Worth a look if in the area.

Dir: 2m NE of Chorley. Drive to the end of White Coppice, a small group of houses near the motorway. The crag will be seen on the R by the river running into Anglezarke reservoir, to the W of Anglezarke Moor. [LNW]

Summit Quarry:
OS.109 GR.948 196   [62]

A very good gritstone quarry, 30–40ft, offering about 70 routes in all grades, but with an abundance of VS routes. Well worth a visit.

Dir: 4.5m NE of Rochdale. Take the A6033 through Littleborough and on for 1.7m to the bridge crossing the Rochdale Canal at The Summit pub. Here take a footpath on the L over the bridge, which leads up the hill and to the crag in about 10 mins. [LNW]

Swineshaw Quarries:
OS.109 GR.998 992 [63]

A good area for bouldering, a few easy climbs on gritstone. There are two quarries situated at about 750ft.

Dir: 2m E of Stalybridge just above the Walkerwood reservoir. Take the B6175 NE for about 1m to some sharp bends, just after here on the R a small road leads up to the reservoir. The quarries are reached in about 1m along this road. [LNW]

Tonacliffe Quarry:
OS.109 GR.883 176 [64]

A 20–30ft quarry, offering nearly 40 routes in the Diff to E2 grades, a lot of very good climbs at VS. Worth a trip for any lower-grade climber.

Dir: 2m NNW of Rochdale. Take the A671 100yds beyond the junction with the B6377, fork R on to Tonacliffe Road and after 0.3m park at the foot of Highpeak Lane. Walk up to the top of the hill and the quarry. [LNW]

Trough of Bowland Quarry:
OS.103 GR.628 519 [65]

A limestone quarry with about a dozen routes of grades Diff to E1, 30–70ft. Top-roping is often sensible here since the rock is interesting towards the top.

Dir: 9m NW of Clitheroe. From Dunsop Bridge take the small road NW to Sykes, the quarry is 200yds past the houses on the R. [LNW]

Troy Quarry:
OS.103 GR.763 235 [66]

A good quarry of fine gritstone with about 60 routes, 30–60ft. There are a few Diffs and Severes, but on the whole the climbs are VS upwards with a fair number of Extremes and one E5, 6b. The crag faces S, dries out quickly and is warm on a sunny winter's day. Well worth a visit.

Dir: 1.5m WNW of Haslingden. From the A677 at Haslingden take the B6232 W for 1.7m, turn R up Thirteen Stone Hill. This leads to a track which leads to the quarry in 400yds. [LNW]

Warland Quarry:
OS.103 GR.948 201 [67]

A small crag of excellent gritstone, offering about a dozen routes, VS to E1. The quarry has two tiers, of which only the bottom one is climbed. Not a bad crag.

Dir: 5.5m ESE of Bacup. From the roundabout at Todmorden take the A6033 S for 3.4m through Walsden and to Warland. Just past Bird in the Hand pub take the bridge over the canal and follow for 200yds up the hill to a corrugated-iron cottage on the R. A track leads off here to the quarry. Beware of the dog! [LNW]

Whiston Quarry:
OS.108 GR.483 923 [68]

Not a very large quarry, only a few routes. But up to 80ft on sandstone not dissimilar to that of Pex Hill, some good climbing in the 5b grade.

Dir: 1m E of Prescot. From Junction 7 on the M62 take the A57 N through Rainhill, continue for another mile to the hospital. Turn R on to the B5201, after 300 yds turn R on to a small road which leads to the quarry. [LNW]

Widdop:
OS.103 GR.935 326 [69]

A good outcrop on the moor overlooking Widdop reservoir, N-facing at 1,100 ft. Not the place for a bleak winter's day. Some very good rock offers about 30 climbs when in condition, all grades up to E3 with some harder problems, 30–100ft. On the other side of the road to the N is an outcrop known as **Scout Crag – Widdop**, and **Jackson's Ridge**. These both offer plenty of bouldering and being S-facing are often a very good alternative to the larger and colder Widdop. Worth a visit.

Dir: 6m E of Burnley. Go to Widdop reservoir and the crag is easily visible. Cross over the dam and follow the track to the crag. By carrying on along the track, up the valley on the L, and taking the path around the hill in an easterly direction, one can reach Gorple outcrop in 15 mins, visible to the L. [YG]

Wilton Quarries: Restriction
OS.109 GR.700 133 [70]

The local shooting club has agreed shooting times and if firing is in process it is suggested that climbing be restricted to quarries 1 and 4, as a safer pastime.

	Wilton 3	Wilton 2
Wed	10.30–Sunset	2 30–Sunset
Fri	10.30–Sunset	2.30–Sunset
Sat	10.30–5.30	Midday–Sunset
Sun	Sunrise–1.30	10–Sunset

The quarries here are numbered 1–4. The largest is Wilton 1 with over 200 routes in it. There are over 400 routes in the quarries altogether, and enough to keep any standard of climber busy for quite a time. The routes vary quite a lot in length but generally are around 30–60ft. The walls face many aspects and it is easy to find climbs in or out of the sun as desired. They are generally sheltered and dry out very quickly. There is very good bouldering to be had by all. Definitely worth a visit.

Dir: 3m WNW of Bolton. Take the A675 NW from the town, 2m after the A58 ring road take the small road going sharply back L, to the quarries in 0.5m. Wilton 1 is on the L and the others are on the R. [LNW]

Woodhouse Scar:
OS.104 GR.082 235 [71]

A small gritstone crag, offering about 50 climbs in all grades to E4, most around 30ft. Some very good bouldering to be found here also. The crag

has a habit of becoming green and unclimbable. Worth a visit after some dry weather.

Dir: 1.5m SSW of Halifax centre. From the A58 at Sowerby Bridge railway station take the main road towards Elland, after 1.4m take the road going off to the L up a hill; take the 1st L after 100yds and the crag is up on the R. [YG]

Woolley Edge:
OS.110 GR.307 137 [72]

Some small 20ft gritstone outcrops in the trees, offering some good problems, good for bouldering. A picnic area. Worth a visit if passing on the M1 having been rained off elsewhere.

Dir: 5m NNW of Barnsley. From Junction 38 on the M1 take the small road leading NE to Woolley. After 1m turn L at a crossroads, then R after 0.3m to a lane which leads to the crag on the R. [YG]

Worlow Quarry:
OS.110 GR.037 103 [73]

A small gritstone quarry, offering about a dozen routes, Diff to E2, 20–40ft. Worthwhile if only for a few really good VS climbs.

Dir: 8m WSW of Huddersfield. Take the A62 to Marsden, then a small road on the L past Marsden golf course on the L. The quarry is shortly on the R. [LNW]

LANCASHIRE NORTH

This area is predominantly limestone of quite high quality. There are, however, serious exceptions. Beware of Warton Main Quarry and White Scar, I will say no more.

Baycliff New Quarry:
OS.96 & 97 GR.287 727 [74]

A small quarry that offers few routes but some good traversing.

Dir: 3.5m S of Ulverston. Take the A5087 S to Baycliff, turn R into the village, then R again on to a small lane that leads to the quarry. [LNW]

Birkrigg Quarry:
OS.96 & 97 GR.281 746 [75]

A very good quarry, offering endless amusement and plenty of good bouldering for everyone. NW-facing at 200ft altitude. Worth a visit if it's cats and dogs in the Lakes.

Dir: 2m S of Ulverston. Take the small road going S out of Ulverston towards Scales. At the turn-off

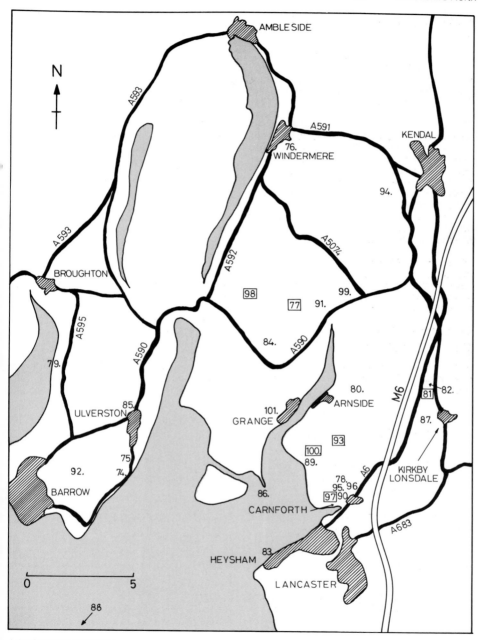

LANCASHIRE NORTH

to Great Urswick the crag can be seen to the L. [LNW]

Brant Fell:
OS.96 & 97 GR.409 962   [76]

A great crag, which gives some very fine bouldering and a nice view.

Dir: 1.5m from the centre of Windermere. Leaving Bowness on the A5074 turn L on to the B5284 and after 0.5m turn L up a lane through a small wood. A track leads up to the fell, and the crag is seen on the summit. [LNW]

Chapel Head Scar: Restriction
OS.97 GR.443 862   [77]

There is a bird ban here, no climbing 1 Mar.–1 Aug. The crag is in a nature reserve and consequently plants and trees should be left well alone. The best crag in the area to the S of the Lake District. There are about 80 routes here, 100–50ft grades, in the grades VS upwards, a handful of routes around V Diff to keep others occupied for a short while. The best routes are in the E3 upwards category, about 40, and there are some fine E6 climbs also. SW-facing, nearly at sea-level, steep but solid limestone. Protection in general is good, with bolts on the harder routes. Definitely worth a visit. The saviour of the Southern Lakes for the E5 limestone addict.

Dir: 6m SE of Kendal. Turn off the A590 and take the small road to Witherslack Hall, park. Just to the R of the hall entrance follow a track off to the R for a few yards, a footpath leads off L and up to the crag in 5 mins. [LNW]

Crag Foot:
OS.97 GR.479 737   [78]

A W-facing crag, offering about 10 climbs in the VS to HVS grades, 40–60ft. Worth a visit for the HVS climber.

Dir: 2.5m NNW of Carnforth. From Carnforth there is a small road that runs parallel to the railway going to Silverdale. Take this for 2m, passing woods on the R, and carry on for another mile to a sharp L-hand bend. The crag was 200yds back, you passed it on the R. It is rumoured that there exists a crag called **Barrow Scout Cove** on the R before the crag and the limekiln, with a few routes around VS. [LNW]

Dunnerholme:
OS.96 GR.212 797   [79]

A limestone crag offering some climbing and bouldering for all the family. Quite pleasant.

Dir: 7m N of Barrow-in-Furness. Half-way between Ireleth and Soutergate is a track which leads off W to Grange Marsh Farm, the crag is visible beyond this. [LNW]

Fairy Steps:
OS.97 GR.487 789   [80]

A 20–30ft crag, with about 30 routes in the lower grades, V Diff to HVS. Definitely worth a visit and the quality of the rock lends itself to soloing. Plenty of problems.

Dir: 5.5m N of Carnforth. From Milnthorpe take the B5282 for 2.7m and through Storth, turn L up a small road which immediately bends R. After 0.4m turn L up a road for 0.3m to a T-junction and Hazelslack Farm. Here straight ahead a footpath leads to the crag after about 600yds. [LNW]

Farleton Crag:
OS.97 GR.539 796   [81]

Some excellent rock up to 60ft, however nearly all of the 50 or so climbs are only 30ft high. The routes are from Diff to HVS with a lot at VS. Faces SW and very quick to dry. Worth a visit for the VS climber.

Dir: 4.5m WNW of Kirkby Lonsdale. Leave the M6 at Junction 36 and head S on the A6070 for 2m to Holme Park Farm on the L. Go up the track and park just past the second gate in about 0.5m. The crag is up and to the L from here, above the lower band of cliffs, 10 mins. [LNW]

Farleton Quarry:
OS.97 GR.536 809   [82]

A small limestone quarry, offering a handful of routes in the low grades, Diff to Severe, and an Extreme.

Dir: 5m WNW of Kirkby Lonsdale. Leave the M6 at Junction 36, go to the village of Farleton and park. The quarry is behind, to the SE of the village. [LNW]

Heysham Head:
OS.96 & 97 GR.407 617   [83]

Some small sandstone outcrops, 20–5ft high and about 200yds long, with lots of very good boulder problems. Worth an evening visit.

Dir: 4.5m W of Lancaster. Go to the far W of Heysham and the cliffs are by the coast. Park to the S and walk N up the coast, 5 mins. [LNW]

High Newton Crag: Access
OS.96 & 97 GR.404 828   [84]

Please do not park on the grass verge below the crag. A good quarry, about 40ft high and offering about 10 routes, V Diff to E1, 5c. Worth a visit if raining in the Lakes.

Dir: 3.5m N of Grange-over-Sands. Take the A590 to High Newton, the crag lies a few hundred yards to the S on the E side of the road. High Newton has a pub. [LNW]

Hoad Slabs:
OS.96 & 97 GR.296 790   [85]

Some popular slabs, 70–90ft, offering half a dozen routes, Diff and 4b–5a. Quick drying. Most of the climbs are worth doing.

Dir: 0.5m NE of Ulverston. Leave the town on the A590 N and the crag is clearly visible on the L by the big hill. [LNW]

Humphrey Head Point:
OS.96 & 97 GR.390 740   [86]

A sea cliff in a fine position with some very good routes indeed, about 15 routes here, all E1 upwards to E4. W-facing and non-tidal. The crag has not been over-popular in the past years, who knows why. Worth a visit.

Dir: 3m SSW of Grange-over-Sands. The climbing is on the W side of the sharp point, a road 0.3m W of Allithwaite leads S to the head. [LNW]

Hutton Roof Crags:
OS.97 GR.554 781   [87]

Lots of small limestone crags to explore at will, 20–30ft high and offering plenty of scope in the lower grades.

Dir: 4m W of Kirkby Lonsdale. Drive to Hutton

Roof, the crags are on the hillside to the W of the village.

Isle of Man:
OS.95   [88]

There is quite a bit of climbing here but it is of questionable merit and because of lack of space it has been omitted from this guide. The climbing is very quiet and peaceful, and to this purpose it is better left to those in search of vertical tranquillity.

Dir: 70m W of Lancaster. A boat is generally necessary to reach the island. [LNW]

Jack Scout Cove:
OS.97 GR.459 736   [89]

Almost a sea cliff, SW-facing and quite different. The crag is prone to rockfall but the routes are solid. About 40 routes in the lower grades Diff to E1, but offering most to the VS leader. A very quiet and scenic spot.

Dir: 3m NW of Carnforth. From Silverdale a small road leads down to the S point past a caravan site in 1m. At the S point the crags are on the R, looking out to sea. [LNW]

Millhead Quarry:
OS.97 GR.498 715   [90]

A small 40ft quarry, offering half a dozen routes in the Diff to VS grades.

Dir: 0.5m N of Carnforth. From the A6 in the town turn L past the station then go under two railway bridges and take the second turning on the R. From the end of here a footpath leads across to Warton, the quarry is about 2 mins walk along it. [LNW]

Millside Scar:
OS.97 GR.451 845   [91]

A crag which has received variable opinions. S-facing and 60ft high. There are a handful of routes around E4 plus a Severe, also an upper tier with a couple of easy routes around E1.

Dir: 7m SSW of Kendal. Drive to the village of Millside just off the A590, go through the hamlet to a dead end. From here a footpath leads up to the crag above. [LNW]

Stainton Quarry:
OS.96 GR.243 727 [92]

A limestone quarry, offering about half a dozen routes in the grades Diff to HVS with most of the climbing being around VS. Apparently there is more scope.

Dir: 4m NE of Barrow-in-Furness. From Dalton-in-Furness take the small road to Stainton with Adgarley, the quarry is straight on and obvious. [LNW]

Trowbarrow Quarry:
OS.97 GR.481 758 [93]

A good quarry that looks like a desolate lunar landscape. There are almost 100 routes, genuinely at all grades. Well, they are all easy to be honest, from Diff to E3. Varying lengths, 40–120ft, in general quite long though. Faces all directions and dries very quickly. Worth a visit if you are blind, best for the HVS climber.

Dir: 3m NNW of Carnforth. Take the A6 N from Junction 35a for 2.9m, a small road leads off L to the village of Yealand Redmayne. After 0.7m turn R at the T-junction, follow this round keeping L on the road to Silverdale for 1.5m and park. A path leads off through the woods to the R and the quarry in a few minutes. [YL]

Underbarrow Scar:
OS.97 GR.486 915 [94]

A limestone crag, 60–100ft high, offering about a dozen routes Mod to E4, 5 in the very easy grades. Not a bad spot, W-facing.

Dir: 2m WSW from Kendal town centre. From the town take the small road L off the ring road towards Underbarrow, after 1.6m park at a car park. Walk on for 100yds and a path on the L leads off to the crag. [LNW]

Warton Main Quarry:
OS.97 GR.492 144 [95]

This crag does not merit inclusion, it is positively horrible and should be filled in to make way for a giant superstore, furniture warehouse or car park for Carnforth. Of the 50 routes here all are loose and lethal, 4b to 6a, and up to 300ft. The BMC should declare this a climbing disaster area.

Dir: 1m WNW of Warton. Leave Warton preferably in the opposite direction to the crag. [LNW]

Warton Pinnacle Crag:
OS.97 GR.492 727 [96]

A small crag, 20–30ft and in the trees, offering about 25 routes in the lower grades, Diff to VS. Worth a visit for the Severe and VS leader.

Dir: 1m NW of Warton. Locate the Black Bull Inn – which should be easy enough – then leave it (desperately) from the L-hand end on a well-worn path to the main quarry, on to the ridge and a group of prominent limestone boulders. The crag is about 200yds NW of here in the trees. Alternatively, go R (NE) from here and in about 200yds reach **Warton Upper Crag**, very similar and of the same appeal. [LNW]

Warton Small Quarry:
OS.97 GR.498 724 [97]

An excellent quarry, offering short 20–30ft routes, all worth doing and most possible solo. 40 routes, Diff to HVS, but most in the easier Severe grades. Quite polished but still a fun place. Best in the village, superb on a winter's day.

Dir: At Warton, 1m N of Carnforth. Locate the Black Bull Inn and the crag is behind it. [LNW]

Whitestone Crag:
OS.96 & 97 GR.397 849 [98]

A good crag with about 10 routes, 80ft, in the lower grades, V Diff to HVS. Well worth a visit for the low-grade climber.

Dir: 9m SW of Kendal. From Newby Bridge take the A590 SE to High Newton, turn L and go up the valley, fork L after 400yds. After 1m follow the track leading off up to the L for 600yds, the crag is 400yds on the L. [LNW]

White Scar:
OS.97 GR.459 853 [99]

I suggest that if anyone recommends White Scar to you, it is perhaps because they have a peculiar sense of humour. It is not a crag on which to lark around, indeed it can be positively dangerous to one's health. There are some 10 routes here, verging on the Extreme upwards, 90–200ft. Access is problematic.

OPUS, 6a, Almscliff. (Climber Joe Healey, Photo David B A Jones) (See over.)

Dir: 6m SW of Kendal. From the A6 take the A590 for 3m to a turning on the R just past the A5074 turn-off. This leads to a footpath to the crag. Approach to the face is often made by abseil, 300ft and left in place. Helmets are essential. Wonderful crag, eh? [LNW]

Woodwell:
OS.97 GR.465 743   [100]

A 20–30ft crag, offering plenty of climbing, half in the lower grades Severe to HVS, and half in the 5b to 6a grades. About 60 climbs in total and some good problems. A pleasant spot, worth visiting if passing.

Dir: 4m NW of Carnforth at Silverdale. Leave Junction 35a on the M6 and go N on the A6. Turn L and go through Warton on to the road to Silver-dale, pass over the railway crossing to a T-junction. Turn L and then in 0.2m L again, in 0.3m a footpath signposted to Woodwell is seen. When parking, please use spaces provided or carry on around the road to park in a responsible place. [LNW]

Yewbarrow:
OS.96 & 97 GR.405 782   [101]

A small crag, 30ft, with about 10 routes, Diffs, Severes and HVSs.

Dir: In Grange-over-Sands. From the town take the road towards Cartmel, then turn R down Eden Mount Road. At Charney Well Lane walk down past a house to the woods and the crag. [LNW]

8 Yorkshire

GRITSTONE

Almscliff:
OS.104 GR.268 490   [1]

A very traditional crag with a great reputation. About 100 routes in all grades on this natural outcrop, 30–50ft high and very well protected. The crag faces in most directions but generally W. The climbing is very good from strenuous to delicate. Most of the routes, however, demand a typical Yorkshire, thuggish, blunt approach for the easiest success. The crag is very exposed and dries instantly after rain if even the slightest breeze is blowing. Always worth a visit.

Dir: 5m ENE of Otley. Take the A659 to Pool, then turn L on to the A658 going NE. At Huby turn L and go through the village on the small road to Stainburn, after 1m the road bends to the L and the crag is on the R in 1 min. [YG]

Ash Head Crags: Access
OS.99 GR.144 754   [2]

The crag is on a grouse-shooting moor, duck if in season. A crag with about 15 climbs in the grades Severe to HVS, 25–50ft of walls and buttresses. The main overhangs are breached by Thunder Crack at VS. 1,300ft, worth a visit on a sunny day.

Dir: 11m WNW of Ripon. From Masham on the A6108 take the small roads to Leighton reservoir. The road bends round and crosses over a branch of the reservoir, follow it up for 2m and you can look across L and almost directly S to the crag just over 1m away. Carry on the road for 1m, passing across a bridge over a stream. A footpath on the L leads across the moor to a small gully and then up to the crags. [YG]

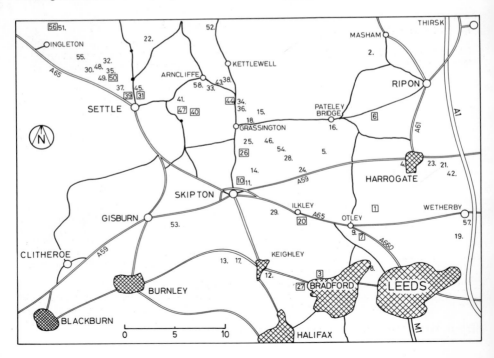

Baildon Bank:
OS.104 GR.150 390   [3]

A series of sandstone quarries, offering about 200 routes in all grades. The crag is hardly the most scenic spot in the N of England but does offer some very good bouldering and climbing. The routes are 30–50ft with mostly good holds on strong rock, however top-roping from the trees above the crag can help one venture on to harder technical climbs.

Dir: 4m NNW of Bradford. From the A6308 enter Baildon on the B road, 300yds before the round-about in the town centre the crag can be seen on the L. [YG]

Birk Crag:
OS.104 GR.278 547   [4]

Some small, isolated boulders, offering about 30 routes and problems. Worth an evening visit.

Dir: 1.5m W of Harrogate. From the town centre take the B6162 for 1.3m from the roundabout to a turning on the R, which leads in a straight line almost to the crag in about 600yds. [YG]

Brandrith:
OS.104 GR.153 564   [5]

Some small outcrops, offering a handful of interesting routes.

Dir: 10m ENE of Skipton. From the A59 at Blubberhouses – what a silly name – take the small road leading to the W side of Thruscross reservoir for 1m. The crag can be seen on the moor to the L, 5-min. walk. [YG]

Brimham Rocks:
OS.99 GR.208 647   [6]

The best gritstone outcrop in the world, in fact the Milky Way. The climbing here is very good but the geological make-up of the area is superb. Lots of buttresses with paths running between them, problems at every turn. Absolutely varied climbing throughout, over 200 listed climbs, 30–50ft at all grades with thousands of boulder problems. The rocks can get green in winter, but nearly always offer some good rock to climb on. Good running on the moors nearby and around the outcrops. A must for climbers and the family.

Dir: 9m NW of Harrogate. Take the B6165 to Summerbridge, where a small road on the R leads up the steep hill to the rocks in about 1.5m. The area is owned by the National Trust, please use the car park. [YG]

Caley Crag:
OS.104 GR.231 444   [7]

One of the best bouldering areas in the country. There are 50 or so climbs, but most of these are just large boulder problems. A rope is useful here for the unsteady and novice, not for the hard climber. Boulders up to 50ft high on the main craggy section, with smaller ones scattered around the fern fields. A lot of problems are well polished, as with Almscliff, so there is no excuse for having even a hair out of place when cruising a problem. The crag is generally N-facing but one can usually find some problems which are in the sun, or at least dry.

Dir: 2m ESE of Otley. The crags are just to the S of the A660 between Leeds and Otley, 1m before the roundabout when entering Otley. Park at the side of the road and walk to the crag in 3 secs. [YG]

Calverley Quarry:
OS.104 GR.201 377   [8]

A disused gritstone quarry, offering a handful of climbs of 60ft, with reasonable interest. All grades, but some quite difficult climbs.

Dir: 4m NE of Bradford. From the roundabout at Calverley take the A657 NW for 0.8m, then the small road on the R just past the church. This leads round to the L after 400yds and into the woods. Before crossing over a bridge, the quarry is in the woods to the R in a few mins. [YG]

Chevin Crags:
OS.104 GR.209 444   [9]

A soft buttress offering about 10 climbs, Severe upwards, and several more smaller problems. There is also a sandstone quarry next to the crag with 15 or so routes in all grades, treat the rock with caution. Plenty of problems and bouldering also. Together both are worth a visit.

Dir: 1m SE of Otley. From the town centre off the roundabout take a small road heading SE towards East Carlton, after 1m up the hill, where it steepens, the crag and quarry are on the R. [YG]

Crookrise:
OS.103 GR.987 558 [10]

A very good crag in a superb position. There are nearly four score routes here in all grades, 30–50ft. The V Diff to VS grades are served particularly well. At 1,300ft, SW-facing and good, solid, clean rock. Worth a visit.

Dir: 2.5m N of Skipton. Drive to Embasy, from here take the moor road to the car park at Embasy reservoir. The moor ahead has the crag of Deer Gallows on it up to the R, not to be confused with Crookrise. Follow the ridge on the L of the moor to the summit in 15 mins. Crookrise crag is below this to the L. [YG]

Deer Gallows:
OS.103 GR.995 555 [11]

A small crag, 100ft long, with about 25 routes in the lower grades, Diff to HVS. S-facing and of a pleasant outlook. Worth a visit in combination with Crookrise.

Dir: 2.5m N of Skipton. Approach: see Crookrise. [YG]

Druid's Altar:
OS.104 GR.093 399 [12]

A good bouldering area on some slabs and buttresses. Very exposed but quick to dry. Enough to entertain the serious boulderer.

Dir: 2m ESE of Keighley. From Bingley take the B6429 SW for 200yds, then turn R on to the smaller road, Alter Lane. This leads to the crag on the R in 0.9m. [YG]

Earl Crag: Access
OS.103 GR.988 429 [13]

The crag is on private property and visits by large and especially rowdy groups are not welcome. Please do not aggravate the situation, approach by footpath. A crag of many buttresses, offering about 50 routes in all grades, with plenty of bouldering. N-facing at 1,000ft, can be cold in winter. Very good on a summer's day.

Dir: 5m W of Keighley just W of the good viewpoint. From the main A629 at Glusburn turn on to the A6068, after 2m at Lanes Ends a road leads off L up the hill towards the crag. Drive on to the L end and approach climbs by the footpath

which leads in from the L, the easiest way anyway. [YG]

Eastby:
OS.104 GR.023 549 [14]

A lovely crag, facing SE with a pleasant angle for a change. About 30 climbs up to 70ft in the lower grades. There are a few hard climbs, but the Severe and VS climber will feel at home here, also some good Diffs. Can get green and slippery but are easy to top-rope. Dries quickly.

Dir: 3.5m NE of Skipton. Drive to Embasy then take the small road crossing the moor towards Appletreewick. After 1m reach the village of Eastby, after the houses turn L up the steep hill and the crag is 400yds on the L. Also one can reach Halton Heights Quarry by carrying on the road for 0.7m to the end of the wood on the L. About 10 climbs on sandstone, 30ft. [YG]

Great Wolfrey:
OS.99 GR.063 674 [15]

This crag is remote and not even to be approached on anything other than a good, sunny day. The crag faces SW and is 30–40ft high. The climbing is around Diff standard with some harder up to VS. Worth a visit, if only for the complete loneliness factor.

Dir: 11m NNE of Skipton, 1.5m N of the Grimwith reservoir. From the B6265 a track leads up to the reservoir. On the other side of the river Dibb is a long track which leads up on to the moor. From here walk in wellies across the moor to the crag on the R directly N in 30 mins. [YG]

Guisecliffe:
OS.99 GR.166 633 [16]

If you are planning to climb in the Amazon jungle for any length of time, a few evenings here would be time well spent. The rest of us will meet you in the pub later. 100 routes of all grades, 40–90ft, NE-facing. Leech lotion and magnesium malaria tablets essential here.

Dir: 10m NW of Harrogate. Take the B6165 and turn off L at Glasshouses, just before Pateley Bridge. Follow the small road down the hill over the river, bear R, then keep going L and up the steep, twisting hill. That is the crag on the L, believe it or not! A footpath leads along the top to the 'better' parts of the crag. [YG]

Hawkcliffe Crag: Restriction
OS.104 GR.041 440   [17]

This crag lies on private land and permission to climb must be sought before approaching it. Some buttresses with a good 30 routes on 20–70ft.

Dir: 2.5m NW of Keighley. Take the A629 towards Steeton, 1m from the town turn L to Utley. From here take the small road towards Steeton, after 1.2m Tower Farm is on the R and so are the crags. Enquire at the farm. [YG]

Hebden Ghyll:
OS.98 GR.026 641   [18]

A small crag with about 15 routes in all grades from Diff to Extreme, up to 60ft but generally around 30ft. SW-facing and at 900ft. In condition for most of the year and worth a visit for anyone.

Dir: 8m NNE of Skipton. Take the B6265 to Hebden. From the village drive N up the valley for about 500yds to an obvious parking spot. The crag is up on the R and is easily reached by walking up the valley and then cutting back. [YG]

Hetchell Crags:
OS.104 GR.376 424   [19]

A small gritstone crag, offering about 30 routes, 30ft high. The rock here is much softer than most gritstone crags and care should be taken accordingly. A nice selection of routes in all grades from Diff to 6a. Worth a look.

Dir: 4m SSW of Wetherby. From Collingham take the A58 S to Bardsey, turn off L on to the small road going up the hill and R towards Thorner. Follow the road through some trees after 0.8m, past a road leading off L to Bramham, continue for 0.4m and park. A footpath on the R leads to the crag in the wood in about 5 mins. [YG]

Ilkley:
OS.104 GR.125 465   [20]

One of the best and most popular gritstone areas N of Leeds. There are over 200 climbs here in all grades and none ever seems really easy. There are various areas all within a few minutes of the Cow and Calf Hotel, a serious threat to a day's climbing, especially in winter. There is a natural crag on the moor called the Cow and Calf, which has the classic Desperate Dan E6, and about 20 easier routes. There is a quarry to the L, which is sandstone and offers some very good crack climbs up to 60ft high. Going 0.5m to the W are **Rocky Valley Crags**, which are 6 buttresses and about 45ft high.

Dir: 1m SW of Ilkley. Follow the small road signposted Cow and Calf from the town centre. [YG]

Knaresborough:
OS.104 GR.351 566   [21]

A large 80ft sandstone cliff of variable quality, to be treated with caution. An HVS takes the obvious line up the centre.

Dir: Just a few hundred yards S of the centre of Knaresborough. From the centre take the B6163 S for 200yds to the river Nidd. The crag lies above the river to the N. Please do not park at the side of the access road at the base of the cliff. [YG]

Pen Y Ghent:
OS.98 GR.836 732   [22]

The gritstone outcrop with the most exposure in Yorkshire. A crag of mixed quality, offering about 15 routes, Diff to VS, around 80ft. The rock in places is not firm and care should be exercised. At 200ft and W-facing. Best in summer. On the E side is a limestone outcrop, offering a couple of 100ft routes at VS and E2. Dubious.

Dir: 6m N of Settle. Drive to the village of Stainforth, off the B6479 take the small road NE which goes to Halton Gill. Park after 3m and walk up the big bugger on the L, the crags are on the other side. [YG]

Plompton Rocks:
OS.104 GR.356 537   [23]

A small, vegetated crag with some problems.

Dir: 3m ESE of Harrogate. Take the A661 SE from Harrogate to the junction with the B6163, carry on for 0.4m, then turn L down a lane to Plompton Square. Here a track leads off L into the woods and a lake where the crags lie. [YG]

Raven's Peak:
OS.104 GR.141 554   [24]

A small, clean outcrop, offering about half a dozen routes in the grades Severe to HVS, 20–50ft. A pleasant spot, worth a quick visit.

Dir: 9m ENE of Skipton. Take the A59 E for 8m. W – here a road leads off to the moor, stay on the main road and the crag is 1m further on the L. [YG]

Rolling Gate:
OS.98 GR.001 602   [25]

A crag with a score of routes in the lower grades, Diff to Hard Severe, up to 70ft high. Situated on the moor at 1,300ft, NW-facing, cold on a cold day, and even colder on an even colder day. A pleasant cliff on which to bumble around, some good easy bouldering to be found also.

Dir: 6m NNE of Skipton. Drive to the small village of Thorpe, at the S end of the village follow a track which leads S up the fell, then bear round to the R. The crag is 1m from the end of the track. Bit of a hike but worth it for the seclusion. [YG]

Rylstone:
OS.103 GR.983 576   [26]

A very good outcrop of clean and solid rock, about 50 climbs in the lower grades, Diff to VS. There are harder climbs but this is generally not the crag for the stick insect. NW-facing and best on a good, sunny afternoon in midweek, with some cheese and a glass of 10-year-old port. Worth a visit.

Dir: 4m N of Skipton. Take the B6265 towards Rylstone, park 0.3m before the village, where track leads off to the R (N). Take the track for 400yds, the crag is high up on the fell to the L. Best bet and easiest way is to follow the track up the fell, then cut across on the public footpath to the crag. Most Yorkshiremen take the direct route. [YG]

Shipley Glen:
OS.104 GR.131 389   [27]

A very pleasant and well-regarded bouldering area with plenty of fun for all. The crag is a series of small buttresses, which offer about 5 problems each, over 100 routes in all but none over 20ft. A rope can be useful since the landings are not always comfortable and the finishes leave you in awkward positions. Not to be missed.

Dir: 1.5m NW of Shipley. From the roundabout at Baildon take the small road going W above the river Aire towards Eldwick, after 1.8m park on the L on some open ground. The glen is down to the L from here. [YG]

Simon's Seat:
OS.104 GR.079 598   [28]

About 35 routes in all grades, but particularly good in the lower grades around Severe, 30–70ft. The crag is at 1,600ft on the moor and can be quite cool at times. All round a very worthwhile crag.

Dir: 7m NE of Skipton. Take the B6160 N from Bolton Abbey for 3.4m to a turning on the R to Appletreewick, after 1.3m a small track bears off R to Howgill Farm. From here a track leads up through the woods to the crag, about a mile up to the L. [YG]

Windgate Nick:
OS.104 GR.072 472   [29]

Some small, lichenous buttresses offering routes of up to 50ft in the grades Severe to HVS. The routes are on N-facing, natural gritstone. Best kept for that good, long, dry spell in December!

Dir: 3m W of Ilkley. Leave Ilkley on the A65 NW, after 1m turn L on to the small road going over the moor to Silsden. After 2.3m turn R at a small crossroads and follow this lane for 0.5m to a sharp L-hand bend in the road. Here a footpath leads straight on up to the rocks on the moor above. [YG]

Limestone

The Yorkshire limestone is rated by most Extreme climbers as the most demanding rock in the country. In past times the routes have often been very bold as well as hard. Now, with the widespread use of bolts, nearly all the hard routes are quite safe. There are quite a few easy routes on the limestone which are well worth doing, however they rarely take the very good lines. These are reserved for Extremes usually, and hard ones at that. There is plenty here to keep the visiting 6b climber occupied. Double ropes are almost essential on most climbs. Most of the bolts are quite recent and very strong.

Ash Tree Crag:
OS.98 GR.758 376 [30]

A good crag for the not-so-hard climber feeling out of depth in the vertical limestone of Yorkshire. The crag faces S and dries quickly, 30–50ft with a score of routes, Diff to VS, but most in the easier grades. Worth a visit.

Dir: 4m SE of Ingleton. Drive to Clapham and park. Take the bridleway heading SE towards Austwick from the N end of the town, after 300yds turn L on to a track called Long Lane, the crag is up on the R about 700yds away. [YL]

Attermire Scar:
OS.98 GR.834 642 [31]

One of the better areas in Yorkshire to climb. There are over 200 routes here in all grades from Diff to E5, with most being in the lower grades, Diff to HVS. SW-facing and quick to dry, but at 1,200ft and quite exposed. Not really for the cold winter days, although there is some very good bouldering to be found here. Worth a visit.

Dir: 1.5m NE of Settle. Take the small road up the steep hill leading out of the village towards Airton. After 0.9m a track leads off to the L and the crag is soon seen up on the L. [YL]

Beggar's Stile:
OS.98 GR.781 722 [32]

A 60ft wall along the rambling and broken Moughton Scar. There are about 10 routes here of grades V Diff to E2. A pleasant SW aspect and quite isolated. Worthy of climbing, pleasant for an afternoon.

Dir: 6m NNW of Settle. Drive to Austwick then take the L turn just past the village school, which leads up to Crummack Farm after 2m. From here the crag is over to the R at the end of the valley, 1m, 15-min. walk. [YL]

Blue Scar: Restriction
OS.98 GR.938 708 [33]

Birds here, no climbing 1 Mar.–1 Aug. Why this crag needs a restriction, though, amazes me – it deserves to remain thoroughly unpopular. It is loose, devoid of bolts and dries out only occasionally. There are hard routes worth top-roping, but bring a bolt kit with you to put in a safe belay at the top. There have been some 50 routes climbed here, 60–100ft – about one is worth doing and that is the route back down to the pub in Arncliffe. Worth a visit if you like serious 6b climbing, or in a hot, dry spell for top-roping. There are easier routes of very limited merit in the middle grades.

Dir: 8.5m NE of Settle. From Arncliffe take the road on the S side of the river going SE, after 1m the crag is on the R. Ask at the farm buildings for permission to climb here. [YL]

Bull Scar:
OS.98 GR.986 675 [34]

A very good crag for the beginner or those leaders of a nervous disposition. Quite a few Diffs on this W-facing easy-angled buttress, with some harder lines including an HVS. Worth a visit.

Dir: 10m WNW of Settle. Go to the village of Conistone just off the B6160. A footpath leads directly W from the village to the crag in 5 mins. [YL]

Crummackdale: Access
OS.98 GR.782 703   [35]

The crag is on private ground. Permission, which is nearly always given, can be sought from Mr Morphet, Town End, Austwick, tel. Clapham (04685) 2880. The name of this crag is shortened from Crummy Rock Dale – need I say more? It lives up to expectations in fine style, you are invited to take a hold home with you. About 35 routes, 50–150ft, in grades VS to E4, S-facing. Some of the HVS routes are worth thinking about, but in general a crag to forget.

Dir: 5m NNW of Settle. From Austwick take the small road to Wharfe. Here a track leads N up the valley, the crag is 400yds up on the R. [YL]

Dib Scar:
OS.98 GR.990 663   [36]

A small version of Malham Cove. About 15 climbs here, 60–100ft, VS to E5. Most are worth doing but none are really thrilling. A good position, though, facing W and quick to dry. It has been reported that helmets are useful on the R-hand side, so one can only presume that the rock or the protection is suspect!

Dir: 11m E of Settle. At Grassington take the small road that runs parallel to the B6160 to Conistone. After 2.3m the wood on the R ends, and the crag can be seen up on the R. [YL]

Feizor Gap:
OS.98 GR.790 681   [37]

A small crag, offering a handful of climbs in the lower grades, Diff to VS. W-facing, in a very pleasant surrounding and very handy. If going to Pot Scar worth taking advantage of this one in the evening sunshine.

Dir: 3.5m NNW of Settle. Drive to the village of Feizor, bear round to the L and the crag is reached shortly. [YL]

Gate Cote Scar:
OS.98 GR.971 703   [38]

There are about 50 climbs on this crag, of which maybe 25 are worth doing in the lower grades, Severe to HVS, 30–70ft. There are also a couple of easy Extremes. E-facing, the lower parts are sheltered by the woods, but in bad weather or an E wind this is definitely a place to avoid. Good for the HVS leader who wishes to miss the crowds and likes early mornings.

Dir: 10.5m ENE of Settle. Heading N on the B6160 the road bears R over a bridge where a small road goes L to Hawkswick. 1m further up the B road the crag can be seen directly at the top of the woods on the L. Around the ridge to the L is the crag **Knipe Scar.** This is in most parts loose and unattractive – there is one small, compact buttress which offers a few routes around HVS worthy of ascent – just. [YL]

Giggleswick Scar:
OS.98 GR.800 658   [39]

A series of crags running up the side of the A65 out of Settle to the NW. About 120 routes in total of all grades. The first crag reached is Giggleswick South, 30–70ft. The first rock, known as the Low Level Crag, has about 30 climbs around VS. Further up is the High Level Crag, which sports about 30 good routes, HVS to E3, on clean rock and stays dry quite often. Further up still is Giggleswick North, offering climbs in all grades from Diff to E5, around 80ft. The area as a whole is worth a visit.

Dir: 2m NW of Settle. Take the A65 from the metropolis of Settle, pass under the railway to the S crag in 1.8m and the N crag in 2.8m. [YL]

Gordale Scar:
OS.98 GR.916 641   [40]

This crag is very impressive. Any climber who is not an E6 leader, upon looking up at the huge, overhanging walls, will not even think of climbing here. One should not be daunted by this, however, since there are many easier routes on the walls outside the gorge, and these are quick to dry and catch a lot of sun. The main gorge, though, has a waterfall running through it and for most of the year down the walls also. During the dry spell in the summer the river will dry up and the walls dry out to give some of the most demanding routes in Britain. They are nearly all 150ft, single- or double-pitch E6 and E7 climbs. The L wall has some quite serious routes as becomes apparent in the first 30ft. The R side of the gorge is quite steep and needs arms that do not give up. The hard routes on the R side never see on-sight cruises! About 90 routes on the wings, 20–100ft, in all grades from Diff to E1, with a few E2s and E3s. About 30 routes in the gorge, on average E5, 150–250ft.

Dir: 6.5m E of Settle. From Malham take the small road leading off E to Lee Gate and the gorge. After 0.9m one can park at a bend in the road, usually chaos. The gorge is directly ahead N up the stream and comes into view after 5 mins. By walking up through the gorge and following the river for 1m, the crags of **High Stoney Bank** and **Low Stoney Bank** are reached. These 70ft crags offer a dozen or so routes each in the middle grades, but need a good, dry spell. Nice and secluded after Gordale. [YL]

Great Close Scar: Restriction
OS.98 GR.901 667 [41]

This crag is used by birds to nest, a climbing ban operates 1 Mar.–1 Aug. A very good crag, offering lots of climbs in the lower grades. There are about 50 climbs, about 80ft, Diff to E1, with a couple of good E3s also. Most of the routes are worth doing. A pleasant setting, facing SW, and with quite good protection on mostly sound rock. Dries out quickly. Worth a visit.

Dir: 5m ENE of Settle. Park at the bend in the small road just to the SE of Malham Tarn. A footpath leads N to the crag, which overlooks the tarn and is situated on the E side, 10 mins. [YL]

Grimbald Crag: Restriction
OS.104 GR.362 558 [42]

The crag is on a caravan site and climbing is only allowed out of season, no climbing 1 May–1 Oct. About 50ft of softish rock, offering a score of routes in the middle grades. Worth a miss.

Dir: 1m SE of Knaresborough. Take the B6164 and after 0.4m reach the river Nidd. On the R is the caravan site and crag. [YL]

Hawkswick Crag: Restriction
OS.98 GR.946 715 [43]

The BMC have agreed the following access arrangement for unknown reasons: large parties and dogs are banned, and in Nov., Dec. and Jan. you may only climb on Sundays! A long rambling crag, reaching up to 60ft in most parts. There are over 100 climbs here in the lower grades, Diff to HVS, and about 10 Extremes up to E3. The climbing is generally V Diff or VS depending on the size of weakness in the cliff. The top can usually lack suitable belays, bring a bolt kit. Facing SW over the beautiful valley, the place to potter around all day on easier routes.

Dir: 9m NE of Settle. From Hawkswick there is a small road running up the R-hand side of the valley to Arncliffe, take this for 1m to the R-hand end of the wood on the R. Here, through an iron gate, a path leads up to the crag. [YL]

Kilnsey Crag: Access
OS.98 GR.974 681 [44]

There used to be a restriction here preventing climbing at weekends, but this has now been lifted. To prevent any access problems, please park to the N of the crag and take special care not to block the road in any way. Along with Malham and Gordale this crag offers plenty to the rock superstar. The crag is quite steep indeed, the top even overhangs slightly. About 60 routes, E4 upwards to E7 and above! There are also a couple of easier routes to solo around E1 before warming up on the E4s. E-facing, best on a warm summer's afternoon. The routes are quite hard, consequently bolts are in favour here.

Dir: 10m ENE of Settle. The crag is obvious from the pub in the village. Drive to the N end of the crag and then park about 200yds further on at a parking spot. [YL]

Langcliffe Quarry:
OS.98 GR.825 665 [45]

A quarry and a natural edge, offering about 50 climbs, Severe to 5c. To top-rope the harder routes would seem sensible due to the frailty of the rock. Worth thinking about.

Dir: 1.7m N of Settle. From just outside Settle take the B6479 N through Langcliffe, carry on for 0.8m and the quarry is on the R. Access is by going through the rubbish tip on the R. Wonderful setting. Is this your favourite crag? [YL]

Loup Scar:
OS.98 GR.029 618 [46]

About a dozen routes in the E2–E5 grade, 40–70ft, with access being governed by the state of the river. Very sheltered and S-facing, also quite steep.

Dir: 7m NNE of Skipton. Drive to the village of Burnsall, park. Walk upstream for 300yds and the crag is on the opposite side. There is also a footbridge 500yds further on. [YL]

LE MAXIMUM, E6, 6c, Malham Cove. (Climber Joe Healey, Photo David B A Jones)

Malham Cove:
OS.98 GR.897 642 [47]

Malham Cove at first sight looks so impressive that to stand at the foot of the central wall is quite forbidding. The climbing, though, rates from excellent to very disappointing, 300ft high with nearly 200 routes, VS upwards. The hard routes, of which there are many, are brilliant, and should be on the tick list for any visiting superstars, especially the route controversy at E9 7a, the most impressive climb in the country at the end of 1988. Lots of E6 climbs, most impossible on sight, even by the best. The other routes on the wings tend to be disappointing. The rock is often poor and starts are unprotected, resulting in several injuries over the years. The easier climbs also tend to have single moves which are ridiculously hard and spoil the route. The crag is best suited to the E5–E6 climber since many of the easier Extremes are quite serious and in need of many bolts. The Yorkshire attitude is commonly to make the routes as serious as possible so as to stop any chance of further ascents. However, the fact that no one can cruise E5, 6b ensures that those climbs and above are very well protected. The cove gets a lot of sunshine and dries out very quickly.

Dir: 5m E of Settle. Drive to Malham and follow signs or the crowds of tourists to the cove. The best introduction is on the R wing. To the centre and the L are the big walls which have the hard routes on. [YL]

Norber Scar:
OS.98 GR.768 697 [48]

A smallish crag of two buttresses, a L one 100ft high and a R one about 50ft high. The L buttress offers a handful of HVS climbs and one E3. The R buttress offers half a dozen Severes with a couple of HS and VS routes. The crag faces S with a fine view. Treat the rock with reasonable caution. Worth a jaunt.

Dir: 5.5m NNW of Settle. Go to Austwick, follow the Helwith Bridge road for 100yds, then turn L just past the village school. After 0.3m a footpath leads up to the crag on the L in about 5 mins. [YL]

Oxenber Scar: Access
OS.98 GR.779 683 [49]

It is requested that the walls here should not be climbed over in order to gain access to the crag, however desperate you are. A short crag, 30–55ft, offering about 40 climbs in the grades Diff to E2 and quite evenly spread. The crag faces W, dries out quite quickly and in most places is solid. There is some vegetation but this hinders little. The crag is quite sheltered and pleasant. Worth a visit.

Dir: 4m NW of Settle. Take the A65 then turn off to Austwick after 4.3m. Go down this lane for 0.5m and park at a track on the R before the bridge. Follow this track on the R for 400yds turn, go straight on, then fork R after 300yds and follow a footpath to the crag, reached in 5 mins. [YL]

Pot Scar:
OS.98 GR.795 678 [50]

A crag in a better situation than Giggleswick Scar, away from the road. The crag faces S and dries out quickly. About 50 routes, 30–50ft, Diff to E1. Definitely worth a visit for the VS leader and anybody who likes a good, easy crag, uncommon in Yorkshire. Also see Feizor Gap.

Dir: 3m NE of Settle. Take the A65 for 3.3m from the railway bridge in the town. Here a road leads off R to Feizor, take this for 0.7m to a parking spot. The crag is straight ahead. [YL]

Raven Scar:
OS.98 GR.722 747 [51]

A very long crag, yet low in height, 30–40ft. Offers many routes, of which there are about 20 from Severe to E4. NW-facing and generally away from the crowds. Handy if you get turfed off Twistleton Scar. Worth a wander.

Dir: 3m NE of Ingleton. Take the B6255 in a NE direction, after 2.5m is a quarry on the L and a parking spot. Alight here and walk up and to the R, the crag is reached in 5 mins. [YL]

Strans Ghyll:
OS.98 GR.915 785 [52]

A gorge offering about 1,000ft of scrambling in the Mod–Diff grade. Worth a gripper on a rainy day.

Dir: 11m NNE of Settle. Drive to the village of Hubberholme, take the small road leading NW for 0.7m to the gorge on the R. [YL]

Thornton-in-Craven Quarry:
OS.103 GR.912 489   [53]

A quarry offering quite a bit of climbing, up to 150ft in all grades on an easy-angled slab. The protection is none too good, so bring a top rope if you want to enjoy yourself. Worth a visit.

Dir: 1.5m N of Earby. Drive N on the A56 to Thornton-in-Craven. Go into the village where the Pennine Way walk goes through, the quarry is just off to the R of this, going in a N direction. [YL]

Troller's Gill:
OS.99 GR.069 620   [54]

A small crag, 30–60ft, offering a dozen climbs, VS to E5. Most are worth doing with some classics at E4. The gorge allows climbing on both sides and is quite sheltered. Worth a visit.

Dir: 8m NE of Skipton. From Appletreewick take the small road over the moor due N towards the B6165. After 2m a footpath leads off R by a stile to the gill in 5 mins. Alternatively, take the small road but, instead of turning up the hill, cross the moor and carry on up, bearing L into the small valley to Ridge End. Walk up the valley to the N and the crag in 15 mins. [YL]

Trow Gill:
OS.98 GR.754 717   [55]

A crag with about a dozen routes, 60–100ft, HVS to E5. Most of the routes are good and are in the low E grades. Slow to dry, but in a dry spell worth a visit.

Dir: 4m ESE of Ingleton. Drive to Clapham. Take the footpath up the valley to the N, which leads to the gorge and crag in 25 mins. [YL]

Twistleton Scars: Access
OS.98 GR.711 759   [56]

The crag is on private land and access to it must first be approved by the farmer at Twistleton House Farm beneath the crag. A long rambling crag, SE-facing, 30–60ft. Few of the 150 or so climbs here are memorable, but climbing is nevertheless quite enjoyable. The rock is good in most places and there is easily enough to warrant never treading on poor rock. Most of the climbs are in the Diff to HS category, a fair few VS and harder climbs but nothing to tax the forearms even slightly. Always worth a visit.

Dir: 2m NNE of Ingleton. From the town a small road runs up parallel with the B6255 to beneath the crag. The farm is along here. [YL]

Wetherby:
OS.105 GR.406 479   [57]

A very good outcrop for bouldering and traversing, in a handy position.

Dir: On the SE side of Wetherby. From the S turn off the A1 ring road and go straight in towards the town centre. After crossing over the river turn first R to the car park and the crag is on the R. [YL]

Yew Cogar:
OS.98 GR.918 707   [58]

Previously dismissed as loose and unworthy of a visit, climbers have seen fit to list about 10 routes in the E3–E5 standard on the R-hand end of the crag up the steep buttress. About 80ft and faces NW. Worth a look.

Dir: 8m NE of Settle. The crag lies about 1m on the S side of the impressive valley running SW from Arncliffe. The best approach is from the village itself, park here by the pub — handy for the disillusioned retreat. Walk up the valley for 1m to the crag. [YL]

9 Lake District

The Lake District is the wettest part of England. It has, though, some of the best crags in the country and certainly the most beautiful scenery. A real mixture is offered to the rock climber that necessitates a careful gamble to gain dividends. The summer months are undoubtedly the best times to visit the Lakes, but preferably outside bank holiday periods. Each area has its own merits but, as a rule of thumb, the farther west you go the fewer people and the less tourism. The towns of Ambleside and Grasmere are the hot spots in this respect, even so Ambleside offers good shops, cafés and an eccentric cinema.

The choice of crags is huge but can be split into high and low level. The high-level crags can take up to 3 hours to walk to, and can be a very wet return trip. I have tried to make it possible for crags to be located without an OS map, but if you only buy one map in the whole of England I recommend this one since the tourist map covers the whole Lake District and is well worth the money. A lot of the crags can be reached from many points, but the descriptions given are usually the quickest and easiest. If the crags are not in sunshine they can be very cold and take several days to dry out after a wet spell. The low crags are invariably quite busy, especially in the Langdale and Borrowdale areas, and they should be saved for those days which might turn wet and nasty. I have tried to mention all of the low-level crags but only most of the larger high-level ones to save space.

Most routes in the Lakes are not sustained, but they require a good head and an ability to read an easy line up the cliff. Protection is varied and bolts are non-existent. Few would disagree that *when* you get a good day in the Lakes it is the finest climbing area in Britain. A useful tip: many of the high crags dry out to an arid state and having to walk back down 1,000ft for a drink of water is horrendous, so in summer carry water up with you. For the opposite conditions – which are more likely – climbing the easy routes in the wet proves satisfying to some with the great mountaineering urge. Fair enough, but care should be exercised since most of the crags in the wet become greasy and slippery, as do insurance companies when it comes to paying out a claim.

SOUTH WEST LAKES

This area covers climbing which can be easily accessed from Wasdale campsite at the N end of Lake Wastwater. To reach this lake

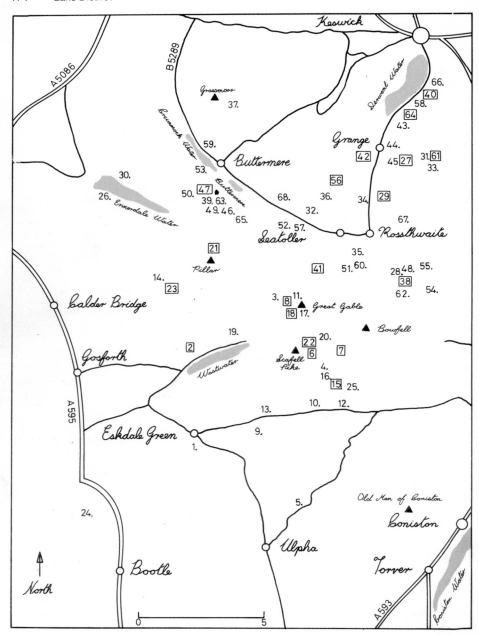

LAKE DISTRICT WEST

takes a good hour from Ambleside and most people who climb in this area base themselves at Wasdale in a tent or hotel. There is a climbing shop here and the town of Gosforth is the nearest place you can buy anything else. The climbing is virtually all on high crags, so when you come here you should expect to do a lot of walking – and drinking.

Brantrake Crag:
OS.96, TM3 GR.145 984   [1]

A good roadside crag, offering good climbing on 3 different outcrops. About 20 routes in total from Diff to 6b slab desperates. The lower and upper crags will accommodate the Diff leader, whilst the main wall offers some good 60ft slab routes. NW-facing and handy for the evening before a good session at The George IV.

Dir: 1m S of Eskdale Green. Leave The George IV pub (!) at Eskdale Green and take the small road going S over the river Esk. After 200yds fork R and the crag is 500yds on the L. [SDE]

Buckbarrow:
OS.89, TM3 GR.138 060   [2]

A popular crag in recent years, with a good many hard routes S-facing, about 40 routes, 100–200ft, Severe to E5 spread quite evenly across the grades. Worth a visit, something here to suit anyone.

Dir: 1.3m NNE of Nether Wasdale. Approaching Wastwater from Gosforth, take the road that goes to the N of Nether Wasdale, 1.5m after the fork the crag can be seen up on the L. Walk to the crag in 15 mins. [GG]

Boat Howe Crags:
OS.89 & 90, TM3 GR.199 110   [3]

Not a great crag, NE-facing at 2,000ft and of a broken nature, but offering some pleasant climbing in a wonderful position overlooking the Ennerdale valley. About 20 routes, 100–200ft, in the lower grades Diff to H Severe, with a few routes up to HVS. Quite remote and rarely sees climbers, good for peace and quiet.

Dir: 1.5m NNE of Wasdale Head. From Wasdale Head take the footpath up the R valley towards Sty Head, after 1m turn L up the smaller valley on a path to the R of the stream. At the top of the valley turn L and go around the mountain, the crag will be seen high on the L after about 300yds. 1.3 hrs. [GG]

Cam Spout:
OS.89 & 90, TM3 GR.216 057   [4]

Most regard this crag as a haunt for esoteric habitués practising Druid Naturalism. It was here in June 1893 that Edgar C. Blatenthwistle carried out his act of interminable doing and left a scar on the Cumbrian fellside that most would think of as a geological formation. Those who can abide the incestuous dark past of this SE-facing crag, 210ft, 10 routes around HVS, may well find their midsummer destiny here.

Dir: 4m NE of Boot. Approach: see Esk Buttress and High Scarth Crag. [SDE]

Dunnerdale:
OS.96, TM3 GR.215 954   [5]

This valley, one of the most beautiful in the Lakes, offers plenty of short climbs on little cliffs spread around the hillside. The crags offer no climbs of great distinction, but an alternative to the popular areas. It has always been a case of wandering around finding the odd outcrop with a couple of routes on. Long may it stay that way.

Dir: 7m N of Broughton in Furness.

East Buttress
OS.89 & 90, TM3 GR.215 067   [6]

A stupendous crag, offering most of the finest high-level hard routes in the Lakes. Wait for a dry spell, even so it is a very windy crag and can dry out in hours. A high crag, rather dirty after winter, E-facing and often bitter in the afternoon. Routes at 120–250ft, VS minimum, about 50 routes up to E6. Many of the routes are classics and quite steep, all go as expected for difficulty. Always worth a visit, attack it with oomph!

Dir: 2m SE of Wasdale Head. Approach: see Scafell Crag. [SDE]

Esk Buttress:
OS.89 & 90, TM3 GR.223 065 [7]

An excellent crag with the finest position in the Lake District. S-facing, about 30 routes H Severe to E5, 250ft. The climbing is good, but does not match the position except for the harder routes, E3 upwards. The two classics, Humdrum E3 and The Cumbrian E4, take the centre of the two obvious walls. It is the most remote crag in the Lakes, so much so that nobody ever goes there except on a superb day. Expect to find it very busy.

Dir: 4.5m NE of Boot, marked Dow Crag on the OS map. Go equipped for a good 12-hr day. From Boot drive W up the valley for 2.3m to the river Esk at Brotherkeld, park. Go up the valley to the N, after 0.5m Yew Crags can be seen up to the R and after 1m Heron Crag can be seen on the L side of the valley. Carry on and after 2m follow the main river to the L and start the uphill slog. After 2m more the path levels out into a fantastic valley, the crag Cam Spout is up to the L. Walk for 1m up the valley to the crag, which is seen straight ahead. This valley bottom can be very wet indeed. 2 hrs without rests. [SDE]

Gable Crag:
OS.89 & 90, TM3 GR.213 105 [8]

A good crag with some high-quality routes around the VS grade. About 40 routes, 150–250ft, in all grades Diff to good Extremes. The crag is quite steep and is best for the H Severe climber who is quite competent. The crag is at almost 3,000ft and N-facing, and for most of the year is best avoided. However, in June on a fine afternoon the sun will warm the crag up perfectly to one of the best spots in the Lakes, and in these conditions it is always worth visiting.

Dir: 1.9m NE of Wasdale Head. From Wasdale Head take the footpath up the R valley towards Sty Head, after 1m take the footpath running up the valley to the L. From the top of the valley turn R and take a footpath, after 500yds the crag can be seen high on the R. By continuing around the valley the crags of Green Gable can be seen leading up to the summit of the next mountain after the col on the R, Green Gable. [GG]

Gate Crag:
OS.96, TM3 GR.184 996 [9]

A line of 50–150ft, NW-facing crags. Quite low

down and offering about 25 routes in all grades V Diff to E4. A fair number around E1, the best of which are to be found at the R-hand end. The big trouble with the crag is that you can see the pub at Boot from the climbs and the attraction often becomes too great, even before you do a route.

Dir: 1m SSE of Boot. From the village take the track S to St Catherine's Church, walk upstream for 600yds, then cross by the bridge and follow the path up to the crag. [SDE]

Goat Crag – Eskdale
OS.96, TM3 GR.208 018 [10]

Nothing here for the super spurter but some good easy-angled slabs, 150ft, offering plenty of climbing to novices and leaders up to Hard Severe. W-facing and quite pleasant.

Dir: 2m ENE of Boot. Take the road going E for 1.5m, then fork L up the small lane. The crags are up the hillside to the L, 10 mins. [SDE]

Green Gable Crags:
OS.89 & 90, TM3 GR.214 106 [11]

A good alternative to Gable Crag since it faces W and catches the sun after midday. A high crag again, at almost 3,000ft, offering about 10 routes in the Diff to Severe grades, with one VS. Climbs are between 100–150ft. Nothing particularly difficult, but for a party of mixed ability this and Gable Crag can offer a sociable afternoon's cragging.

Dir: 2.1m NE of Wasdale Head. Approach: see Gable Crag. [GG]

Hard Knott Crag:
OS.89 & 90, TM3 GR.228 016 [12]

A 100ft crag, offering about a dozen routes in the grades Severe to E3, most between HVS and E2. The routes on the whole are quite strenuous. W-facing and quick to dry, a crag worth remembering and worth a visit.

Dir: 3.5m E of Boot. Take the small road going E to the Hard Knott Pass. Driving up the pass, the crag is on the L almost at the top. [SDE]

Hare Crag:
OS.89 & 90, TM3 GR.200 013 [13]

A small 60ft set of crags on which slab climbs

TOPHET WALL, Severe, Napes Crags, Great Gable. (Climber John Kingston, Photo Ian Roper)

...dominate. Plenty for everyone, Diff to E2, about 20 routes with no horrors. SW-facing and handy, worth a visit.

Dir: 1.5m E of Boot. Take the road for 1.5m to just past the youth hostel and the crags can be seen up to the L, 5 mins. [SDE]

Haskett Buttress:
OS.89, TM3 GR.155 114 [14]

A somewhat broken buttress, but nevertheless offers some challenging climbs. About half a dozen routes, 200–350ft, in the grades around Severe and VS. A high, N-facing crag.

Dir: 2.7m NW of Wasdale Head. Best taken in the course of a good day's walk. Park in the car park 1m before the end of Wastwater on the L. Walk up the fell to the L and follow the ridge all the way up and down to the summit of Steeple at the N end. The crag is down to the L in the cove and is easiest approached by the ridge on the R. About 1.5 hrs. [PR]

Heron Crag – Eskdale:
OS.89 & 90, TM3 GR.222 030 [15]

Quite a good crag, offering many climbs of quality which its appearance undermines. Not unduly steep but offers nothing to the Severe leader, all of the 20 or so routes here are between VS and E3, 2,000ft. SE-facing and very tempting if you know how far Esk Buttress actually is. Worth a visit. Further up the valley on the same side in about half a mile is Round Scar. This crag offers very good rock and plenty to accommodate the Severe leader.

Dir: 3m ENE of Boot. Approach: see Esk Buttress, but go up the L side of the valley. [SDE]

High Scarth Crag:
OS.89 & 90, TM3 GR.215 040 [16]

Quite a hike up to this one. About 10 routes, V Diff to VS, and a couple of E2s, 70ft. S-facing and a good bet on a chilly, sunny day in either spring or autumn. There is also a 40ft wall worth playing around on at **Silverybield Crag**, which is 500yds up and to the R of this crag. Some good 5b and harder problems.

Dir: 3.5m NE of Boot. Take the road E from Boot for 2.5m and park. Take the valley to the N and immediately cross over the river Esk on the footbridge. Take the footpath up the valley for about 600yds, then attack the hill to the L on the footpath. After 15 mins the path levels out and turns to the R, the crag can be seen straight ahead to the L of the footpath. You can reach the crag Cam Spout by carrying on the footpath, and also Esk Buttress in about 6 days. [SDE]

Kern Knotts:
OS.89 & 90, TM3 GR.216 094 [17]

In my humble opinion this is the best small crag in the Lakes. A grand position and fantastic rock, it was a pity when half of the crag fell down. The L-hand part offers half a dozen climbs, 120ft, around VS, which catch the sun all day. On the E face there are classics, VS to E3, 70–150ft. A must for the VS climber.

Dir: 1.8m ENE from Wasdale Head. Approach: see Napes Crags.

Napes Crags:
OS.89 & 90, TM3 GR.211 099 [18]

This crag is referred to by most as Great Gable, since it is the most important crag on the parent mountain. A high crag, offering climbs up to 350ft in a splendid position. S-facing, but beware – many of the good climbs are on the gully wall, which loses the sun around midday. About 30 climbs on the main buttress, Severe to E5, and a good 20 climbs on the crags to the W of the main buttress up the ridges. Also about 5 climbs up Napes Needle. One of the best crags in the Lakes.

Dir: 1.6m ENE from Wasdale Head, on the S side of Great Gable. A footpath to the S of Great Gable leads up the valley to the R and on the L side of the stream to Sty Head. Follow this 6ft-wide track all the way up the side of the mountain, after 2m and just before the col take the path going back L. After 500yds the crag of Kern Knotts is reached, carry on up the side of the mountain to the large obvious crag. The Needle is just a bit further on. 1.5 hrs. One can continue up the side of the fell by various ridges to the crags just before the summit, **Westmorland Crags**. All routes around Diff to V Diff, an interesting way up this most majestic of mountains. [GG]

Overbeck – Dropping Crag:
OS.89, TM3 GR.169 078   [19]

A good crag if you are short of time, 30-min. ascent. W-facing, solid rock, with about a dozen routes in the V Diff to VS category, 100–60ft. A crag worth remembering if visiting Wasdale and you get delayed.

Dir: 1.4m SW of Wasdale Head. Drive up the side of Wastwater to a car park 1m before the end of the L-hand side. From here a valley leads off to the L, take the footpath up the valley for a few hundred yards, then go up the ridge and the crag will be seen on the hillside to the L. [GG]

Pike's Crag:
OS.89 & 90, TM3 GR.210 073   [20]

This crag is worth listing separately to the other crags in the close area since it faces W, dries out far more quickly and is generally more pleasant to climb on. Forget people going on about Scafell and enjoy your day's climbing here. About 25 routes in the lower grades, Mod to VS, 150–350ft. Excellent around Diff to Severe. Worth a visit.

Dir: 1.8m SE of Wasdale Head. Approach: see Scafell Crag. [SDE]

Pillar Rock:
OS.89 & 90, TM3 GR.172 123   [21]

Most people are impressed by this huge piece of rock so long as their visit is on a good, sunny day. After Napes Needle it must have more history attached to it than the whole of the rest of the Lake District put together. The climbing is quite good in most places, indeed some of the routes are quite exceptional, but the main reason for the stature attached to the rock itself is the fine setting it commands over Ennerdale. The rock has over 100 routes, mostly 300–500ft long. All standards of routes, Mod to E3 at least, but the best routes are in the lower grades around V Diff and it is the climber of this standard who will probably benefit most from a visit. Catches the afternoon sun. There are many other crags in the area of a broken, smaller nature, offering end-less Diffs and Severes. Explore at will.

Dir: 2.5m NNW of Wasdale Head. Take the valley to the L from Wasdale Head, after 1m follow the R-hand valley all the way up to the top. Turn L along the ridge and after 0.5m a path will be seen dropping down to the R and around to the crag in 1,000yds. The rock itself looks like a lump on the side of the mountain. 2 hrs. [PR]

Scafell Crag:
OS.89 & 90, TM3 GR.209 068   [22]

One of the best crags in the Lakes. A high, steep and uncompromising crag, N-facing and with climbs up to 250ft. There are a good 70 climbs on the main face and outlying crags to either side. The main crag offers little worth doing below Severe, but at VS and E1 upwards there are some classic climbs and none too difficult. Worth a trip only on very good weather. The crags off to the R are known as **Shamrock**, just to the R of the main cliff, and **Black Crag**, about 300yds further round to the R.

Dir: 1.7m SE of Wasdale Head. From the car park at the end of the lake by Wasdale Head a footpath goes up to Scafell Pike via Lingmell Gill. Take this all the way up the valley to the top, crag is unmistakable on the R 15 mins. To the L is Pike's Crag. Carry on over the col and down a very short way to the R for East Buttress. [SDE]

Steeple:
OS.89, TM3 GR.158 116   [23]

There are several crags here in the valley to the N of the peak of Steeple. High and N-facing, they all have a somewhat cold atmosphere, but offer some good routes in the lower grades. About 30 routes in total, climbs vary in length up to 350ft and a Severe leader should be able to cope with any of the routes here on the three crags. A good alternative to Pillar Rock, which can be packed full of climbers.

Dir: 2.3m NW of Wasdale Head. From Wasdale Head take the valley up to the L going to Mosedale. Follow the footpath straight up the valley to the top, Windy Gap, drop down the other side slightly and go around to the L. The first crag encountered is **Black Crag – Steeple**, further around at the back of the cove is **Scoat Fell Crag**, and on the ridge all the way round is the crag called **Steeple**. 1.5 hrs. [PR]

Waberthwaite Wharry:
OS.96, TM3 GR.113 944   [24]

Not a brilliant quarry, but somewhere to boulder away the hours in winter if it is too cold to venture on to the high crags. A top rope can also be of use here, as the longer problems are not worth dying for.

Dir: 4m N of Bootle. Take the A595 N for 4.7m to a turning on the L to Hall Waberthwaite. Follow this for 100yds, then R into the quarry, past the first and into the second. [SDE]

Yew Crags – Eskdale:
OS.89 & 90, TM3 GR.222 022   [25]

Some rather unattractive, NW-facing, crags, offering about 10 climbs on the cleaner sections, Severe to E2, about 100ft.

Dir: 3m ENE of Boot. Approach: see Esk Buttress. [SDE]

NORTH WEST LAKES

This area consists of the climbing which is easily accessible from Borrowdale valley at the southern end of Derwent Water. There are a lot of low-level crags here, of which most are W-facing and very quick to dry, bearing in mind that Borrowdale is the wettest valley in England. If the sun shines it is absolutely beautiful and a great place to climb.

Angler's Crag:
OS.89, TM3 GR.099 151   [26]

About 30 climbs, Diff to E1, on this 100ft crag on the edge of Ennerdale Water. The crag is N-facing and often wet and slippery. In the dry, however, it is good fun and worthy of a short visit.

Dir: 2m ESE of Ennerdale Bridge. From the village take the small road going W to the end of the lake and a car park. Follow the footpath around the S shore of the lake to the crag in about 1m. [PR]

Black Crag – Borrowdale
OS.89 & 90, TM3 GR.263 172   [27]

One of the best crags in the valley for the Extreme leader. Of the 40 or so routes, 20 are Extreme. There is also a good selection of VS and HVS routes and the classic 350ft Severe, Troutdale Pinnacle. The climbs are all around 300ft and offer adequate protection. NW-facing, best in the afternoon.

Dir: 4m S of Keswick. Take the B5289 S for 3m to the Borrowdale Hotel. Here a track leads off up the valley to the woods, a footpath bears up and L to the obvious crag in the valley in about 20 mins. Up to the R is Great End Crag. [BOR]

Bleak How:
OS.89 & 90, TM3 GR.273 124   [28]

Quite a good evening crag, NW-facing and offering some pleasant slabby routes around the lower grades, HVS to E4, 100ft. The rock is good and sound, and clean for the area. Worth a visit.

Dir: 1.8m SSE of Rossthwaite. Take the B5289 further S for 0.3m to a small lane on the L, follow this to some parking places at the end. Carry on down the valley by foot to where the river forks, the fell in between has a path running up the R-hand side of the nose to the crag quickly. By continuing up the path one reaches the crags at the top of the fell, Eagle Crag to the L and Heron Crag to the R. Further along the fell on the R at a high level is Sergeant's Crag. [BOR]

Bowderstone Crags:
OS.89 & 90, TM3 GR.256 165   [29]

An area of immense popularity with just about everyone. **The Bowderstone** itself is a boulder 40ft wide and some 20ft high, with a lot of hard bouldering on it. Bowderstone Crag is up the hill from The Bowderstone and offers about 25 routes in the lower Diff grades and up to Hell's Wall E6, W-facing and sunny. Also there is **Woden's Face**, a small, popular buttress with some 60ft Diffs and Severes, excellent for beginners. **Quayfoot Buttress** offers 15 routes around 100ft in the HVS upwards grades. A very good area.

Dir: 4.5m S of Keswick. Take the B5289 S for 5m to a car park on the L just past the turn-off to Grange. Here a footpath leads off S through the woods past Woden's Face to The Bowderstone, then a path can be taken on the L up to the Bowderstone Crags. Alternatively, one can go L from the car park, and up above in the trees is Quayfoot Buttress. [BOR]

Bowness Knott:
OS.89, TM3 GR.111 154   [30]

A group of three crags low on the hillside, offering around 20 routes, Diff to E2. The crags are W-facing, dry quickly, a few minutes from the road and quite pleasant. Climbs are from 80–350ft. Worth a visit for anyone Diff upwards.

Dir: 2.6m E of Ennerdale Bridge. Take the road which goes around the N side of the lake, the crag is on the L at the start of the forest. There is a car park at the bottom. [PR]

Brown Dodd:
OS.89 & 90, TM3 GR.268 178   [31]

Some vegetated buttresses, offering 10 climbs of around 120ft in the lower grades VS to E1. NE-facing at 1,000ft. If it were not for the beautiful view, there would be no reason to climb here.

Dir: 3m S of Keswick. Approach: see Reecastle Crags. [BOR]

Buckstone How:
OS.89 & 90, TM3 GR.223 143   [32]

A large and steep crag with some interesting climbing. The rock in most parts is of dubious nature and should be treated accordingly, with dynamite preferably. SW-facing and dries quickly, easy walk from the road, very easy access back to the brilliant pub at Buttermere. A score of 200ft routes, VS upwards. A challenging cliff, and absorbing at VS.

Dir: 3.5m SE of Buttermere. Take the B5289 to the top of the Honister Pass, walk back into the valley along a track, then across the scree to the crag. [BEC]

Caffel Side Crags:
OS.89 & 90, TM3 GR.269 175   [33]

The crags on the W side of the Watendlath valley are quite awful and climbing here on these E-facing, vegetated, snivelling 100ft cliffs is often thoroughly unpleasant. The protection is less than obvious, and quite frankly I suggest you climb elsewhere.

Dir: 3.7m S of Keswick. Approach: see Reecastle Crags. [BOR]

Castle Crag – Borrowdale:
OS.89 & 90, TM3 GR.249 159   [34]

A crag in an impressive position with fab views. Not a lot else to commend it: variable rock, scrappy buttresses huddled together, about 20 routes Severe to E3, mainly in the HVS category. Protection in parts is not at all obvious – does it even exist?

Dir: 1m S of Grange. From the café at Grange take the footpath going S by the river, after 0.5m a campsite is reached. Carry on and take the footpath on the R in about 200yds, after 400yds the crag can be seen on the L. [BOR]

Combe Ghyll:
OS.89 & 90, TM3 GR.250 120   [35]

This is the name given to the valley situated between Stonethwaite and Seathwaite running S. The L side of the valley offers some excellent climbing, W-facing, in the easy grades Diff and V Diff. Areas of note are: **Glaciated Slab** and **Intake Ridge**, about 10 routes, Mods and Diffs, 100ft; **Twa Hummocks**, about 8 routes, Mod to Severe, 200ft; **Dove's Nest**, 5 routes, Mod to Severe, 200ft. The crags on the R side are dealt with separately.

Dir: 2m SSW of Rossthwaite. Take the B5289 for 1m, where a footpath leads off to the L and up the valley. The Glaciated Slab is immediately up on the L. Walk up into the valley floor, nearly 1m, here the crags up on the L offer the rest of the climbing in the lower grades. [BOR]

Dale Head Crag:
OS.89 & 90, TM3 GR.225 156   [36]

Of all the rock on the N slope of Dale head, this is the most significant buttress, easily spotted by the masses of vegetation all over the rock. Dries out very slowly. About a dozen routes in total, around Severe to HVS, 150–300ft. After a pleasant walk up the valley the best decision would be to carry on walking, preferably in the direction of a tavern.

Dir: 2.7m S of Little Town. From the village take the track running down the valley to the S, the crag is at the head of the valley. [BEC]

Dove Crag – Grasmoor:
OS.89 & 90, TM3 GR.177 206 [37]

A large crag, NE-facing, with a handful of routes in horrible gulleys, VS–HVS, 240ft. For the earth dwellers.

Dir: 2.3m N of Buttermere. Take the B5289 N for 2.3m to a parking spot. Here a path leads off up the fell to the R and to the summit of Grasmoor, 2,791ft. The crag is over on the N side. [BEC]

Eagle Crag – Borrowdale:
OS.89 & 90, TM3 GR.278 121 [38]

A fair crag but, being NE-facing and at 1,500ft, it rarely comes into condition, and when it does there always seems to be warmer and more attractive rock elsewhere. Suitable in a very good, long summer. On the lower crag 5 easy Extremes, 120–50ft; on the main crag about 30 routes, all above HVS to E5, around 150ft.

Dir: 2m SSE of Rossthwaite. Approach: see Bleak How. [BOR]

Eagle Crag – Buttermere:
OS.89 & 90, TM3 GR.172 145 [39]

A very large and impressive crag that offers little in the way of good climbing. N-facing, vegetated and consistently damp, this cliff will never become popular. About 30 routes, 200–500ft, Severe upwards to E3. The dirtiest crag in the Lake District.

Dir: 1.6m S of Buttermere. Take the B5289 to Gatesgarth at the S end of the lake. Take the footpath running around the S end, then up the path on the fell to the R, going beneath some small crags to a high valley, Birkness Combe. Straight ahead is Eagle Crag, to the R is Grey Crag and to the L is Sheepbone Buttress. All are reached in about 1 hr. [BEC]

Falcon Crags:
OS.89 & 90, TM3 GR.272 206 [40]

There are two W-facing crags here, Lower Falcon and Upper Falcon. They offer similar climbing, the lower being perhaps the looser of the two. There are about 50 climbs, of which most are on the lower crag, 150–250ft. The climbing is not well protected and one should be very aware of this. Belays at the top are hard to find so longish ropes are advised.

Dir: 2m S of Keswick. Take the B5289 S to Derwent Water, after 1.7m the road runs along the side of the lake, and shortly there is a turning off up to the L (to Watendlath) and a car park. From here the crag can be reached by walking back L and up the fellside. [BOR]

Gillercombe:
OS.89 & 90, TM3 GR.221 124 [41]

Most of the climbs on this crag are long – indeed many would say 400ft too long – but nevertheless Diffs and Severes abound on this broken crag in a fine setting. For the more ambitious there are a few easy Extremes on the R wall of the crag to the N end, around 150ft. About 20 routes in total. There is often vegetation, as is typical for a mountain crag. E-facing, a good crag for the early risers.

Dir: 1m W of Seathwaite. From the houses a footpath runs off to the W and over the river by a footbridge, then straight up the fellside beside the stream. After 0.5m the path levels out into a high valley, the crag is high on the R. Allow 15 mins to 1 hr. [BOR]

Goat Crag:
OS.89 & 90, TM3 GR.245 165 [42]

The only crag of real significance on the W side of the Borrowdale valley. There are some classic hard routes here, none of which are any harder than E3 it is rumoured. The crag also has many small buttresses surrounding it, which offer plenty of routes in the VS to E1 standard. The main crag, some 300ft high, is very imposing when you are actually on it, with about 20 middle-grade Extremes. To be kept for those really scorching summer days.

Dir: 0.7m SSW of Grange. The crag is to the S on the side of the fell. Follow the track going S from the village, a path goes up the fellside on the R to the crag in 10 mins. The ridge before is referred to as Knitting How and offers some very good Diffs around 150ft. [BOR]

Gowder Crag:
OS.89 & 90, TM3 GR.266 187 [43]

One of the very good crags in the area. W-facing and offering a score of 200–300ft routes in the middle grades VS, HVS and E1. There are a few harder climbs, but the crag lends itself to VS and HVS climbs. Rarely does one have to resort to small holds, just marginal runners. Worth a visit. There is a lot more climbing in the area on the looser, more vegetated crags **Lodore Crag**, opposite, and **Hogs Back**, the obvious ridge. Routes in all grades, one can explore at will. A very beautiful area.

Dir: 3m S of Keswick. Take the B5289 S for 3m to the Lodore Hotel on the L. Here a footpath leads off beside the river on the E side of the crag in 5 mins. [BOR]

Grange Crags: Access
OS.89 & 90, TM3 GR.258 177   [44]

There have been reports here of difficulty with access, the nature of which is unclear. Proceed with courtesy. There are about 50 routes here, 50–100ft, mostly VS to E2 but with a few easier climbs. NW-facing and very close to the road.

Dir: 3.5m S of Keswick. Take the B5289 for 3m to the Borrowdale Hotel on the L, carry on for 0.4m. Here a track on the L leads off up the valley, continue around for another 100yds to a parking spot. The crags are directly above. [BOR]

Greatend Crags:
OS.89 & 90, TM3 GR.260 170   [45]

A large, NW-facing crag with some very good routes. About 20 routes, all HVS upwards with the exception of a Diff, about 250–300ft long. Vegetation is an ongrowing problem. Worth thinking about.

Dir: 3.5m S of Keswick. Approach: see Black Crag. [BOR]

Green Crag:
OS.89 & 90, TM3 GR.201 132   [46]

A big N-facing crag, offering a dozen routes between VS and E4. Protection is often very elusive amongst the heavy vegetation. Very slow to dry, but a fantastic position nevertheless.

Dir: 3m SSE of Buttermere. Take the B5289 for 2m to Gatesgarth, then take the valley ahead, Warnscale Bottom. The crag is at the head of the valley to the R of the footpath in 40 mins. By carrying on up the footpath to the small tarns, the crag of **Round How** can be seen over to the L. This has about 5 Diffs, 100ft, on good rock, but still N-facing. [BEC]

Grey Crag:
OS.89 & 90, TM3 GR.172 148   [47]

The best crag in the Buttermere area. Good, sound, clean rock which dries quickly. SE-facing and worth an early start. A score of routes in the lower grades, Mod to VS, but most being Diffs. Great for the inexperienced climber and the VS leader who enjoys being the super crag-rat. Worth a visit.

Dir: 1.4m S of Buttermere. Approach: see Eagle Crag. [BEC]

Heron Crag – Borrowdale:
OS.89 & 90, TM3 GR.274 121   [48]

A broken crag offering about 10 routes, 250ft, in the lower grades around Diff to VS, on the main crag; and about 10 more routes in the HVS–E2 grades, 100ft, on the upper tier to the L of the crag. W-facing and dries quickly.

Dir: 2m SSE of Rossthwaite. Approach: see Bleak How. [BOR]

High Crag:
OS.89 & 90, TM3 GR.183 145   [49]

Quite a good crag but a bit cold generally, NE-facing at 1,600ft. The rock is generally sound and clean though! About 40 routes in all grades, with some classics at VS to E1, 100–200ft. In nice weather worth a visit.

Dir: 2m SSE of Buttermere. Take the B5289 for 2m to the end of the lake at Gatesgarth. From here a footpath leads across the end of the lake and to the fell in the S, take the L path up the fell and the crag is on the R at the top in 30 mins. [BEC]

High Stile:
OS.89, TM3 GR.166 146   [50]

Some good Diffs high on the S side of High Stile. The routes are 100–180ft, on very good, clean rock, S-facing and with a fantastic view. Superb if included on a day's walk around High Stile. Worth visiting.

Dir: 1.6m SSW of Buttermere. Take the track from the village S between the two lakes and up the fell straight ahead. From the summit the crags are just over and down to the R. [BEC]

Hind Crag:
OS.89 & 90, TM3 GR.238 112   [51]

A good spot for the mountain scrambler. A handful of 600ft Diffs and Severes. The climbing is quite broken but good sport on a cold day if you want to keep moving. SW-facing and a pleasant way to climb up Glaramara. Round in the gully there are a couple of E1s, 200ft, on the obvious wall.

Dir: 0.5m SSE of Seathwaite. Walk up the valley for 200yds to a path which leads up the fell on the L, the crag is high above. There is also some good Diff climbing to be found on Aaron Crag, which is at the top of the fell splitting the two valleys. Short but on good rock, often referred to as **Grains Ghyll**. [BOR]

Honister Crag:
OS.89 & 90, TM3 GR.214 143   [52]

If you are in search of a thoroughly miserable day's climbing then come to Honister Crag. A crag which is damp, cold, covered in excrement, and a great long hike up from the road is the reward for those who set forth in search of Lakeland rock on the N side of Fleetwith Pike. Half a dozen routes around 5a, 250ft – interesting!

Dir: 3m SE of Buttermere. Take your limousine on the B5289 to the top of the Honister Pass. The crag is high on the S side of the pass due W about 1m, best approached from the top of the fell then bearing down to the R at the col. [BEC]

Ling Crag:
OS.89, TM3 GR.155 182   [53]

The best wet-weather crag in the valley. E-facing but beside the lake in a nice position on a walkers' highway. Some slabs at Diff standard to occupy all novices, and steep walls with half a dozen routes around HVS, 140ft. Something for everyone.

Dir: 1.3m NW of Buttermere. From the village take the path running along the E side of Crummock Water to the crag in 1m. [BEC]

Linning Crag:
OS.89 & 90, TM3 GR.283 113   [54]

A remotely situated crag, which walkers tend to fall off in the mist when coming down the footpath – it is marked going over the cliff. Gets a bit mossy, but in general is very good rock and provides enjoyable climbing. About 15 routes in the lower grades, Mod to HVS.

Dir: 3m SE of Rossthwaite. Approach: see Long Band crag. [BOR]

Long Band Crag:
OS.89 & 90, TM3 GR.282 125   [55]

A small but impressive crag in a very nice position. SW-facing and some 100ft high, this crag offers a handful of routes in the E4 category, and with limited protection. Gear is minimal and abseil inspection advised.

Dir: 2m SE of Rossthwaite. Carry on S along the B5289 for 0.4m, then turn off L to Stonethwaite and park. Walk up the valley and where it splits take the L branch, the crag is up on the L. Continue along the valley floor and up the path for another mile to Linning Crag, 1 hour. [BOR]

Miner's Crag:
OS.89 & 90, TM3 GR.231 157   [56]

This crag is perhaps the best of a group of four, all W-facing and quite reasonable. About 50 routes in total from Diff to E3, but nearly all in the Diff and Severe grades. All the routes dry very quickly and are climbed rarely. A good spot to get away from it all.

Dir: 2m S of Little Town. Take the track leading S down the valley, after 2m this turns into a footpath and passes a rocky buttress low on the L. Soon after the crags are seen high on the L: **Grey Buttress**, then **Red Crag**, then **Waterfall Buttress**, and then at the end **Miner's Buttress**. [BEC]

Moss Crag:
OS.89 & 90, TM3 GR.212 147   [57]

A misplaced name perhaps, for a worthy little crag. In a good summer the rock dries well and offers about 15 good 80ft routes, HVS upwards, with also a couple of easier Severes. Very handy and worth a visit if passing.

Dir: 2.5m SE of Buttermere. Take your hackney carriage along the B5289 for 3m to the bridge crossing the stream. The crag is on the fellside up to the R, 10 mins. [BEC]

National Trust Crags:
OS.89 & 90, TM3 GR.268 196   [58]

These crags are situated in the trees, W-facing and at 500ft. There are about 20 routes up to 100ft, Severe to E2, with a few pleasant climbs. However, the crags are generally loose and serious, and the rock offers little in the way of natural protection.

Dir: 2.5m S of Keswick. Take the B5289 S for 2m to where it runs beside the lake, follow the road over a small hill, then back beside the lake again to a car park shortly on the L. Walk up to the crags in the woods. From the top of the crag there are fine views over the lake. [BOR]

Rannerdale Knotts:
OS.89, TM3 GR.163 184   [59]

Not a lot of climbing, but low level and close to the road. A V Diff and a few VSs, 100ft. NW-facing and average.

Dir: 1.2m NW of Buttermere. Take the B5289 N, just after a R-hand bend in the road the crags can be seen on the fell to the R. [BEC]

Raven Crag – Borrowdale:
OS.89 & 90, TM3 GR.248 114   [60]

A large, broken crag, offering routes of all grades. About 30 routes, mainly Diff to VS but also with a couple of easy Extremes, 100–500ft. NE-facing and best in a good summer.

Dir: 2.2m SSW of Rossthwaite. Approach as for Combe Ghyll to the valley floor, Raven Crag is at the end of the valley high on the R. [BOR]

Reecastle Crags:
OS.89 & 90, TM3 GR.273 176   [61]

A good, small crag of solid rock, close to the road and W-facing. About 30 climbs around 100ft, mainly in the low Extreme grades with a few desperates and a few Severes and VSs. Worth a visit.

Dir: 3.5m S of Keswick. Take the B5289 S to the Borrowdale valley, after 2m take a fork going up towards Watendlath, and 2m later the crags are seen directly on the L. On the opposite side of the valley is Caffel Side Crag and to the far R-hand end of this are the Brown Dodd Crags. [BOR]

Sergeant's Crag:
OS.89 & 90, TM3 GR.274 114   [62]

Quite a pleasant crag, even though the climbing is somewhat broken. There are about a dozen routes, mostly around Severe with a few Diffs and HVSs. Good crag for the lower-standard climber. The easy routes are very long with the harder routes being quite short, 100ft. NW-facing at 1,200ft, great view.

Dir: 2.5m SSE of Rossthwaite. Approach: see Bleak How. [BOR]

Sheepbone Buttress:
OS.89 & 90, TM3 GR.179 144   [63]

The smallest of the three crags in Birkness Combe, offering about 10 routes, either easy Extremes or Diffs and Severes, 100–200ft. NW-facing and catches the afternoon sun in summer, the rock is clean and dries quite quickly. Often the best crag in the combe.

Dir: 1.6m S of Buttermere. Approach: see Eagle Crag. [BEC]

Shepherd's Crag:
OS.89 & 90, TM3 GR.263 185   [64]

The most popular crag in the whole of the Lake District, and generally the first to dry after rain. A mere 30 seconds from the road, W-facing and with about 100 routes of all grades from Diff to E6. The easy routes are excellent 150–200ft climbs, the harder routes tend to be short and technical. All the routes are very polished and most are very good. Many of the hardest routes are top-roped and because of the local dislike of bolts I recommend that you continue their tradition.

Dir: 3.2m S of Keswick. Take the B5289 S to the far end of Derwent Water and the Borrowdale Hotel. The crag is back along the road overlooking the lake. A pleasant spot, but can get very crowded with tourists. [BOR]

Striddle Crag:
OS.89 & 90, TM3 GR.204 139   [65]

A broken crag, but offering about a dozen climbs in the lower grades, V Diff to VS, 200ft. SW-facing with a very fine view.

Dir: 2.7m SSE of Buttermere. Take the B5289 to

the S end of the lake and the group of houses known as Gatesgarth. Take the footpath leading up the valley to the R side of the fell in front, after 1.5m the crag is over on the L. [BEC]

Walla Crag:
OS.89 & 90, TM3 GR.274 212   [66]

A reasonable, W-facing crag with about 15 routes, VS to E2, 130–200ft. The cliff is quite vegetated in parts and if damp can lead to some interesting situations. There is a gully which goes at V Diff, but otherwise this is not a cliff for the novice.

Dir: 1.5m SSE of Keswick. Take the B5289 S from Keswick for 1.4m to a National Trust car park on the L. The crag is to the L above the trees and a path leads up to it through the woods. [BOR]

Yew Crag – Borrowdale:
OS.89 & 90, TM3 GR.264 152   [67]

Not a bad crag in parts, W-facing and 100–170ft. A handful of Diffs and Severes with a

couple of HVS routes on the steeper parts of the crag. Quite good for beginners.

Dir: 5.3m S of Keswick. Take the B5289 S to Rosthwaite and the worst pub in the Lake District. From here a footpath leads up the side of the fell towards Watendlath, the crag is on the R after about 0.5m. [BOR]

Yew Crags – Buttermere
OS.89 & 90, TM3 GR.219 147   [68]

These W-facing crags offer messy climbing on mossy rock with little character. About 20 climbs, of which 5 are below VS and the rest around E1, 150ft. Hardly the centre of the world's climbing.

Dir: 3m SE of Buttermere. Take your Batmobile on the B5289, up the Honister Pass. After 3m the road crosses a stream, carry on for 0.8m where the crag can be seen up on the L. To the R about 400yds is the crag of Buckstone How, which is best reached by a track from the top of the pass. [BEC]

SOUTH EAST LAKES

This is by far the most popular area in the Lake District for climbers, walkers and tourists. The climbing is very varied and for the most part is excellent. The three principal areas are Langdale, Coniston and the Hodge Hall slate quarries. Dow Crag at Coniston is perhaps the best crag in the Lakes with superb climbing in every grade. The higher crags at Langdale offer the better rock to climb on, even so many of the cliffs give exciting exposure. There are few really hard routes, but ample in the lower grades to E4. For the hardest routes in the area visit Hodge Close, a slate quarry with a large pool of water at the bottom, an eerie setting – the fastest-drying crag in the immediate area. All the routes are serious and top-rope inspection is almost essential. One of the best fell runs in the Lake District is here, Coniston–Wetherlam–Old Man–Coniston, great for relaxation on a summer's evening.

Black Crag – Rydal:
OS.90, TM3 GR.362 108   [69]

A steep, SE-facing crag, offering a handful of climbs VS to E4, 100ft. Very rarely crowded. Needs an effort, 1 hr at least.

Dir: 3m N of Rydal. Approach: see Erne Crag. [BEC]

Black Hole Quarry:
OS.90, TM3 GR.314 028   [70]

An impressive quarry, offering a handful of routes around E3, 120ft. S-facing and quick to dry, but varying protection, proceed with caution. Worth a snoot.

Dir: 0.3m S of Little Langdale. From the village –

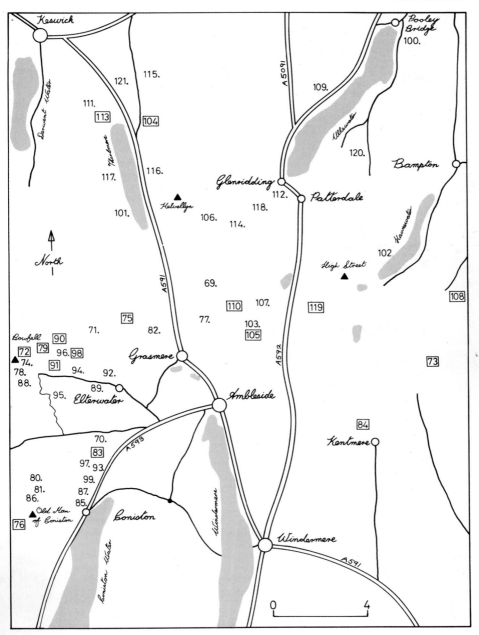

LAKE DISTRICT EAST

and pub! – take the small lane running S. After 400yds cross over the river on the footbridge and take the footpath running up the hill to the R, the quarry is reached after a few minutes. [SDE]

Blea Crag – Easdale:
OS.90, TM3 GR.301 080   [71]

This gets the Worst Crag of the Area award, not to mention the bloody long walk to get to it. 200ft high with a V Diff and a couple of HVSs. N-facing, well vegetated and often very damp. To be avoided at all costs.

Dir: 2.3m WNW of Grasmere. Take the small lane leading up the valley to the NW, Easdale. Take the footpath along the valley floor on the L side of the river, after 800yds take the L fork up the hill to Easdale Tarn. From the tarn the path splits and the L branch goes up to Blea Crag. The wiser people would take the R branch. 1.5 hrs. [GL]

Bowfell Buttress:
OS.89 & 90, TM3 GR.245 069   [72]

The classic crag of the area. NE-facing with a dozen routes around Diff to Severe and the odd Extreme, 200–350ft. All routes worth doing. A very impressive high-mountain crag which needs good weather, a must in anyone's climbing years.

Dir: 6m W of Elterwater. Approach: see Neckband Crag. [GL]

Buckbarrow Crag:
OS.90, TM3 GR.483 073   [73]

An excellent crag, SW-facing and hidden away from the main hordes of climbers in this remote valley. About 30 routes, Diff to E4, 100–300ft. Good rock and a pleasant spot.

Dir: 1m N of Sadgill, 7m ENE of Ambleside. Park at Sadgill and walk up the valley to the N for 1m. The crag is up on the R from here. [BEC]

Cambridge Crag – North Buttress:
OS.89 & 90, TM3 GR.245 069   [74]

A high crag with a couple of very good routes, a Severe and a V Diff. The North Buttress to the R of the crag offers 10 climbs, quite a bit harder, VS to E3. NE-facing and quite technical climbing, routes 100–400ft.

Dir: 5.3m W of Elterwater. Approach: see Neckband Crag. [GL]

Deer Bield Crag:
OS.90, TM3 GR. 303 096   [75]

An interesting crag with routes of very great interest. About 10 interesting Extremes, 5 not-so-interesting Extremes, and half a dozen pleasantly interesting lower-grade Severes, 200ft. NE-facing and quite cool, but perfect on the summer scorcher of a day. Worth an interesting visit.

Dir: 2.5m WNW of Grasmere. Take the track NW to the Easdale valley, follow this for 2.5m and the crag will then be seen up on the L, 1.5 hrs. [GL]

Dow Crag:
OS.96 & 97, TM3 GR. 264 977   [76]

One of the finest crags in the Lake District. E-facing and best in the morning. To climb all day here needs a very warm afternoon indeed. There are 5 large buttresses with almost 100 routes in all grades, 250–350ft. The best climbs are to the L of the crag and they keep the sun longest. The central buttress has the classic Murray's Route, Severe, but is crossed by so many routes that I have witnessed 14 people at one belay – complete chaos as most had double ropes. A crag not to be missed.

Dir: 2.5m W of Coniston. From the town take a small lane signposted Walna Scar Track past the Sun Hotel, follow this up the hill and through some gates to park on some grass. A path then leads off W, fairly level, after 1m the path turns R uphill and goes up to a lake called Goats Water. There are no streams at the crag, which should now be obvious. Up well to the L in the next cove is the small **Blind Tarn Crag**, a handful of VS to E1 climbs, 120ft. Not in the same class as Dow. [SDE]

Erne Crag:
OS.90, TM3 GR.359 087   [77]

A fair crag, SE-facing and quite steep, lending itself to hardish climbing. About 10 routes, VS to E2. The best climbing is to be found on the L side of the crag. Worth a visit.

Dir: 1.6m of Rydal. Park at the car park in Rydal. Take the track going N up the valley, after 1m it becomes a footpath and climbs the fellside to the L. Erne Crag is high up to the L and can be recognised by the area of whitish rock on the L-hand side. To reach Black Crag continue up the ridge and follow this to the head of the valley, the crag is about 1.5m further on with the same aspect as Erne Crag. [BEC]

Flat Crags:
OS.89 & 90, TM3 GR.245 069 [78]

A good crag living up to its name quite adequately enough for most. High and NE-facing. There are about 10 climbs here, Diff to E5, 150ft. There are only a couple of easy routes, most are around E1.

Dir: 5m W of Elterwater. Approach: see Neckband Crag. [GL]

Gimmer Crag:
OS.89 & 90, TM3 GR.277 070 [79]

Few would dispute that this crag would rate in the world's top 50 crags. It is a crag of magnificence and splendour, and sheer delight to climb upon, W-facing at 1,600ft. There are about 60 routes mainly up to VS with half a dozen Extremes, E1 to E3. The climbs are not difficult and the situation, high on the side of the Langdale Pikes in the evening sun, can be enjoyed in a relaxed frame of mind.

Dir: 3.5m WNW of Elterwater. Take the B5343 W from Elterwater to the car park at the end of the road, Old Dungeon Ghyll. From here Raven Crag overlooks the pub in fine fashion. Take the footpath up towards Raven Crag, then bear L on to another footpath signposted Gimmer Crag. After walking up the side of the fell for hours the crag is reached in about 1m. Keep going L and the cliff will become apparent. 45 mins. [GL]

Great How Crags:
OS.96 & 97, TM3 GR.277 998 [80]

Some extensive crags, offering about half a dozen V Diffs and a couple of E1s, 200ft. SE-facing and quite secluded. Not very popular even though the rock is quite good. There is also **Little How Crag** off to the L, less broken and offers perhaps better climbing, plenty in the lower Severe and Diff grades. Worth a visit for some pleasant climbing.

Dir: 2.3m NW of Coniston. Take the track going up the Coppermines valley, continue up past the youth hostel on the footpath to Levers Water, a small dammed lake. The crags are at the N end, Great How to the R and Little How to the L. [SDE]

Grey Crag – Coniston
OS.96 & 97, TM3 GR.282 987 [81]

An excellent crag for the VS leader, worth a special trip. About 25 routes from Diff to HVS, 15 at VS, 140ft. SE-facing and good, solid rock. The theme of the routes is Wagner's *Ring*, come here in search of Brünnhilde.

Dir: 1.5m WNW of Coniston. Approach is best made on a white horse, bearing in mind that a hasty retreat could prove necessary in the likely event of rain and consequential flooding. From the town take the track going NW up the Coppermines valley. After 1m a youth hostel is reached, the crag is straight on and up to the L beneath Leves Water. By following the stream up to the L the slightly vegetated **Cove Crag** is reached, good climbing around HS. To the R of the Grey Crag across the streams is **Kernel Crag**, which offers a handful of E2s and Diffs, NE-facing. Generally the whole area has lots of small crags worth bouldering around on. [SDE]

Helm Crag:
OS.90, TM3 GR.325 089 [82]

Quite a good, small 100ft crag, SW-facing and offering about 10 routes in the lower grades, Diff to VS. Worth an investigation.

Dir: 1m NW of Grasmere. From the town a small road goes up to the Easdale valley. As this turns into a footpath the crag can be seen over to the R, about 100yds behind a quarry. [GL]

Hodge Close Quarry:
OS.90, TM3 GR.316 016 [83]

Most people regard this as a place definitely to avoid at all costs. This is very understandable but since top-roping is great fun, Hodge Close should become more popular. A bolts blitz on the existing routes would see this become the most popular Extreme crag in the Lakes. It catches the afternoon sun, dries out instantly and is very sheltered, 25 seconds from the car. The protection in general is terrible, and if you are squeamish, do not be a second. Sticky boots essential, plus a towel and a 40ft piece of rope to make top-roping easy. There are about 40 routes from E1 to E6, and about 30 routes on the outlying smaller quarries all of a similar nature, 150–200ft.

Dir: 2.5m N of Coniston. Take the A593 N for 1.5m to the second lane on the L, follow this seemingly for ever, keeping R, and arrive at the quarry after 2.2m. **Parrock Quarry** is just to the N and **Peatfield Quarry** is just to the W, both only a few minutes' walk. [SDE]

Iving Crag:
OS.90, TM3 GR.453 049   [84]

One of the best crags in the eastern Lake District. Steep and uncompromising, E-facing and good rock. Protection here needs a desperate review, be prepared for interesting situations. About 20 routes, Severe to E6, but mainly in the E grades 1 and 4, 30–60ft, with good bouldering in the area as well.

Dir: 0.5m NW of Kentmere, 5m E of Ambleside. From the church in the pub-less village a track leads N up the valley. For alternative amusement one can go due W from the church down a lane to its end in 0.5m, then continue a short while to the impressive **Brockstone**, a very good, large boulder, offering good bouldering in all grades. [BEC]

Long Crag:
OS.96 & 97, TM3 GR.299 984   [85]

Not a crag to rave about. SE-facing, vegetated and broken, offering about 10 routes, Diff to HS, 150ft.

Dir: 0.5m N of Coniston. Take the track going up to the Coppermines valley for 200yds, here a footpath goes off to the R and along the R side of the fell. Long Crag is on the L in about 300yds, then Mart Crag 500yds on, and finally Yewdale Crag another 500yds on. [SDE]

Low Wether Crag:
OS.89, 90, 96 & 97, TM3 GR.284 000   [86]

A nice remote crag at 1,700ft and E-facing. Quite a bit of climbing, about 8 routes in the low grades, Diff to Severe, 100–250ft. Broken and slightly vegetated, the norm on such a pleasant mountain crag. One for the summer.

Dir: 2m NW of Coniston. Take the track leading up the Coppermines valley and follow a footpath

leading around the youth hostel to the R. This leads up to a higher valley where the crags are on the L-hand side. [SDE]

Mart Crag:
OS.96 & 97, TM3 GR.305 989   [87]

A broken, mossy crag with sufficient vegetation to make earth dwellers feel at home. Half a dozen routes, VS to E1, 150ft, SE-facing. It would seem a pity to spoil a pleasant walk.

Dir: 0.8m N of Coniston. Approach: see Long Crag. [SDE]

Neckband Crag:
OS.89 & 90, TM3 GR.261 061   [88]

Quite a good NE-facing crag, offering some quite hard climbing for the general area. About 20 routes, VS to E4, with most of the routes being in the low Extremes, 130–300ft. In good weather worth a visit, preferably after a dry spell also.

Dir: 4.5m W of Elterwater. Take the B5343 to the W end of the Langdale valley to the car park. From here the valley runs W and splits after 0.5m, go straight up the ridge in front known as The Band. After 1m reach the first summit, the crag is just down to the R (N), 1 hr. To reach the other Bowfell crags carry on the ridge for another mile and bear off R below the top on a path which leads to below the crags, first Flat Crags then Cambridge Crag immediately after. Cross the scree shoot to the bottom of the formidable-looking Bowfell Buttress. 1.5 hrs. [GL]

Oak Howe Needle:
OS.90, TM3 GR.305 055   [89]

A fine, small needle, offering some short climbs. Some climbing is also to be found 300yds to the S of this on **Spout Crags**. Various routes, a couple of VSs and E3s. E-facing and average.

Dir: 1.5m WNW of Elterwater. From Chapel Stile take the track which crosses over the river and goes up the valley on the opposite side to the road. After 0.5m the crags can be seen high on the fellside to the L. [GL]

Pavey Ark:
OS.89 & 90, TM3 GR.286 080   [90]

A very good summer crag but quite a walk up

from the valley bottom, SE-facing and large. There are about 80 routes here, 100–300ft: easy routes tend to be on the L side around Diff to HS; on the R and steeper sections there is an abundance of Extremes, E1 to E6, mostly around E2–E3. The climbing on the hard routes is continuous and often with sustained interest. The easier routes are quite rambling. There is also the classic Easy, Jacks Rake, the R to L diagonal climb. A great crag to visit.

Dir: 3.4m NW of Elterwater. Take the B5343 down the Langdale valley for 3m to the New Dungeon Ghyll. Here a path goes up the ghyll and to Langdale Tarn, passing Tarn Crag on the R almost at the top of the ghyll. Upon reaching the tarn the crag is opposite and fairly obvious. [GL]

Raven Crag – Langdale
OS.89 & 90, TM3 GR.285 064   [91]

The most accessible crag in the Langdale valley, S-facing and offering some 70 routes in all grades from Diff to ES, 100–200ft. The rock here is somewhat suspect and soloing cannot be recommended, some of the routes are also quite pokey. A great crag nevertheless, worth a visit.

Dir: 3m WNW of Elterwater. Approach: see Gimmer Crag. [GL]

Raven Crag – Walthwaite:
OS.90, TM3 GR.325 058   [92]

Mostly easy climbs, 10 routes, Diff to VS, 100–50ft. Easy access from the road and S-facing. Worth a visit in the evening after a rainy day.

Dir: 0.6m N of Elterwater. Take the B5343 towards Chapel Stile, then turn off R in the village and R again to a small lane, which leads to the crag in 300yds on the L, up on the fellside. [GL]

Raven Crag – Yewdale:
OS.89 & 90, TM3 GR.312 002   [93]

An impressive crag when viewed from the road, but only offering reasonable climbing. Although low down and SE-facing, the crag only seems to come in condition when the high crags do. About 20 routes in the grades HS to E2, 150–80ft.

Dir: 2m NNE of Coniston. Take the A593 N for

about 1.4m to the second small lane on the L. Follow this for 600yds and the crag can be seen on the R. [SDE]

Scout Crag:
OS.89 & 90, TM3 GR.298 068   [94]

One of the best small crags for beginners in the Lakes. A handful of Diffs and Severes with good variations to be tried at will. About 10 routes, 150ft and S-facing. About 100yds up to the R is another buttress, offering a very good VS in the dry season. Excellent crag.

Dir: 2.3m NW of Elterwater. Approach: see White Ghyll. [GL]

Side Pike:
OS.89 & 90, TM3 GR.293 054   [95]

Not a great crag, but nevertheless offering plenty of amusement to the Severe leader. Half a dozen routes around the Severe grades, 100ft. Worth a visit during a dry spell.

Dir: 2m NW of Little Langdale. Take the small road going W towards the Wrynose Pass then after 0.9m turn R to Langdale up a small road. Follow this to a cattle grid in 1.6m, the crag can be seen over to the R on the fell called Side Pike. [GL]

Tarn Crag:
OS.89 & 90, TM3 GR.290 073   [96]

Another excellent small crag, offering about 8 very good Diff climbs of 150–250ft. S-facing, quite sheltered and accessible, but higher than Scout Crag. Worth a visit.

Dir: 3m WNW of Elterwater. Approach: see Pavey Ark, 25mins. [GL]

Tilberthwaite Quarries:
OS.90, TM3 GR.305 008   [97]

A slate quarry with about 30 routes VS upwards to mid-Extremes. The routes are quite small, 40–60ft. Maybe worth a visit, somewhere to puke after a really good session in The Black Bull at Coniston.

Dir: 2m NNE of Coniston. Take the A593 N for 1.3m, then the small lane on the L to a car park on the L after 0.9m. The quarry is above the old slate tips, following the footpath. [SDE]

White Ghyll:
OS.89 & 90, TM3 GR.297 071   [98]

One of the most impressive crags in the Lakes. Being tucked up high in a gully keeps the crag away from any tourists having heart attacks wandering up to Langdale Tarn, and also shelters the crag from most of the cold winds in autumn, spring and even summer! The cliff is W-facing and in two sections, a lower and upper crag, both very good. In total about 60 routes, all grades Diff upwards, 150–250ft. The lower crag offers the easier climbing, but there are VS routes which weave their way through the overhangs on the upper crag. The best routes are to be found on the upper crag and all 30 or so routes from VS to E4 are worth doing. A great crag.

Dir: 2.3m NW of Elterwater. Take the B5343 going W down the Langdale valley and park after 3m at New Dungeon Ghyll. From here a footpath leads off up the ghyll, go to the R of this and up the next valley along, due N. The footpath goes to the R of a group of trees and then up into the gully. Scout Crag is over on the R at this point if you are feeling nervous. Follow the gully and the crag is high on the R side. 30 mins. [GL]

Yewdale Crag – Coniston:
OS.96 & 97, TM3 GR.309 991   [99]

The best of the small crags on the W side of this valley. SE-facing, 150ft, with half a dozen routes, Severe to E1. Still has a large touch of the Perthy Thwowers.

Dir: 1m NNE of Coniston. Approach: 1m NNE of Coniston. Approach: see Long Crag, or quicker by driving up the A593 for 1m and the crag can be seen up on the L. [SDE]

NORTH EAST LAKES

A quiet area with some very good climbing on out-of-the-way crags. The climbing to be found around the N end of Thirlmere is quite popular because of the ease of access. The crags in the Ullswater valley are less frequented but are the answer for getting away from the smog at the weekend. The crags to the east often stay dry when Scafell is getting a right plastering: Threshwaite Cove is a very good example of this, one of the driest areas in the Lakes. Patterdale and Glenridding are completely tourist-ridden and dead in the evening. The trip south to Ambleside or Troutbeck is well worth the drive.

Arthur's Pike:
OS.90, TM3 GR.463 217   [100]

Some small crags on the side of Barton Fell. NW-facing with a handful of routes around Severe and below. Worth a look if passing.

Dir: 2m SSW of Pooley Bridge. Take the small road running down the S side of Ullswater for 2m to Thwaitehill Farm on the L. The crags can be seen above on the hillside to the L. [BEC]

Birk Crag – Grasmere:
OS.90, TM3 GR.317 135   [101]

Only three routes here, 2 VSs and an E3, 140ft. All good routes, though, and worth doing. E-facing, quick access and good, clean rock.

Dir: 4m NNW of Grasmere. Take the A591 N for 3m, turn L on to the small road going around the lake and after 1m the crag can be seen up on the L. [BEC]

Birk's Crag – Haweswater:
OS.90, TM3 GR.468 128   [102]

A small, NE-facing crag with a handful of 150ft routes, HS and HVS. A very quiet setting and of low altitude. Good-quality rock.

Dir: 1m WSW of the hotel on Haweswater. Drive to the hotel on the E side of the lake and the crag can be seen to the SW directly above a copse of trees on the W side. Drive to the S end of the lake and take the lakeside footpath to beneath the crag. [BEC]

Black Crag – Dovedale:
OS.90, TM3 GR.378 116   [103]

A 100–20ft crag with half a dozen routes in the lower grades, Diff to Severe. Appearing somewhat vegetated, it does offer good sport in a dry spell. SE-facing and best on the L-hand side.

Dir: 3m SSW of Patterdale. Approach: see Dove Crag. [BEC]

Castle Rock:
OS.90, TM3 GR.322 197   [104]

One of the great crags in the Lake District. A visit here is a must for anyone seeking the ultimate fulfilment from rock climbing. The crag is steep and offers little below VS on the main face. The S crag to the R, though, offers plenty in the lower grades. There are about 50 routes, 200ft, averaging E1. Even the E3s here feel like E1, simply very good easy climbing in the Extreme grade. The VS climbs rage through savage territory, seeking the pleasant pastures above the crag. Wonderful setting, fine views, and a sunny situation. A crag for everyone, worth a champagne visit.

Dir: 4m SE of Keswick. Take the A591 S to Legburthwaite, 4m, then turn L on to the B5322. After 0.4m the crag can be seen over on the R, 5-min. walk please. [BEC]

Dove Crag – Ullswater:
OS.90, TM3 GR.375 110   [105]

A crag for the super-spurter super cruiser. NE-facing, 100–250ft routes of testing, overhanging, adrenalin-driving, exhilarating rock romping. More 3-star routes on this crag than in the rest of the Lakes. About 20 routes, Diff to E6, but half are E4 and above. Its cool aspect, though, demands a good, dry spell, but if it rains you are not going to get wet here. Good crag.

Dir: 3.3m SSW of Patterdale. Take the A592 S for 3m to the pub on the R at Brothers Water. Follow the track W across the valley for 500yds, then turn L and take the footpath that goes up diagonally through the forest. After 0.7m Gill Crag is on the R, carry on for another 0.5m to Black Crag on the R. Continue around L to the head of the valley and Dove Crag should be quite obvious. 40 mins. [BEC]

Eagle Crag – Grisedale:
OS.89, TM3 GR.357 143   [106]

A good crag up this very scenic valley, E-facing but without the usual flora and fauna. There are two parts of the crag, but only the S part is worth climbing on. About 20 routes, 150–230ft, in the middle grades, VS to E3. There are a couple of Diffs worth doing but the HVS leader upwards will feel at home here. Protection is occasionally difficult to find.

Dir: 3m WSW of Patterdale. From Patterdale go N on the A592 for 0.5m. Take the valley on the L for 2.5m to where a big stream comes down from the R. The crag is straight ahead up the fell. Directly on the opposite S side of the valley is Saint Sunday Crag, a long line of dark crags at the top of the ridge. [BEC]

Gill Crag:
OS.90, TM3 GR.387 119   [107]

A good crag, honest. S-facing with a handful of climbs around Diff and an HS, 160ft. Definitely the place to bring a novice to have a very pleasant day, also quite a quick walk. Always worth a visit. 20 mins.

Dir: 2.3m SSW of Patterdale. Approach: see Dove Crag. [BEC]

Gouther Crag:
OS.90, TM3 GR.515 127   [108]

One of the more secluded areas of the Lake District. A NW-facing crag of good sound rock. Climbs 60–180ft in all grades from Diff to E4, about 50 in total on different buttresses. Worth a visit, especially if it is drier in the E than the W.

Dir: 10m S of Penrith, 3m WSW of Shap. From Shap drive N to Rosgil and take the low road towards Bampton. After 0.3m the road turns R, then after another 0.3m turn L on to the small lane going up the Swindale valley. After 3m the crag can be seen up the L. Cross the river by the footbridge and take the path to the L of the stream, then cut across to the crags. [BEC]

Gowbarrow:
OS.90, TM3 GR.414 206   [109]

This roadside, S-facing crag remains as popular as ever. Great as a winter retreat, sheltered and well polished. There are about 30 routes, Diff to

E1, on the three buttresses going up the hillside, 60–120ft. Good for beginners, keep for that cold day in autumn or spring.

Dir: 2.5m WSW of Watermillock. Take the A592 S from the hamlet for 2.5m and the crag can be seen above on the R. [BEC]

Hutaple Crag:
OS.90, TM3 GR.367 120   [110]

A large, 300–400ft, NW-facing crag with lots of easy routes. The crag is not without vegetation and appears to be favoured in particular by mountaineers. A score of stealthy routes in the grades Diff to E2, with HS being particularly well served. All the crags in the head of this valley offer quite similar climbing and are all either in or out of condition together. All are worth a visit on a good summer's day.

Dir: 3m SW of Patterdale. Take the A592 S from Patterdale for 0.8m to a car park. Take the valley running SW, Deepdale, for 2m to where the valley steepens. The buttress in between the two valleys is Hutaple Crag. Beneath this, low down, is **Mart Crag**, very good. The cove up to the L has **Scrubby Crag** in it on the R-hand side, which also offers good climbing, and at the back of that cove is **Hart Crag**, a steep and compact cliff offering good Severes. [BEC]

Iron Crag:
OS.89 & 90, TM3 GR.297 193   [111]

An above-average crag on the L- and R-hand sides, forget the rubbish in the middle. E-facing and quietly tucked away up a scenic valley. All routes are Extreme, mainly E1, 4, 5 and 6, about a dozen in total, 150ft. Well worth a morning visit.

Dir: 3.5m SSE of Keswick. Take the A591 S and continue for 2m from the top of the hill after leaving town. At the beginning of the big forest on the L is Shoulthwaite Farm, take a footpath running alongside its R edge going directly S for 1m. The crag is up on the R from here. [BEC]

Raven Crag – Keldas:
OS.90, TM3 GR.387 165   [112]

A very handy crag, offering a couple of routes around E1, 40ft. E-facing and best on the L-hand side. Worth a glimpse.

Dir: 0.2m S of Glenridding. Park in the S end of the village. The crag can be seen above the village to the S, up in the trees. [BEC]

Raven Crag – Thirlmere:
OS.90, TM3 GR.304 188   [113]

A very good crag indeed, offering some excellent hard routes in the high E grades. Little here below VS, about 25 routes to E6, 150–200ft. The crag is very imposing and some of the leads have interesting situations, just keep cool. Not a good crag for soloing. E-facing and often a bit cold in the afternoon, however, enough warmth is usually generated when struggling up the routes, and especially the scree leading up to the crag.

Dir: 3m SSE of Keswick. Take the A591 going S, after 3m take the small road on the R for 1m. The crag should be visible up to the R overlooking the lake, 5 mins. [BEC]

Saint Sunday Crag:
OS.90, TM3 GR.368 137   [114]

A very good crag for the easy-grade climber. More renowned for its winter gullies, it does offer some 20 routes in the Diff and Severe grades in a good summer. NW-facing with routes 100–200ft.

Dir: 2.5m SW of Patterdale. From the village of Patterdale take the A592 N for 0.5m, then take the track on the L into the Grisedale valley. After 400yds a path goes off to the L and up the obvious big ridge, take this ridge for 2m to near the top. The crags are down to the R and are easily reached by traversing in. [BEC]

Sandbed Ghyll Crag:
OS.90, TM3 GR.322 215   [115]

Not a large crag, but a good one for the Extreme climber. About a dozen climbs, VS to E5, of which 10 are Extreme, 100ft. NW-facing and generally in good condition, superb rock with good protection. This one is a definite on the tick list.

Dir: 4m ESE of Keswick. Take the B5322 going N from Legburthwaite for 1.9m and to the farm on the R. Immediately on the R follow a ghyll up to a high level and the crag is on the R side of the ghyll. [BEC]

Swirl Crags:
OS.90, TM3 GR.324 156   [116]

Some great small crags in a very fine position. 20 routes, Severe to E4, spread quite evenly. The climbs are only about 60ft long but pack a lot of entertainment in. W-facing and very good rock, simply heaven. Worth an evening jaunt.

Dir: 6m SSE of Keswick. Take the A591 going S for about 6m to a car park at the start of the forest either side of the road. Take the footpath up the L side of the forest, then along the top to reach the crags in 20 mins. [BEC]

Thackmell Crag:
OS.90, TM3 GR.309 156   [117]

Fairish climbing on this E-facing cliff. About 10 routes in the VS to E1 grades, with a couple of E3s for good measure, 60–120ft. Worth exploring on a poor day.

Dir: 6m NNW of Grasmere. Take the A591 N for 3m, turn L on to the small road going round the lake. Follow this for 3m to a lay-by and the Launchy Gill trail on the L. Take this up the hill for just over 500yds, then the L fork which leads towards the crag on the R. [BEC]

Thornhow Crag:
OS.90, TM3 GR.382 154   [118]

A good crag for the lower-grade climber and of easy access for this area. A handful of Diffs and Severes, 100–200ft, NW-facing and pleasant.

Dir: 1m WSW of Patterdale. Take the A592 N from Patterdale for 0.5m. Turn left up a small road which becomes a rougher track, Thornhow Crag is just up on the L. **Harrison's Crag**, with similar aspect and climbing potential, is another 500ft up the fellside. [BEC]

Threshthwaite Cove – Raven Crag:
OS.90, TM3 GR.420 112   [119]

A very good crag completely away from the tourists. About 15 routes, E2 to E6, 200ft but not much here below E4. Do not expect loads of protection here, however the climbing is very good, bold but safe – just. But then again . . . ! SE-facing and ideal on a good, sunny morning. Go for it.

Dir: 1.5m SSE of Hartsop. Park in the village at the National Trust car park, which is off the main road. Take the footpaths up the valley and as the valley splits take the R branch. The crag is passed on the R after 1.5m and is unseen until passed. A very large, flat face to the R of a gully. [BEC]

Thrang Crags: Restriction
OS.90, TM3 GR.431 177   [120]

Permission must be sought from the farm before climbing. Varied climbing in the middle grades, about 30 routes Severe to E5 but nearly all above VS and E1, 100–150ft. E-facing, a great crag for the low E-grade climber. Worth a visit.

Dir: 1m S of Martindale. From the small village drive S for 1m on the small road towards Dale Head, the crags can be seen up on the R. [BEC]

Yew Crag – Thirlmere:
OS.90, TM3 GR.307 207   [121]

Not a very good crag and definitely worth missing if in the area, especially in light of the other climbing on offer. About 10 routes, 170ft, Severe to E2. W-facing and sprouting plenty of green veggie stuff.

Dir: 3m SE of Keswick. Take the A591 for 3m to a lay-by just before the start of the dual carriageway. A footpath off to the L leads below the crag. [BEC]

10 North of England

This area is the least climbed in all of England and Wales due to its distance from the major centres of population. Quick access to the area is improving with the modernisation of the A1, but it will still be a long time before you can do London to Bowden Doors in 3 hours. The climbing in general is very good but not very large. If one could be guaranteed a good summer, bouldering here would be very good. There is plenty to do in this largely undiscovered area. New crags are still being found and will no doubt be well documented in the climbing magazines and forthcoming separate area guides.

WEST PENNINES

This area, to the north east of the Lake District, offers some very good climbing but most of it should come under the heading of bouldering. A top rope here is quite adequate, and in many cases it is preferable: the rock is rarely strong enough to take falls, the climbs are quite short and the tops very accessible. The rock varies from very good sandstone to awful stuff, and then up to quite reasonable limestone just west of Carlisle. The area is often quite deserted except for a few good evenings in summer and is the ideal place to boulder in peace.

Argill Beck:
OS.91 GR.858 133 [1]

Quite an impressive limestone crag, E-facing but quite loose in places. A handful of routes in the grades VS upwards, 60ft.

Dir: 6m ENE of Kirkby Stephen. From Brough to the N take the A66 E for 5.5m, then the small road on the R towards Barras for 300yds down a hill to a T-junction. On the R is a track which leads off NW parallel with the A66 to the top of the crag in about 600yds. [NOE]

Armathwaite:
OS.86 GR.505 453 [2]

One of the great bouldering areas in the N of England. The crag has some 100 routes in all grades from Diff to E6, but the harder routes are done either as top-rope problems or solos. 10–50ft sandstone cliffs and boulders situated in pleasant woodland. SW-facing and good at any time of the year, midges get a bit hungry in summer months though.

Dir: 9m N of Penrith. Take the A6 N to High Hesket then turn off R to Armathwaite. At the village turn R, go over the bridge, park. A footpath leads down under the bridge and along the S bank. Follow this into the trees keeping R on a well-worn path to reach the crag in about 10 mins.

Caldbeck Moor Quarry:
OS.85 GR.287 402 [4]

Not one of the greatest limestone quarries in the world. There are about 10 climbs, 20ft Diff to VS, and some good traversing.

Dir: 5.5m SSE of Wigton. Take the B5304 S out of town to the A595, cross straight over on to the small road going to Caldbeck. Follow this to a bend after 0.6m, carry on to the L for 0.9m and a small crossroad. Turn R here, after 0.7m take the

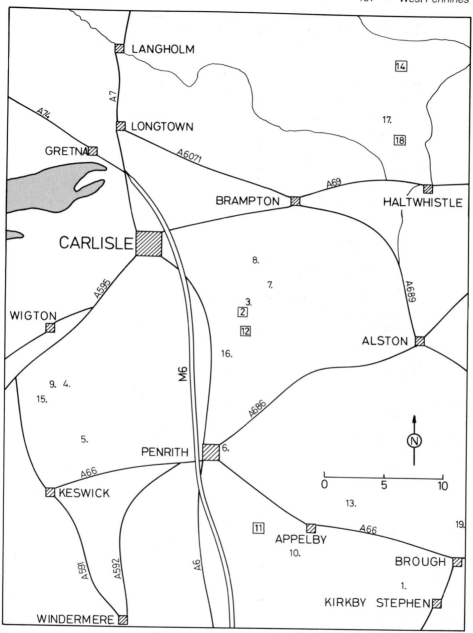

WEST PENNINES

L fork and follow this long, straightish road for 2.3m. Here a track on the R leads to the quarry. [NOE]

Carrock Fell:
OS.90 GR.355 324   [5]

Some quite reasonable climbing to be found on several outcrops on the E side of this fell. About 20 routes, 60–150ft, Diff to VS.

Dir: 15m SSW of Carlisle, 0.5m NW of Mosedale. Drive to Mosedale and the crags can be seen on the side of the fell to the NW. [BEC]

Cowrake Quarry:
OS.90 GR.531 308   [6]

Quite a good sandstone quarry with about 20 routes in the grades 3b upwards, 15–25ft. Ideal for an evening's bouldering and, being S-facing, good on that cold winter's day. Quite sheltered also.

Dir: 1m ENE from the centre of Penrith. From the large roundabout to the E of the motorway take the A686 for 1.9m. At the pylons turn L on to a lane and follow for 0.9m to a footpath on the R which leads up to the quarry. [NOE]

Cumrew Crag:
OS.86 GR.562 502   [7]

A limestone crag on the side of the Pennines at 1,000ft and SW-facing, part natural edge and part quarried. Quick to dry and with a good sunny aspect, this makes up for the walk to the crag. About 20 routes, of which most are in the easy grades, Diff to Severe, 30ft. A pleasant spot worth a visit for the Severe leader.

Dir: 13m NNE of Penrith. Drive to the village of Newbiggin on the B6413, turn R into the village and carry on for 300yds to park at the start of a track to a wood on the L. Take this track up beside the stream for a while, then fork L and follow the path to the crag in about 5 mins. [NOE]

The Gelt Boulder:
OS.86 GR.567 553   [8]

A very good limestone boulder, offering steep and excellent problems, 20ft. Worth a boulder.

Dir: 16m NNE of Penrith, 10m E of Carlisle. Drive to Castle Carrock on the B6413. From the village take the road going E to the river Gelt, where the road turns R. After 1.2m park. Walk straight on down to the river, cross over the bridge and turn R to go upstream for about 400yds to the boulder. [NOE]

Headend Quarry:
OS.85 GR.250 408   [9]

A limestone quarry, offering about 30 routes, Mod upwards to Extreme, with a good selection of Diffs. S-facing and dries out quickly. Worth a visit for the Diff–VS climber certainly.

Dir: 5.5m S of Wigton. From Mealsgate on the A595 take the B5299 to Boltongate, carry on for 1.3m and then turn L to Sandale. After 100yds fork R, go up the hill and follow the road round to the quarry, which is on the R near the top of the hill. [NOE]

The Hoff:
OS.91 GR.677 180   [10]

A small 20ft crag of conglomerate limestone with about 20 routes in and around the Severe grades. The rock is pocketed and quite rough, though unfortunately it is not reliable! However, it does face SW and dries very quickly. Not a bad crag in winter for a bit of amusement.

Dir: 2m SSW of Appleby-in-Westmorland. Take the B6260 from the town S for about 2m to the village of Hoff. Just before reaching the village the crag can be seen on the R. [NOE]

Kings Meaburn – Jackdaw Scar:
OS.91 GR.618 213   [11]

A different crag this one: a 30–40ft limestone crag resting on a bed of sandstone. The rock overhangs at the start with interest and then goes to limestone which cannot be regarded as totally solid! About 50 climbs across the grades.

Dir: 4.5m W of Appleby-in-Westmorland. Take the small road through Colby to Kings Meaburn. At the village turn L down the hill to a ford across the river, the crag can be seen to the R. [NOE]

Lazonby:
OS.86 GR.527 423   [12]

A large escarpment of sandstone running along the W side of the river Eden. 100–30ft high buttresses, offering about 50 routes in all grades. The rock is quite soft here and although one can lead it is wiser to top-rope routes. Quite a spectacular crag, definitely worth seeing.

Dir: 8m N of Penrith. From Lazonby take the small road which passes over the railway to the N, running up the side of the river to the L of the railway. Cross over the railway, then continue for 2.3m and park. Take a track going off to the R, which leads down some steps to the crag. [NOE]

Murton: Restriction
OS.91 GR.743 228   [13]

The crag is on an army firing range, keep out if the red flag is flying. A limestone crag which starts off solid at the bottom and becomes interesting towards the top. About 10 routes, 40–60ft, in the Severe to HVS grades. SW-facing with a fine view.

Dir: 3.5m ENE of Appleby-in-Westmorland. Take a small road to Murton. The crag can be seen on the fell to the N from here, 10 mins. [NOE]

Padda Crag:
OS.86 GR.650 788   [14]

Some excellent sandstone of the Northumberland variety. There are some 40 routes here, Diff to 5c, 20–30ft, with countless problems. S-facing at 1,100ft, a bit cold and damp in winter but gets the sunshine. A very remote crag, do not get caught here without an umbrella. Worth a visit.

Dir: 10m NNW of Haltwhistle, 1.5m NW of Churnsike Lodge. Take the small road from Gisland to Churnsike Lodge. Follow a track W for 0.5m, past a demolished barn on the L, then turn R up another track for 0.9m, where the crag can be seen on the R. [NOE]

Park Head: Access
OS.85 GR.336 405   [15]

The crag is on private ground, the farmer is very happy for climbers to use the crag so long as they are courteous enough to ask at the house beforehand. A good limestone outcrop, 15–25ft high, some quarried and some natural. There are some 15 or so routes around the Severe grade, but in general it lends itself more to bouldering. A very nice situation, SE-facing. Worth a boulder.

Dir: 7.5m SE of Wigton. From Carlisle take the B5299 SW for 9m to the junction with the B5305. Go straight over and carry on to a bend in 1.1m, here turn L up a small road to Park Head. Keep on this track for 0.5m and then follow it round to the R and a farm. From here the crag can be reached in a few minutes by keeping on the track to the R. [NOE]

Scratchmere Scar: Access
OS.90 GR.514 380   [16]

Permission to climb must be sought from Mr Atkinson at the farm. A fair crag with a lovely setting and facing SW, good on a winter's day. About 20 climbs of which most are in the easier grades and very good for the beginner, 20–30ft high. A better alternative than a horrible walk in the rain in the lakes for a group of enthusiastic beginners.

Dir: 4.5m N of Penrith. From Plumpton on the A6 take the B6413 for 1m, where the crag can be easily seen. Approach is by a footpath that goes through gates and not over walls please. [NOE]

Spadeadam Crag:
OS.86 GR.637 694   [17]

A couple of 20ft sandstone buttresses, offering about a dozen climbs in all grades from Severe upwards to 6a. A pleasant situation and worth a visit.

Dir: 5.5m NW of Haltwhistle. Take the B6318 to Gisland, then take the small Butterburn road running N. Keep on this to a sharp R-hand bend after 1.6m, carry on for 0.5m to a lay-by. Here a path goes down to the R and the river, the crag is on this side. [NOE]

The Tipalt: Restriction
OS.86 GR.673 671   [18]

Permission to climb here must be sought from the farm over the road, and is freely given. Climbing is to be found here on sandstone, walls, roofs and everything to keep one amused for several hours, except the finishes – beware. NW-facing but still manages to stay quite dry for most of the time. About 20 routes, 20–40ft, Diff to VS and countless harder problems. Worth a visit.

Dir: 3m NW of Haltwhistle. From Greenland on the A69 take the B6318 E up the hill for 0.5m, then turn L on to the small road. Follow this for

1.3m and the crag will be seen very close to the road on the R. [NOE]

Windmore End:
OS.91 & 92 GR.825 166 [19]

Climbing of limited interest on this extensive limestone escarpment. About 100 routes, 20–60ft, in all grades from Diff to HVS. There are plenty of Diffs and Severes to keep one happy. SW-facing at 1,200ft, dries out very quickly but can get quite cold here in the winter months.

Dir: 6m NNE of Kirkby Stephen. From Brough to the N take the B6267 for 2.2m, the crag can be seen on the R here. The better climbing is to be found at the R end. [NOE]

DURHAM–CLEVELAND

Although these areas fall into separate climbing guidebooks, a small amount of thought would indicate that all the climbing is of a similar nature and could easily come under one guidebook. All the crags are no more than 1 hour from Middlesbrough. Nothing to rave about here, but some very good small crags in very pleasant surroundings. Plenty of bouldering in the summer months; in winter choose your crags carefully. Plenty of climbing in general if you are in the area, but to travel all the way from Bristol, say, or further afield is perhaps not using your travel resources to their best advantage.

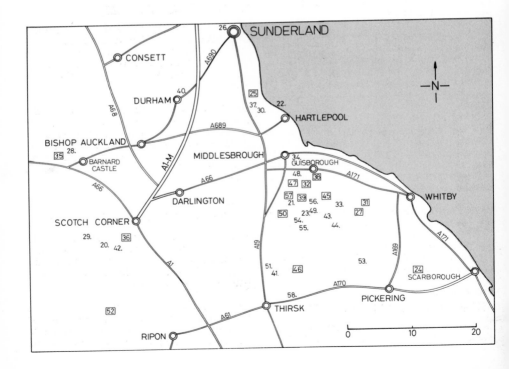

Appelgarth Crag:
OS.92 GR.118 016   [20]

A limestone crag which tends to be rather prone to ivy and loose rock. However the angle is quite accommodating and these distractions can be dealt with. About 40 routes, 30–40ft high, mostly in the Diff and Severe grades. Although there are some harder, this is a crag for the low-grade climber to enjoy. S-facing and quite pleasant, even in winter. Good on a cold day.

Dir: 3.5m W of Richmond. From the town a small road runs parallel to the N of the A6108. Take this for 3.7m to a footpath on the L as you come down into a small valley. This path goes around to the L and the crag in about 5 mins. [NOE]

Beacon Scar:
OS.100, see TM2 GR.460 998   [21]

A damp, wooded, green crag facing NW. In a dry spell the climbing here is very good and well worth the visit, at other times best to give it a miss. About 40 climbs, lots of Mods and Diffs, all climbs through to HVS and a couple of easy extremes to E3, 40–70ft. Beware of the finishes, some are not all that solid.

Dir: 7m SW of Stokesley. Take the A172 S to Swainby, turn L into the small road bearing R towards Osmotherley, after 1.5m park on the R. Here a footpath goes up the ridge to the top of the hill and the crag is just on the other side, 10 mins. [NYM]

Blackhall Rocks:
OS.93 GR.470 394 HT–1.55   [22]

Some good-quality limestone, in places on the sea. Best not at high tide. Various cliffs along the coast provide good entertainment, traversing being the most popular activity.

Dir: 5m NNW of Hartlepool. Take the A1086 N for 3m from the edge of Hartlepool to Blackhall Rocks, turn R on to a small road that goes under the railway. After 400yds a track L leads down to the coastline and the crags. The best areas lie to the N of this, about 500yds away. [NOE]

Botton Head:
OS.93, TM2 GR.592 019   [23]

A N-facing crag, offering about 30 routes in the Diff grade, 29–35ft. One can easily nip off and conquer the highest point in Cleveland, just to the S of here at 1,490ft. A nice crag, but in need of a very good day.

Dir: 6m SE from Stokesley. For access one can approach as described for Turkey Nab and take in most of the crags in the area. For a quicker route take the B1257 S from Great Broughton for 3m to a car park. Follow the footpath leading up the ridge to the L (SE) and along to the high summit, the crag is on the L in 30 mins. [NYM]

Bridestones:
OS.94, TM2 GR.873 915   [24]

A good area of softish sandstone, offering about 30 climbs of 15–20ft, generally in the 5a and 5b grades. Worth a visit.

Dir: 7m NE of Pickering. Take the A170 to Thornton Dale, then the small toll road leading up to Stain Dale for 5m to a car park on the L. There are notices giving directions to the rocks 1m N of here. [NYM]

Castle Eden Dene:
OS.93 GR.429 392   [25]

Some esoteric crags in the woods. There are quite a few crags, giving about 50 routes, 30–50ft, of all grades from Severe to Extreme. The area will not appeal to all, but the setting is peaceful and the limestone is reasonably steep in places.

Dir: 7m WNW of Hartlepool. Take the B1281 going E from the A19 by the golf course, after 1.1m at Castle Eden turn L up the road to the castle. From here one can walk down to the river, the crags are scattered along both sides of the riverbank. The better crags tend to be upstream. [NOE]

Cleadon Crags:
OS.88 GR.385 640   [26]

Some small limestone crags around the village of Cleadon. Rarely do the crags exceed 20ft in height, but a good 200 problems, 3a upwards. They are S-facing and present good winter bouldering. Worth a visit if passing.

Dir: 2m S of South Shields. From the roundabout at the S end of South Shields, where the A1300 and A1018 cross, go E to the next roundabout in 0.2m. Turn R and go down the road for 0.2m, then turn L along the N side of Cleadon Park. After 400yds a footpath on the R leads to **Quarry Buttress** and **Anders Buttress**. By following the path across the road to the L and the golf course, you can reach **Golf Course Crag** in about 10 mins. There are also small outcrops to the S of the golf course. Explore at will. [NOE]

Clemitt's Crag:
OS.94, TM2 GR.709 037   [27]

Some good, solid sandstone, which for the most part is clean and very worthwhile. SE-facing, with about 30 routes spread over the grades Diff to E2, 25–40ft. Worth a visit for most.

Dir: 10m SSE of Guisborough. From Danby take the road going E out of the village, under the railway, and immediately turn R and then L on to the small road which leads S on to the moors. Follow this for 3.4m to a parking spot on the L. Here a footpath leads L and to the crag. The footpath on the R leads to **Camp Hill Crag**, about 20 shortish climbs, VS to E3, and W-facing. Pleasant. [NYM]

Cotherstone Crag:
OS.92 GR.018 198   [28]

An outcrop of suspect sandstone, 20 Diffs and Severes up to 40ft. Worth a miss.

Dir: 3m NW of Barnard Castle. From the town take the B6277 to the village of Cotherstone — good pub and a far better idea. Park at the top end by the village green. Take a footpath to where the rivers meet, cross one and then the other, and turn R and follow the river down-stream for 400yds to the crag. [NOE]

Crag Willas:
OS.92 GR.975 012   [29]

A high gritstone outcrop, 1,800ft up. Quite small, mostly around 10–30ft, but offering some 60 routes and lots more problems. The crag is quite a long escarpment in several sections and S-facing. Lovely remote setting, good place to boulder in the summer.

Dir: 12.5m W of Richmond, 2m NW of Keaton. Turn off the B6270 at Healaugh and take the small road to Kearton. Follow the road to the head of the valley in 0.7m, the crag is up the valley 1m on the R-hand side (N). [NOE]

Crimdon Dene:
OS.93 GR.476 370   [30]

A couple of good limestone buttresses, offering some of the best climbing in the area. The dozen or so routes tend to be quite hard due to the steep nature of these crags, however, there are a few Diffs on Ramp Crag, 20–40ft. Worth a visit.

Dir: 3.5m NW of Hartlepool. From the last roundabout on the A1086 leaving Hartlepool carry on N for 0.8m to beside the railway bridge. Here the valley to the L has two crags: **Overhang Crag** on the S Bank and **Ramp Crag** on the N bank. Both can be reached in minutes from here. [NOE]

Danby Crag:
OS.94, TM2 GR.730 068   [31]

About 60 climbs in the lower grades, Diff to VS, mostly below HS, 20–30ft. Not a bad crag but N-facing, one to avoid when a cold N wind is blowing.

Dir: 9.5m ESE of Guisborough. Drive to the village of Danby and take the small road going E towards Houlskye, passing under a railway after 1.2m. After 0.4m there is a track and a footpath on the R which lead up to the crag in 10 mins. [NYM]

Easby Moor Area:
OS.93, TM2 GR.593 097   [32]

There is plenty of climbing in this area to entertain the V Diff climber and the VS tiger on several outcrops, some of which are natural and others quarried. Nearly all the routes are very small, around 20ft, but are worth a day's fun scrambling and soloing. About 60 routes in total, generally SW-facing and can be very pleasant on a sunny winter's afternoon as protected from the cold NE winds. Worth a visit, good area to bring a novice.

Dir: 4m SW of Guisborough. Take the A173 S to Newton under Rosebury. Here up to the L is Roseberry Topping, reached quite obviously. Carry on for 1.2m to Great Ayton, bear L to the station and go over the railway to a car park in 1.7m. A footpath leads around the hill to the S and goes above all the crags. [NYM]

Esklets:
OS.94, TM2 GR.662 020 [33]

A good area with about 20 climbs and plenty of bouldering on two W-facing outcrops. All grades from Diff to 6b on routes which do not exceed 20ft. Worth a look if passing.

Dir: 9.5m ESE of Stokesley. Drive to Westerdale. From here a small road runs S down the valley to the SW for 1.5m. From the end of the valley there is a public footpath down the valley to the S and up to the ridge. The crag is high on the L. 20 mins. [NYM]

Eston Nab:
OS.93, TM2 GR.566 183 [34]

When they built the dual carriageway here they made a major mistake in building it around the crag. This crag is similar to the Avon Gorge Crags in aesthetic delight and commands a beautiful view over the pretty village of Middlesbrough, the edges of the buildings softened by the smog-filled air. A delight. The climbing here is somewhat dubious and best left to those who like the element of chance in climbing. Most routes are around 40ft in the grades Diff to HVS, and there are about 50 in total.

Dir: 4m ESE of the town centre. From the A19 take the S ring road for 7m to the roundabout just before Lazenby. Turn L on to the B1380 and after 0.7m take the turning on the L which goes back to and under the ring road. The rocks on the hill to the S can be reached from here. [NYM]

Goldsborough Carr:
OS.92 GR.954 175 [35]

A good gritstone crop, only 15–20ft high but offering plenty of climbing with about 50 routes in total. At 1,200ft up, gets chilly in winter, but a lot of the climbs face S and, being short, are still fun on the cold winter days. Easy and hard problems, something here to occupy everyone. Worth a boulder.

Dir: 6m W of Barnard Castle. Take the B6277 out of Barnard Castle to Cotherstone, here turn L on to the small road that leads up to Hury reservoir. Go along the S side of the reservoir, follow the road L for 1m and park. Take the footpath going S (Pennine Way) up to the crag in about 5 mins. [NOE]

Hag Wood:
OS.92 GR.134 009 [36]

This is the best crag in the immediate area, offering about 60 climbs, Diff to Extreme. Limestone, quite solid but verging to loose on the finishes. Nearly all the climbs are around 50ft and there is much here to occupy the Severe and VS leader. NW-facing and quite quick to dry. Not bad as a winter crag either. Worth a visit.

Dir: 2.5m W of Richmond. Take the A6108 W for 2.5m to a picnic spot in the woods on the L. The crag is here in the woods. [NOE]

Hesleden Dene:
OS.93 GR.456 371 [37]

A mixed area with some good rock and some poorer. A handful of routes on the two crags here. Although Jack Rock, 120ft, is more imposing, the better climbing is to be had lower down the valley on The Buttress, 25ft. Here the rock is very good and offers some very good bouldering on a few outcrops. Worth a few hours to boulder around.

Dir: 4m NW of Hartlepool. Drive to Hesleden Dene from the B1281. Here a small road leads down to the river and the few houses at Monk Hesleden. **Jack Rock** is just down on the N side of the river, follow the path down by the river for about 10 mins to **The Buttress** on the S side of the river. [NOE]

Highcliffe Nab:
OS.94, TM2 GR.610 138 [38]

A very good sandstone crag, offering some very fine climbing. N-facing and best in the summer months, in fact a delight. About 80 climbs in all grades from Diff to E5, 30–70ft. The harder routes can often be quite bold, and those wishing to top-rope will find a 30ft length of rope for the belay very useful since the top does not lend itself to many natural belays. The crag has a fine view and is exposed, drying quickly and also getting cold quickly. Worth a visit.

Dir: 1.5m S of Guisborough. Leave the town SW on the A173. After 0.5m turn L to Hutton Village, 1m, park. Take a forest track up through the woods, bearing L when it splits to the crag in about 10 mins. [NYM]

Ingleby Incline:
OS.94, TM2 GR.604 039 [39]

A long, rambling crag with several buttresses, offering plenty of climbing in a good position. About 60 routes all in the lower grades, Mods, Diffs and Severes, 15–45ft. W-facing and catches the sun well. A very pleasant crag.

Dir: 5.5m SE of Stokesley. Approach: see Turkey Nab. [NYM]

Kepier Woods:
OS.88 GR.288 438 [40]

A really good, small sandstone crag of about 20ft. There are about a dozen climbs Severe to VS and as many harder problems. All the climbing is in a pleasant situation and dries out very quickly. Worth a visit to boulder.

Dir: 1.5m NE of Durham centre. The crags lie in the woods off the L of the A690 dual carriageway, half-way to the motorway junction. There is a car park to the L just before the slip road going off to Carville. From here a footpath leads off into the woods and down to the crags in about 10 mins, just upstream. [NOE]

Kepwick Crag:
OS.100, TM2 GR.467 905 [41]

A small crag consisting of three bays with climbing of 15–30ft on half a dozen routes, HS to E1. Not bad, handy for the A19.

Dir: 7m ESE of Northallerton. Drive to the village of Kepwick, the crag is easily reached just to the SW of the village on the hillside. [NYM]

Marske Quarry:
OS.99 GR.991 114 [42]

A crag for the leader who has no brain cells whatsoever. This limestone crag is positively dangerous and will no doubt attract a certain number of people – not me. 20 Diff routes to 90ft.

Dir: 4m WSW of Richmond. Take the A6108 towards Downholme, about 1m before the village the quarry will be seen on the L just by the road. [NOE]

Middle Head Crag:
OS.94, TM2 GR.631 011 [43]

A small 30ft sandstone crag, offering about 20 routes in all grades to E2 on a series of buttresses. Good rock and S-facing, an ideal spot for the good winter's day. Plenty here for all, worth a visit.

Dir: 8.5m SE of Stokesley. Drive to Church Houses on the S side of Farndale and Westerdale Moor, then up the Farndale valley which is directly to the NW. After 3m the road ends and the crag is directly in front at the head of the valley in 20 mins. [NYM]

Oak Crag:
OS.94, TM2 GR.685 963 [44]

A few buttresses high on the moor, offering about 10 routes in the Diff and Severe grades, 20–40ft. Not far from the road.

Dir: 12m SE of Stokesley. Go W for 8m to the village of Castleton, then take the small road going across Westerdale Moor. Follow this for 7m to a parking spot and viewpoint (second *en route*), carry on for 1.8m and park. From here walk R (W) across the moor to the crag in 5 mins. [NYM]

Park Nab:
OS.94 TM2 GR.611 086 [45]

A very fine sandstone crag, offering good, clean, solid rock. About 30 routes from Diff to HVS, with a handful of Extremes to E3, 20–30ft. Always worth a visit.

Dir: 4.5m S of Guisborough at the viewpoint. Drive to the small village of Kildale, 300yds to the W of the village take the small road which leads up the hill to Baysdale Abbey. Walk across the hill to the crag. [NYM]

Peak Scar:
OS.100, TM2 GR.527 884 [46]

The North York Moors have never been famous for limestone crags, but this crag saves the day in many ways. Most of the climbs are around 100ft and in the lower grades, about 70 routes in total. There is vegetation at either end and the crag is in general need of more traffic. For the VS climber the crag is very popular, also surprisingly solid. N-facing. Worth a visit.

Dir: 7m NE of Thirsk. Take the B1267 N from Helmsley for 3.3m, then the small road that forks off to the L. Follow this down the hill, over the bridge on the L and carry on for 1.2m to a T-junction. Turn L up the steep hill and continue to a parking spot on the R in 1.6m. The crag is down to the R. [NYM]

Raven's Scar – Hasty Bank:
OS.93, TM2 GR.566 037   [47]

One of the best outcrops in the area. The crag is sandstone and generally green in appearance. It is N-facing and takes a few days to dry after rain, but in summer during a dry spell the crag gives superb routes in all the grades up to 6b. About 60 routes, 30–60ft, with the best routes perhaps being in the harder grades. Worth a visit.

Dir: 4m SSE of Stokesley. Take the B1257 S for 3m to a parking spot and picnic site on the L. From here a footpath goes off R (W) above the forest. The first crag reached is **Landslip** on the brow, with about 10 low-grade routes. Further round is Raven's Scar, reached in about 10 mins, and by carrying on for another 5 mins one comes to The Wainstones. [NYM]

Roseberry Topping:
OS.93, TM2 GR.579 126   [48]

On this sandstone outcrop one is quite possibly going to die if attempting climbs on the S face. There is some rock worth climbing but still caution should be taken. About a dozen routes in the lower grades, Diff to VS, 30ft. A good slab offering a couple of routes – the best here-abouts. Worth a visit to reach the summit of the fine mountain.

Dir: 3m SW of Guisborough. Approach: see Easby Moor area. [NYM]

Rud Scar:
OS.94, TM2 GR.606 025   [49]

Two separate N-facing outcrops of about 20–40ft. About 40 routes in the lower grades, Diff to VS, a bit more here for the VS climber than at the neighbouring Ingleby Incline. Quiet spot.

Dir: 6m SE of Stokesley. Approach: see Turkey Nab. [NYM]

Scugdale:
OS.93, TM2 GR.520 004   [50]

An area of sandstone crags stretching along the hillside for about 1m and offering over 100 climbs in all grades. The crags face SW, are often dry, and hence very popular. The area has been compared to Fontainebleau but given the choice I would not think twice. Rarely does the rock exceed 20ft in height, but the interesting moves make up for this. A great spot for everyone. Individual areas are known as **Stoney Wicks**, to the R; **Barker's Crags**, in the middle; **Scot Crags** to the L; and **Snotterdale** around in the valley to the L. 10-min. walk.

Dir: 5m S of Stokesley. Take the A172 S to Swainby. Here turn L and follow the small lane L up the valley through Huthwaite and on to the end in 3m. The crags are up on the L. [NYM]

Silton:
OS.99, TM2 GR.448 940   [51]

A few buttresses offering about a dozen routes in the lower grades, Diff to Severe, 30–40ft. Worth a visit if passing.

Dir: 5m E of Northallerton. Drive to Over Silton, approach from the S if coming from the A19. The crags can be seen in the woods to the N of the village and are reached by a forest track at the N end of the village. [NYM]

Slipstone Crag:
OS.99 GR.138 821   [52]

A very good gritstone crag with about 100 routes to 20ft and at least as many problems. All grades from Diff to 6a with a good 70 routes in the lower grades below VS. Plenty of good bouldering here and a nice SW-facing position for the colder months. Worth a detour.

Dir: 14m NW of Ripon, 1m NE of Colsterdale. From Masham on the A6108 take a small road leading W through the village of Healey to the fork leading to Colsterdale. Take this going R for 1.7m to a parking spot on the R. Walk along the road for 300yds where a footpath leads off up to the R and the rocks in about 5 mins. [NOE]

Thorgill Crag: Restriction & Access
OS.94, TM2 GR.713 959   [53]

The crag has nesting birds, no climbing 1 Apr.–

RADICAL SMEG MONSTER, 5c, Slipstones. (Climber Joe Healey, Photo David B A Jones)

1 Aug. There have been access difficulties here in the past: there is only a public footpath some 200yds to the L of the crag and the easiest but less obvious approach to the crag is from the top. NE-facing at 1,000ft, quite chilly at times. 15–40ft routes in grades Diff to HVS. Worth a visit.

Dir: 9m NW of Pickering. Drive to Rosedale Abbey, go S from the village past the pub and up the steep hill, the crag is on the R. Continue up to the top, where a track leads off to the R and the top of the crag in 10 mins. [NYM]

Tranmire Rocks:
OS.93, TM2 GR.575 006   [54]

A band of sandstone outcrops, 15–25ft high and about 300yds long. About 40 routes mainly in the lower grades around Diff, but some harder problems up to 5b. A good situation, facing SW and very scenic.

Dir: 6m SSE of Stokesley. Take the B1257 S for almost 8m to Seave Green, turn L and go up the small road for 0.4m. Here take public footpath up the hill to the L of the crag and then bear along R on the other public footpath to the crag. [NYM]

Tripsdale:
OS.100, TM2 GR.583 987   [55]

Some quite large climbs for the area here in this very quiet valley. About 10 routes, 15–60ft, Diff to VS. W-facing and on the 1,000ft contour.

Dir: 7m SSE of Stokesley. Take the B1257 S for about 11m to Grange. Here turn back L and park, or drive 1m up the valley to Hagg House Farm and seek permission to park there. The crag is in the valley to the L, about 1m. [NYM]

Turkey Nab:
OS.93, TM2 GR.598 060   [56]

A good outcrop, offering W-facing routes with a wonderful view. About 10 routes, Severe to HVS, 30–40ft high. Handy and pleasant.

Dir: 4m SE of Stokesley. Take the small road to Ingleby Greenhow, then follow the road out of the village to the L and then R, and to the hill overlooking the crag, which is to the R. To the L is **Battersby Crag**, which has a handful of similar routes. To reach the other crags in the area carry on R up to the ridge on the Cleveland Way. After 1.5m Ingleby Incline is on the R and, as the valley turns to the R (W) the crags at the head of the valley are Rud Scar to the L and Botton Head to the R. About 45-min. walk to the furthest from the car, a good day is advisable. [NYM]

The Wainstones:
OS.93, TM2 GR.559 036   [57]

A popular spot with some 60 routes from Mod to E4. Most of the routes are in the lower grades but this is generally a crag for everyone to visit and enjoy. 30ft in most places and N-facing.

Dir: 4m SSE of Stokesley. Approach: see Raven's Scar.

Whitestone Cliff:
OS.100, TM2 GR.507 836   [58]

Why anybody has ever bothered to climb here defeats me – this is definitely Loony League territory. The smallest hold the rock can support is about 3a. The largest cliff in the area up to 120ft and offering some 50 routes. W-facing and catches the sun well. That's the only good bit, do not expect to enjoy this crag.

Dir: 5m E of Thirsk. Take the A170 E from Sutton-under-Whitestonecliff for 3m to the top of some sharp bends and a parking spot. Walk N to the crag in 10 mins. [NYM]

NORTHUMBERLAND

The climbing in Northumberland is mostly on sandstone with a few exceptions on the west side of the county. The routes are generally short and difficult, but offer a more relaxed approach to climbing than the big limestone cliffs in England. Because of the low level of many crags here the northern latitude is less important, but even so in winter there is quite a bit of snow. The best bouldering in the country can be found on the more northern crags, and these are worth a visit at least once in a lifetime even if you live in the south of England. To those uninitiated the area is quite large and the crags of Bowden and Kyloe are still a good hour's drive to the north of Newcastle. People do use top ropes on the routes that they find very hard and this seems quite sensible since the placing of bolts on the rock here would scar and ruin what are beautiful, undamaged boulders and crags. A friendly area in which to climb, and quite varied given that the rock is of only one type.

Back Bowden Doors:
OS.75 GR.065 336   [59]

A very good crag and a lot more sheltered than its neighbour, Bowden Doors. SW-facing and quite high, reaching a full 50ft in places. Very good climbing on about 60 routes in all grades, but quite strenuous. Some very good roof problems here. Always worth a visit.

Dir: 4m ENE of Wooler. Approach: see Bowden Doors. [ND]

Berryhill Crag: Access
OS.74 GR.938 403   [60]

Please ask permission at the farm before climbing. A pleasant, S-facing crag, offering about a dozen routes in the lower grades, Diff to 5a, 25–50ft. There is a lot of scope for shorter climbs and bouldering here, but the rock is not over-strong so top-roping should not be ruled out.

Dir: 8.5m SSW of Berwick-upon-Tweed. Take the B6354 S to Duddo, continue for 1.4m passing the bends in the road to a track leading off L to a farm. The crag is just beyond the farm. [ND]

Bowden Doors:
OS.75 GR.070 326   [61]

A very open and exposed crag which dries out instantly. SW-facing and very good rock, with over 100 routes in all grades from Diff to 6c, 30–40ft. One of the best crags in the area, not to be missed.

Dir: 4m ENE of Wooler. Turn off the B6348 on to the B6349 and continue for 4m, the crag can be seen on the L. Please be careful of fences and walls. To reach Back Bowden Doors carry on the road for another 200yds, turn L and after 1m a path leads down the edge of a forest to the crag, 5 mins. [ND]

Callerhues Crag:
OS.80 GR.854 862   [62]

One of the great crags in the area, SW-facing at 1,000ft. About 60 routes and lots of very fine bouldering. There is not a lot here for the low-grade climber but one can always struggle up the 5a climbs on a top rope. Worth a visit, beautiful spot.

Dir: 16m NNW of Hexham, 2m NNE of Bellingham. Take the B6320 N from Bellingham for 2m, the crag can be seen on the opposite side of the valley to the R. Carry on for 0.5m to a track on the R, follow this for 600yds, then bear R on the well-worn Pennine Way footpath to below the crag. 20 mins. [ND]

Causey Quarry:
OS.88 GR.204 560   [63]

A quarry receiving mixed opinions. Mostly soft rubbish, but with a top rope plenty of good climbing can be found here. It is requested, though, that you use a long sling at the top to prevent undue wear. Sandstone up to 60ft with about 40 routes and endless variations. Worth a trip if stuck in Newcastle.

Dir: 2m N of Stanley, 5m S of Newcastle. Take the A6076 N from the roundabout at Stanley for 2m to Causey. Turn R down a track here and a path leads to the quarry. [ND]

Coe Crag:
OS.81 GR.074 073   [64]

Some quite good sandstone, offering about 20 good routes in all grades but little worth doing

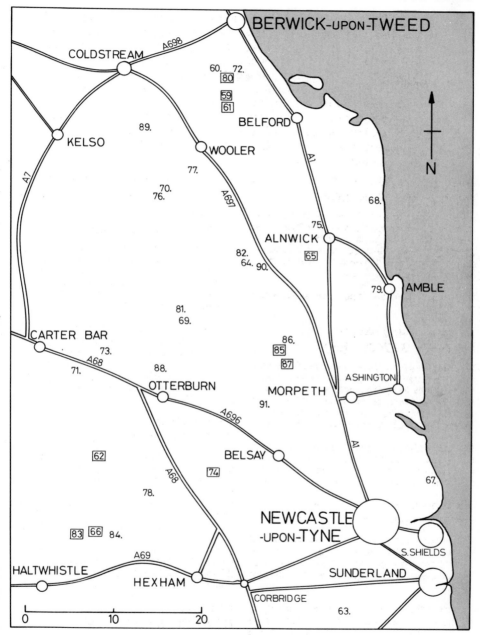

NORTHUMBERLAND

RADICAL YOUTH, 5c, Bowden Doors. (Climber David Jones, Photo Joe the Radical)

below Severe, 40–50ft. NW-facing and quite high at 1,000ft, climbing here achieves an almost alpine experience – well, compared with the other crags in the area. Worth a visit.

Dir: 8m WSW of Alnwick. Bit of a walk. Go N up the A697 from the crossroads with the B6341 for 0.5m, then fork L on to the small road. After 200yds follow the track leading off L through the forest, under the pylons and up the hill, bearing to the R. 1.5m from the road the path reaches the ridge and the crag is on the N side just to the R. [ND]

Corby's Crag:
OS.81 GR.127 101   [65]

A very good crag with about 60 climbs in all grades and some very good bouldering also. Quite steep, 30–50ft, and facing NW. Quite sheltered but best in the late afternoon. Very handy for those who dislike walking.

Dir: 4m SW of Alnwick. Take the B6341 for 4m and the crag is on the L, just after the end of the long, straight bit. [ND]

Crag Lough:
OS.87 GR.765 679   [66]

A well-established crag of quartz dolerite, up to 80ft in height. About 100 routes in all grades Diff upwards, something for everyone here. N-facing over a lake. Bad in the summer months for midges. Worth a visit, quite popular.

Dir: 11m WNW of Hexham. From Haydon Bridge take the A69 going W to Henshaw, turn R and go to the B6318. Carry straight over and up to a car park in about 300yds. From here walk E along the ridge to Peel Crag in about 30 secs and Crag Lough in about 15 mins, overlooking the lake. [ND]

Crag Point:
OS.88 GR.343 763   [67]

A sandstone sea cliff of negative worth next to the town of Seaton Sluice. 50ft of vertical terror and most probably doom!

Dir: 8m NE of Newcastle city centre. Go to Seaton Sluice. [ND]

Cullernose Point:
OS.81 GR.261 188   [68]

I can only recommend that after reading this description you erase this crag from your memory. A dangerous, E-facing sea cliff, 60ft of poor rock overlooking the cold North Sea. About 15 routes with 4c–5b moves, serious!

Dir: 5m NE of Alnwick. Turn off the B1340 and drive to Craster. Just before entering the village there is a road on the R which goes down to the coast. The crag is between here and the village. [ND]

Drake Stone:
OS.80 GR.921 044   [69]

A large sandstone boulder, 20–30ft and offering plenty of climbing and bouldering for everyone.

Dir: 26m N of Hexham, 1m W of Harbottle. Drive W from the village of Harbottle for 0.3m to a car park. Here a footpath leads off L and up the hill to the crag. [ND]

Dunsdale Crag:
OS.74 GR.897 235   [70]

A 70–100ft, S-facing volcanic crag, with rock not above suspicion. Nevertheless there are many routes here in the lower grades around Diff and Severe. At 900ft its situation is low for the area but it still gets any bad weather that is going. If it is a nice day Henhole is more worth the trip.

Dir: 7m SW of Wooler. Approach: see Henhole Crags. Walk up College Burn, after 2m take the bridge across the river and follow the valley leading off to the L. In almost 1m and just turning the bend the crag is seen up and to the L. [ND]

Ellis Crag:
OS.80 GR.747 011   [71]

An impressive 20ft buttress, SE-facing at 1,600ft with a fine view. Affords about a dozen routes. Worth a visit if Great Dour Crag is out of bounds for the day.

Dir: 26m NNW of Hexham, 1m S of Catcleugh reservoir. Go to the E end of the reservoir and the crag is on top of the big hill to the S. [ND]

Goats Crag: Access
OS.74 GR.976 370   [72]

Please seek permission from the farm and help maintain the good relationship with the farmer. Another good sandstone crag in this area around Lowick. Quite small, 20–30ft, and only offering about two score routes across the grades. S-facing and quick drying. Worth a visit.

Dir: 10m S of Berwick-upon-Tweed. At the Barmoor Castle crossroads near Lowick take the B6525 S for about 0.5m, turn R on to the small road going towards Milfield. After 2.2m a track leads off to the R and a farm, park. Walk to the crag in about 10 secs. [ND]

Great Dour Crag: Restriction
OS.80 GR.792 030   [73]

Birds nest here, no climbing 1 Mar.–1 Aug. Also the crag is in an army firing range – tough on the birds! Most of this crag leaves much to be desired. There are however parts worth climbing, in all grades up to 50ft. NW-facing and at 1,300ft, stays damp quite often. In a good spell of fine weather in summer it is worthy of a look. Also see Ellis Crag.

Dir: 25m NNW of Hexham at Dour Hill. From Rochester continue up the A68 for about 4m to a small road on the R opposite the caravan site. Take this for 1m and the crag can be seen across the valley [ND]

Great Wanney:
OS.80 GR.935 835   [74]

A very good area, offering the nearest really good climbing to Newcastle. 60–70 climbs in all grades Diff to 6c, 30–50ft. Quite exposed at 1,000ft and steep, offering easy routes to those with big biceps. Always worth a visit, excellent for bouldering.

Dir: 11m N of Hexham, just N of Sweethorpe Loughs. Take the A68 to Ridsdale, carry on for 0.4m to just round a bend, then turn R and follow the small road for 1.6m and park. Here a public footpath leads almost S and up to the crags in 10 mins, just. [ND]

Heckley Crag:
OS.81 GR.187 165   [75]

A very small crag of overhanging sandstone with a handful of routes on it. Handy if passing through to relieve that desperate climbing urge when bored stiff driving up the A1.

Dir: 2m N of Alnwick. Take the B6341 from the roundabout at the N end of the town. After 1m a track and footpath lead off to the R and the crag in 5 mins [ND]

Henhole Crags:
OS.74 GR.888 203   [76]

Volcanic rock and an exposed position at around 2,000ft make this a crag for the summer. Crags reaching up to 150ft in places give a fair selection of routes in the lower grades, especially around Severe. About 30 climbs worth doing. Can be very pleasant on a nice day as it faces S and dries out fairly quickly. A good mountain experience.

Dir: 8m SW of Wooler. Take the B6351 from the A697 just N of Woller for 3m, passing through the village of Kirknewton, then take a small road L up a steep hill to Hethpool and park. Walk up the College Burn for 4.5m, as the valley turns to the L at the end the crag is seen high on the L. About 2 hrs. [ND]

Housey Crags:
OS.75 GR.957 218   [77]

Some small outcrops of volcanic rock reaching up to about 40ft. A good spot for beginners with about a dozen routes around Diff–V Diff. NE-facing at 1,300ft, but a lovely setting.

Dir: 5m SSW of Wooler. From the town leave S by the small road leading to Middleton Hall, here turn R to Langleeford. This road goes over a steep hill and into Harthorpe Burn, follow it for 2m to the bridge at Langlee. Here a footpath goes diagonally up the hill and to the R side of the stream. Follow this for 20 mins then bear off R to the crags. About 30 mins. [ND]

Howelerhirst Crag:
OS.80 GR.787 830   [78]

A good 40ft sandstone outcrop with about 10 routes on it in the middle grades, VS to 6a. W-facing and excellent for bouldering in the afternoon. Worth a glance.

Dir: 15m NW of Hexham, 3.5m W of Bellingham. Take the small road to Helseyside, carry on for

1.4m to a footpath going off to the L and up a valley by a stream. Follow this after parking and the crags are up on the L, 10 mins. [ND]

The Jack Rock:
OS.81 GR.235 044   [79]

A sandstone crag offering about 30 climbs of 40ft in the grades Severe upwards. The crag is quite steep and does not lend itself to easy routes, or even routes easily climbed. Worth a look.

Dir: 2m W of Amble-by-the-Sea. From Acklington to the S take a small road leading N for 1.5m and turn off L to Morwick Mill. The crag is downstream on the S bank, 5 mins. [ND]

Kyloe Crags:
OS.75 GR.040 395   [80]

There are two crags here **Kyloe Crag** and **Kyloe in the Wood**. Kyloe is 30–50ft high and offers some very good climbing in all grades, very sheltered and facing SW. The latter crags are in the woods, stay dry in rain and are a must for the 6a, b, c, boulderer, 30ft high offering 100 short hard powerful routes. Both worth a visit.

Dir: 9m SSE of Berwick-upon-Tweed. From Lowick on the B6353 go E for 1.3m, turn R and after 0.3m a track leads off to the L and the crags in about 5 mins. Kyloe Crag is obvious. The crags in the wood are reached by taking the small road for 0.9m to a gate on the L with some fire beaters. A track leads into the forest, after 5 mins bear R on a track marked WS 7, the crag is reached in 5 mins. [ND]

Linshiels Crags: Restriction
OS.80 GR.897 054   [81]

A group of three crags on an army firing range, red flags will be flying if the range is being used. Overnight bivouacs are not wise. Some good climbing to be found, about 30 routes in all grades, 30–50ft. The crags face different directions and although they are at 700ft high one can usually find shelter somewhere. A remote spot as with South Yardhope.

Dir: 26m N of Hexham, 2m W of Alwinton. From Alwinton drive to Linshiels. The crags lie 1m to the SE from here. [ND]

Maiden Chambers:
OS.81 GR.048 076   [82]

A good, clean sandstone crag in the woods, offering some very good climbing. About 20 routes in all grades with plenty of problems as well. Worth a look.

Dir: 9.5m WSW of Alnwick. From Whittingham just off the A697 take the small road going to Callaly. Pass through the hamlet, after 1.5m Lorbottle Hall is passed on the L and the road does a sharp R turn going away. Here a footpath goes off to the L and up into the woods and the crag in 10 mins. [ND]

Peel Crag:
OS.87 GR.755 677   [83]

Generally the same as Crag Lough but more broken and vegetated. N-facing with about 80 routes, half of which are in the lower grades around Severe. See Crag Lough.

Dir: 11.5m WNW of Hexham. Approach: see Crag Lough.

Queen's Crag:
OS.87 GR.795 706   [84]

Permission to climb must be sought at Sewing Shields Farm. A very good small crag, only 20–30ft high but offering plenty of climbing in all grades Severe upwards. Plenty of good bouldering also, SE-facing. Worth a visit.

Dir: 10m WNW of Hexham. From Low Brunton just N take the B6318 from the roundabout W for 7.1m to a track which leads off to the R. Follow this to some small woods, go around them and continue N, in 100 yds you will be able to see the crag over to the L in about 600yds. [ND]

Ravensheugh Crag:
OS.81 GR.012 988   [85]

Good, compact sandstone cliffs at 1,300ft, N-facing. There are about 100 climbs here in all grades, easy to very hard. A fantastic view and well worth the walk on a fine day at any time of year.

Dir: 14m NW of Morpeth. Approach: see Simonside. [ND]

Sandy Crag:
OS.81 GR. 968 972 [86]

There are about 30 routes here of mixed quality and difficulty, 20–70ft. The bouldering, however, is very good indeed, some of the best in the county. Worth a visit.

Dir: 16m NW of Morpeth. Take the B6341 SW from Rothbury for about 6m to the village of Hepple. Carry on for 1.5m to a track which leads straight on where the road goes over a bridge. The track leads to Midgy House after 0.7m, the crag is on the hill up to the L. [ND]

Simonside:
OS.81 GR.025 988 [87]

A fairly good crag with lots of climbing in all grades, about 80 routes, 20–50ft. N-facing and 1,300ft up, not the place to go in winter except on a walk to Selby's Cove.

Dir: 14m NW of Morpeth. From Rothbury drive to Great Tosson. Here a path leads directly up the hill to the S and the col, separating the two summits of Simonside to the L and Ravensheugh to the R (W), 30 mins. Also you can carry on S from here for almost 1m down the hill to the crag of **Selby's Cove**, which is a lot more sheltered and faces SW, about 20 routes in all grades, 40ft. Worth a visit if the wind is too cold or strong on Simonside, but 45 mins back to the car. Good for a walk on a nice winter's day. [ND]

South Yardhope: Restriction
OS.80 GR.924 006 [88]

The crag is on an army firing range and it is generally recommended not to enter if a red flag is flying. A good sandstone crag, NW-facing and at 1,000ft. Not as many holds here as at most places and the climbs tend to be in the harder grades. There are a few Diffs but moves are usually 4b upwards. Best in the afternoon. Nice view, worth a visit.

Dir: 20m N of Hexham, 5m NNE of Otterburn. A small road leads from Hepple to Holystone. Turn L into the village, L past the pub and down the Yardhope valley. After 2m a road can be taken L down the valley to North Yardhope, the crag is on the S side of the valley. [ND]

Spindlestone Crag:
OS.75 GR.152 338 [89]

A rather broken crag, but nevertheless offering about 10 routes up to 50ft in the lower grades, Diff to Severe with 2 VSs. The Crag is S-facing but is not over-solid. Worth thinking about!

Dir: 10m ENE of Wooler. From Belford take the B1342 and after 2.1m turn R to Spindlestone. Turn L and a footpath leads to the crag. [ND]

Thrunton Crag:
OS.81 GR.075 096 [90]

A reasonable crag consisting of several buttresses on a ridge with about 30 routes in all grades Diff upwards, 30–50ft a fine view and facing NW at 800ft.

Dir: 7.5m WSW of Alnwick. Go to Thrunton, which is just off the A697, through the hamlet and after 0.4m take the L turn after the hill to the top, the best route between buttresses. 10 mins. [ND]

Wolf Crag:
OS.81 GR.975 882 [91]

A reasonable spot for some bouldering and easy routes up to 20ft high. NW-facing and handy from the road, just outside the army firing area. Worth a look if passing.

Dir: 14m W of Morpeth. From Knowesgate go NW on the A696, continue for 1.9m to the start of a forest set back on the R, park. The crag is 300yds to the R at the edge of the forest. [ND]

Appendices

I GUIDEBOOKS TO ENGLAND AND WALES

[AVC]   Avon and Cheddar–1989
[BEC]   Buttermere and Eastern Crags – 1987
[BOR]   Borrowdale – 1986
[CDU]   Carneddu – 1975
[CGY]   Clogwyn Du'r Arddu – 1989
[CL]   Clwyd Limestone – 1989
[CSC]   Cwm Silyn and Cwellyn – 1971
[CV]   Chew Valley – 1989
[CWP]   Cornwall – West Penwith – 1984
[DG]   Derwent Gristone – 1985
[GG]   Great Gable – 1977
[GL]   Great Langdale – 1989
[GO]   Gogarth – 1989
[GSW]   Gower and South East Wales – 1983
[HEL]   Helsby and the Wirral – 1976
[KB]   Kinder and Bleaklow – 1989
[LLD]   Lliwedd – 1972
[LLP]   Llanberis Pass – 1987
[LNW]   Lancashire & North West – 1983, 1989
[LNWS] Lancashire & NW Supplement – 1986
[LPI]   Lleyn Peninsula interim guide – 1979
[LU]   Lundy – 1985
[MW]   Mid Wales – 1989

[NOE]   North of England – 1980
[ND]   Northumberland – 1989
[NDC]   North Devon and Cornwall – 1989
[NWL]   North Wales Limestone – 1987
[NWS]   North Wales Supplement – 1982
[NYM]   North York Moors – 1985
[OGW]   Ogwen – 1982
[PCH]   Peak Limestone Chee Dale – 1987
[PSO]   Peak Limestone South – 1987
[PST]   Peak Limestone Stoney – 1987
[PE]   Pembroke – 1986
[PR]   Pillar Rock – 1977
[SDD]   South Devon and Dartmoor – 1985
[SDE]   Scafell, Dow and Eskdale – 1988
[SG]   Staffordshire Gritstone – 1989
[SNE]   Snowdon East – 1970
[SS]   Southern Sandstone – 1989
[STA]   Stanage – 1989
[SWA]   Swanage – 1986
[TGM]   Tremadog and the Moelwyns – 1989
[WYE]   Wye Valley – 1987
[YG]   Yorkshire Gritstone – 1982
[YL]   Yorkshire Limestone – 1985

II WEATHER FORECAST TELEPHONE NUMBERS

Mountain-top weather forecasts:
North Wales – Snowdonia: Llanberis (0286) 870 120
Lake District National Park: Windermere (096 62) 5151

Weathercall: This service is quite chatty and long. The best on offer and run by the Meteorological Office – excellent.

Weatherline: This service is run by British Telecom. It is short and a good idea if you only have 10p.

III CLIMBING WALLS

Three-Star Wall*
London: Brunel University Sports Centre (0895) 52361

Two-Star Walls**
Ambleside: Charlotte Mason College (0966) 33066
Birmingham: Ackers Trust (021) 771 4448
Bradford: Richard Dunn Leisure Centre (0274) 307 822
Cambridge: Kelsey Kerridge Sports Hall (0223) 68791
Cardiff: Channel View (0222) 394 317
Carlisle: The Sands Centre (0228) 27555
Guiseley: Airborough Leisure Centre (0943) 77131
Manchester: Altrincham Sports Centre (061) 928 2217
Preston: West View Leisure Centre (0772) 796788
Sheffield: Sheffield Polytechnic (0742) 368 116
              Sheffield YMCA (0742) 684 807 – Late 1989
Stourbridge: Stourbridge Leisure Centre (0384) 456 000

One-Star Walls*

Bournemouth:	Ferndown Sports Centre (0202) 877 193
Bristol:	Bristol YMCA (0272) 716 749
Buxton:	Whitehall Centre (0298) 3260
Canterbury:	University of Kent (0227) 53598
Capel Curig:	Plas Y Brenin Outdoor Centre (06904) 214
Caernarfon:	Plas Menai Centre (0248) 670 964
Cleethorpes:	The Lindsey School (0472) 694 835
Crewe:	South Cheshire Tertiary College (0270) 69133
Darlington:	Dolphin Leisure Centre (0325) 60651
Egremont:	Pelhamhurst School (0946) 234
Ellesmere Port:	Ellesmere Port Indoor Centre (051) 355 643 214
Hatfield:	Hatfield Polytechnic (07072) 79461
Leeds:	Leeds University Sports Centre (0532) 431 751
	Rothwell Sports Centre (0532) 824 110
London:	Downside Settlement (01) 407 0093
	Harrow School (01) 422 2196
	Imperial College (01) 581 5111
	Jubilee Sports Hall (01) 836 4007
	Michael Sobell Centre (01) 607 1632
	Sutton Youth Centre (01) 642 0634
Manchester:	Abraham Moss Centre (061) 740 1491
	University Armitage Centre (061) 224 0404
Mansfield:	Westfield Folkhouse (0623) 660 611
Nottingham:	Hucknall Leisure Centre (0602) 640 641
Scunthorpe:	West Common Sports Hall (0724) 865 407
Southend:	Rochford Sports Centre (0702) 204 7777
Stalybridge:	SIDS Centre (061) 338 3528
Stanley:	Louisa Sports Centre (0207) 30311
Stoke:	Newcastle, Keele University (0782) 62111
Sunderland:	Outdoor Activities Association (0783) 657 630
Swindon:	Link Centre (0793) 871 111
Totnes:	Totnes Community Centre (0803) 862 399
Whitehaven:	Whitehaven Sports Centre (0946) 5666

IV TRANSLATIONS OF USEFUL TERMS

English	French	German	Italian	Spanish
About	À peu près	Herum	Circa	Cerca
Above	Au dessus	Über	Sopra	Encima
Access	Accès	Zutritt	Accesso	Accesso
Approach	Approche	Zugang	Approccio	Entrada
Ban	Interdit	Bann	Proibire	Prohibición
Bear	Aller	Vorgehen	Procedere	Arrum Barse
Beck	P. rivière	Flup bach	Ruscello	Riachuelo
Beginning	Commencement	Anfang	Origine	Principio
Below	Au dessous	Unten	Sotto	Abajo
Bend	Courbe	Kurve	Curva	Comba
Bolt	Boulon	Bolzen	Bullone	Tornillo
Boulder	Gros rocher	Felsblock	Rocca	Peñasco
Buttress	Éperon	Strebepfeiler	Contraforte	Estribo
Climb	Escalade	Klettern	Scalata	Subida
Continue	Continuer	Weitrgehen	Continuare	Continuare
Corner	Coin	Winkel	Cantuccio	Ángulo
Cove	Anse	Kleine Bucht	Piccola Baia	Abra
Crux	Noeud	Schwierigkeit	Nodo	Duropunto
Direction	Direction	Richtung	Direzione	Curso
Double	Double	Doppelgänger	Doppio	Doble
Down	Descendre	Hinuter	Scendere	Vello
Dozen	Douze	Dutzend	Dodici	Docena
Drive	Conduire	Fahrweg	Guidare	Passeo
Easy/ier	Facile	Leicht	Agevole	Fácil
Face	Façade	Oberfläche	Facciata	Fachada
Facing	En face à	Blicken	Davanti a	Enfrente

English	French	German	Italian	Spanish
Fell	Côte	Hügel	Colle	Cerro
Follow	Suivre	Folgen	Seguire	Seguir
Footpath	Sentier	Fussweg	Sentiero	Vereda
Fork	Branche	Abzweigung	Fenditura	Bifurcación
Further	Plus loin	Weiter	Piu lontano	Mas alla
Gill	Petite vallée	Klein Tal	P. vallata	Barranco
Granite	Granit	Granit	Granito	Granito
Gritstone	Roche gravier	Griesstein	Grana Pietra	Arenaroca
Gully	Ravin	Schlucht	Burrone	Hondomada
Half	Moitié	Hälfte	Meta	Medio
Hamlet	Hameau	Dörfchen	P. Villaggio	Villorio
Hard	Difficile	Schwer	Difficile	Duro
Head, Point	Source, Cap	Spitze	Punta	Punto
Hill	Colline	Hügel	Collina	Cerro
Hold	Serrer	Halten	Serrare	Asidero
Interesting	Intéressant	Interessieren	Intersessante	Interesante
Junction	Jonction	Kreuzung	Congiunzione	Union
Lane	Ruelle	Gasse	Vicolo	Senda
Large	Grand	Gross	Grande	Grande
Ledge	Rebord	Felsvorsprung	Ripiano	Borde
L, left	Gauche	Links	Sinistra	Izquierdo
Lichen	Lichen	Moos	Lichene	Liquen
Limestone	Pierre à chaux	Kalkfels	Calce Sasso	Calceroca
Loose	Lâche	Löse	Libero	Suelto
Map	Carte	Landkarte	Carta	Mapa
Moor	Lande	Moor	Brughiera	Páramo
Mountain	Montagne	Berg	Montagna	Montaña
Opposite	Opposé	Gegenuber	Opposto	Opuesto
Outcrop	Affleurement	Felsnase	Rupe a picco	Peña
Overhang	Surplomb	Überhang	Incombere	Colgar
Parallel	Parallèle	Parallel	Paralello	Paralelo
Park	Stationner	Parkplatz	Parcheggio	Estacionamiento
Pitch	Section	Schnitt	Sezione	Sección
Pocket	Poche	Tasche	Tasca	Bolsillo
Poorly	Mauvais	Schlecht	Male	Enfermo
Protection	Protection	Schutz	Protezione	Protección
Quarry	Carrière	Steinbruch	Cava	Cantera
Reached	Atteint	Erreicht	Arrivata	Aleanzado
Restriction	Restriction	Einschränkung	Restrizione	Restricción
Ridge	Arête	Kamm	Cresta	Lomo
R, right	Droit	Rechts	Destra	Derecha
Ring road	Rue cercle	Ringstrasse	Strada Circ.	Circopista
River	Rivière	Fluss	Flume	Rio
Road	Route, Rue	Strasse	Strada	Camino
Rope	Corde	Seil	Corda	Cuerda
Routes	Routes	Richtungen	Via	Ruta
Runner	Protection	Schutz	Protezione	Protección
Safe	Sauf	Sicher	Sicuro	Seguro
Sandstone	Roche sable	Sandfels	Pietra Sabbia	Arenaroca
Scar	Rocher	Nabre	Picco	Peña
Score	Vingt	Zwanzig	Venti	Veinte
Scrambling	Escalade	Klettern	Scalata	Trepa
Sea	Mer	See	Mare	Mar
Serious	Sérieux	Schwierig	Grave	Serio
Sharp	Tranchant	Scharf	Acuto	Agudo
Side	Flanc	Seite	Fianco	Lateral
Single	Seul	Einzig	Singolo	Solo
Slate	Ardoise	Schiefer	Ardesia	Pizama
Small	Petit	Klein	Piccolo	Peqeno
Solid	Solide	Fest	Solido	Sólido
Start	Commencement	Anfang	Partenza	Principio
Steep	Vertical	Steil	China	Escarpado
Straight	Ligne droite	Direkt	Diretto	Derecho
Stream	Cours d'eau	Wasserlauf	Corrente	Arroyo
Tides	Marée temps	Ebbe Zeit	Marea.Epoca	De Marea

English	French	German	Italian	Spanish
Towards	Envers	Gegen	Verso	Hacia
Town	Ville	Stadt	Citta	Ciudad
Track	Trace	Feldweg	Cammino	Sendero
Turn	Tourner	Umdrehung	Girare	Vuelta
Until	Jusqu'a, au	Bis	Fino a	Hasta
Up, Upper	En dessus	Auf	Piu in Alto	Superior
Various	Varié	Verschieden	Diverso	Vario
Village	Village	Dorf	Villaggio	Pueblo
Volcanic	Volcanique	Vulkanisch	Vulcanico	Volcánico
Walk	Marche	Lauf	Cammino	Paseo
Way down	Descente	Abstieg	Discesa	Bajada
Zawn	Caverne-mer	See-Höhle	Cavernamare	Cueva de Mar

V LIST OF CRAGS AND CLIMBING AREAS